Myths and Traditions of the Arikara Indians

Sources of American Indian Oral Literature

EDITORS

Douglas R. Parks
Raymond J. DeMallie

This series offers new editions of works previously published,
as well as works never before published,
on Native American oral tradition.

Myths and Traditions
of the Arikara Indians

Douglas R. Parks

University of Nebraska Press
Lincoln and London

E
99
.A8
T 7325
1996

⊛ The paper in this book meets the minimum requirements of
American National Standard for Information Sciences—
Permanence of Paper for Printed Library Materials,
ANSI Z39.48-1984.

Library of Congress Cataloging-in-Publication Data
Traditional narratives of the Arikara Indians. Selections.
Myths and traditions of the Arikara Indians / [edited by]
Douglas R. Parks.   p.   cm.—(Sources of American Indian
oral literature) "A one-volume selection of narratives
reprinted from volumes 3 and 4 of Traditional narratives
of the Arikara Indians"—Pref. Includes bibliographical
references (p.   ) and index.
ISBN 0-8032-3712-X (cl: alk. paper).—
ISBN 0-8032-8742-9 (pa: alk. paper)
1. Arikara Indians—Folklore.   2. Arikara mythology.
I. Parks, Douglas R.   II. Title.   III. Series.
E99.A8T7325   1995   398.2′08997—dc20
95-43855   CIP

TiweNAsaakaríčI nikuwetiresWAtwaáhAt:
AniinuuNUxtaahiwaáRA.

Today we remember them,
the ways of the old ones who were:
The good ways that were ours.

FROM THE SONG
MEMORIAL TO THE OLD SCOUTS

Contents

Introduction to Arikara Oral Traditions

Myths and Traditions

AN OPENING PRAYER

NARRATIVES OF THE PAST

Of Mysterious Incidents

TALES

Of Human Actors

Of Coyote

Of Others

SONG

Illustrations

Maps

Plates

Table

Preface

Myths and Traditions of the Arikara Indians is a one-volume selection of narratives reprinted from volumes 3 and 4 of *Traditional Narratives of the Arikara Indians* (Parks 1991). The latter work, a four-volume set comprising 156 oral narratives, is the only comprehensive collection recorded in the native language of the major genres in the historical and literary tradition of the Arikaras, a historically important northern Plains people who for centuries have lived along the middle course of the Missouri River and today still live by its waters in west-central North Dakota, where Garrison Dam forms Lake Saka-kawea, the reservoir that now divides the Fort Berthold Reservation. Through the contributions of numerous tribal elders, the narratives, both in the original publication and in this abridged edition, range in content from mythology and other folkloristic genres to historical accounts and cultural descriptions, embodying a rich selection of what has survived into the late-twentieth century of the fundamental attributes as well as the topical diversity and range of stylistic variation of traditional Arikara oral literature.

In the original publication, volumes 1 and 2 present linguistic transcrip-tions of the Arikara oral tape recordings of the narratives accompanied by literal word-by-word English translations. The narratives of a single individual, Alfred Morsette, Sr., constitute volume 1, while the narratives of ten other contributors comprise volume 2. Volumes 3 and 4 present free English trans-lations of the stories paralleling the arrangement of the first two volumes. An extended introduction in volume 3 serves the entire collection, covering a variety of topics designed to aid the reader to understand the narratives as fully as possible and to appreciate them as historical and literary documents. To contextualize the collection, the introduction begins with sections that provide a cultural and historical overview of the Arikara people, the history of past documentation of Arikara oral traditions, and short biographies of the narrators who contributed stories to the present collection. Against this background there follows a discussion of the structure of the narratives and their English presen-tation. Here the topics include a characterization of the nature of the collection, the principles guiding the translations and redactive forms of the narratives, the salient features comprising the Arikara oral literary style, the structure and content of the narratives, and a depiction of the performance situations in which these oral traditions were told. That introduction, revised slightly, is reprinted at the outset of the present volume.

Because the style and structure of Arikara oral narratives differ so dramatically from those to which English readers are accustomed, and because the social and cultural world depicted in the traditions differs even more dramatically from that of contemporary America, the narratives presented here require careful study. Comprehension and appreciation of the subleties that characterize the Arikara oral literary style may be difficult for readers accustomed to the usual collections of American Indian tales rewritten to conform to Western literary conventions. Nevertheless, to be truly understood Arikara oral literature must be approached in its own terms; and for English readers this effort means understanding the uniqueness of Arikara culture—particularly, to the extent possible, its worldview and concerns—and accepting unfamiliar linguistic expression and literary form.

The reward for the effort to understand the narratives as fully as possible will be at once enlightening and satisfying, since the accounts recorded here enable the reader, in a manner not otherwise possible, to enter into another cultural world and obtain a glimpse of a lifeway now lost to contemporary society. Arikara life of the nineteenth century, like that of American Indian peoples generally, has transformed dramatically. Many cultural institutions have persisted, but the concerns of everyday life, together with Arikara cultural consciousness and its traditional expressions, have been adapted to the modern world we all now share. The only published record of the Arikara past from Arikara perspectives is the one recorded here in the words of the last generation of speakers of the Arikara language, who have repeated in traditional form the stories—religious, legendary, historical, anecdotal, and humorous—that they remembered, stories that formed an intimate, fundamental part of the expression of Arikara culture as it was formerly lived.

Acknowledgments

Many Arikara people have contributed to this collection of narratives. Foremost among them are the eleven narrators who shared their stories: Alfred Morsette, Lillian Brave, Ella P. Waters, Dan Howling Wolf, Dan Hopkins, Matthew White Bear, Mary Gillette, William Deane, Sr., Eleanor Chase, Esther Perkins, and Joe Fox. Especially impressive are Mr. Morsette's contributions, which constitute more than half of the collection. He was a true raconteur who faithfully remembered the stories told him by older generations, and he was committed to the task of preserving this record of Arikara history. Mrs. Brave and Mrs. Waters, both exceptionally knowledgeable about Arikara traditions, also recorded numerous stories that they remembered in order to make the collection as representative and complete as possible. For them, as for all those individuals whose stories are a part of this collection, these traditional narratives represented a precious, intimate, and fundamental embodiment of their identity as Arikaras, and the decision to share their stories was not lightly undertaken. Theirs was a desire to record and preserve this oral heritage as a gift to future generations, that others, particularly their descendants, might gain some understanding of an Arikara world that is now a part of the past. It is a gift that is sincerely appreciated, especially since of all these narrators only Mrs. Brave and Miss Perkins lived to see the project to completion; and the passing of these traditional storytellers signals a major transition in the cultural life of the Arikara community.

Fundamentally important, too, were the efforts of various translators— Ella P. Waters, Lillian Brave, Angela Plante, Fannie Whiteman, Nellie Yellow Bird, John Fox, and Melfine Everett—who conscientiously assisted in the demanding process of transcription and translation of the stories. To Mrs. Waters, in particular, I am grateful for an unfailing devotion to this project, which spanned more than a decade of work, lasting until shortly before she passed away in 1983. Without her collaboration, and later that of Mrs. Brave and her daughter Angela, who have worked with me subsequently, this collection of narratives would never have achieved its present state.

Over the years many other individuals in the Arikara community have provided hospitality and assistance, as well as extending many other courtesies to me, all of which have made my work there both pleasant and gratifying. It would be impossible to list everyone, but foremost among them are three individuals now deceased—Mabel Howling Wolf, Wilena Little Soldier, and Alice White Bear—all of whom were warm, generous people and fluent speakers of their language. Other people who have been equally generous with time and friendship include Ramona Flute, David Ripley, Marie Wells, Tom Wells, Florence White, Fannie Whiteman, and Delilah Yellow Bird. To all of them I wish to extend my sincere thanks and express the hope that this volume does not disappoint their expectations.

Appreciated also is the official support and encouragement of several Fort Berthold tribal organizations. In 1977 the Fort Berthold Tribal Council gave an endorsement by resolution of my linguistic project, and in 1980 tribal chairman Austin Gillette kindly wrote a strong letter of support for the expansion of the linguistic work to document Arikara culture as well, and especially the oral narratives presented here. The White Shield school board and district superintendent, both representing the Arikara community on the Fort Berthold Reservation, have given equally strong support on numerous occasions over the past fifteen years. Among the many school board members who have been particularly helpful are Robert Fox (deceased), Donald Malnourie, Gerald White, Edmund White Bear, and Delores Wilkinson.

It is also a pleasure to acknowledge the critical comments of many colleagues. Wallace Chafe and Ives Goddard offered suggestions on an earlier version of the manuscript that improved the presentation, while over the past decade my work with the texts has benefited from discussions with Raymond J. DeMallie, A. Wesley Jones, David S. Rood, and Allan R. Taylor. The introduction and translations herein have, in particular, been improved by the careful readings and thoughtful comments of Raymond DeMallie.

I am grateful to Christina Burke, Rita Crouch, Ronald R. Royce, and Robert Thompson, all of the American Indian Studies Research Institute (Indiana University), who helped prepare this volume for publication.

I wish to express my appreciation to each of the individuals and organizations providing the maps and illustrations enhancing the presentation. The maps in the introduction, which illustrate important landmarks in Arikara history, were drawn by Rachael Freyman (Indiana University). Historical photographs were provided by the North Dakota State Historical Society and the Custer Battlefield Historical and Museum Association. Contemporary photographs of North Dakota landmarks were provided by Raymond T. Haas (Annapolis, Maryland), and photographs of several narrators were provided by

Faye Seidler of Faye Portraits, Inc. (Garrison, North Dakota), Louis Garcia (Tokio, North Dakota), and James Vranna (New Town, North Dakota).

I am grateful to Lori Grove for the drawing used on the section divider pages throughout the book. The design is taken from the decorative strips on a pair of Arikara men's leggings, collected by George A. Dorsey, in the Field Museum of Natural History, Chicago (no. 15328). The strips are of porcupine quillwork in yellow, red, green, and purple, edged with dark blue seed beads.

Support for my study of the Arikara language and specifically for the collection and preparation of the texts came from a variety of sources, including grants from the following agencies: National Endowment for the Humanities, divisions of Research and Educational Programs (1972-1978); Department of Education, Title III (1974-1979) and Title VII (1984-1988); Smithsonian Institution, Urgent Anthropology Program (1977-1978); and North Dakota Arts Council (1982-1983). It is a pleasure to acknowledge their generous support, without which this collection would not have been possible. Three institutions—Mary College, now University of Mary (Bismarck, North Dakota), White Shield School (Roseglen, North Dakota), and Indiana University (Bloomington)—have also generously provided essential support and assistance that is gratefully acknowledged.

Sound Key

	ARIKARA	APPROXIMATE EQUIVALENT
Short Vowels:	a	ago, father
	e	bed
	i	police, pit
	o	wrote
	u	flute
Long Vowels:	aa	spa
	ee	neighbor
	ii	machine
	oo	go
	uu	rude
Consonants:	č	which
	h	hit
	n	no
	s	sit
	š	ship
	w	will
	k	skill
	p	spill
	t	still
	r	Spanish pero
	x	German ich, acht
	'	oh-oh (glottal stop)
Others:	^{i}	(raised ^{i} not pronounced)
	^{u}	(raised ^{u} not pronounced)
	æ	bat
	ą	French ans
	ų	French un
	´	(primary stress)
	CAPITALS	(whispered sounds)

Other Symbols and Conventions

SYMBOL	EXPLANATION
« »	Transition appearing at top or bottom of a page (see p. 62)
« « « » » »	Major transition separating episodes (see p. 62)
[ ]	Explanatory material not in the narrative tellling
< >	Supplementary details or narrative in Alfred Morsette's stories that come from his English versions (see p. 64)
Bold sans serif typeface	Narrative told from a first person perspective (see pp. 65-66)

Introduction to Arikara Oral Traditions

"The desire to preserve to future ages the memory of past achievements is a universal human instinct," wrote James Mooney (1898:141) in the opening line of his *Calendar History of the Kiowa Indians,* the first comprehensive attempt to construct an American Indian tribal history by using native as well as Euro-American written sources. For the Kiowas those native sources were what Mooney called "calendar histories," pictographs drawn on hides or paper that recorded a significant event for a given period—a month, a season, or a year. Like the winter counts of the Sioux and many other tribes, those calendars were mnemonic records of past events that were exhibited at frequent intervals during winter evenings when older men and warriors would recite the traditions represented by the pictographs.

Not all Plains tribes, unfortunately, kept such tangible records formulating tribal history and aiding in its perpetuation, but they all had what the Kiowa pictographs brought to mind: mythic and historic oral traditions that were the substance of the tribe's historiography. Thus Mooney, in his description of the Kiowa calendars, was presenting in essence a collection of oral traditions, albeit ones that because of their chronological sequencing were more systematically organized from the perspective of Western scholarship than most American Indian traditions.[1]

This introduction first appeared in volume 3 of *Traditional Narratives of the Arikara Indians* (Parks 1991). It has been revised and slightly updated for this edition, which comprises selected stories from the earlier work. Readers should note that throughout the introduction, numbered references cited within parentheses refer to the numbers of the narratives in the original edition of *Traditional Narratives of the Arikara Indians.* The stories selected for inclusion in the present volume have been renumbered. Therefore, in order to identify stories referred to by number in this introduction, readers should consult the Concordance (pp. 375-80), which facilitates cross-reference between the narratives in the original, complete edition and those in this abridged edition.

1. Other tribes also used mnemonic devices to aid in the retention and recitation of ritual knowledge. The Arikara sacred bundle of the Eastern (*huukaawirát*) band, for example, contained a sheaf of thirty-four small sticks that were laid out whenever the

This volume presents another Plains historiographic tradition, that of the Arikaras, frequently called Rees, a group of people who have lived in what is now the Dakotas for well over two centuries and who are closely related linguistically to the Pawnees of Nebraska and more distantly to the Wichitas and Caddos of the southern Plains.[2] All these peoples—Arikaras, Pawnees, Wichitas, Caddos, as well as the extinct Kitsais—composed the Caddoan language family and, until the late eighteenth century, formed a nearly unbroken population continuum extending over the tall grass prairies of the eastern Plains from the Dakotas to Texas (Lesser and Weltfish 1932). That continuum was the historical result of a gradual northward movement from the southeastern Plains of the Caddoan peoples who were the ancestors of the Arikaras and Pawnees. For the Arikaras, who were in the vanguard of that movement, the gradual northwestward course along the Missouri River was divinely sanctioned and became a religious symbol around which they organized their historical traditions.

A Cultural Overview

Arikara culture developed over many centuries during which their ancestors cultivated the soil of the Missouri River bottoms in what is now South Dakota, where the women planted gardens of corn, squash, and beans. The crops they raised allowed these people a more sedentary and secure lifestyle than that of their nomadic neighbors, who subsisted almost exclusively on the wandering herds of buffalo. There, generally on bluffs overlooking the west bank of the river, Arikaras built their permanent villages of earth lodges. These large, dome-shaped dwellings stood some fifteen feet in height and thirty feet in diameter, supported by four central posts and a circle of smaller posts at the periphery, and were covered with rafters, over which were layers of sticks, grass, and finally prairie sod. In the early eighteenth century a typical village was a hamlet of perhaps thirty-five such earth lodges arranged randomly. Somewhere near the center there generally was a ceremonial struc-

---

bundle was opened and its ritual recited. Each stick symbolized a portion of the bundle's set of religious teachings as well as stages in the development of the world (Gilmore 1929).

2. In the eighteenth and nineteenth centuries the Arikaras were also frequently referred to as Arikarees, a name that had many variant spellings (see Hodge 1907-11, 1:86). The name Rees, a shortened form of Arikarees, is said to have been the form used by early French Canadian traders (Lewis and Clark in Moulton 1987, 3:400) and is commonly used on the Fort Berthold Reservation today by both Arikaras themselves as well as Mandans and Hidatsas.

ture, today called the Medicine Lodge, identical in shape to the residential lodges but much larger in size, having a diameter of up to sixty feet and a capacity to accommodate as many as six hundred people. Later in the eighteenth century, when more easterly tribes like the Sioux pushed westward onto the Plains, intertribal warfare intensified. The Arikaras then concentrated in larger communities, each fortified by a surrounding ditch and palisade to afford protection against enemies, particularly against those tribes from the east who had already obtained European firearms.

Throughout the early eighteenth century the Arikaras had a population of at least 10,000 people living at any one time in twenty to perhaps as many as forty villages extending along the Missouri from the White River north to just above the Grand River. That population was not only much larger but also more diverse than it was a century later. It was not a single, unified tribe but rather comprised aggregates of villages organized into seven or perhaps a dozen bands, some of which—but certainly not all—may have been allied (Parks 1979a). The names of ten of those social units have survived into the twentieth century:

awaáhu (no translation) [3]
tUhkaatákUx 'Village Against A Hill'
NAhuukaátA 'By The Water'
čiNIhnaahtákUx 'Ash Tree On A Hill'
tUhkAsthaánu' 'Buffalo Sod Village'
naakaríkA 'Tree Branch Sticking Out'
huukaawirát 'Eastern'
warihká' (no translation)
šitⁱniišápIt 'They Broke The Arrow'
wiita'uúxU 'Long Haired Man'

Two other names have been recorded but not corroborated by more than one source: *nakaanústš* 'Little Chokecherry' and Scirihάu, a name of uncertain derivation but said to mean 'Coyote Fat' [4] (Gilmore 1927:345).

The population was dialectally diverse as well. Precisely how diverse is unknown today, but based on statements from fur traders and words recorded

---

3. The usual translation for this name is 'Left Behind,' based on an association with the stem *huunawaa* 'to leave behind, abandon.' It is not certain, however, that the name in fact derives from that stem.

4. The first element of this form is *sčirir*, the stem for 'wolf, coyote,' and the second part appears to be related to the descriptive stem *ahiht* 'to be fat.' Perhaps Gilmore was attempting to write *sčiri'ahIt*, a word not recognized by modern speakers.

early in the nineteenth century it is clear that there were at least two major dialect groups, one whose speech was more closely related to that of the Pawnee groups to the south and another whose speech diverged more sharply from Pawnee and more closely resembled that of contemporary Arikaras (Parks 1979b). Less striking dialectal distinctions must have existed within those larger speech groups as well, for in 1804 the fur trader Pierre-Antoine Tabeau, who lived with the Arikaras for two years, wrote:

> The Loups [Skiri Pawnees] and all the different Panis [Pawnees] now on the river Platte, made, undoubtedly, with the Ricaras but one nation which time and circumstances have, without doubt, insensibly divided. The language was originally the same; but, like that of all nations, it has undergone such great changes that it has left many different dialects. Each of the tribes has its own particular one so that no one can say that he knows the Ricara language; for it would be necessary that he should understand in ten different ways the greater number of the words, in which the common etymology is scarcely to be recognized. The pronunciation especially differs markedly. [Abel 1939: 125-26]

Several fundamental features distinguished eighteenth-century Arikaras from neighboring tribes. The most prominent distinctive cultural traits were corn cultivation—clearly an ancient feature of Arikara life that was deeply embedded in the people's ceremonial life—and patterns of ceremonial and political organization.

Although Arikaras planted other crops as well—squash, beans, and sunflowers—in tribal religious life none of them assumed the fundamental importance of corn. The plant was personified and deified as Mother Corn, a bestower of culture and a protector of the people. Mother Corn was intrinsic to religious rites, most of which corresponded to the cycle of corn growth, the teachings of Mother Corn, and the invocation of her assistance. The pervasive role of corn in Arikara life was, moreover, manifested in economy and life-style. Buffalo hunting, while certainly important for subsistence, was not the protracted activity that it was among the Pawnees and other horticulturalists to the south. Corn afforded an economic surplus that attracted nomadic tribes from the high plains to the Arikara villages on the Missouri to barter. In the late eighteenth century those tribes included the Kiowas, Comanches, Plains Apaches, Arapahos, Cheyennes, and others whose names are no longer identifiable today, all friends of the Arikaras, as well as various Sioux bands, sometimes friendly but more often hostile. The nomadic hunters brought to the Arikaras their products of the chase—dried meat, hides, furs, and buckskin clothing decorated with quill work—as well as horses from the southwest, in exchange for which the Arikaras bartered their garden produce and the native tobacco they also grew. So intrinsic, in fact, was corn to the life of Arikaras that it was for them a metaphor for life itself, one that was recognized by other Plains peoples as well and was manifested in the Plains sign language designation of Arikaras as 'corn shellers.'

Another striking feature of Arikara culture was a divinely sanctioned religious and political organization. Early in human history, when the ancestors of the Arikara people lived underground, the Chief Above *(neešaanu' t^{i}načitákUx)* sent to them Mother Corn, who with the assistance of various animals led them out into the world and along a path beset with many obstacles to reach the land where they lived in the eighteenth century. Finally she gave these ancestors of the Arikaras their religious teachings and ceremonies as well as corn and other plants to cultivate. Through her, too, the Chief Above ordained the office of chief *(neešaánu'),* the man who would be the people's protector and leader. To him and his lineal descendants was entrusted the sacred bundle, representing the power of the Chief Above and the teachings of Mother Corn; it was to serve as a palladium that drew the people of the village together, binding them as a social unit and giving focus to their religious life (G. A. Dorsey 1904a:12-32).

Village chieftaincy, a hereditary position, was a status passed down through the male line and was apparently symbolized by family ownership of the village sacred bundle.[5] Through achievements in war other men could become chiefs, who were then leaders in political and social affairs, but their positions could not be inherited; only village chieftaincy was hereditary (Holder 1970:41-45).

Although the chief was the lineal descendant of the original owner of the village sacred bundle, he did not necessarily know its rituals. That knowledge belonged to a leading priest *(kunahUxčitawí'u'),* whose position also tended to be hereditary in the male line and who actually conducted the ceremonies of the bundle. His duties, like those of the chief, were prescribed at the time of Creation: he was a mediator between the deities and the people. The rituals that he and his assistants conducted in the Medicine Lodge were solemn, measured liturgies composed of offerings and sacrifices interspersed with long cycles of songs recounting events in mythological times, when the world was forming, as well as recitations of the moral teachings given the people by Mother Corn. The purpose of such ceremonies was to gain the attention of the deities—of the Chief Above, Mother Corn, and a host of spiritual beings—and by supplication, sacrifice, and acknowledgment of their deeds to gain the deities' favor, resulting in good fortune and assistance in the people's food

---

5. For Arikaras, there is insufficient ethnographic data to confirm that bundles were the property of the chiefs' families, but for Pawnees the association of bundle with village chief is amply documented (Dorsey and Murie 1940; Holder 1970:41-45).

quest and in their social needs. Early each spring the ritual calendar began with a renewal of objects in the bundle, proceeded to a series of spring and summer ceremonies marking stages in the planting and cultivation of crops (especially corn), and then continued on to activities associated with the summer hunt. In early fall the ceremonial season concluded with a thanksgiving ritual for bountiful crops, after which life in the winter villages in the Missouri bottom lands was ritually dormant, punctuated by short buffalo hunts on the plains.

Contrasting with Arikara religious life, represented in each village by a sacred bundle and its priest, was the institution of healing, represented by medicines and doctors. Both institutions, the religious and the medical, although conceptually separate, were nevertheless symbolically united in the Medicine Lodge, where the rituals of both were always conducted. The Medicine Lodge was, consequently, the paramount symbol of Arikara social and cultural solidarity.

In Arikara society, doctors *(kunaá'u')* were men not necessarily born to that status but who generally obtained their powers to cure and perform mystical feats from other doctors or from membership in a doctor's society, whose powers ultimately derived from animals. Doctors whose powers came from the same source formed associations. Some doctors, such as those having horse or snake medicine, for example, formed loose associations that in the late nineteenth century were of relatively recent origin. Other doctors, however, belonged to older, established societies that had assigned seating positions in the Medicine Lodge for those ritual occasions when its members met there. In the late nineteenth century eight societies comprised the Medicine Lodge— Ghost, Blacktail Deer, Shedding Buffalo, Cormorant, Duck, Owl, Din Of Birds, and Bear—in addition to a group of leading doctors who sat at the altar. Every year during late summer these societies met in the Medicine Lodge, and for a period of a month the doctors lived there, where they performed dances, rituals, and legerdemain daily. Unlike religious rituals, which were solemn, repetitive acts, the doctors' performances emphasized drama. To the accompaniment of song and dance, body parts would appear to be severed, then miraculously reattached; a person would be shot and apparently killed, then be brought back to life; a plant would appear to grow before the eyes of spectators. Those and many other remarkable feats gained Arikara doctors not only the respect and awe of their own people but of others as well, both neighboring Indians and, later, European visitors (Maximilian 1843, 2:394; Curtis 1907-30, 5:70; W. Hoffman 1884; Will 1934:39-48).

Integral to Arikara social organization were secular men's societies (*naaníšu'*), many of which were influential in village sociopolitical affairs. Although membership in some Arikara societies was based on age—a feature characteristic of Mandan and Hidatsa societies—there also existed an older form of societies conceived to be coordinate units, like their Pawnee counter-parts. Thus, although the Crow Shin society, for example, was comprised exclusively of boys, most organizations had adult members of all ages and individuals were free to leave one society to join another whenever they wished.

The men's societies were military as well as social organizations. Each society had a distinctive staff or lance, usually decorated with feathers, which served as its insignia. Members of each society shared distinctive dress and sometimes had a special style of wearing their hair or painting themselves. Each society also had its individual musical instruments as well as its own dances and songs. Members of a society met frequently to sing and at times to parade through the village, dancing as a group. Although all the men's organizations had military functions, certain ones like the *Taroxpa* were noted for their bravery in battle. On war parties men grouped themselves into their societies, which rivaled one another in battle and marched together in formation on triumphal return to the village. On communal hunts one of the societies was chosen to act as the camp police.

Although an Arikara village was conceived to be a large kin group, all of whose members were related, the basic unit of social organization was an extended family of some fifteen to twenty people who lived in an earth lodge. At its head was an older woman, who had built the lodge, and her husband. Since sororal polygyny was common, the older woman's sisters might reside there as well. The generation below this couple included unmarried sons and one or more daughters, together with their spouses if they were married, and below them a third generation, their children. The most common postmarital residence pattern was matrilocal, where a man joined his wife in her mother's lodge, although occasionally a couple would set up its own household or even more infrequently a woman would join the household of her husband's family. Whatever the residence pattern, however, the lodge was the property of the women.

The Arikara kinship system, which shared several features common to all Caddoan peoples, was bilateral and generational. Conceptually a father's brother was a father, a mother's sister was a mother, a man's brother's child was his child, a woman's sister's child was her child, and, finally, children of siblings of like sex were siblings to each other. These features extended thoughout the system to all collateral kin lines. Although a father's sister was termed a mother, a mother's brother was called uncle.

Between relatives, social behavior was patterned, characterized by either a respect or joking relationship. A respectful relationship obtained between children and their parents, as well as between other individuals to whom the parental and child kin terms were extended. Although a man could not remain

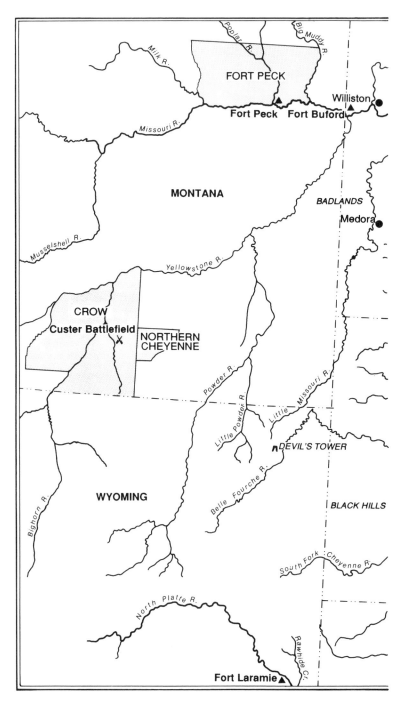

Map 1. The Northern Plains in the Late Nineteenth Century. Shown are the 1897 reservation boundaries.

0   50
miles

NORTH DAKOTA

N

Minot●   Souris R.

Devils Lake

FORT BERTHOLD   DEVILS LAKE

DOG DEN BUTTE
▲Fort Stevenson
Fort Berthold

KILLDEER
MOUNTAINS
Knife R.
▲Fort Clark

Sheyenne R.

VIRGIN'S BREASTS BUTTES
Heart R.   ∩∩   ●Bismarck
LITTLE HEART BUTTE ∩   ▲Fort A. Lincoln
Cannonball R.
EAGLE NOSE BUTTE ▲ Fort Rice

Grand R.
                        ▲Fort Yates
         STANDING ROCK

SOUTH DAKOTA

Moreau R.

CHEYENNE
RIVER

Cheyenne R.
                   Fort Pierre▲ ●Pierre

James R.

Bad R.
                   LOWER BRULE   CROW CREEK

BADLANDS
White R.

PINE RIDGE   ROSEBUD

Missouri R.

Niobrara R.

alone with his sister and generally spoke only minimally with her, close ties among siblings were highly valued. Brothers, who were expected to maintain the family's honor, had a close relationship in which there was a lifelong respect for seniority. Brothers-in-law were also the closest of friends. A respectful relationship analogous to that between younger and older brother was that between nephew and maternal uncle. At puberty, in fact, a boy would go to live in the lodge of his uncle or older brother and there be instructed in the arts of manhood. A joking relationship, in contrast, was obligatory between grandparents and their grandchildren. In contrast with those relationships was the strict taboo against communication between son-in-law and mother-in-law that forbade the former to speak to his mother-in-law or remain alone in the lodge with her.

A Historical Overview

In the late eighteenth century the Arikara experienced the first of a series of major upheavals that over the next century ultimately shattered their way of life. In 1780–1781 a smallpox epidemic swept over the Plains, inflicting untold casualties among sedentary tribes like the Arikaras. There may have been even earlier, equally deadly epidemics, for the fur trader Jean Baptiste Truteau, who lived among the Arikaras from 1794 to 1796, stated that they had suffered three epidemics before his residency there. Truteau claimed that before those smallpox outbreaks the Arikaras counted 4,000 warriors and lived in thirty-two large villages, but when he was with them, most of the survivors were living in two villages at the mouth of the Cheyenne River, while two additional small groups had gone off, one to reside with the Mandans in the north and the other to visit the Skiri Pawnees to the south; he estimated their population at that time to be 500 warriors, or about 2,500 people in all. The Arikaras, however, anticipating a major onslaught by the Sioux, abandoned the two Cheyenne River villages in 1796, abruptly ending Truteau's stay. Some went north to the Mandans and others went west to the Cheyennes.

In 1804, when Tabeau established residency among the tribe—the same year Lewis and Clark visited them—the Arikaras were again living on the Missouri, now in three villages just above the Grand River, one on modern Ashley Island above the mouth of Rampart Creek and the other two villages four miles north on the west bank of the river. They were still residing there in the two upper villages on the west bank when Henry Brackenridge and John Bradbury traveled up the Missouri in 1811, but the island village had been abandoned some time earlier. During the following decade the Arikaras continued to live in those villages above the Grand River, but in 1823 their life there was disrupted when hostilities broke out with William Ashley's party of fur traders ascending the Missouri. The encounter resulted in the deaths of some fifteen members of Ashley's expedition and immediately prompted a U.S. military expedition to retaliate against the Arikaras. Commanded by Colonel Henry Leavenworth, the American force of 275 men was joined by 750 Sioux. After sustaining Sioux attacks and several days of shelling by the troops, the Arikaras abandoned their palisaded villages under the cover of night, shortly after peace negotiations collapsed, and fled north to the Mandan and Hidatsa villages (Morgan 1964).

George Catlin found the Arikaras living again in the Grand River villages in 1832, but when Prince Maximilian ascended the Missouri in 1833 he recorded that they had moved from the area the preceding year. Driven away by fear of the more powerful Sioux, crop failure, scarcity of buffalo, and potential harassment from American troops in the aftermath of the Leavenworth campaign, most of the Arikaras had gone south to live near the Skiris on the Loup River in Nebraska. In 1835, however, after friction broke out between them and the Skiris, the Arikaras moved into western Nebraska and eastern South Dakota, where they lived for two years as nomadic hunters.

In 1837 small Arikara groups began moving back to the Missouri, continuing their gradual northwestward movement up the river, to settle as a tribe at Fort Clark, the American Fur Company post near the mouth of the Knife River, where the Mandans lived. Immediately upon settling there that year, however, smallpox broke out, brought upstream by a fur company steamboat. The resulting epidemic took a heavy toll on the horticultural tribes of the middle Missouri. The Arikaras lost one half of their population; only some 1,500 survived. Mandan mortalities, however, were even grimmer: some 90 percent of their people perished, reportedly leaving fewer than 150 survivors (Hodge 1907-10, 1:798). Demoralized, the remaining Mandans abandoned their village at Fort Clark and many moved north to join the Hidatsas; later, after a fire destroyed the old Mandan lodges, the Arikaras established their village at Fort Clark, where they remained for over two decades.

Three persistent pressures continued to afflict Arikara life at Fort Clark and took even greater tolls on their already diminished population: crop failures; epidemic diseases that included measles, cholera, and smallpox; and constant Sioux raiding. Finally in 1861, after Fort Clark was abandoned by the fur traders and burned by the Sioux, the Arikaras moved upriver once again, this time to build two villages on the bank opposite Like-A-Fishhook Village, in which both the Mandans and Hidatsas were living. A year later, after more Sioux threats, the Arikaras crossed the Missouri to join them, creating in Like-A-Fishhook a combined village in which each of the three tribes maintained its own section. There the Arikaras constructed a Medicine Lodge and tried to

Plate 1. Views of Like-A-Fishhook Village in 1872. *Left*, Arikara section, showing palisade in foreground, log cabins and earth lodges in background. *Right*, Arikara section, showing drying scaffolds in foreground and log cabins in background. Photographs by Stanley J. Morrow, courtesy State Historical Society of North Dakota.

Plate 2. Views of Like-A-Fishhook Village in 1872. *Left*, Arikara Medicine Lodge with sacred cedar tree and rock in front of entryway. *Right*, Hidatsa section, showing drying scaffolds in foreground and earth lodges and log cabins in background. Photographs by Stanley J. Morrow, courtesy State Historical Society of North Dakota.

recreate their old way of life. At first they were plagued by continuing attacks from the Sioux, but during the following decades their lifestyle was more drastically altered by Euro-Americans. Most previous contact with Americans had been with but one group, the fur traders, who had no intention of radically altering the native lifestyle; now, on a reservation guaranteed them in 1870 by a treaty with the U.S. government, contact occurred with diverse elements of an expanding American society—Indian agents, the military, missionaries, teachers, and settlers—all exerting strong pressures to modify native cultural patterns.

Changes came rapidly for what were now called the Three Tribes[6] on the new Fort Berthold Reservation, the boundaries of which were legally establish-ed in 1870.[7] Intertribal warfare, long a bane to the horticulturalists, effectively came to an end after the 1876 military campaign against the off-reservation Sioux and the Battle of the Little Big Horn, in which Arikara scouts served the U.S. government. Once peace was achieved, erstwhile enemies became friendly visitors, and groups of Sioux and Assiniboines, in addition to other previously friendly peoples, came to Fort Berthold to socialize—to visit, dance, and tell stories—while Fort Berthold peoples reciprocated with visits of friendship to neighboring reservation communities in the Dakotas and eastern Montana. The most fundamental changes, however, were ones affecting native culture. Of them, perhaps the most profound was land allotment, the plan of the U.S. government to move Indian families out of tribal settlements and onto individually owned plots of land that they were to farm. The first group of villagers to leave Like-A-Fishhook were Arikara families who took up farm-steads in 1884; by 1886 the entire Arikara section of the village had been abandoned, thereby ending the community mode of living that the tribe had always known. Equally profound, but not nearly so abrupt, was the elimination, at least overtly, of Arikara religious and curing practices symbolized by the Medicine Lodge. Following Office of Indian Affairs policy, public ceremonies in the Medicine Lodge were finally suppressed by the Indian agent in 1885, at the same time that families were taking up their allotments.

Shortly after the settlement of families onto individual farmsteads, day schools were established that gave a new focus to community life on the

6. Later they were officially designated the Three Affiliated Tribes.

7. The first recognition of the territorial claims of the Three Tribes was in the 1851 Fort Laramie Treaty. The boundaries it defined, and the revised ones of 1870, created a reservation that extended on its eastern border from the Missouri River south to the Heart and Little Powder rivers, and on its western border north along the Powder and Yellowstone rivers to the Missouri. The boundaries of this reservation were modified on three subsequent occasions—in 1880, 1891, and finally 1910—in each instance reducing its size. (See map 2.)

reservation at the end of the nineteenth century, a focus that has continued to the present.[8] The first school was opened in 1895 in the Arikara settlement near the site of old Fort Berthold. Both the school and the settlement there were named Armstrong. Shortly afterward schools were built at Independence, a Mandan and Hidatsa settlement west of the Missouri; at Elbowoods, which was established in 1892 as the site of the new Fort Berthold agency and which became a Hidatsa settlement; and at Shell Creek, another Hidatsa settlement, where most of the members of Crow Flies High's dissident band located after they returned to the reservation in 1894. In addition to the communities that developed around these schools and that later became seats of reservation districts, several other district communities took form: Beaver Creek, an Arikara community; and Red Butte (now Twin Buttes), Little Missouri (or Short River), and Santee (later Lucky Mound), all primarily Hidatsa and Mandan settlements. In addition to the schools in four of them, the initial core of each community was a dance hall (a round wooden structure for dances and other community events) and generally a trading post or store. Later, churches were built in some of the communities like Armstrong (later named Nishu), Red Butte, Independence, and Little Missouri (later called Charging Eagle); and a post office, in addition to the one in Elbowoods, was opened in Armstrong. By 1937 each of the eight communities had a day school.

During the first half of the twentieth century, Arikara life on the Fort Berthold Reservation was dominated by efforts to implement government Indian policy charted at the end of the previous century: to educate Indians, primarily by teaching them manual trade skills, and to train them to become successful, independent farmers or livestock ranchers—goals that sought to merge Indian people ultimately into rural American society. Agency and government programs met with general success, although some fundamental aspects of traditional Indian culture continued to survive, often in spite of vigorous agency efforts to suppress them. So vigorous, in fact, were those attempts that in 1902 they prompted the anthropologist George A. Dorsey to remark in a letter to Commissioner of Indian Affairs William A. Jones:

> To me, one of the most pitiable things which I have ever seen in all my dealings with the Indians is that of a tribe like the Arikara, for instance, who have been hounded by the missionaries and by their agents for a period of

8. Earlier schools on the reservation were a day school at the agency, first opened in 1870 but operating only sporadically; one established at the Congregational mission in 1876; and another constructed at the Catholic mission in 1889. When the army closed Fort Stevenson on the eastern border of the reservation, the agency opened a boarding school in the old buildings in 1883 and operated it until 1893, when the main part of the plant burned down.

Territory established by Treaty of 1851

Reservation Boundaries 1870

Reservation Boundaries 1880

Reservation Boundaries 1891

Map 2. Changing Fort Berthold Reservation Boundaries, 1851–1891.

Map 3. Fort Berthold Reservation and Vicinity in the Early Twentieth Century.

thirty or forty years, and who have been made to think that they had absolutely no right on this earth to think about their own gods, who have literally been compelled to hide away all their religious paraphernalia; and whatever of their rites or ceremonies they have held they have held with fear and trembling—and yet, the Arikara are truly Indians in that feeling and belief as are any Indians of this Continent. [G. A. Dorsey 1902]

Despite the agency and missionary efforts to eradicate Arikara religious traditions, however, at the turn of the century there were attempts in the Beaver Creek district to revive them. Two prominent ritual leaders, Crow Ghost and Red Star, for example, had dreams in which they were given dance songs (story 32); Crow Ghost tried to revive older ceremonies; and a young woman named Winnie Enemy Heart had a vision in which she was told that Arikaras should return to their former ways. Moreover, in 1910 the Arikara Medicine Lodge was revived for Edward Curtis so that he could photograph and describe its rituals for the Arikara section of his multivolume set *The North American Indian* (Curtis 1907-30, 5:59-100). It was a revival that continued sporadically until the early 1930s.

The Arikara population, which had reached an all-time low of 379 in 1905, began a slow, steady rise, but simultaneously, Arikara intermarriage with Hidatsas and Mandans increased, blurring many of the distinctive cultural differences among the three tribes, even though each continued to maintain its own communities.

In 1953 still another major upheaval—the last of many—affected life for the Arikaras and their Fort Berthold neighbors when the U.S. Army Corps of Engineers constructed Garrison Dam on the Missouri just below the southeastern boundary of the reservation. Built for flood control and for water diversion to central North Dakota farming areas, the dam created Garrison Reservoir, now called Lake Sakakawea, which flooded all the Missouri bottom lands on the reservation. For the Three Affiliated Tribes, all of whose communities were located in those bottom lands, the flooding necessitated a massive relocation to the upland prairies surrounding the new reservoir. It also meant that the reservation was divided into discontinuous segments even more remote from each other, separated by a lake too wide to span feasibly with bridges. The result of the relocation was only an approximate replication on the prairies of the old communities in the river bottoms. Elbowoods and the agency, as well as the Shell Creek community, were reestablished in New Town in the Northern Segment of the reservation, which continued to be primarily Hidatsa in population. Nishu (formerly Armstrong), the primary Arikara community, moved to the Eastern Segment and became White Shield, named after the prominent nineteenth-century Arikara chief. The old communities of Beaver Creek, Red Butte, and Little Missouri in the Southern Segment joined to form

Plate 3. Partial View of Elbowoods, Fort Berthold Reservation, North Dakota. Photograph ca. 1911, by Fred Olsen, courtesy State Historical Society of North Dakota.

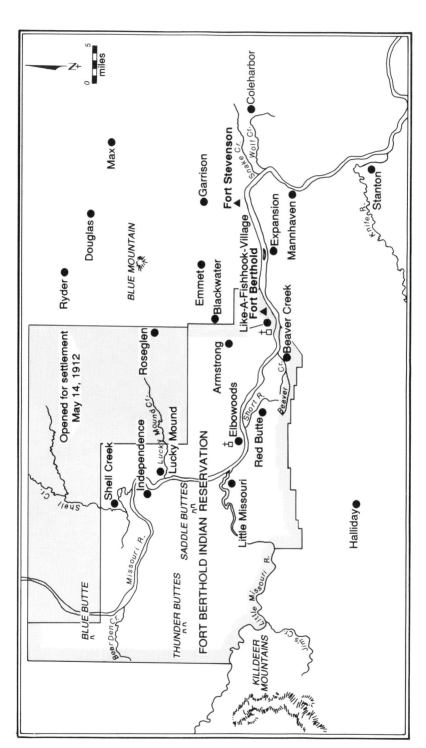

Map 4. Fort Berthold Reservation in the Early Twentieth Century.

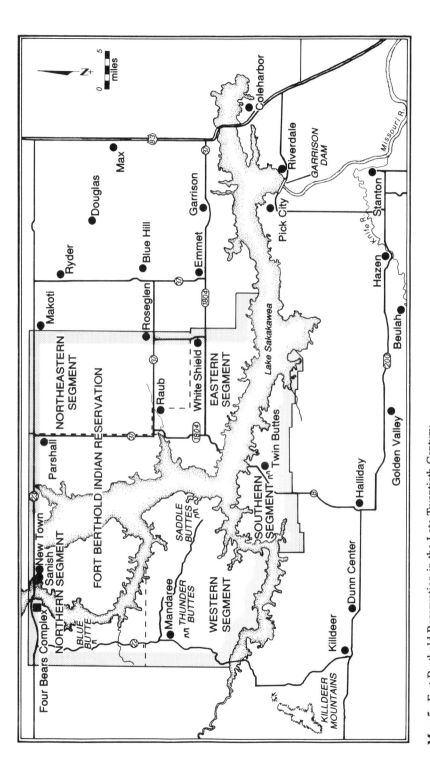

Map 5. Fort Berthold Reservation in the Late Twentieth Century.

the new community of Twin Buttes; the Hidatsa community of Independence was reformed as Mandaree in the Western Segment; and Lucky Mound was moved to the new Northeastern Segment. As before, the core of each new community was its school, together with housing for teachers and tribal members, and a community hall in which dances, funerals, community meetings, and other social events were held.

Thus by the mid-twentieth century the Arikaras had relocated as a group for perhaps the final time in their gradual movement north. It was a journey that had commenced untold centuries in the past, before their modern identification as Arikaras had taken form, when they and their close relatives the Pawnees lived somewhere farther southeastward in what must have been the homeland of all the Caddoan peoples. The original group or groups who ultimately became the Arikaras were the vanguard of those Caddoans who migrated north to Nebraska and beyond and who were settled along the Missouri River in South Dakota in the eighteenth century when Europeans first encountered them. From the late eighteenth to the late nineteenth century, a combination of disease and warfare decimated their population so that what had formerly been dialectally, and perhaps culturally, diverse people became an amalgam that would henceforth be considered a single tribal entity. However, no matter the specific stimuli—disease, enemies, famine—their history throughout this period continued to be the story of a northwestward migration along the Holy Water, the Missouri River, in a general movement enshrined in myth and ordained in religious belief that has culminated in their present location in west central North Dakota.

Recording Arikara Oral Traditions

For a tribe that has received so little attention from anthropologists and other cultural recorders, the body of documented Arikara oral traditions is both surprisingly extensive and yet frustratingly meager—extensive in a comparative Plains context because there is at least one large collection that was recorded at the turn of the century, and yet meager because even at this relatively early date the stories were collected at the end of a tradition that, while still alive, would not long remain viable.

Jean Baptiste Truteau, during his late-eighteenth-century visit, was the first outsider to record an Arikara myth. In a discussion of Arikara religious beliefs in his "Description of the Upper Missouri" (Parks in press), he presented as an illustration of Arikara religious traditions an abbreviated account of the origins of horticulture and of human subsistence on game animals followed by divine instructions for ritual worship of the Great Holy. In their journals nearly a decade later, Lewis and Clark also mentioned an Arikara tradition, a story about a young couple who turned to stone, which was related to them during their brief visit with the tribe on their way up the Missouri (Moulton 1987, 3:169).

Other Arikara stories published in the nineteenth century include the myth of Long Teeth, recorded by the physician Walter Hoffman in 1892, as well as a small number of other stories that appeared sporadically during the last two decades of the nineteenth century in the *Word Carrier*, a newspaper serving the Dakota Mission of the Congregational and Presbyterian churches and printed at Santee, Nebraska. These stories, which include the genesis tradition as well as several myths and fables, were recorded by the Congregational missionary Charles L. Hall and his wife, who first went to the Fort Berthold Reservation in 1876. Hall was not one of those exceptional missionaries who truly appreciated Indian culture and attempted to preserve a record of the vanishing lifeway of the people he served. For him there was no compromise in his missionary calling: the new must replace the old; cultural surrender must be unconditional. And yet, despite his inflexible stance, there was a curious ambivalence toward Indian culture that, for example, inspired him and his wife to record and preserve through publication some of the religious beliefs of the Arikaras.

In 1903 James R. Murie, a mixed-blood Skiri Pawnee educated at Hampton Institute in Virginia and at that time assistant to the anthropologist George A. Dorsey of the Field Columbian Museum in Chicago, visited the Fort Berthold Reservation to make a record of Arikara folklore and ceremonialism as well as to purchase material culture specimens for the museum.[9] The material he recorded, which marked the first modern anthropological study of the Arikaras, was to contribute to Dorsey's broad descriptive and comparative study of the mythology and ritualism of the Caddoan tribes. Murie had begun collecting Pawnee oral traditions three years earlier—an effort that over a five-year period resulted in two published volumes of Pawnee traditions[10]—and in the course of a three-month visit to Fort Berthold he recorded eighty-two stories, which were published by Dorsey in 1904 under the title *Traditions of the Arikara*.

Here was a large, representative collection of the repertoire of traditional Arikara folklore at the turn of the century, at a time when the last Arikara Medicine Lodge was a disappearing ruin and a log church had already been built to serve the tribe. Murie's narrators were prominent tribal members, who included Bear's Head, Four Horns (Four Rings), White Owl, Many Foxes,

9. For a biography of Murie, see Murie (1981, 1:21–28).

10. *Traditions of the Skidi Pawnee* (G. A. Dorsey 1904b) and *The Pawnee: Mythology (Part 1)* (G. A. Dorsey 1906a).

Yellow Bull, Yellow Bear, Strikes Enemy, White Bear, Snowbird (Nice Voiced Elk), Enemy Heart, Sam Newman (Two Hawks), Joe Reed (Red Hail), and Andrew Little Crow. Some of them as young men had been on war parties, and many were traditional ritual leaders and doctors. Four Rings, for example, was the keeper and priest of the Eastern bundle. Some were educated and were fully bilingual in Arikara and English; but most spoke little or no English, so that Murie, who according to Dorsey had overcome the differences between Arikara and Pawnee speech, took the stories down in an English translation that apparently closely followed the narrated Arikara.

After Murie, no one made further efforts to record substantial amounts of Arikara oral traditions. Edward Curtis, who collected material in 1907 for the Arikara section of *The North American Indian*, did record three long stories, including a version of the genesis tradition, which he published in 1909. And in 1910, when the anthropologist Robert Lowie spent several days interviewing Bear's Teeth, an elderly Arikara man, on the topic of tribal societies, he obtained several stories that he subsequently published (Lowie 1915).

Although not yet oral traditions, the reminiscences in *The Arikara Narrative* are an important part of Arikara oral history. They record Arikara participation in Lieutenant Colonel George Armstrong Custer's 1874 and 1876 campaigns and represent the final major effort during the early twentieth century to preserve tribal history. Finding that Arikara service in those campaigns and their perspective on them had been overlooked by historians, in 1912 O.G. Libby, then director of the North Dakota State Historical Society, gathered together in the house of Bear's Belly the surviving scouts who had served under Custer at Fort Abraham Lincoln. Libby recorded their reminiscences and published them as a volume in 1920.

During the 1920s the ethnobotanist Melvin R. Gilmore frequently visited the Arikaras at Fort Berthold to record material on a variety of topics, including religion, botany, and social organization. Although he, too, recorded a small number of oral traditions incidental to other projects, one, the genesis myth associated with the Eastern bundle, was published as a separate article (Gilmore 1929). In it Gilmore presented the myth and described the ritual transfer of a sheaf of thirty-four willow sticks from the bundle's priest, Four Rings, to himself. The set of sticks were what the priest would lay out during the bundle-opening ritual to represent stages in the narrative of the beginning and development of all things in the world. Presented in the article in English translation is a recitation of this cosmogonic component, which was integral to Arikara religious ceremonialism.

More recently, in 1938 the anthropologist Preston Holder spent six months at Fort Berthold studying Arikara culture, and during the course of that work he wrote down in English a small miscellaneous collection of stories that remain unpublished.

Finally, two short selections of Arikara interlinear linguistic texts were recently published as part of a representative collection of Caddoan texts (Parks 1977). One set consists of three narratives collected by Allan R. Taylor in 1960, and the second comprises seven texts, all of which are earlier versions of narratives in the present collection.

Recording the Collection

Despite more than a century and a half of unrelenting assaults on Arikara society by human foes and disease, and despite their cooperativeness with the U.S. government and their more positive attitude toward acculturation than most other Plains tribes adopted in the late nineteenth century, many Arikaras clung tenaciously to their language and distinctive cultural traditions. As a consequence, when I first went to North Dakota in 1970 to begin a study of the Arikara language, there were some two hundred speakers, twenty to thirty of whom still used an older form of the language and remembered many traditional stories.

Over the ensuing two decades I have been engaged in an effort to help preserve as much of this linguistic and historiographic heritage as possible. At the outset my goals were purely academic—to document oral traditions in the language as one means of preserving a linguistic record of Arikara speech. But it soon became apparent that many people in the White Shield community, still maintaining its distinct Arikara identity, were keenly interested in having both their language and their cultural traditions not only preserved but also taught in the tribal school, so that their children would be able to learn there what elders at home were no longer able to teach: their tribal linguistic and historical heritage. Hence my effort developed into a more broadly based one involving many Arikara elders and other individuals in the community.

History of the Project

The history of this project began in Pawnee, Oklahoma, on a hot August evening in 1969, when I went to the home of Dolly Moore, with whom I had regularly worked on the Pawnee language, to bid her farewell before my return to California. Visiting her from North Dakota was a gregarious Arikara friend, Fanny Whiteman, who took a lively interest in our linguistic project and suggested before I left that if I should ever come to North Dakota to study Arikara she would introduce me to her mother, Clara Perkins, an elderly and fluent speaker of the language. Anxious to undertake comparative work with this language, which grammatically is almost identical to Pawnee but is not mutually intelligible with it because of various sound shifts and changes in the meanings of words, I traveled to North Dakota the following summer to spend two weeks there recording Arikara vocabulary from Fanny and her mother. During my visit, Dan Howling Wolf, a blind man then in his sixties, came to Fanny's when she told him I wanted to record Indian stories and songs. Over two evenings we tape-recorded fourteen stories, most of them about Coyote and Scalped Man but including others, as well as forty-six personal songs of military servicemen—the modern equivalent of old warrior songs.

My first visit to North Dakota established warm friendships which developed into obvious mutual enthusiasm for continuing the study of Arikara, but I was not able to return there for a year and a half. Meanwhile, in the fall of the following year, Fanny's mother passed away before we had the opportunity to continue our work.

Nevertheless, in January 1972, during the winter academic break, I flew to Minot, North Dakota, and then took a bus to Parshall, where I stayed two weeks with Fanny and her father. During that visit Dan and Mabel Howling Wolf and another elder couple, Matthew and Alice White Bear, came to stay for several days. During the daytime we recorded vocabulary, and in the evenings we recorded more stories. Dan told nine, which together with the ones he had told previously, form the inventory of his narratives in this collection. Matthew told eight, four of which are presented here. Subsequently, Fanny and Alice worked with me for several days at transcribing and translating several of them before I had to return to my teaching duties at Idaho State University.

In early June I came back to Parshall and remained in North Dakota throughout the summer. First I continued to work with Fanny and Alice, taking up the linguistic work where we had left off in the winter. Then in early August I visited Mary Gillette, daughter of Little Sioux, an Arikara scout and prominent doctor, and herself a conservative elder member of the community who always participated in traditional affairs. I wanted to record songs and suggested offhandedly that she might, for example, know a lullaby. She mistook my request, however, thinking that I had come to ask her to sing a medicine song for newborn infants that she knew, and set a later date for me to return. When I arrived at her home, accompanied at her request by Fanny, who would be a witness to what she did, she performed a ceremony preparatory to the recording and then sang for me her medicine song preceded by a prayer (narrative 146). Afterward she recorded two stories and a love song with an accompanying explanation in Arikara, all of which are included here.

During that August Fanny took me to White Shield to introduce me to her aunt, Ella Waters, an octogenarian who was noted as a medicine woman and tribal ceremonial leader. We stayed two days at Mrs. Waters's home, working all day and into the night. The experience was exhilarating for me because in Mrs. Waters I had found a person who not only spoke Arikara without peer but who also, because she had previously worked with anthropologists, was sensitive to what I wanted to know and seemed genuinely to enjoy the linguistic endeavor. We arranged to continue working together for the duration of my stay that summer.

I returned to North Dakota the following June (1973) and took up residence in Garrison, a small town twenty-two miles east of White Shield. From there I drove daily to White Shield, a regular commute made whenever I worked in the community over the ensuing eleven years. For a short time while we worked together, Mrs. Waters lived in a house in White Shield, while her own house on a farm four miles west of the community was being renovated. Once the renovations were completed, she moved back to the farm, where we continued our collaboration in a peaceful setting with rare interruptions. There, interspersed with other linguistic endeavors over the course of the summer, I recorded eleven stories. Sometimes her grandson's wife, a young Sioux woman from Manitoba, together with her son, would be present, but frequently I would be the sole member of the audience—an audience which in either case did not understand the narration—told in her living room with its windows open to let the warm summer winds provide a refreshing air flow. After recording the stories, I transcribed and translated them with Mrs. Waters's collaboration.

During the spring of 1974 I accepted a position at Mary College (presently the University of Mary), a small, private school in Bismarck, North Dakota, to direct an Indian language program established by Elaine A. Jahner (now of Dartmouth College). The goal of the program was to develop college-level pedagogical materials for the languages native to North Dakota so that courses in those languages could be offered as part of the college's developing Indian Studies program, initiated at a time when there was an awakening interest in tribal heritage among Indian students in the state. During the first year of this program, my work, together with that of Janet Beltran, a curriculum designer and writer, was to concentrate on Arikara, but a year later, in 1976, two additional linguists, Robert Hollow and A. Wesley Jones, were added to the staff to prepare reference and teaching materials for the two other Fort Berthold languages, Mandan and Hidatsa. The initial goal of the program was subsequently widened to include the preparation of elementary language lessons that could be used in reservation school classrooms in White Shield, Twin Buttes, and Mandaree. To achieve these goals, two complementary efforts were required: working with older speakers to record various linguistic data—vocabulary for dictionaries; phrases, sentences, and verb paradigms for grammars; and traditional narratives for historical and literary preservation—and developing language lessons derived from the linguistic data and other material collected specifically for that purpose. Thus, over the next few years the agenda was established.

Relocating to Bismarck prevented me from working at Fort Berthold during the summer of 1974, but the new position in North Dakota was to afford me the opportunity to work on the reservation throughout the year rather than solely during the summers and to become acquainted with a wider range of people there—tribal officials, school personnel, and members of the Arikara community. As a result, interest in the linguistic project increased, developing it into a more community-based endeavor rather than solely an academic one.

In June 1975 I returned to live in Garrison for a three-month period, during which I recorded another story from Mary Gillette, a number of stories from Mrs. Waters, and three stories from William Deane, Jr., an elderly man with whom I had become acquainted.

The following year, 1976, marked another significant milestone in the project. One day, when casually chatting with John Fox, a prominent member of the White Shield community, he suggested one of his brothers, Alfred Morsette, as a potential source of traditional stories. Although I had never heard of his brother before, I followed the lead. In August I visited him at his home in a remote area west of Twin Buttes in the Southern Segment of the reservation and explained to him the linguistic work I was doing and my desire to record traditional Arikara stories. His response was heartening: he said he knew many old stories about the Arikara past, ones told to him by his grandparents who had reared him and by many other men now deceased, and he would be glad to record them so that there would be a history of the tribe. He insisted, however, on one modification in my plan: I had only asked him to record stories in Arikara, but he wanted to record them in English as well so that anyone who did not understand Arikara—and from his perspective that was nearly everyone in the world—could listen to them. That day we recorded three narratives, all historical in a Western sense, describing the Arikara separation from the Pawnees, the Fort Laramie Treaty of 1851, and the two Custer campaigns culminating in the Battle of the Little Big Horn. Each one was told first in Arikara and immediately afterward in English, a routine subsequently followed every time we recorded stories.

Over the next four years Alfred and I met many times, but always during the winter, which was loosely defined as any time between October and March, since he wished to follow the old custom of telling stories only during that season. At first I traveled to his home, where during each visit we would generally record from two to five narratives, depending on their length. Later, as we became better acquainted, Alfred came periodically to Bismarck—initially, to stay with his son and, later, after he had taken me as a son, to stay with me at my home. On such occasions we would chat and review Arikara vocabulary during the day, and after supper in the evening we would record stories. I would turn on the tape recorder when he was ready, and then he would proceed to narrate, frequently closing his eyes and folding his arms as he recited from memory the details of the story, told, as he would say, exactly as he had heard it. Some stories he had been told only once or twice while a child or youth; others were accounts he had heard later in his life. He had repeated many of the stories to his own children when they were growing up, but many had not been related to anyone since he had heard them originally, so the latter required thoughtful preparation before recording. Then, about ten thirty at night, after recording for several hours, Alfred liked to have "a little lunch" and coffee and then chat until bedtime. In the morning he would always rise early and sit in the dining room singing Arikara songs until breakfast.

Between 1976 and 1979 Alfred recorded a total of sixty-one stories in Arikara. During that period, as well as later, he also recorded a number of others that were told only in English and are not included here. The number of stories in his repertoire is impressive, especially given their nature and detail. Certainly no other contemporary Arikara, even those older than he, matched Alfred in the number and variety of stories remembered, all told in a fine narrative style characteristic of an older, all-but-forgotten oral tradition. For him, knowing them was a source of great pride. So, too, was his phenomenal memory for songs. A singer most of his life, he was noted not only for his fine voice but also for his vast repertoire of songs. After he heard a song, he once told me pridefully, he "soaked it up like a sponge" and retained it in his memory. And indeed he demonstrated this capacity one week in spring 1978 when he came to Bismarck to record old songs, most of them no longer remembered by his contemporaries. One set consisted of twenty Pawnee grass dance songs introduced to the Arikaras before the turn of the century; two other groups were also grass dance songs—one set those of Crow Ghost and the other those of Red Star—which were dreamed at the turn of the century (narrative 32). Most of them had not been sung in years. During that week Alfred recorded the old grass dance songs as well as many others representing other genres, for a total of over two hundred songs, and afterward told in English the story behind each one.

In 1977 I also recorded a sample of stories from several other individuals in order to insure that the text collection would be representative of the contemporary Arikara community and illustrate individual variation in both narrative type and style. In September I arranged to meet with John Fox and

Dan Hopkins at Fox's house in White Shield. There, in his living room, we recorded all afternoon, the two men alternating stories. They each told four. One evening later that month I visited Joe Fox, a grandson of Lowie's informant, Bear's Teeth, at his home in Drags Wolf Village west of New Town. On that visit he recorded two stories, one of which is included in this collection. Again one evening in the fall Mrs. Waters and I went to Drags Wolf Village to visit Eleanor Chase, another fine Arikara speaker who had a strong interest in her heritage. Although, she told us, she wished we had given her advance notice so she could have thought about stories, she recorded three of them. Finally that year Mrs. Waters and I visited her niece, Esther Perkins, who then lived across the street from Mrs. Waters's new apartment in a housing development two miles southeast of White Shield. Esther had been crippled all her life and had never attended school. Consequently she grew up speaking only Arikara, learning English later in life. On this visit she took us to her bedroom, where we would be away from the young children playing, and there recorded two stories.

Through winter 1978 Mrs. Waters stayed in Bismarck, where she could work regularly with the language program, aiding in the development of an introductory Arikara language textbook, tape recording lessons, and co-teaching with me an Arikara language course for Mary College students and interested adults. During this period she and I also worked daily at transcribing and translating Alfred Morsette's stories as well as ones that I had recorded earlier from Dan Howling Wolf and others. Mrs. Waters, in fact, assisted me in the transcription and translation process with nearly all of the stories in this collection, with the exception of Lillian Brave's, which are described below. The following year Mrs. Waters returned again to Bismarck for various periods of time to continue the work we had begun the previous fall. At the culmination of this work in spring 1979, at the annual Mary College Indian Student Powwow, she adopted me as a member of the tribe and gave me the Arikara name White Crow *(kaakaataaká)*.

The final chapter in the history of this collection began in 1983, when I came to Indiana University and at the same time began working part-time with a newly funded bilingual education program in the White Shield Elementary School. My goals with the program were to provide further language teaching materials—among them illustrated elementary bilingual readers and a bilingual dictionary—and to complete the preparation of this collection of texts. Shortly after the project began, Fanny Whiteman began working with the program and spoke to her aunt, Lillian Brave, then in her mid-eighties, about recording some of her stories to be included in the collection. And there began a significant new dimension to the project, since Mrs. Brave was an exceptionally fine speaker of the language—Ella Waters had mentioned to me years earlier that Lillian "spoke the old language"—and knew many old stories. Like Alfred Morsette, she would tell stories only in the winter.

Over a period of several days in January 1984 I recorded nine narratives from Mrs. Brave in the kitchen of her daughter Angela Plante. On each occasion there were at least three of us present—Angela, Fanny, and myself—as well as occasional grandchildren and other relatives, creating an appreciative audience for Mrs. Brave. Afterward I transcribed and translated the stories with the assistance of both Lilly and Angela. In February, after I had returned to Indiana, Angela recorded another seven stories from her mother and mailed the tape to me. In February 1987 I returned to Parshall, where we recorded six more narratives, all of which, together with the ones previously mailed to me, were then transcribed and translated as before. At the same time Angela shared with me a cassette tape on which in 1975 she had recorded a particularly meaningful story (69) from her mother, and together the three of us transcribed and translated it.

The Narrators

Alfred Morsette, Sr. (Not Afraid Of The Enemy), whose band affiliation was Awahu, was born September 26, 1911, north of Elbowoods in McLean County on the Fort Berthold Reservation. His father was Fred Fox (Holy Owl), the son of John Morsette (Chippewa Child), a Métis from the north, and Squash Blossom, an Arikara woman. His mother was Blanche Meyer, whose father was white and whose mother was Skunk Woman. Alfred lived with his grandparents—Squash Blossom and her second husband, Short Bear, both of whom spoke no English—until he went to Pierre Indian School in South Dakota. There he remained for eight years. When he returned home to the reservation, he lived with an uncle and learned to ride and break horses and then worked locally as a hired hand. At the same time he also took up boxing, but later quit it after losing one eye in an accident. In 1934 he built a house in the old Beaver Creek district from logs that he himself cut and lived there for four years as a bachelor; then in 1938 he married Lena Hunts Along, a Hidatsa who was the daughter of John Hunts Along and the granddaughter of Buffalo Paunch. In that same year Alfred was laid off from his job as a night watchman in Elbowoods and subsequently planted his own gardens, raised horses and cattle, and worked at various odd jobs.

After Garrison Dam was built, Alfred moved to the Southern Segment of the reservation, in a remote area east of Twin Buttes where many other families from Beaver Creek relocated. When I first visited him in 1976, Alfred's son Roy and his family were also living in his home. His wife, Lena, had

Plate 4. Alfred Morsette, Sr. (*Paatúh Kananuuninó,* Not Afraid Of The Enemy). Photograph by Douglas R. Parks, 1980.

passed away many years earlier. After several years he moved into an apartment for senior citizens in the Twin Buttes community, where he remained until his death on December 15, 1989, at the age of seventy-eight. He and his wife had seven children, two sons and five daughters.

An abiding interest in his Arikara heritage distinguished Mr. Morsette's life, an interest that was cultivated from the outset by his grandparents, who were conservative members of the Arikara community and provided an environment for him early in life that was rich in traditional culture. Not only did his grandparents and the relatives and friends who visited them serve as sources for traditional narratives, but when he was a child his grandmother also encouraged him to go to older relatives to learn songs and stories. By the time he was fourteen he was sitting at the drum, joining in the singing, an activity he continued throughout his life. One of his favorite pastimes, he used to reminisce, was getting together with friends on winter evenings—with such men as Wallace Hand, Billy Lockwood, Vincent Malnourie—who used to come across the river to gather around the drum and sing for pleasure. When he was younger, Alfred was recognized as one of the very best singers on the reservation, and throughout most of his life, whenever he attended a dance or celebration, he always went to the drum. Because of his good voice and his ability to remember songs, the older officiants at traditional religious rituals would also ask him to sing. Moreover, he used to assist his uncle Snowbird, an Arikara ceremonial leader in the Beaver Creek district, in the performance of such rituals as the death feast, which was prepared for a deceased person immediately after burial (see narrative 107); from Snowbird he also acquired the right to the song that accompanies the smudging of a drum, a ritual that must be performed preceding a dance after the death of a tribal member.

The stories told by Mr. Morsette and presented in this collection represent the full range of Arikara oral traditions. Many of them, particularly the myths, were no longer known or remembered by any of his contemporaries. These are stories that he learned from his grandparents, his father, his uncle Snowbird, and other prominent members of older generations, including Many Foxes, Running Wolf, and Jackrabbit. No doubt in large part because Arikara was Alfred's first language and the one in which he was most comfortable speaking, but also because his narratives were memorized texts, the vocabulary and grammatical constructions in the narratives are rich in older forms, many of which are no longer used by contemporary speakers; and the narrative style is similarly diverse and eloquent, reflecting an ease of expression in Arikara not found among most speakers of his generation.

What also distinguished Alfred from most contemporary Arikara speakers, in addition to fluency in the language and prodigious knowledge of stories and songs, was his attitude toward proper cultural behavior, an attitude that certainly affected this project. He insisted that the stories he recorded must provide a true representation of Arikara history from an Arikara perspective— something he felt had never been recorded—and to that end he contributed a broad range of narratives always told in what he characterized as the proper manner: told a few at a time in the winter and recited in culturally correct form, just as they had been told to him. Many Arikaras, some older than he, had a more relaxed attitude toward Arikara traditions—not just story telling, but behavior as well—and when they neglected or fell short of traditional expectations, Alfred was always critical of them, sometimes outspokenly.

Ella P. Waters (Yellow Bird Woman) was born on the Fort Berthold Reservation in 1889. Her father was Paul Yellow Bear (*kuuNUxtAhkáta,* Yellow

Plate 5. Ella P. Waters *(StikUstAhkáta,* Yellow Bird Woman). Photograph by Douglas R. Parks, 1973.

Bear), a noted Arikara doctor and later in his life a lay reader in the Episcopal church on the reservation. Her mother was Prairie Sod Village Woman, a name designating the band to which she and Ella also belonged, since band membership descended in the female line. After attending the Congregational mission school at Fort Berthold, Ella was a student at Wahpeton Indian School in South Dakota. Not long after returning home, her parents arranged her marriage in the traditional manner to Albert Simpson, an older Arikara man trained as a blacksmith and who owned a store in Beaver Creek. For several years he also served as the McLean County assessor.

Both Ella and her husband took a keen interest in traditional Arikara life, especially in its religion, doctoring, and social activities. As a young man in the decade before 1920 and later, Mr. Simpson had been an interpreter for the ethnobotanist Melvin Gilmore on his frequent visits to the reservation, and at times Simpson himself had served as consultant for Gilmore. With Ella assisting him, Simpson learned what he could from the older men who were traditional doctors, in particular Bear's Belly and Yellow Bear, and kept several of them, including George Howard, Sr., and Crow Ghost, in his home when they were elderly; later, after these men died, Simpson carried out many of the rituals they had conducted and healed people with the medicines he had obtained from them. Ella, for her part, used to take food to the doctors in the revived Medicine Lodge, manifesting what she characterized as "having holy feelings." In the preface to one narrative (108), in fact, she tells that beginning at the age of eighteen she regularly went to the Medicine Lodge to fast, make sacrifices of food and goods, and ask the doctors' societies for blessings. Later she, too, became a doctor; and then just before the death of her aunt, Julia White Bear, the sole female member of the Ghost Society, Mrs. White Bear gave her position in this doctor's society to Ella.[11]

Throughout her life Ella Waters was prominent in the Arikara community. From the 1930s to 1953, when Garrison Dam was constructed, she and three other women (Hanna Fox, Daisy Ross, and Mary Lockwood) formed the female chorus *(swakaatakúxu')* for the Dead Grass Society, a men's dance organization that was also influential in community affairs. Like her father, she was active in the Episcopal church throughout her life. During World War II she was president of the Nishu chapter of the War Mothers.

When I first met Mrs. Waters in 1970, she had recently lost her third husband, Levi Waters. For the next decade she continued to live on their farm four miles west of White Shield; then in 1980 she and her daughter Grace moved into an apartment for senior citizens in White Shield. Throughout the fifteen years of our friendship, Mrs. Waters was a ceremonial leader for the Arikara community, maintaining such traditions as the death feast and the public bestowal of Arikara names on individuals—rituals formerly performed by men but which by then only she knew and had the right to conduct.

Because of her intense, lifelong desire to learn and maintain Arikara traditions, Ella Waters was unsurpassed over the last two decades of her life as a source of information on the Arikara language, and particularly on older usages. A proud, confident woman, she always responded unhesitatingly and authoritatively to language questions, and she translated the stories of other narrators, no matter how challenging to understand, with ease and a strong

11. Most of the medicine societies had one female member.

Plate 6. Lillian Brave (*StičiišáxkUx*, One Kernel Of Corn Woman). Photograph by
Raymond J. DeMallie, 1990.

sense of what was correct Arikara speech. After I began to work with her, she
became completely dedicated to the project of preserving the Arikara language
through whatever media were available—written stories, a dictionary, class-
room materials, tape recordings, personal instruction—and with a clear,
unflagging sense of mission she always gave highest priority to this endeavor,
most of the products of which, unfortunately, she did not live to see completed.
Ella passed away in 1984, at the age of ninety-five.

  Lillian Brave (One Kernel Of Corn Woman), whose band affiliation is
čiNIhnaahtákUx, was in 1991 the oldest living Arikara speaker. She was born

July 20, 1899 in her parents' home in Elbowoods. Her father was Sam Newman (Two Hawks), an educated Arikara man who frequently interpreted for government officials and also served as Hidatsa interpreter for anthropologist Alfred Bowers in his studies of that tribe during the 1930s. Lilly's mother was Jenny Strikes Enemy (Squash Blossom), whose father was Black Trail, a leading Arikara doctor and nineteenth-century political leader who was one of the signatories to the Fort Laramie Treaty. While Lilly was growing up, several prominent Arikara ritualists stayed at her parents' home, among whom were Weasel Heart, Little Crow, and Crow Ghost. Crow Ghost, a cultural revivalist, taught the men in the family the ritual for opening a sacred bundle, how to sing Sage (purificatory) and other ceremonial songs, and recounted numerous traditions. It was in this environment—a home in which some of the most prominent, conservative Arikaras lived, men who were determined to maintain their traditions despite the radical social changes engulfing their lives—that Lilly lived during her early years, save for the periods when she attended boarding school, first at Wahpeton and then later at Bismarck Indian School. And it was this environment that enabled her to become familiar with many facets of traditional Arikara life unknown to most of her contemporaries and that instilled in her a strong, lifelong Arikara identity. It was this environment, too, that nurtured her conservative Arikara speech, which has many old features not found in the speech of her contemporaries.

Mrs. Brave lived most of her life in the Elbowoods community, but after construction of the dam she moved to Parshall, where she continues to live. Although she began work with me relatively late in the course of this project, Lilly, like Ella Waters, has demonstrated a deep, serious commitment to it, a commitment that is a measure of the importance she attaches to her language and culture. She nevertheless loves to clown and joke, often bawdily, and is deftly able to enliven any social situation, no matter how serious, without trivializing it. The latter trait, combined with her solemn, earnest attitude toward her language and culture, have made Lilly an extraordinarily pleasurable person to work with.

Lilly was formerly married to the late John Bad Brave, a noted Hidatsa traditionalist, and has two daughters, one of whom (Angela Plante) speaks Arikara fluently.

Mary Gillette (Red Eagle Woman) was a cousin of Lilly Brave and a classmate as well when they both attended Wahpeton Indian School. She was born in Beaver Creek district on April 4, 1899. Her mother was Sioux Woman, a first cousin of Jenny Newman. Like Mrs. Newman, her band affiliation was *čiNIhnaahtákUx.* Mary's father was Little Sioux, an Arikara who was part Sioux. He served as an Indian scout in the 1876 campaign against the Sioux

Plate 7. Mary Gillette *(SteetAhkaswáhAt,* Red Eagle Woman). Photograph 1973.

and was a traditional doctor who owned both horse and snake medicine.[12] Mary was married first to Walter Plenty Chief and later to Albert Gillette. She lived in Nishu until the dam flooded the river basin in 1953, when she moved into Parshall, the first Indian to live in this small town that has only recently

12. Various individuals owned these medicines, and those who possessed one of them (e.g., snake medicine) formed a loose-knit society. They were not, however, members of the older, established doctors' societies that had positions in the Medicine Lodge. A short biography of Little Sioux, which he apparently dictated, appears in Libby (1920:191-193).

Plate 8. William Deane, Jr. *(Skána NareešaáNU,* Lone Chief). Photograph courtesy of Faye Portraits, Inc., Garrison, North Dakota.

been recognized to be within the borders of the Northeastern Segment of the reservation. Parshall was her home from that time until her death on July 26, 1976, at the age of seventy-seven.

A close friend of both Ella Waters and Lilly Brave, Mary Gillette shared with them a deep sense of pride in her Arikara heritage. When I first visited Fort Berthold, she was recognized as one of the most knowledgeable members of the community and an excellent speaker of the language—one who, as I learned, spoke slowly and precisely, always with exceptional clarity. She was also a gregarious individual, generous to friend and stranger alike, who was noted for usually having a pot of food simmering on the stove and for inviting friends who passed by her house to come in to eat. Whenever I visited at her home, she was unfailingly cordial and warm, an outgoing person whose conversations in a heavily accented English were always spiced with humor, and who was happy to contribute her knowledge to this project.

William Deane, Jr. (Lone Chief) was a proud, serious man, then in his late seventies, when I knew him. He was born July 11, 1897 at Armstrong. His parents were William Deane, Sr. (He Is Yellow), an Arikara subchief, and Grace Parker. After attending day school at Armstrong, Bill Deane, too, went to Wahpeton Indian School to complete his education. From 1917 to 1918 he served in the U.S. Army, and upon discharge he returned to Fort Berthold, where in 1920 he married Leona Yellow Bird.

Throughout most of his life, Bill ranched. He started the first Hereford ranch on the Fort Berthold Reservation and operated it until his retirement in 1960. In his youth he was noted as an outstanding saddle bronc rider and, like many young men on the reservation, competed in rodeos in North Dakota and surrounding states. Later he became involved in tribal government and served on the tribal council, holding the position of treasurer. He also held positions with the Bureau of Indian Affairs as relocation officer and credit officer. An active member of the local chapter of the American Legion, he served as its commander several times and helped to reorganize the post at White Shield. He also served as precinct committeeman for the Republican Party from 1942 until his death.

Bill Deane was a member of the Prairie Sod Village band. The last tribal subchief, he possessed the personality traits traditionally associated with that status: generosity, thoughtfulness, and security born of confidence. Although he devoted most of his life to ranching and tribal government, he was an active participant in Arikara tribal functions. He spoke fluent Arikara and Hidatsa, as well as English, and when I came into the community he was recognized as a linguistic and cultural authority.

Dan Howling Wolf (Standing Wolf), born on April 11, 1906, in the Nishu community, was the son of Lawrence Howling Wolf (Bear Crosses The Water), a minister of the Nishu Congregational Church, which was a branch of the reservation mission at Elbowoods. His mother was Stella Rogers (Curlew Woman). In 1927 Dan married Mabel Bear, daughter of Floyd Bear, who in turn was the son of Sitting Bear, the leading Arikara chief at the end of the nineteenth century and the son of Son Of Star. For most of their lives, Dan and Mabel lived in the country near Nishu, where Dan ranched, working cattle and horses, and did a little farming. From 1931 until 1953 he was a member of the Nishu singers, a group of younger men who succeeded the older

Plate 9. Dan Howling Wolf *(Sčiri TeéRIt,* Standing Wolf). Photograph ca. 1950, courtesy of Diane Howling Wolf.

Grass Dance society singers in the community and included Vincent Malnourie, Harvey Hopkins, Dan Hopkins, Davis Painte, and Marvin Painte. After
the Nishu community relocated to the present White Shield area, Dan
continued singing with those men, who then came to be known as the White
Shield singers. Most of his sons also took up singing, and today several of
them are active members of the White Shield singers.

When I first met Dan, he was living in the country several miles west of
White Shield. Although blind, he was still an active singer and was a fluent
speaker of Arikara who loved to tell stories, be they traditional Arikara or contemporary ones. He was, like Alfred Morsette, a generation younger than the

Plate 10. Dan Hopkins *(WáRUx Tuutiiká'At,* Rabbit Goes In The Middle). Photograph courtesy Faye Portraits, Inc., Garrison, North Dakota.

more elderly speakers like Ella Waters, Lilly Brave, and Mary Gillette. Yet he and Mabel spoke Arikara in the home, one of the few families to maintain active use of the language. As a consequence, their older children speak Arikara, and the younger ones understand it. Dan was an amiable, generous person, always helpful to anyone who approached him. He passed away on July 5, 1974, at the age of sixty-eight.

Dan Hopkins (Rabbit Goes In The Middle), a World War I veteran, was born on August 26, 1900, in Nishu. He was the son of Ernest Hopkins (Snowbird) and Ida Sherwood (Chippewa Woman), and was an Awahu band

Plate 11. Matthew White Bear *(kuúNUx šinaatíRA,* He Is Together With The Bear). Photograph courtesy Faye Portraits, Inc., Garrison, North Dakota.

member. In 1930, after two previous marriages, he married Ruth Eagle. Except for the period of his military service, he was a lifelong resident of the Fort Berthold Reservation, where he ranched and farmed. When I became acquainted with him, Dan was living alone in the country, several miles west of the homes of Mrs. Waters and the Howling Wolfs. A contemporary of Dan Howling Wolf, he, too, was a singer most of his life. Before Mrs. Waters passed away, he learned from her the ritual for the death feast and conducted it occasionally during the several years before his death. He passed away on November 26, 1982, at the age of eighty-two.

Plate 12. Eleanor Chase *(SkuuNUxtaáka,* White Bear Woman). Photograph 1970s, courtesy of Yvonne Merrick.

Matthew White Bear (Together With The Bear), born May 31, 1900, in Elbowoods, was the son of Paul White Bear *(kuuNUxtaáka,* White Bear) and Annie Sitting Bear (Yellow Calf Woman), and was a member of the *čiNIh-naahtákUx* band. He was a nephew of Sitting Bear and a descendant of White Shield and Son Of Star, all prominent nineteenth-century Arikara chiefs. In 1924 he married Alice Eagle, and together they lived on a farm near Nishu, not far from the site of old Like-A-Fishhook Village, where Matthew raised crops and ranched and was active in the Catholic church.

When I met the couple in 1970, they were living on their farm southeast of White Shield. Both were noted for their knowledge of Arikara culture. They spoke their language fluently, and Matthew had in his keeping a tribal pipe and a sacred bundle. He was a quiet, reflective man who spoke softly, sometimes almost in a whisper. Alice was an active, prominent member of the White Shield community; and Matthew, by virtue of his father's social position, was himself a leader in the Arikara community throughout his life. On January 21, 1975, he passed away at the age of seventy-four.

Eleanor Chase (White Bear Woman), born April 12, 1906, was the daughter of Red Bear and Julia Bull Neck.[13] Her parents, too, were prominent members of the Arikara community at Fort Berthold. Her father served as a scout under Lieutenant Colonel George A. Custer on his 1876 expedition to the Little Big Horn and was appointed tribal judge in 1915. Julia Red Bear, her mother, worked with Melvin Gilmore and later Preston Holder when those two anthropologists visited the reservation.

After attending Flandreau Indian School, Eleanor worked as a cook and matron at Pierre Indian School in South Dakota. Later she returned home to Nishu, where she worked as a cook at the day school. In 1929 she married Joseph White Bear, Sr., who farmed near Nishu, but he passed away four years later. In 1940 she married Frank Chase, a Mandan from the Twin Buttes community. After their marriage the couple lived near Nishu, where they farmed. Throughout her life Eleanor maintained a strong interest in Arikara ways, an interest that after her marriage to Frank Chase was expressed in part by her beadwork and by her participation in Indian dances. After dam construction the couple moved to Bear Den, and, later, after the death of her husband, Eleanor moved to Drags Wolf Village, where I visited her in 1977. She was a large, outgoing, confident woman who spoke clear, crisp Arikara at a rapid tempo, certainly faster than any other speaker I ever heard. She passed away on December 31, 1980.

Esther Perkins (Young Elk Woman) was born in her parents' home in the country near Armstrong on March 15, 1916. Her father was Henry Perkins (Afraid Of The Soldier), an older brother of Ella Waters; and her mother was Elizabeth Price. Because Esther was born with a congenital ailment that prevented her from walking, she did not attend school. During her early childhood she lived with her grandfather Yellow Bear and his wife, both of whom spoke no English, and consequently she grew up speaking Arikara as her first language. Later, when living with her parents, who spoke English as well as Arikara in the home, she learned English by listening to them.

13. A short biography of Red Bear, apparently one he himself dictated, appears in Libby (1920:200–202).

Plate 13. Esther Perkins *(Sweeháni', Young Elk Woman)*. Photograph by James Vranna, 1991.

Esther lived with her parents until they died, and since then has lived with a sister and her family. Despite her handicap, she is always cheerful and jocular. She, like most in her family, is active in the Episcopal church in White Shield.

Joseph Fox (Little Elk) was born January 8, 1904, in Nishu, where he was reared. His father was Isaac Fox (Red Fox); his mother, Julia (Last Child). After attending Bismarck Indian School, he returned to the Fort Berthold Reservation and in 1920 married Susan Many Bears. They farmed in the Nishu area until 1943 and then moved to Minot, where Joe worked in construction.

Plate 14. Joe Fox *(Wáh KananiRIhuúNU,* Little Elk).

In 1963 he moved back to the reservation and lived first in White Shield and later in Drags Wolf Village.

Throughout his life Joe was noted as a good dancer. He was, in fact, the last surviving member of the Grass Dance society. I knew him from only one visit to his home in 1977, when he recorded two stories and a song. Those recordings proved him to be a fine speaker of Arikara, whose diction was unsurpassed for clarity and smoothness of delivery. He passed away on September 21, 1978.

Nature of the Collection

A Typology of Arikara Oral Traditions

In 1976, when I first approached Alfred Morsette with my request to record traditional Arikara stories, his response revealed a fundamentally different perception of what I wanted. He translated the Western category of "traditional story" into something meaningful from an Arikara perspective, and replied that he would be happy to tell stories of the Arikara past—those he had learned from his grandparents and other individuals of preceding generations— so that there would be a written history of the tribe. For him the stories that he would tell were *history*, not myths, tales, or other folkloric categories. Similarly, Lillian Brave made the same identification of oral traditions with history, although she revealed her understanding of Arikara historiography through an example. Before commencing our first recording session, she asked what precisely I wanted her to tell. I asked her to relate something about Arikara history, about some incident that had actually occurred in the tribal past. For several minutes she sat silently and then began to recount a story (70) about a brother and sister mesmerized by an elk spirit and subsequently given power by that animal. From a Euro-American perspective this narrative is a myth, but for Mrs. Brave, as for any older Arikara, this is an account of a historical event, an important incident that happened in the past—in a time very different from today—when an elk bestowed supernatural power on the brother and sister, who in turn conveyed certain traditions to the Arikara people. For Arikaras this story, together with the total aggregate of those known to their people, preserved over countless generations through oral transmission, constitute their history.

All the narrators in this collection classified oral traditions into two fundamental categories: true stories; and tales or, as Arikaras call them in English today, fairy tales. In Arikara the latter are termed *naa'iikáWIš*. True stories have no special denotation. If one must specify a story as true, he simply says, *tiraanaáNIš* 'It is true.' Thus, true stories are, to use a linguistic expression, an unmarked category, whereas tales are marked by a denotative term, so that unless an Arikara story is characterized as or known to be a tale, it is assumed to be true.

True stories. True stories cover a wide range of themes but are not subcategorized into named types. There is, however, again a native distinction between two general types: the sacred story that tells about "holy" or mysterious events in the past, and the nonsacred story that is not as remote in time and lacks the overriding supernatural element of sacred traditions— generally what from a Western perspective would be called historical narratives. Although most stories fall clearly into one of these two general categories, and although finer subgroupings within each type can be distinguished, Arikaras have no more than a general sense of such a classification, which is based primarily on named protagonists or on functions such as explanations of the origin of particular institutions. The boundaries between types are not hard and fast, but rather blend into one another, so that in actual fact sacred and secular stories and their subtypes form a continuum along which stories cluster, a continuum which, in the last analysis, is for Arikaras a single category: the true story or history.

The most specialized type of sacred story is the genesis tradition, or the traditions associated with the tribal sacred bundles. Formerly, when Arikaras lived in autonomous or semi-independent villages, each village had its own sacred bundle that symbolized the history of the group and its covenant with the deities. The origin of each village traced back to a supernatural experience or encounter, during which the deity instructed the dreamer to make a bundle of objects, some to recall what happened in the dream and some to be used in subsequent rituals. As a result of the decimation of the Arikara people in the late eighteenth and nineteenth centuries, by the early twentieth century all these village origin stories, except for that of the Awahu, were apparently lost. What did survive, however, was a genesis story that accounts for the origins and migration of all the Arikara people, a story that may have formerly belonged to one band. This tradition was recorded from many individuals in the late nineteenth and early twentieth centuries (Hall 1891:32; Grinnell 1893:122-128; G. A. Dorsey 1904a:12-35).

Another type of sacred story comprises what are generally termed myths—traditions of incidents that occurred during a period before the earth had fully taken its present form, before or at a time when human institutions were developing. Arikaras refer to this as the holy period, the time when mysterious events occurred. Stories set in this era are said to be holy (*tiraa'iitUxwaá-RUxti'* 'it is a holy story'). It was a time when animals were the actors in dramas and deities came down to earth from the heavens above, when animals killed humans and buffalo ate people rather than the reverse—a period when a dangerous natural world was evolving into the present one in which man hunts animals and rides horses and lives much as he did previous to the arrival of Euro-Americans.

A third type of sacred story is the legendary event. Here there are several discreet types to be distinguished. One of the most common is the etiological narrative that accounts for the origin of a particular rite or tradition. This is a dream or vision story that relates a supernatural encounter between a human and some animal spirit or other agency who teaches an Arikara a ritual for the benefit of the tribe. Related to this type is the dream story, in which a poor boy or some hapless young man stumbles upon an animal or other supernaturally endowed agent whom he is able to help or please and who subsequently pities him—or "blesses" him, as Arikaras say in English today—by endowing him with supernatural powers for hunting, warfare, or healing, and becomes his spiritual helper. A third type of legendary narrative is one that recounts some supernatural occurrence, as when, for example, a priest pouts and turns into stone or a girl is shamed and turns into stone.

In contrast to these sacred stories are the nonsacred ones, which in general describe events that are more recent in time and, more importantly, do not have a predominant supernatural component—although nearly every story has some supernatural reference. War stories, which relate incidents that occurred during the period of intertribal warfare, form a prominent group. So also do narratives describing recent historical events such as the Arikara tribal migration to Pawnee country immediately after the Atkinson campaign, the Fort Laramie Treaty, or the Custer campaign. Still another group of nonsacred stories are personal anecdotes, generally telling of a supernatural encounter but lacking the bestowal of power—what might be characterized as testimonials to the existence of supernatural beings or events, to phenomena that ostensibly are humanly inexplicable—the sort of attestation that assures people that the world about them is still imbued with mysterious power and that skepticism is foolish.

Tales. As with true stories, there are different sorts of tales, but most common are those that have the trickster Coyote or some other animal as protagonist. Unlike many other tribes, the Arikaras do not put Coyote into the role of a divine being. He is endowed with mysterious power *(waaRUxtii'u')*, but he is always portrayed as a tricky, deceitful character who tries to outwit others but invariably bungles and generally dies through his own folly. Only secondarily is he a transformer. Frequently these tales are etiological ones that end with an explanation of some feature of the natural world, but on the whole Arikaras attach little significance to Coyote stories since they are primarily told to evoke laughter or to entertain children. Alfred Morsette, in fact, told me that it would be a waste of time to record them, even though he always relished a good Coyote story.

Other stories, like that of Bounding Head, are more like European Mother Goose stories and, like Coyote tales, were told on winter nights for diversion, frequently to lull children to sleep. Unlike Coyote and other animal tales, however, they are not humorous but have a more serious, often frightening, tone and a primarily human cast of characters. The characters in these tales are often the same ones that appear in myths, and so these stories sometimes seem to be categorically transitional between myth and tale. In one version of the

Bounding Head story (6), in fact, the narrator states in his introduction that "I certainly never saw him [the one-eyed Bounding Head], but I have heard of him through the stories they used to tell about him." Because of this and a similar ambivalence expressed by some narrators toward the historical validity of many stories that otherwise would unequivocally be considered to be tales, these stories have been arranged with the myths in this collection with the caveat that the line between myth and tale is fine indeed. What are true myths for some Arikaras today are tales for others. For many stories, in fact, it is doubtful that consensus in regard to their historical validity could be achieved now—or even, perhaps, could ever have been achieved in the past—since in no culture does everyone hold identical beliefs.

The oral traditions in this collection are grouped by narrator and then arranged to reflect the basic Arikara distinction between true stories and fictional tales. These two divisions are designated here as Narratives of the Past and Tales, respectively. Within the category of true stories are four types, which again reflect the genres discussed above: Of Ancient Times (myths); Of Power Bestowed (legends); Of Historical Events (historical narratives); and Of Mysterious Events (anecdotes of supernatural occurrences). A fifth type, designated Of Ritualism, also fits into the category of true stories. These narratives include descriptive accounts of ritual procedures like personal name bestowal (107, 108), prayers (110, 144), song texts (146, 147), and an account of the origin of the death feast (107). In contrast to true stories, tales, the second major division of narratives, are grouped by protagonist: Coyote, Stuwi, and others, the latter of whom may be other animals or human characters. Table 1 (below) summarizes the classification of Arikara oral traditions in this collection and the content of each category.

Characters

Although many of the same characters reappear in the myths and tales of all Plains tribes, albeit with different names, each tribe has its own set of favorite characters that recur in many stories and thereby become distinctive in the traditions of that people. The Mandans, for example, have Corn Silk Woman, a beautiful young woman transformed from corn, about whom there are many accounts (Beckwith 1937; Bowers 1950; Lévi-Strauss 1968:314-23). Other tribes tell of this same woman—Corn Woman among the Arikaras and the Omahas, Reed Woman among the Sioux, for example—in the widely diffused story of the corn wife and buffalo wife—but she appears in only this one story and no others. The Sioux, for another example, have the mythical Double Face, who appears sometimes as a man and sometimes as a woman in numerous stories and is peculiarly Sioux even though, like the Mandan Corn

Table 1. Typology of Arikara Oral Traditions

Arikara Classification	Table of Contents Designation	Narrative Type
TRUE STORIES	NARRATIVES OF THE PAST	
Sacred	Of Ancient Times	World origins, mythic dramas
	Of Power Bestowed	Visionary encounters, legends
Nonsacred	Of Historical Events	Historical narratives
	Of Mysterious Incidents	Supernatural occurrences
TALES *(naa'iikáWIš)*	TALES	
	Of Coyote	Trickster tales
	Of Stuwi	Trickster tales
	Of Others	Animal tales; adventure stories

Silk Woman, Double Face parallels characters in the traditions of other tribes (Deloria 1932).

In Arikara stories, too, there are familiar characters, ones who return again and again in different narratives; some are named and some are nameless. The named characters appear primarily in two groups of stories, myths and tales, although some of them occasionally occur in legendary stories as well. Nameless persons are most frequently the protagonists of myths and legendary stories and are often a favorite personality type representing an actor in an old story whose name has been forgotten or perhaps may never have existed, or designating an actor in a story borrowed from another tribe whose name would lack significance in its new social context.

Named characters. Among the most common of the named characters is Lucky Man *(wiitakaWAhaánu'),* whose name, according to Mrs. Waters, signifies a person who is a successful hunter and is able to provide for his family. He is a good man, whom Mrs. Brave characterized as "sort of a chief," indicating that he is wealthy and never in want, and is always willing to share what he has with other people and help those in need. His roles vary from being the father of a protagonist (e.g., 4, 64, 65) to being a protagonist himself (e.g., 69).

Stays In The Lodge Dressed In Finery *(tshaahkaákUx)* is another stock character who is a frequent protagonist. Said by some Arikara narrators to be a Hidatsa character incorporated into Arikara stories, he is portrayed as a young dandy who stays at home, spending his days on the earth lodge roof and never venturing from the village with war parties or hunters. Although he represents the antithesis of what a young Arikara male should be, Stays In The Lodge always vindicates his aberrant social role, which is invariably a mask for a person who possesses mysterious power.

Bloody Hands *(štaanápaa'At),* the Burnt Belly of Skiri folklore and Wets The Bed of Wichita stories, is a favorite personage, an archetype of the widespread Plains poor boy. Known also as Hands *(štaánu'),* a shortened form of his name, he is a small, poor boy who lives with his grandmother in a tipi among the dung heaps on the outskirts of the village. Although in some stories (4, 5) his physical appearance is not mentioned, he is usually said to be short, ugly, and swaybacked and to have a scarred potbelly and deformed feet. His grandmother, too, is short and heavyset, with a large stomach. Despite his ugliness and poverty, Bloody Hands has mysterious powers that always enable him and his grandmother to triumph in situations where other, socially more fortunate individuals fail.

Old Woman Spider *(suxtiikIsíš),* a spider who appears in the form of an old woman, is in some stories a neutral, background character who helps people to accomplish an otherwise insurmountable task (e.g., 85, 89), while in others she is an evil personage who, like the spider, ensnares adversaries in her web (e.g., 62, 65).

A ubiquitous character, uniquely Arikara and Pawnee, is Scalped Man *(tshunúxu'* 'scalped one'), who appears in a variety of roles.[14] "Scalped one" is the term for a person who was scalped in warfare but who, though mistaken for dead, somehow survived, generally, it was believed, through the act of some supernatural agency like Night. Of such a maimed person it was said, *tí' ičiwiniítu'* 'He is transformed; he is different,' signifying the belief that he was no longer human but had become a spirit forever doomed to live a solitary existence outside the pale of human society, shunning human contact. Arikara and Pawnee traditions about Scalped Man abound. In some anecdotes and stories he is a historical character, sometimes simply a misfortunate person who survived scalping and is later accidentally encountered by someone, while at other times he is a malevolent spirit who steals human possessions as well as women and children. In the latter role he is a bogeyman, an object of fear whom parents frequently used to threaten misbehaving children. In still other stories Scalped Man is a legendary figure who is the benefactor or bestower of

14. A fuller discussion of the scalped man appears below and in Parks (1982).

supernatural power on some man, generally a solitary hunter, who discovers him and receives war or healing powers in return for keeping his existence secret. Occasionally, too, Scalped Man appears in myths (e.g., 1) and tales (e.g., 81), in which he may be either a serious or comic character, becoming in the latter role a trickster much like Coyote, who bears little or no resemblance to the historical personage.

Occurring in several myths are two men who are said to be stars in the heavens associated with the buffalo on earth and who come down to earth, where they appear in human form. They are holy men who have supernatural powers, particularly the ability to summon buffalo herds, powers which they use to save people from starvation. Consequently they are portrayed as benefactors. In none of the stories in which they occur (15, 16, 85), however, are they named; in the Arikara versions they are referred to simply as "two men" or as "fathers" of the protagonist, while in English Mr. Morsette speaks of them as the "two holy men" and "star fathers." They appear in Mandan and Hidatsa myths, too, in which they are named Two Men (Beckwith 1937:43–52, 257–58; Bowers 1965).

Coyote *(sčiríhtš)* is the Arikara trickster who, like the animal after which he is named, is noted primarily for his cunning and deceit, particularly in his quest for food and sex, and his wild conceits. He is known by two other names that are also used in these narratives, Mischievous Coyote *(sčiRIhtšutaRA-háxu')* and Coyote Chief *(sčiRIhtšuneešaánu'),* the latter a name frequently used when referring to him in English. Mrs. Brave characterized Coyote by a single term, *aawaanúx* 'foxy, tricky,' while Eleanor Chase said of him, "Coyote is the one we have who always does wrong things . . . who has no sense and who does mischievous things." In the conclusion to one Coyote story (60), Alfred Morsette gives a similar portrayal: "That is the way Coyote was, always telling lies when he was looking for food for himself." Despite his trickiness and virtual indestructibility, Coyote is always overcome, either by his own ineptitude or by an adversary; and although he generally dies at the end of a story, he is never ultimately vanquished.[15]

For one narrator, Mrs. Brave, a character epitomizing the traits of Coyote is Wolf *(sčiRIhkaapinát),* whom she portrays as "the main Coyote, who is the *really* tricky one." At the outset of several of her stories (75–78) she interchanges Wolf and Coyote as protagonist but eventually settles on Coyote as the name she uses throughout the remainder of the tales. Although no other

---

15. A classic description of the Winnebago trickster, who is not unlike the Arikaras' Coyote, appears in Paul Radin (1956). For a more recent comparative study of Coyote in American Indian folklore see "The Natural History of Old Man Coyote" by William Bright (1987:339–87).

narrator represented in this collection employs Wolf as the trickster, her usage and insistence that Wolf is the real trickster are significant in light of a parallel role Wolf was formerly said to play in Pawnee tales:

> There is reason to believe that, while the Pawnee were in Nebraska, the Coyote was rarely or possibly never used in connection with these [trickster] tales, and that they were called instead Wolf tales, the Wolf being the mean trickster and not the Coyote. These Coyote or Wolf tales, in general, suggest to the Pawnee the mischievous performances of the Wolf sent by the Wolf-star, who, in attempting to steal people from Lightning, introduces mortality on earth, and through Lightning's failure to sacrifice Wolf the earth becomes subject to warfare and death. Thus the original wolf is a transformer of far-reaching consequences and at the same time a veritable trickster. [G. A. Dorsey 1906a:10-11]

Another character who appears only in Mrs. Brave's stories is Kit Fox (*pAhkátš*), whom the narrator describes as "the littlest fox" and red in color. He is a comic character and Coyote's nemesis, always mocking Coyote and giving him away by announcing his foibles publicly. Although no other contemporary Arikara narrator tells stories in which Kit Fox appears, the character is undoubtedly an old one. His name appears in Maximilian's Arikara vocabulary recorded in 1833, where it is translated as 'god.'[16] Even earlier, in 1796, Truteau mentioned what must be the same character in his description of doctors' performances in the Medicine Lodge, when he wrote that "two young men, the most sprightly, to whom they give the name of 'little foxes,' imitate and mimic the gestures and contortions of the others [doctors] almost as clowns among our comedians mimic the actors" (Parks in press).

A female character who appears in tales is Stuwi (*stuúWI*), whose name has no translation.[17] She is a sexually loose, meddlesome woman who is something of a clown. Mrs. Brave characterizes her as a 1920s flapper who tempts men and fools people, while Mr. Morsette similarly likened her to a modern go-go dancer or stripper. Like Coyote, Stuwi is said to be tricky (*aawaanúx*). Because of her overtly sexual nature and the reticence of most narrators to tell such stories, there are only two about her in this collection. In one (81) the Stuwis of the world are portrayed as responsible for creek water,

16. Maximilian (1843, 3:211) recorded the name as "pachkátsch," with the note that *ach* was pronounced as the German guttural. In the orthography used here the word would be *pAxkátš*, differing slightly from the form used by Mrs. Brave.

17. The Pawnee equivalent of Stuwi is *Ctú'u'* (Witch Woman), who has the same attributes of the Arikara character. For a description of her, see George A. Dorsey (1904a:334).

which they cause to flow by urinating, while in the other (80), a fine example of ribald humor, Stuwi is a sexually insatiable woman.

In addition to the foregoing personae, every story has its distinctive character who generally does not appear in other narratives. Among the best known of the mythical ones who are named are Bounding Head *(pAxukúku')*, Shwahit *(šwaáhii'It*, no translation), Old Woman's Grandson *(súxtIt iNAhniítš)*, and Long Teeth *(aáhčes)* and his brother, Drinks Brain Soup *(pAxčiRAhčiíka')*, each of whom has a consistent portrayal in all the versions of the story in which he or she occurs.

Unnamed characters. In Arikara mythical and legendary traditions unnamed protagonists are far more common than named ones. Among the stories recorded by Alfred Morsette, for example, primary characters are named in three myths and are unnamed in nine, and similarly they are named in ten legends but are unnamed in twenty-six. Such unnamed characters are referred to simply as a boy, a young man, or a man, or, if female, as a girl, a young woman, or a woman; and frequently the designations boy and young man, or young man and man, are used interchangeably in the same story for the same individual, as are also the parallel female sets, girl and young woman, or young woman and woman. In some stories (e.g., 23, 46, 90) the name of the protagonist or another character is not given until the very end of the narrative, where its specification typically serves as part of the conclusion.

Secondary characters in such stories are almost always unnamed, too, depicted only as, for example, a young man, boy, or woman, depending upon the person's sex and age, and perhaps referred to as 'the one who was his companion' or some similar descriptive designation. Frequently, however, secondary characters are relatives of a major character, and then kinship terms are used when referring to them.

Character types. Arikara traditions, like oral traditions throughout the world, usually lack character development. In most Arikara stories, in fact, characterization of the personality of the protagonist or members of the supporting cast generally consists of a simple summary statement. The named characters discussed above, like Bloody Hands, Coyote, and Stays Inside The Lodge, are culturally renowned personae representing types with which all Arikaras are familiar, so that it is unnecessary to describe them. Most stories, however, have a protagonist who appears in only that narrative. Since that narrative generally depicts only the protagonist's actions, the listener must construct a visualization of the character on this basis alone and never becomes intimately acquainted with the individual or directly learns his motivations. There is, nevertheless, among the many characters in the "true" stories of this collection, a small number of recurrent personality types that typify Arikara oral tradition and, significantly, contrast with the personality norm in Arikara society.

A favorite Arikara literary figure is the poor boy, represented archetypically by the mythical Bloody Hands, who, despite an outward appearance of ugliness and poverty, is in reality a handsome young man endowed with mysterious powers that enable him to accomplish feats beyond the capabilities of men who are socially prominent. The poor boy character is represented equally well in the tale of Eats Ashes (144), who also lives in poverty with his grandmother. After befriending a wealthy boy who has everything, Eats Ashes determines to go on a war party with his companion to accomplish something noteworthy. Although his grandmother futilely tries to dissuade him from going, she finally gives him a burnt marrowbone to take on the expedition. Its ashes are to be his food, but in fact the bone is the source of his power, enabling him to kill many of the enemy and return to the village as a person of renown who is given a seat among the chiefs. The protagonists of many other stories are similarly poor but achieve fame after some supernatural power pities them.

Many stories recount the exploits of young men who are socially deviant: those who are lazy, reclusive, backward, or even retarded. Eats Ashes, the triumphant poor boy, for example, is also characterized as backward. The story of Young Hawk (28) tells of a lazy young man who is mysteriously endowed with hawk power that enables him to achieve success in war, while in the account of the origin of the Hidatsa Crazy Dog Society (30), the young man who is chosen to forewarn his people of an impending attack on the village is a disinterested fop. Representing the dandy who never ventures from the village is Stays In The Lodge Dressed In Finery. Others like him are the boy with the feathered staff (23) and the boy who had coyote or wolf power (156). All are reclusive young men who, though seemingly unmanly in their behavior, have power that ultimately allows them to achieve success in war and vindicate their socially abnormal manner. At the extreme of this type is the simple-minded, or actually retarded, young man (96) who once ate snake flesh and subsequently became a snake himself. After he was put into the Missouri River, he was thereafter commemorated by warriors who made offerings to him whenever they wished to cross the river safely.

The reckless young man, sometimes arrogant but always a foolish daredevil, is another typical protagonist spanning the temporal range of Arikara traditions. Mythically, he is represented by the wild Long Teeth, who brashly leads his brother, Drinks Brain Soup, into one dangerous adventure after another. In legend the same character type appears frequently. The story of the two Foolish Ones who killed the beloved snake child (14, 88) provides an example in which such behavior was institutionalized in a men's organization and, in this story at least, brought grief to the Arikara people; while the story of Red Dog and the Four Stars (18) illustrates this personality in a man who also had the power to call the buffalo, a power which he used successfully to save his people from starvation. In another example, the story of a wild buffalo (134), the protagonist is a poor daredevil who teases the fearsome animal despite the warnings of his companions. Although the buffalo chases him for countless miles and kills his horse, it ultimately pities the young man and enables him to achieve success in war.

The foolish daredevil personality is depicted in war stories, too, in which the deeds of reckless young men figure prominently. Exemplifying this personality is the account of a Sioux attack on Like-A-Fishhook Village (47), in which the enemies lay in ambush on the bank of the Missouri opposite the village and used decoys to lure impetuous young Arikaras into their trap. Despite the warnings of older, experienced warriors, according to Mr. Morsette's account, "there always are some who won't heed what they are told," and they rashly gave chase to the decoys. Three of those brave but reckless Arikaras were killed. As a matter of interest, the same scenario in which Sioux attackers lured reckless young Arikaras into their traps on the bank opposite the village is a familiar one that was first described in 1796 by the fur trader Truteau (Parks in press) and was reiterated throughout the nineteenth century in the accounts of white observers on the Upper Missouri.

A related character type common in Arikara literature is the skeptic who scoffs at conventional wisdom—the individual who does not believe in spirits and in the mysterious power resident in holy objects. Such a skeptic is the leader of a war party in an Arikara version of the story of the gigantic snapping turtle (25), a widespread legend on the Plains. When the party encounters a large, strange object—the something-out-of-the-ordinary sort that typically marks it as holy—the leader, characterized as a nonbeliever, cannot resist the temptation to climb up onto it despite the admonitions of one member of the group who has appropriate respect for the holy. The leader's skepticism, of course, proves to be fateful for both himself and the companions who follow his lead. A similar, common type of tradition is exemplified in the account of a young man who does not believe in ghosts until he encounters one (56). That encounter proves to be fateful, too, until the young man acknowledges the ghost's existence and pays it proper respect, after which the man enjoys success in hunting and as a result becomes a believer.

Another character recurring in Arikara traditions is the man who, after being pitied by some animal or other supernatural being, abuses the powers conferred on him until he becomes thoroughly evil. Such individuals appear frequently in myths as the antagonist. The story of the man with the sharpened leg (8) is a short but typical example. In it a young man courts a beautiful young woman, and after he marries her the father-in-law pursues him to kill him with his leg, just as he has done before to many other young men. This young man, however, is saved by the tree that had previously given the father-in-law his power, since the tree is finally outraged by the older man's repeated evil deeds. Many legends also tell about a pitiful young man who is given power and for some time afterward performs good deeds with it, but finally begins to abuse it. Sometimes, as in one version of the young man pitied by a wild buffalo (134), his behavior simply becomes reprehensible; but at other times, as in the story of Mice Mouth (20, 89, 112), his actions become so intolerable that he must be killed.

The chief's—or alternatively a wealthy man's—daughter is another
Although most of the prominent character types in Arikara oral traditions are male, there are at least two recurrent female roles. The more stereotyped one is the outcast grandmother who lives in poverty with her grandson, either Bloody Hands or another poor-boy character like Eats Ashes. In most of the stories in which she figures, the grandmother usually serves as a counterforce to her grandson's ambitions, always trying to dissuade him from attempting to achieve his aspirations. So, for example, in Lillian Brave's stories of Bloody Hands (64-68) and Mary Gillette's story of Eats Ashes (144), the grandmother initially scoffs at her grandson's presumption to want to go on the warpath like young men of higher social station do; in one story (68), in fact, she steadfastly forbids it, ultimately to her everlasting regret. Also characteristic of her in this role is her pride in—or perhaps resigned determination to uphold—her impoverished lifestyle; so that, even when her grandson does achieve social prominence (e.g., 64, 66), she refuses to leave her humble lodge among the dung heaps to live in a better one among the wealthy families. Despite her destitute state, however, in some stories the grandmother, like her grandson, possesses mysterious power that she finally demonstrates. Before Eats Ashes goes on the warpath, for example, his grandmother gives him a marrowbone that miraculously enables him to kill many enemies and become a great warrior.

The chief's—or alternatively a wealthy man's—daughter is another common female character whose customary role complements that of the protagonist. This young woman, often a background character with little or no involvement in the action of a story, is always beautiful and unmarried; her ultimate fate is to be the wife of the protagonist, often the lowly poor boy, who wins her in marriage through his exploits.

Translation and Presentation

All the narratives in this collection were recorded in Arikara, the first language of each narrator and the language in which each one learned the stories. Most of Alfred Morsette's and one of William Deane's stories were afterward retold and taped in English as well, providing parallel versions of a substantial portion of the collection, but the Arikara versions, which are to a large extent memorized texts, are the primary documents that preserve the stories in the original language without the interpretive reworking that characterizes versions either translated into or told in English. The English versions are thus primarily of comparative interest and illustrative of the differences between accounts told in the original and in a second language.

In the original edition (Parks 1991), the narratives are presented in two forms. One is an interlinear format that consists of a systematic phonetic transcription of the naturally told Arikara together with an accompanying word-by-word literal English translation conveying the grammatical and semantic content of each word. This paired-line format, standard for the publication of linguistic texts, provides both an accurate written version of the oral documents and an English translation that allows for their future linguistic and literary study and interpretation. The interlinear presentation of the collection appears in volumes 1 and 2 of this work.

The second mode of presentation is a set of free English translations that presents the texts as literary forms. Until recently, when translating American Indian traditions, linguists and other recorders have generally recast them into free English translations that conform to our own standards of good English written style but generally ignore literary devices and stylistic features integral to the native rendition. The results all too frequently have been vapid translations that are neither good stories in English nor faithful representations of the native originals. Over the past few decades, however, a number of literary scholars have become interested in American Indian oral traditions as oral literature, and they have raised the translation process to a new level of concern and sensitivity, insisting on fresh standards that give primacy to native literary features and structure (summarized in Hymes 1981 and Tedlock 1983). The goal of this recent work is, at least ideally, a translated text that is as close to the original as can be achieved in a rendition in another language. It is this goal that has guided the free translations of the Arikara stories presented here.

Where the translations in this collection depart from certain contemporary trends in textual presentation, however, is in redactive form. One recent convention is to replicate the oral performance in written form: pauses, voice modulation, and other performative features are indicated typographically in the translations so that the reader can "participate" in the original performance, reading back from the printed page to the vocal presentation, even though the language of the printing and the auditory medium are removed, and different, from it (Tedlock 1983). The other major approach, in which performative features play no role, is to portray underlying linguistic patterns, marked by morphological and syntactic features such as verbal inflection or sentence initial particles, by numerical repetitions, and a structuring of the narrative into a hierarchy of divisions that includes lines, verses, acts, and scenes, all of which give the text a construction much like a drama (Hymes 1981). Although these two models of redaction differ in the attention they give to performance and linguistic patterns, both share an assumption that native American texts are literary documents that are fundamentally poetic in structure and should be presented in verse, rather than prose, format.

Both of these models have developed out of individual efforts to deal with texts in specific languages.[18] One has evolved out of recordings of narratives performed before audiences, where the performance itself became as important as the words, while the other has developed out of a study of philological texts and oral recordings in which the performative context was minimized. Neither approach seems entirely appropriate to the presentation of this collection of Arikara texts. Although during many of the recordings narrators accompanied their tellings with gestures and dramatic vocal modulation, the recitations were generally subdued, not staged performances, since there was either no audience present (other than the recorder) or it was at most a small, intimate one. Narrators' attention, instead, centered on narrative detail—on remembering all the pieces of the story and rendering as full a version as possible. Similarly, nothing in delivery style or morphological and syntactic arrangements of narrative material suggests a line-verse structure that would more accurately portray an underlying Arikara narrative form than what is achieved in prose.

The presentational format employed here, which evolved out of the translation process itself, recognizes three basic units: sentences, paragraphs, and sections.

Sentence boundaries have been established on the basis of a combination of criteria: pause and intonational contours, occurrence of particle introducers, and grammatical composition. Minimally, a sentence consists of one independent verbal form (i.e., a verb inflected for one of the independent modes) in addition to any number of optional subordinate verbal forms (i.e., verbs in one of the dependent modes). Elliptical sentences, in which the verb form has been omitted, are the exception to the rule. Sometimes they occur in narratives, particularly in statements introducing dialogue, where the speaker's identity is given but the specification of his action—for example, "he said"—is under-

18. Mattina (1987:129-48) and Krupat (1987:113-28) provide recent discussions of alternatives and problems in textual redaction.

stood and therefore omitted. Although Arikara sentences often contain only a single verb, they frequently have, in addition to an independent one, a long string of satellite subordinate forms, some of which translate best into English as independent sentences. Similarly, a sentence may be a concatenation of two or more independent verbs, sometimes, but not always, connected by the conjunctions *na* or *a* 'and.'

Paragraph boundaries are defined by several criteria, the most prominent of which are a variety of transitions. Topical changes, actor and dialogue switches, topical changes within a long dialogue, and temporal and scene changes mark paragraph breaks. Thus paragraphs are generally short, topically self-contained units.

Interacting with these transitions are two forms of discourse bracketing (see Style, below) that frequently introduce and/or conclude a paragraph, thereby helping to define the paragraph as a discourse unit. One form sets off quoted speech: the introductory form is, for example, *witiwaáko'* 'He said,' or *taanikuwitiwaáko'* 'This is what he said,' and the concluding statement is *taanikuwitiwaáko'* 'This is what he said.' An action or series of concatenated actions is similarly bounded by statements like *taanikuwituúta* 'This is what he did.'

In addition to the transitions marked by paragraph breaks there are greater temporal and topical discontinuities—what in drama are changes of scenes or acts. Frequently introduced by a temporal distancing clause like "It was some time later" or "It was a long time later," these shifts from one part of a story to another are indicated here by additional space (i.e., a blank line) between paragraphs. Most stories also begin with an introductory paragraph or section, which backgrounds the narrative and precedes its onset, and ends with a concluding paragraph or section following the end of the story. These introductions and conclusions are also set off by additional space. If that blank line occurs at the top or bottom of a page, where it might not be obvious, a pair of facing guillemets (« ») marks the transition.

In several stories, moreover, there are major transitions between separate episodes that are nearly equivalent to independent stories (see pp. 88–89). These transitions are marked by three pairs of facing guillemets (« « «   » » ») wherever they occur.

One overriding criterion has guided the translation process: to reflect faithfully the original Arikara text. In making the translations, careful effort has been exercised to reproduce the Arikara narrative, with all its complexities and subtleties, as closely as possible in idiomatic English and to maintain the stylistic devices of the original language, even though adherence to those principles has often resulted in a mode of expression that sounds somewhat stilted in English.

The translations, moreover, have been given in formal English since the Arikara speech style is itself formal. In dialogue, however, English contractions are used so that the speech there approximates English spoken style more realistically than uncontracted forms.

Although translations conform closely to the original Arikara, there are a variety of situations in which explanatory information has been inserted so that the English text reads unambiguously. One instance is the specification of a name or noun for an actor who is unspecified in Arikara. Frequently, in Arikara as in other American Indian oral traditions, in describing situations in which individuals are interacting with one another, the names or other nouns denoting the actors are omitted, although sometimes a narrator will use gestures to differentiate among actors;[19] literal translations, therefore, result in an ambiguous interplay of two or more third person singular pronominal subjects (e.g., multiple *he*s and *she*s). For clarity, appropriate designations specifying those actors have been introduced in the translation when confusion would otherwise result.

Similarly, occasional details that are not overtly stated in the Arikara version—details that are generally understood by an Arikara audience and consequently not mentioned, or details that have accidently been omitted in the particular telling but are essential to the story—have been silently provided in the English translation.

An example of an implicit, culturally understood omission occurs in story 140, where the text translates literally as 'thunderbirds were shooting it [a water monster]'; the free translation reads "thunderbirds were shooting it with lightning bolts." Since an Arikara listener understands that a thunderbird shoots lightning bolts, the narrator does not state it explicitly. Likewise, in the opening paragraph of story 142 there is the literal statement, "Then they said, 'Let's go gather ground beans.'" Although the subjects have been identified only as "they" up to this point, the phrase "a group of young women" was added to the free translation since it is culturally understood that women (who happen to be young in this story), and not men or children, would be going to gather the beans. Still another randomly selected example comes from the same story (142) when the protagonist and his three companions discover an apparently unoccupied lodge in their travels. In dialogue the protagonist assigns two of his companions to beds, and then the text reads, "That was the way it was"; to this literal statement the translation adds the explanation, "each had a bed to sleep on," since that is what the Arikara expression implies.

---

19. A common gestural means of differentiating two actors is to use a hand, index finger extended upward, to represent each person and then to move forward the hand that represents the actor who is being referred to or quoted.

An example of a simple explanatory detail that is not explicitly stated in the Arikara but has been supplied in the free translation occurs in story 4 when Long Teeth, one of two protagonists, becomes angry and states, "I have power just like you do." Because it is not immediately apparent who "you" is in this context, a clarifying "he said to the tree" has been added in the translation. Another illustration of a silently added detail appears in story 5 when the protagonist, a star boy who is disguised as a poor, ugly human boy, tries to maintain his disguise by riding a decrepit horse and shooting arrows here and there. After the story had been recorded the narrator explained that the boy had been shooting at prairie chickens, so the translation was expanded to "he . . . began to shoot here and there at prairie chickens."

There is, finally, one additional type of editorial insertion in the free translations that occurs only in the stories told by Alfred Morsette. Occasionally, narrative sequences that range from a sentence to a paragraph or more were accidently omitted in the telling of the Arikara version but were included in the English rendition. When such omissions were deemed important to the story, either as helpful explanations or as integral details, they have been inserted in the free translations and are identified by angled brackets (< >).

In the presentation of the traditions in English translation, each narrative is preceded by an introduction that provides background information intended to facilitate the reader's understanding and appreciation of the story. To this end the introductions vary in content: they may contain comparative observations, clarify obscure references or passages, elucidate relationships among narrative elements, or highlight the significance of the story or an episode in it. Whenever a narrator provided relevant explanatory information outside the recording session, that material is also included.

Style

Perhaps the characteristic that most distinguishes individual American Indian literary traditions is the oral style in which their stories are told. General stylistic features such as narrative perspective, the use of quoted material, narrative sequencing, abbreviatory devices, and numerical patterning, as well as specific morphological and syntactic traits serve to shape what is typically an Arikara story and differentiate its delivery style from that of a narrative in English or other American Indian literary traditions. Since the stylistic features of Arikara have been assiduously preserved in the translations of the narratives in this collection, it is important to recognize and understand them so that for the English reader they are an enhancement rather than an impediment to the appreciation of this literary tradition.

Narrative Perspective

In Arikara a narrative about some past personage or event is usually told in such a way that the teller is distanced from the story line. Generally the teller is repeating what he or she has heard or has been told and relates the activities of the character or cast of the story from a *third person perspective,* in which those actors, even though named, are referred to by the pronouns 'he,' 'she,' 'it,' and 'they.' In Arikara, like many American Indian languages, the narrative is further characterized by what are generally termed evidentials, formal linguistic elements that in different languages may be prefixes, suffixes, or even independent words that usually occur with verbs, tagging their actions as something that the teller has not witnessed or cannot verify from his own experience.

There are two evidentials in Arikara, both verbal prefixes, which occur most extensively in narratives and serve to define a story as a tradition. One is *wi–,* the quotative, which occurs with verbs in the indicative mode and indicates that the speaker is repeating what he heard, not what he observed. The quotative is rarely translated into English by Arikaras. When pressed to explain its use on a verb, they merely attribute it to the story, remarking that it indicates something that is told. It is the equivalent of what in other American Indian languages is frequently translated as 'it is said.' The other evidential, *an–* 'evidential proper,' which usually appears in the form *Ah–,* is prefixed to verbs in modes other than the indicative and signifies that what the verb denotes was not seen by the speaker—that something "apparently" was the case. It, too, is generally not translated; Arikara speakers simply consider it an attribute of the way words appear in a story. Since Arikara speakers do not consider these evidentials as features to be translated into English, both are omitted in the free translations presented in this collection.

Contrasting with this more common narrative perspective in Arikara, however, is an alternative one that is extensively used in historical accounts of war and other incidents that occurred during the nineteenth century. It is a *first person perspective* in which the narrator, rather than distancing himself from the narrative activity, relates it from the perspective of a participant, nearly always a major participant. Here the first person pronoun 'I' predominates, and the third person pronouns are used for other characters in the story. In a narrative told from this perspective, the narrator actually repeats the words of the original actor or participant, telling the story as if the narrator himself had been that person and is now relating what he did and saw. When a narrator recounts a story told in this style, he generally begins with an introductory statement that he is repeating the words of another person, the one who related it to him. So, for example, in story 45, Alfred Morsette begins an Assiniboine war story with the declaration that "Now I am going to repeat the words of my uncle Snowbird," who, as he later explains, had been told the story of a war party that came to Like-A-Fishhook Village sometime during the nineteenth century by the Assiniboine who had led it.

In relating a story from this first person perspective, the narrator does not use the evidential prefixes since he is giving the account from a participatory perspective and thus as something he actually witnessed. Since the narrator is repeating the words of the original participant, in fact, the entire account is one long sequence of quoted speech. Consequently, in translation the entirety of narratives told in this style are set off by double quotation marks, and the speech of other actors in the story is in turn enclosed by single quotation marks. (And if one of those actors repeats someone else's speech, that dialogue is then in turn enclosed by double quotation marks within the single ones.)

Rarely, however, is a narrator entirely consistent in maintaining this first person perspective throughout a long story, since the style apparently requires considerable concentration and effort to execute. Six stories in the collection of sixty-one told by Alfred Morsette illustrate use of this perspective style, and of those six narratives, only two (45, 55) are told entirely within the first person frame. A mixture of perspectives occurs in the other four stories: in one (49) the first person perspective predominates, while in the other three narratives (46, 47, 58) it occurs only sporadically. The same combination of perspectives predominates in Pawnee historical stories as well.

Since the mixture of perspectives in some narratives creates potential confusion for English readers, the first person perspective is set off typographically in these volumes (**using this boldface sans serif type**) to distinguish it from the usual third person perspective. This typographic change occurs in narratives 45–47, 49, 55, 58, and 108–9. In the latter two texts the change represents the actual words recited during the public bestowal of a personal name and contrasts with the narrative description of the ritual procedure in them.

General Features

Direct discourse. One of the most pervasive characteristics of Arikara oral narrative style is its heavy emphasis on quoted speech. So extensive, in fact, is the amount of dialogue in some stories that those narratives take on the appearance of scripts for dramas in which the interplay of dialogue is bound together by a thin narrative thread. Much of the time dialogue is introduced by a statement like "then he said," often preceded by a name or noun designating the actor who is speaking, but almost as frequently there is no introduction. The words of an actor simply appear. Similarly, the dialogue of one character often follows that of another in back-and-forth exchanges throughout which it can become difficult to keep the speakers correctly identified, particularly when the printed rendition lacks the gestures and intonational changes that generally characterize narrative delivery.

This emphasis on dialogue and the attention paid to verbal interaction among characters in narratives correlates with the general tendency in Arikara stories to neglect descriptive detail, a trait once commented on by Mrs. Brave's daughter after we had transcribed a long story. She remarked that "Indian" (here Arikara) stories gloss over many details and that narrators, when pressed, never seem able to provide them. She particularly remembered that as a child when she asked her grandmother about details she had not mentioned in her stories, the grandmother could not provide them, stating that she was just telling the story as she had heard it.

Contributing to the extensive occurrence of dialogue, too, is the lack of any indirect discourse in Arikara. The Arikara equivalent of an indirect statement in English is a direct statement or quotation. The English sentence "He said that he would go there," for example, would translate literally into Arikara as "He said, 'I will go there.' " As another example, the Arikara statement "You'll tell the men, 'This is the kind you should make,' " would translate into idiomatic English as "You'll tell the men that they should make this kind."

The Arikara insistence on direct discourse requires, of course, that quoted material be embedded in dialogue, as the preceding examples show. Such quotations within quotations are common in the language, and freely combine with dialogue interplay, as illustrated in a woman's account of how she had been mesmerized and abducted by a bear:

> Then the woman told what happened. "This is what happened. Here it must have been a bear—a bear—that I had been seeing. Then it was a man who was going into the woods. And it got the best of me. 'I think I'll go there. I wonder who you are, you who are coming out of the woods and then going back into them.'
>
> "This is what I did: I went and walked into the woods. He passed in front of me. And there it was a bear! This is what it said: 'Now you must have come.'
>
> " 'I did come.'
>
> " 'Now let's go over there to my dwelling!' "
>
> "And this is what I did: it took me to its den where you found me. It took me inside where you found me. Now this is what the bear did." [story 119]

Moreover, three levels of embedding are not uncommon, as the following paragraph illustrates. In it a young man is instructing his sister to quiz another sister who had become a bear:

[He said,] "You should go find out things from your bear sister. You must say to her, 'You and I are living here alone. It might happen that the enemy will find us. You say, "They cannot kill me. No one can kill me." However, what will happen if they do kill you? Where can you be wounded?' " [10]

Thoughts, too, are presented as dialogue in Arikara, so that what an actor thinks, wants, or wishes appears in the translations within quotation marks. For example, a young man sees a buffalo in the distance:

Then he thought, "How can I sneak up on you?" [11]

Another example illustrates the common sequence of a stated action followed by the thought motivating it:

The next morning the girl went out. "I think I'll go off for a while! I think I'll look around!" She went up into the hills wandering around, and then went to where her brothers were. [10]

A similar example:

When a party was out going around on the warpath . . . they just did not find anything. Then they started back home. "Let's go home! We haven't found anything." [25]

Because dialogue is such an integral feature of the Arikara oral style, the translations in this collection retain all the direct discourse that appears in the original Arikara, no matter the amount of embedding.

Sequencing. The sequencing of actions and description illustrates yet another fundamental difference between Arikara and Western narrative style. A frequently used technique in Arikara is to state a result *first* and then relate the events or actions that led up to that result, the reverse of normal English style. In Lillian Brave's version of Bounding Head, for example, the listener is first told that Old Woman Spider came and caught in her web the people who were trying to smash Bounding Head, her brother. Then in the next paragraph the narrator goes back in time to relate how the people were trying to smash Bounding Head and nearly did so:

But finally Spider was the one who had caught them. Then they were defeated by him. They were defeated by Bounding Head [i.e., Spider, Bounding Head's partisan]. [62]

The English reader at this point is left wondering, "But I thought that Spider had *already* caught them in her web; is this a second incident?" The answer, of course, is no; the latter sequence actually explains the result that was previously stated.

Another example of stating a result before mentioning the action that led to it occurs when children were misbehaving in the lodge of Fire Maker:

And finally they [the children] were jumping over the fire. Then they were doing it: now they were jumping over the fire.
Then after a while he [Fire Maker] said, "Now, see, you have spoiled it!"
When one of them jumped over it, he farted—a big fart. Then he farted on the fire. [84]

Such narrative sequencing frequently presents the English reader with a story that seems full of contradictions, but which, in fact, are not contradictions at all. Understanding the story requires an appreciation of this sequencing device.

Related to this type of sequencing is another common one in which the actions of an unspecified actor are stated first and only afterward is the actor identified, as in this example:

A man touched him. "Now I've come to tell you. I know what you are seeking. You're seeking your wife. Your wife is not lost. This is what he's been doing. Why, now he's overstepped his limits. A black bear is the one. [22]

Similarly, finer specification or description often follows a more general statement. For example:

Then he went into water. There he crossed to the other side. It was a lake. [20]

Discourse bracketing. A prominent feature of Arikara oral style is to preface an action or sequence of actions with an introductory statement "This is what he did" and frequently to conclude the description with a repetition of the same statement. Alternatively, this formulaic statement may appear only once, either before or after the description of the action. For example:

Now then that is what they did: when spring came, when the green grass came up, he said, "Plant what I gave you!" And then that is what they did. [11]

And as was his custom, he just wouldn't do anything. Whenever the party stopped, he would eat. He would sit there way off somewhere on the prairie.

He would walk around on the prairie at a distance, looking all around. That is what he would do. [28]

The same kind of discourse framing occurs with spoken or thought dialogue as well. A quotation is generally preceded by either "Then he said" or "This is what he said," and frequently it is concluded with a repetition of the same remark. In the following example left and right (i.e., opening and closing) framing co-occur:

> Then the man said, "Hidden Man, I called you purposely since we who live here are always hungry. On this earth you are outstanding in the ways of hunting. And I am hungry as I sit here wanting something to eat. You never think, 'My uncle lives over there,' and you never come." That is what this man was saying. [15]

The following paragraphs illustrate right framing:

> Coyote awoke. He did not have the hoop around his neck. Now he darted around anxiously as he looked for it. "Oh, where could I have dropped it? Oh, I certainly had it around my neck when I lay down." That is what he thought. [12]

> "Oh, why don't you come in? You're causing dirt to drop down on us. I have some meat boiling." That is what she was saying over and over. [12]

Repetition. As a stylistic device, repetition of a statement, either in whole or in part, is commonly used for emphasis, often dramatic in tone, when effected with appropriate voice modulation, as can be seen in the following examples:

> While he was searching around, there lay something on the ground! It was the remains of an elk that had apparently been there a long time. Its bones were there. Its bones were there. The skull was there with the horns still on it. [22]

> Then one of them said, "Hidden Man, we have come purposefully." Then they gave him two arrows. They gave him two. [15]

> Now this is the reason we ride horses: to chase the buffalo as they roam. That is what the plan of the horse was. That was what he planned for himself. [3]

Repetition for dramatic effect and emphasis also occurs in slightly modified restatements, in which a word is either replaced by a synonym or the word order in the restatement is changed, as in the following examples:

> Then all the water disappeared. There was no more water. Wherever the
> creek and river valleys were, the water disappeared entirely. And the boy
> would go to different places looking for water while he just wandered all
> around. When he came to a bank there would be only mud there. [2]

> There he sat on a hill, on a high hill. It was a high hill where he was sitting
> on top. [53]

When the name of a person is first introduced in a narrative, the statement is
commonly repeated with the order of noun and verb reversed:

> Now there once was a man who was chief of them. He was named White
> Horse. White Horse is what he was named. [40]

Verbal repetition is also commonly used to indicate spatial extension—a
long, long ways—as shown here:

> Then Coyote ran off as fast as he could, coming, coming, coming.
>   Now, after four days his strength left him. [1]

> He followed and followed the couple, shooting at the elk until he used up all
> his arrows. [21]

It also denotes temporal extension, as in the following:

> Then the young man cried and cried while he was at the edge of the water.
> Oh, then it became dark. Just before morning the young woman came to the
> surface. [21]

Indeterminacy. An emphasis on specificity characterizes Arikara narrative
style. Verbal accounts must precisely stipulate such details as quantity, location, identification, occurrence, and action. If, for example, a group of men
leaves on a war party, an account of it must specify the number of men in the
party. If they reach a certain location, it must be named. If certain actors are
mentioned, they must be named; and if a certain activity is alluded to, it must
also be described. Frequently, however, a narrator cannot supply such details,
either because he cannot remember them or perhaps because he was not told
them when he learned the story. In such instances, he is constrained to note the
indeterminacy of detail by a special verbal construction in which the verb stem
is preceded by *niikohna-,* a sequence consisting of the general deictic prefix
nii- followed by the dubitative *koh-* and the absolute modal prefix *na-.*

Such formations translate into English in one of two ways. One, which occurs more frequently in these translations, signifies 'whichever,' 'whoever,' 'however many,' or 'whatever,' followed by the English meaning of the Arikara verb, as in the following examples:

> After he lay down and fell asleep, some birds came flying up to Coyote, whatever kind they were. Whatever kind of bird it was, it picked Sun's child up and turned back with him. [1]

> And then they followed behind the group as it went off after the weather was cold in late fall. After leaving the village, they traveled for however many days it was. [15]

> Once when he was traveling around, when he was going around hunting, well, wherever he was going, he crossed the water, wherever it was, to the other side when the ice was floating on the river. [15]

> Then the young man gave it the stick, whatever kind it was. [17]

> Then the other one said, "Now be strong for a while! Our village is close by. You must come there! We're living there with the man who is now my father-in-law"—whatever his name was. [15]

Depending on context, this indeterminate construction sometimes translates into English better as either 'I don't know what/who/which' or 'it isn't known what/who/which' followed by the English meaning of the Arikara verb. The following passages exemplify this translation:

> It occurred long, long ago, somewhere along the way when the Arikaras—the ones I am telling about—were migrating this way upriver. . . . It is not known whether this incident occurred near where we are living today [or whether it happened when we were farther downriver]. [13]

> Then he went to look for a hoop since his son wanted to have one. It was the kind of hoop used in the hoop and pole game. I don't know whether it was a large or small one. [12]

Arikara stories abound with these constructions, which are one of the most distinctive features of their narrative style.

Abbreviatory devices. Arikara narrators employ several conventionalized expressions either for abbreviating narrative repetition or for skipping over stretches of time.

The abbreviation of repetition generally occurs after an actor has undergone some experience, an episode described in the story, and finally returns home, where he relates what has happened to him. Here the actor says, "This is what happened," a conventionalized expression symbolizing the sequence of events he is recounting. The expression commonly occurs at the end of stories, as several examples illustrate. One is the conclusion to a story in which a young man has vanquished his evil father-in-law, then returns to his village with his wife and mother-in-law:

> Then they did it: they arrived at the village. Then they told about it: "This is what happened. So this is what the man who used to come here has been doing." [8]

In another story a boy returns home after a series of adventures in pursuit of his hoop:

> Then he said, "Father, mother, I was looking for my brother, the poor thing, after my hoop disappeared. And I've found him. This is what happened." [12]

Another type of abbreviatory device occurs when the narrator wishes to move from one time period to another. In a story about a woman who was abducted by a bear (142), for example, the narrator, Matthew White Bear, describes how the bear has the woman in its den, and then the narrator wishes to jump ahead to the period after the woman has had a child by it. To do so, he says, "Meanwhile this tale goes fast," and then takes up the narrative from that point. After another episode, the narrator again uses the same device to move the story forward. A similar technique occurs in a true story (148) told by William Deane. There he, too, wishes to take the narrative from the time when a child is small to when he has become older; he states, "As the story goes, it suddenly happened that the child had grown up. Then he became a boy."

Numerical patterning. Two numerals, four and seven, give structure to Arikara traditions. Of the two numbers, four is used far more extensively and figures in most narratives. In the myth of the race between the horse and the buffalo (3), for example, both the animals that race are said to be four winters old, and at the conclusion of the story four horses are said to have their stations in the heavens among the celestial powers, where each is one of the four sacred colors and represents one of the four directions. In the story of Red Dog and the four stars (18), as another example, the numerical pattern of four occurs repeatedly: there are four men, later stars; the wife of one of the stars lays the pipe down in front of the men four times; and Red Dog sends scouts out to look for buffalo four days after he performs a ritual. Likewise, whenever there is a sequence of tests or hurdles in a story, they occur in a set of four, although occasionally in a performance a narrator will inadvertently omit one. So, for example, when the four young women are fleeing from Bounding Head in Mr. Morsette's version (6), they take turns throwing four objects (an awl, comb, knife, and mirror) that create obstacles for him; but in Esther Perkins's version (154), only three young women throw objects (a comb, awl, and a mirror). Likewise, in Miss Perkins's version of the Long Teeth story (155), the two brothers subdue only two holy beings, whereas in most versions of this story the number of encounters is four (or more).

The number seven also occurs in stories but not with the same frequency. In the story of the young man who is pitied by spotted buffalos (17), for example, there are seven animals; and in the narrative of Carries The Antelope (19), the protagonist is confronted with seven paddle-shaped coup sticks, of which he is to choose one.

Morphological and Syntactic Traits

A wide variety of morphological and syntactic features characterize Arikara oral style, giving stories their distinctive texture.

Sentence introducers and connectors. Two interjections, *nawáh* and its shortened form *wah,* are the particles most commonly used to introduce a sentence. They both translate best as 'now' but also convey the meaning 'well,' and are frequently used to open a conversation or greet a person as well as to conclude a conversation or bid farewell. Narrators vary in how frequently they use these particles; some use them very often, others sparingly.

Verbs generally take one of two proclitics that serve to situate a statement in time or to connect it to other statements. One of these is *we-* 'now, at this time,' which has only a vague temporal signification. In addition to 'now,' it also translates into English as the present and past perfect forms of verbs. Arikara speakers occasionally translate it into English as 'now,' but more frequently do not give it any discreet meaning. The other proclitic, *noo-* 'then, and then, so' is a connector that has a fainter semantic force than its English equivalents and that may or may not be preceded by the conjunctions *na* and *a* 'and.' It occurs commonly; in fact, it appears on verb after verb in stories, so that in translation it impresses an English reader as a monotonously redundant feature. Generally it is translated here as 'then' and 'so,' but in many instances it is not translated at all.

Existential constructions. Two existential constructions, each having a distinctive connotation, are prevalent in Arikara narratives. One is the indicative existential, *inoowitii-.* It is composed of the quotative prefix *wi-* and the third person indicative modal prefix *ti-* followed by the sequential *i-;* those elements are preceded by a compounded form of the distal deictic *i-* 'there' and *noo-* 'there.' The construction translates as 'there there [verb]' or 'there he [verb],' and serves to point out emphatically the existence or occurrence of someone or something. Examples of its use are:

> When he went inside where she lived, a heart was hanging there with blood dripping from it. [7]

> Then they were very anxious, so they got up. Then each woman went to her cache pit, and there there were plenty of different kinds of corn, just as the crier had said. [11]

The other construction is the contingent existential, so called because it consists of the independent particle *či* 'here' followed by the contingent modal *i-* and second person subject pronominal prefix *š-* and the evidential proper prefix *an-*. It is translated as 'here it [verb]' and connotes a sense of surprise or of the unexpected, as in the following examples:

> And the children moved toward the woods where the plum bushes were. Then the young girl charged out of the brush, and here she was [now] a bear! [10]

> Then they killed the snake. And here it was the favored child of the snakes, the one that they killed! [14]

The particle *či* 'here' occurs with the absolutive mode *(na-)* as well, and in such combinations the English translations are similar to those of the contingent existential; for example:

> Then her husband said, "And here this is what you are doing when you come here! I'm going to punish that one." [13]

Demonstratives. Demonstrative pronouns are used extensively in Arikara, not only where they are normally used in English but also very often where either the English definite article is used or where in English neither a demonstrative pronoun nor a definite article normally occurs. Proper names and nominal subjects are usually preceded by a demonstrative pronoun, usually 'this one.' In story 1, for example, in most occurrences of the characters' names—Raven, Scalped Man, Coyote, and Sun—there is a demonstrative preceding it that translates literally as 'this Raven,' 'this Scalped Man,' etc. Similarly, in story 2 there are two primary actors, a boy and a spring peeper, and generally when the nouns designating them appear in the narrative, they are preceded by the demonstrative. In these and other instances where a demonstrative is not used in idiomatic English, it is either not translated or is translated as the definite article, whichever is more appropriate.

Exclamatives. Another characteristic feature of Arikara oral style is the prevalent use of four exclamatives, each of which adds a certain emotive tone to statements and which, because they are used far more extensively than similar elements in English, give Arikara narratives a distinctive flavor.

The most common of these interjections are *uu* and *aa,* the equivalents of English 'oh' and 'ah' respectively, which add an element of surprise, intensity, or emphasis to a statement. Exemplifying the use of *uu* is a passage in which Long Teeth suspiciously enters the lodge where Drinks Brains is:

> Oh, the other boy [Long Teeth] looked all around inside the interior of the lodge, at the four main posts; oh, he looked all around. Then he came inside. [4]

In another example from the same story:

> There in the distance was a village. Oh, it was a big village! And then that is where he went. [4]

Examples of *aa* occur in the following, in which Raven instructs Scalped Man to take the hoop:

> And you, Scalped Man, will take the hoop. And after you get out, they're going to chase you. Ah, they're watching. They're watching over him. You'll go in, and as soon as you come out, I'll be right there. You'll put the hoop around my neck and I'll come flying north, ah, for as long as my strength lasts. [1]

A similar interjection is *číríkU* 'oh, my; why!' It, too, adds an element of surprise, as illustrated here:

> And so the spring peeper went to a mud flat where the ground was damp. The spring peeper put its two forelegs into the mud and then backed off. Oh my, then water emerged! And as the water came out, it grew in volume. Why, now this boy began to drink his fill! [2]

Different from these is another exclamative, *wačéh* 'poor thing,' which appears in apposition to an animate noun and is also extensively used. It expresses the narrator's sympathy for a person who, in the Arikara mind, is in a pitiful condition. Sometimes the significance of its use is apparent to an English reader, but at other times it is somewhat elusive, as the following passages illustrate.

> Now the spring peeper, poor thing, became very frightened since the boy was kicking it around, molesting it. [2]

> She caused the village to burn up when the fire swept through it, there where that village was. And it burned everything in it, including the men and women, the poor things, who burned up. Then everything was lost, except for the people, the poor things, who fled in different directions—the ones who ran up the hill or who ran into the water. [4]

> Now I am going to relate a story that my grandmother used to tell. Maybe she is listening now, the poor thing, to what she used to tell when she and I were living alone when my grandfather had gone somewhere. . . . [26]

Decedents. When speaking of someone who is deceased, an Arikara usually qualifies the reference with a past tense participial form, which sometimes is *nuúxU* 'the one who was' and other times is *nuuxAxaáNU* 'the one who was named.' In the introduction to story 24, for example, Alfred Morsette states, "I heard the story from the one who was *[nuúxU]* Bear Goes Out; he was named *[kuwituuxAxaá'A]* Bear Goes Out." Another set of examples occurs in story 104, in which Ella Waters tells about a trip her parents made to the Standing Rock Reservation sometime near the turn of the century. In it she refers to her parents as 'my mother who was' and 'my father who was,' since both were deceased when she recorded the narrative. In the historical narrative about the Fort Laramie Treaty (41) the qualifier 'the one who was named' precedes the first mention of numerous individuals, and at the conclusion of story 53 the narrator states, "This is what I used to hear from the man [who was] named Enemy Heart."

Still another usage for introducing a deceased person's name is what translates as 'they used to call him,' or its subordinate form 'the one they used to call.' These forms also appear in narrative 41; for example, "Then the chiefs summoned another man. They used to call him Stone."

Similar qualifiers that occur in the narratives include 'my father who was living,' (104) and 'when I was the old man's son-in-law' (i.e., 'when my father-in-law was living') (30).

Intensification. In Arikara there are three common ways of intensifying a statement. The one that occurs most frequently is use of the particle *Axtóh.* This particle is, in fact, so extensively used that it, too, gives a characteristic flavor to Arikara narrative style. Most of the time it translates as 'surely, truly, certainly,' as, for example:

"It sure would be nice if it were warm. . . ." [1]

"Say, there surely is a being living who controls things where it is summer." [1]

Then Coyote said, "Truly no one ever overtakes me. . . ." [1]

Occasionally, however, it translates best as 'why, . . !":

> Then this Drinks Brains said, "Why, he said, 'Don't go there!' He doesn't want us to do that." [4]

Another method of expressing intensification is with a negative verb form. A verb inflected for the negative has a double meaning: usually it indicates the negative, but it also sometimes serves to intensify a statement. In the latter instance, the negative form translates into English as a positive statement together with 'really, very, so' or sometimes 'indeed.' Although this archaic usage is no longer understood by most Arikara speakers, it occurs frequently in the narratives of Alfred Morsette and others. Examples are:

> Then these horses, the poor things, became fearful. The buffalo was *so* strong. [3]

> Surely that man who's coming has gone too far. . . . We blessed him previously, but now he's gone beyond the limit with these things that he's been doing. [8]

> Now he threw an awl. And when he threw it where they had just come from, there was a thicket of thorn apple bushes. Oh, there was indeed a multitude of them! [10]

> It was certainly [lit. not] true that this horse was swift when it ran. [50]

Still another way of intensifying an utterance is to lengthen a vowel in a word. So, for example, the adverbial expression *nuu naapakúhtu'* 'long, long ago' can be exaggerated by lengthening *nuu* 'then' to *nuuuu,* the equivalent of lengthening English 'long' to 'loooong.' The same effect can also be achieved by lengthening the vowel of the first syllable in *naapakúhtu',* especially when *nuu* does not precede it; thus, *naaaaapakúhtu'* 'loooong ago.'

Sentence types. Word order in Arikara, as in many polysynthetic languages, is quite free. When a sentence has an independent nominal subject and object, for example, the only requirement is that the subject precede the object, but otherwise nearly every permutation of the two nouns and verb is possible. Speakers concur that no one order is preferable to the others, although each person tends to use certain ones; and speakers do not correlate any of the permutations with specific word orderings in English. Consequently, the English translations here often do not reflect Arikara word order, particularly when an Arikara sentence is long and complex.

The sentences in the translations do, however, reflect the structural complexity or simplicity of the Arikara, and therein lies a basic stylistic contrast in the language. Arikara narrators alternate between sentences that, from an English perspective, are long and unusually complex and ones that are short and simple.

Long, complex sentences occur most commonly in description, where they illustrate a propensity in Arikara to form sentences by stringing many subordinate clauses to a single independent one. The following two paragraphs vividly illustrate this structural preference:

> The young man also had a friend. But his friend was active, going all around, going around hunting and going off on war parties. But this other one was just passive, as they used to say, never going on a war party and never looking for things for his mother and father—just walking around in the village where people made fun of him. [23]

> And when it was morning the man who had had the crippled legs walked around inside. Then he was tremendously thankful, being thankful that he was able to walk all around again after they had made him well—after they had taken away his crippledness. [15]

In stark contrast to complex sentences like the preceding are short, direct ones, which are usually employed in recounting sequences of action. Here, too, the integrity of their simplicity is preserved in the translations, even though the style is not valued in English. The following examples illustrate the concatenation of simple sentences:

> Then the boy went on. Then he went home. Then he went inside. Then he said, "Mother, make a fire! I've returned." Then she said, "Oh, why, they're making fun of me!" [12]

> Then this young man started out. Then he went back to his lodge. Then he untied the dogs. He packed some moccasins. Then he came on. Then he arrived at the village after dark. [22]

More common, however, is a balance between the simple and the complex:

> Then he prepared a sweat lodge. He took the boy inside. He made him vomit everything—the things that he used to eat when he lived in the water of that lake. After he had vomited everything—the worms, frogs, and

whatever other things, everything that he ate—then the man gave him different medicines to drink. [4]

Narrative Structure

Beginnings

Narrators vary in the manner in which they begin their stories. Some open them with a formulaic statement, while others offer an introduction containing background information that situates and authenticates the version of the narrative being told. Still others begin directly with the story.

Unless she is telling historical narratives of recent origin, Lilly Brave illustrates the first-named pattern and nearly always opens her stories, whether true ones or tales, with the formula *kuwiteetuunú'a'* 'the village was coming in a long procession,' an allusion to a village on the march. It has no known historical reference, although it probably refers to the Arikara migration upriver. It is now a formal opening to a story, equivalent to the English 'once upon a time.'

Most narrators, however, generally precede their stories with an introduction. Alfred Morsette prefaces almost every narrative he recorded in this collection with the most elaborately stylized introductions. The prefatory statements of other narrators, although containing some of the same information, never have the detail of his. He generally opens with the statement that he will now tell an old story, which he often characterizes either as holy or one that actually happened, frequently qualifying his statement with an avowal that he did not witness it himself. For myths there may also be a statement that the story occurred during the holy period and involved star beings from the celestial world above. Myths and legends, however, are nearly always said to have occurred "long, long ago when our people were coming this way," the reference being to past centuries when the Arikaras were gradually moving upriver in the northwesterly direction of the Missouri River; this general frame is followed by a more precise locational reference, when it is known. Then Mr. Morsette, like many narrators, generally names the person who told him the story and sometimes tells how he came to hear it. Since the sources of his stories are always people of social rank, who are today, as they were previously, accorded respect, the mention of their names serves to authenticate his stories as well as simply to supply background information. (Sometimes, however, he does not name his source until the conclusion of the narrative.)

Eleanor Chase also begins both the one myth and one tale she recorded with the now formulaic introductory statement that the story occurred sometime "when our villages extended along the Missouri River," an anachronistic localizing term not unlike Alfred Morsette's that refers to a former period when small Arikara villages were strung along the banks of the Missouri.

Other narrators, especially Ella Waters and Matthew White Bear, frequently open a story with one of several closely related verbal forms that translate as 'there was a village.' This statement is often modified by a tribal name or a geographical characterization. Such an introductory line serves to situate the story in an indefinite, or at most a loosely defined, temporal and spatial setting that is usually either unknown or of no concern to the narrator, much like the opening line in English stories, "Once upon a time there was a . . ."

Another term used to situate historical stories is *nuuneesawatuúNU* 'there over the hill,' which Arikaras have used during this century to refer to the location of former Arikara villages at Fort Clark and sites farther south. For Mr. Morsette this term designates the Fort Clark village specifically, but for Mrs. Waters it has a more general reference, denoting village sites along the Missouri below Fort Clark.

Although many tales commence with a short introduction that often includes one of the opening statements characteristic of myths or other narrative types, they generally move directly into the story. In Coyote stories, which comprise the majority of these narratives and are the most stylized of all, the opening line is typically one in which Coyote is said to be wandering around or trotting along, often followed by a picaresque reference to his being hungry as usual—introductory assertions that invariably evoke immediate smiles or laughter from Arikara listeners.

Episodic Structure

Long stories are composite texts of episodes set between an introduction and a conclusion. Even though details may differ, the overall structure of different versions of most stories, particularly myths and tales, whether told by the same or a different narrator, is generally very similar or identical. People learn stories in different forms, of course. Sometimes one person's version is longer than another's and contains embellishments or particulars that do not occur in the other's; or certain details may vary, reflecting the different forms in which myths are told and transmitted. These differences also derive in part from the specific situations in which narratives are told. Depending on such variables as a narrator's mood, memory, or other personal factors as well as the narrative situation itself, the teller may lengthen a story by adding episodes, elaborating on details within an episode, or both, as well as by creating new episodes and details or by utilizing existing ones. Similarly, given the same variables, the narrator may abridge a version to its primary components, omitting one or more episodes as well as neglecting or excluding embellishments and other details considered superfluous to the outline of the story.

Rarely, then, are two recitations of the same story by the same narrator identical in all particulars.

Examples of versions of stories that differ in their episodic structure abound in this collection. The story of the girl who became a bear offers a simple illustration of how details within an episode differ. Three of the four versions of this story (10, 86, 141) are identical in structure except for the one episode in which the bear sister's siblings flee from her. (The fourth version, 151, is radically different.) Two versions (10, 86) have the same sequence of four hurdles that the siblings create for their pursuer before they finally escape by climbing onto a rock that rises into the sky, but the third version (141) omits the obstacles altogether.

Although some stories have a set number of episodes, others have a seemingly indefinite number and thereby allow for greater variability in structure. Two examples are the stories of Long Teeth and Drinks Brain Soup (4, 63, 155) and The Star Husband and Old Woman's Grandson (85, 111), in both of which the young protagonists—two brothers in the former, one boy in the latter—embark on a series of adventures. In one of the versions of the Long Teeth myth (4) four adventures are described, whereas in another version (155) there are only two; moreover, between the two sets there is only one common exploit. A similar contrast occurs in the two versions of Old Woman's Grandson. In one version (85) there are eight episodic adventures, but in the other one (111) there are only four, all of which occur in the longer version. In stark contrast to the versions of these two stories is one telling of the Long Teeth myth (63) that is actually a composite of that myth and the story of The Star Husband and Old Woman's Grandson. In this narrative the two brothers undergo a series of three exploits, of which only one matches any of those in the other versions (4, 155).

The myth of The Star Husband and Old Woman's Grandson illustrates another feature of narrative composition: the creation of a story by combining two different narratives into a single, longer one. This Arikara story, similar to many versions found throughout the Plains (see Lowie 1942; Thompson 1953:93–163), is a composite text of two common myths—one the widespread story of a woman who marries a star and the other, its sequel, a hero tale about the exploits of Star Boy—that are tied together by the survival of the star wife's child when he and his mother drop to earth.[20] Another example of this method of creating one longer story by linking two separate ones is the story of The Young Man Who Became a Snake and Carries The Antelope. Both versions of it presented here—one by Alfred Morsette (19) and the other by Dan

20. The combination of these two stories into a single myth occurs among many Plains tribes, and was not developed by the Arikara alone.

Hopkins (133), which are nearly identical—consist of two subparts that for other Arikara narrators are separate stories: one about a young man who eats snake flesh and subsequently becomes a snake himself and takes up his abode in the Missouri River; and the other about a young man who is taken up into a thunderbirds' nest, where he kills a water monster eating the thunderbirds' children. For Mrs. Waters (90, 96) and Matthew White Bear (140), as well as for other Plains tribes (e.g., Pawnee in G. A. Dorsey 1904b:167-68, Grinnell 1893b:171; Cheyenne in Grinnell 1926:154-57), these are separate stories, but for Mr. Morsette and Mr. Hopkins they have become combined into a single narrative.[21]

Similar in construction is William Deane's version of The Man Married to Buffalo Woman (148), which is a simple juxtaposition of two stories, one an account of a clinging old woman who attaches herself to a young man,[22] and the following one the story of the man who married a buffalo woman; in this telling the two parts are not explicitly related to each other.[23] Another version of the second part of Mr. Deane's story is told as a separate myth by Lilly Brave (69), as in fact it is in many versions among neighboring tribes (e.g., the Omaha in J.O. Dorsey 1890:147-62).

The creation of longer narratives is illustrated here by yet another technique: the combination of different accounts of an event into one story. In his narrative of a nineteenth-century attack on Like-A-Fishhook Village (47), for example, Alfred Morsette gives a loosely integrated account of the attack and its aftermath composed of separate versions that he heard from three older men, each one providing a different perspective on the action. Similar in construction is Mr. Morsette's narrative of Custer's expedition against the Sioux in 1876, culminating in the Battle of the Little Big Horn. This version is actually a conflation of accounts of two separate expeditions in which Arikara scouts served under Lt. Col. Custer's command—the 1874 exploring expedition to the Black Hills and the military campaign against the Sioux two years later—that portrays the two maneuvers as a single one. Two other narratives told by Mr. Morsette, one about Arikara-Hidatsa relations (39) and the other about the Fort Laramie Treaty of 1851 (41), are compositions similarly built up from accounts of many separate events.

21. They are interrelated in Hidatsa myth, too (Bowers 1965:360-62).
22. Lévi-Strauss (1968:54-85) analyzes and traces the distribution of this myth throughout North and South America.
23. A version of this story recorded by Edward Curtis in 1907 also is composed of these two parts, but in it the relationship between the clinging old woman and the buffalo wife is made explicit.

Explanations

Many stories end with a moral or an explanation of why some facet of the world is the way it is today. Myths, which frequently are accounts of the origin of some feature in the physical world, are etiological. The story of "How Summer Came to the North Country" (1), for example, tells how summer was first brought to the northern latitude where the Arikaras were living and why summer and winter have alternated annually ever since. Similarly, the story of the girl who became a bear (10, 86, 141, 151) explains the origin of Devils Tower, a natural landmark in northeastern Wyoming, as well as of the Pleiades. In both stories, these explanations are given at the end. The mythical and legendary stories of the poor boy—Bloody Hands, Eats Ashes, and others—typically, but not always, end with a moral, which is usually that the poor person who is humble ultimately triumphs, as Mrs. Brave eloquently states:

> And now today that is the reason that the person who is poor is the one who becomes a chief. And the one who is a chief is the one who will come last. The poor person is the one who will arrive in the lead. This is the reason that when one of us is poor, that person comes in the lead. For this is what [Bloody] Hands did. [66]

Many legendary stories are also explanatory, particularly those that account for the origin of a rite, a society, or a man's name, or which relate an incident that is reputed to have resulted in a natural feature or landmark. The story of the origin of the Hidatsa Crazy Dog society, for example, ends with the declaration that the incident related in it explains why Doorway songs are sung at night among the Hidatsas. The war story (46) of an Assiniboine of the Watopa band who led a raiding party to Like-A-Fishhook Village and stole two kettles of food from an Arikara lodge illustrates how a man acquired the name Two Kettles, and how the Arikaras gave his people the designation Two Kettles' Village. As still another example, the story of the priest who pouted and turned to stone (53) is typical of several in this collection that account for landmarks.

Tales, like myths, frequently end with an explanation, but in tales this formulaic element tends to be more facile than serious, usually accounting for a mundane phenomenon, and often seems to be tacked on to the story to give it significance more to children than to adults. In Alfred Morsette's version of "Coyote and Beaver" (61), for example, Coyote is ultimately frightened by Beaver's power, and so the narrator ends the tale with the statement "this [incident] is the reason a coyote is afraid; when it sees someone, it runs off." Two other narrators, William Deane and Eleanor Chase, utilize the same formulaic explanation as an ending for two entirely different Coyote stories. Both tales end with Coyote's demise beside a rock, so the incident is cited to explain why people today often find bones lying near rocks. Not unlike these explanations is the one given at the end of the tale of "Fire Maker and Why Children Misbehave" (84), a story of how children once ruined a fire in the fireplace in the lodge of the man who controls fire. Their misbehavior is said to account for why children misbehave today.

Endings

Sometimes narrators end a story with no concluding statement. The story of the man with the sharpened leg (8), for example, simply ends when the protagonist returns triumphantly to his village with his wife and mother-in-law and tells people what happened to him. Sometimes, too, the explanatory statement serves as the finale. Most narratives, however, end with a formal statement like "This is how the story goes," "This is the extent of the story," "This is what happened," or "This is what I used to hear." Alfred Morsette, for example, nearly always uses one or a combination of these forms for a conclusion, any two of which are rarely identical. Other narrators like Mrs. Gillette end their stories with the simple statement *nawáh* 'Now' to indicate the conclusion (e.g., 144-46).

For true stories, in contrast to tales, narrators often qualify the concluding statement by designating the person who told them the story, particularly when that information has not been given in the introduction. Mr. Morsette, for example, concludes one narrative (15) with the statement, "Now this is what I used to hear when my grandmother told the story." He ends another narrative (53) by saying, "This is what I used to hear from the man named Enemy Heart," who was a prominent Arikara doctor and warrior. By specifying the source of the story in such a manner, as noted above, the narrator validates his version, and he may even mention that the person who was its source gave the narrator the right to tell it. Mary Gillette makes this point at the conclusion of her story about Has The Horn and the Sioux raiders (145), when she says, "This is the way Has The Horn used to tell it. She gave me the story."

Still another conclusion to a story is one of the two formulaic statements that signal not only the end of a story but also the end of a narrator's story telling (see pp. 105-6).

Narrative Content

Recognition of both the predominant themes that constitute Arikara oral traditions and the major cultural symbols that pervade them are equally essential to an understanding and appreciation of the Arikara literary tradition. Themes, or topics, are cultural perceptions of natural phenomena and human events, real or imagined, which Arikaras have deemed to be sufficiently significant to remember in tradition and which constitute their notion of history. The cultural symbols imbuing them, in contrast, help to flesh out the themes with distinctively Arikara elements; they are the cultural analogues of stylistic features at the linguistic level. Together, those compositional elements, combined with character types and linguistic features of style, create and define the essence of Arikara oral literature. For Arikaras, that literature fulfills the role of history, and the historicity of stories—evaluated by criteria fundamentally different from Western notions of historiography—is an important measure of their validity. At the same time, Arikara oral tradition does not neglect humor; some stories are told solely for amusement, and humorous episodes are introduced into historical narratives for comic relief.

Cultural Symbols

Holiness. Fundamental to Arikara oral traditions—indeed, permeating almost all of them—is the concept *waaRUxtii'u'* 'mysterious power, holiness, sacredness.' It signifies an awe-inspiring, inexplicable power or quality resident in the forces of the universe *(awaaháxu')*.[24] Those forces or beings, perceived to be animate spirits whom people generally refer to and address by kinship terms, include not only celestial phenomena—stars, Sun, Moon, Rain, Thunder, Night—but such natural features of the earth as rocks, rivers, and trees, as well as animals and birds. They are, in fact, anything in the world that is remarkable or unusual. Each possesses a mysterious power enabling it to effect the extraordinary, to achieve spectacular actions or feats beyond the capabilities or comprehension of human beings. That power may be manifested in what is observable, like the flash of lightning, the ferocity of a grizzly bear, the cure of an herb, or a feat of magic; or it may be exhibited in what is only indirectly apparent but for an Arikara is just as real, like the rain that falls after a ritual has been performed, the death that occurs after a sacrilege has been committed, or the accident that befalls someone after another person who is reputed to possess "medicine" has done something out of the ordinary that appears to be an act of witchcraft.

Arikaras conceive of a supreme power, denoted by several terms. During this century the most common designation for him is the Chief Above *(neešaánu' t*ⁱ*načitákUx,* literally 'this chief who sits above'), but he is also

24. Mrs. Waters and Mrs. Gillette translated *awaaháxu'* and its semantically related form *t*ⁱ*naawaáhAt* as 'the elements,' referring to the elements of the universe that have power. Mrs. Brave's translation, 'the Universe; the amorphous, expansive power above,' is similar.

known as Our Father Above (atí'Ax *tⁱNAxčitákUx*, literally 'your father who sits above'), and in one story in this collection (11) he is also referred to as the Great Holy One *(šeeniiwaaRUxtiNIhuúNU)*. Among elderly Arikaras he is characterized as an amorphous power who is overhead in the heavens and is the ultimate source of the world and everything in it. In story 11, for example, Mother Corn tells the people that he is seen in the sky, that he is the one who put everything in the world, and that he is to be called Father by people here on earth. After recording this story, Alfred Morsette explained that the Great Holy One *is* the Heavens, who looks down on Mother Earth and people here but who does not help people by doing good things for them. Primarily a neutral force, he does not intervene directly in human affairs.

Mother Corn, in contrast, is his intermediary on earth. She is the one who came down to earth from the heavens and is the Mother of people; she is the deity who has helped the Arikara people in the past and continues to help them in times of need. At the beginning of human history she led the Arikaras' ancestors out of the underground world and into the one here on earth; she led them on a journey beset with obstacles to their historic location in the Missouri River valley; she gave them their cultural institutions and moral teachings, and provided them with horticulture, including corn itself. It has been primarily Mother Corn to whom Arikaras have turned for help during the past.

Below the Chief Above and Mother Corn is a host of powers, all of which are subsumed under a general term that occurs in several alternate forms based on the stem *–awaahak* 'to be an expanse.' The most common of those forms are *awaaháxu'* and *tⁱnaawaáhAt*, both of which are translated in various ways by elderly Arikaras, but in essence refer to the totality of powers in the universe.[25] Although today many speakers associate the terms with the Christian Godhead, others recognize the difference between an older Arikara concept of multitudinous powers and the more recent association with a single Christian God. Ella Waters and Mary Gillette, for example, preferred to translate both *awaaháxu'* and *tⁱnaawaáhAt* as 'the Elements,' an English term that they felt encompassed both animate and inanimate powers. And so in one story (99) told by Mrs. Waters, the Elements include the wind, stones, sticks, and straw that blow up into the air and make war whoops when saving the helpless inhabitants of an Arikara village being attacked by a Sioux war party. In the narrative describing her naming ritual (108), moreover, Mrs. Waters distinguishes between two types of Elements, or powers: heavenly and

---

25. The terms are cognate with Pawnee *tiraawaáhat* and *awaáhaksu'*, which are usually translated as 'the Heavens' or 'the Expanse Of The Heavens.' As with Arikaras, many contemporary Pawnees associate Tirawahat with God.

earthly.[26] The former includes celestial beings, such as Sun, Moon, and the various stars, while the latter includes features of the landscape, here enumerated as the Grandfather stones on hillsides and Mother River and those things that are on her banks. Lillian Brave, in contrast, translates both *awaaháxu'* and *t^inaawaáhAt* as 'the Universe; the amorphous, expansive power above,' an English rendering that emphasizes the heavenly powers, although it does not exclude the earthly ones. In interlinear translations in volumes 1 and 2 of the original edition of the narratives (Parks 1991), 'elements' is generally given as the translation for these concepts, following the preference of Mrs. Waters; but in the free translations, 'powers' is the English term used throughout since it is less ambiguous for most readers. Sometimes the distinction between heavenly and earthly Powers is made, and occasionally a modifier like 'holy' is used.

The mysterious powers of the universe are ambivalent—they can be either malevolent or benevolent—and are frequently unpredictable. As malevolent, what is *waarúxti'* is dangerous and to be shunned, unless, of course, a person knows how to handle it properly, as through ritual. To avoid its malevolent effects, a human must treat a force imbued with holiness with respect and maintain a proper distance from it. But mysterious power may also be beneficent, and a person may receive some of this power from the being possessing it. An individual may get it as a token of appreciation after performing some service for the being, as when the poor boy retrieved the children of the distraught mouse couple and for this act was blessed with their power (20); or, more commonly, he may acquire it after making himself pitiable so that the force gives him power out of sympathy for his plight. Fasting on a hill, in a cemetery, or in some other appropriate spot, where the lone supplicant neither eats nor drinks and cries for days and nights, is the institutionalized manner of obtaining a spiritual benefactor and some of its power. The nature of that power varies, naturally, depending on the capabilities of the being who bestows it. At the outset of one story (17), each of four animals endows a young man with its characteristic power. The mountain lion's power is the gift of bravery over the enemy; the eagle's is the ability to hunt proficiently; the rabbit's is fleetness and the ability to overtake someone when running after him; and the ant's is the power to find hidden objects.

Arikara doctors possess more powers than any other members of their society; among them they have all three of the types of power that supernatural beings confer on people. One, already mentioned and undoubtedly the most important, is the power to cure, the methods of which vary from herbal

---

26. Pawnees make the same fundamental distinction between heavenly and earthly powers.

treatment to ritual acts (e.g., story 73). Another is the ability to perform feats of magic, illustrated by the doctors' spectacular public demonstrations in the Medicine Lodge that were staged to convince people of their powers and to inspire awe (e.g., stories 55, 102). Finally, there is the power to 'shoot the spirit' *(assawanik)* of another person, producing a trance state that enables a doctor to render that person passive or helpless and thereby to control his or her behavior. The exercise of this power, translated here as 'to mesmerize,' is exemplified in these narratives only by animals, who generally transform themselves into human beings to mesmerize women and then abduct them (e.g., 21, 26, 70, etc.). In one story (70), however, a brother and sister are mesmerized by an elk spirit so that powers can be conveyed to them—powers that they were to take back to the Arikara people.

Frequently when a person is blessed with power, that power is embodied in a little animal spirit said to reside in the individual's chest, the locus of the human spirit and of emotions. When the little spirit manifests itself, the individual becomes suffused with its power and actually manifests the animal's behavior.[27] Such a transformation is illustrated in the story of an Assiniboine raid (45), when the warriors are "performing the things they say to become holy," thereby taking on the behavior of the animal power each possesses. In this instance the men conjure up the animal spirits within themselves.[28]

Sometimes, however, the spirit overtakes an individual without any conscious effort, exemplified in two anecdotes told by Ella Waters. One incident occurred when an Arikara doctor named Bear's Belly and his wife were visiting her parents and the couple stayed overnight. Mrs. Waters's father, Yellow Bear, and Bear's Belly, who had bear power, slept beside each other on pallets on the floor. During the night, according to her father, Bear's Belly suddenly began to growl and then act like a bear and several times started to bite at Yellow Bear's neck. The next day Yellow Bear recounted the frightening behavior of Bear's Belly when the bear spirit "came on him" during the night.

The other incident related by Mrs. Waters occurred just before the death of Strikes Two *(titaraawičé'),* a doctor who had jackrabbit power. Just before his death while this man lay ill in bed, too weak to move, he asked to be taken outside. Once there, he seemed to regain his strength when, uncontrollably, he proceeded to sit on his haunches and jerk his head while making the cries of

27. The belief in little animal spirits residing in the chest is common among neighboring tribes on the northern Plains (see, e.g., Cooper 1957:283–85, 332 for Atsinas; DeMallie 1984:239 for the Teton Sioux). The Pawnees apparently do not share this belief.

28. Maximilian (1843, 2:343) discusses the same belief in animals in the body among the Mandans and Hidatsas.

a jackrabbit. Then, after the spirit in him "calmed down," he lay down weak again, and no sooner had he been taken back into the house than he died.

Respect. Intertwined in part with the concept of holiness are symbols of respect, which are the same symbols used to honor a person, such as a distinguished visitor. Within the lodge, the west side opposite the entry is the place of honor *(huNAhtAhtiš)*. In the Medicine Lodge the altar is located there and is where the leading priests sit during rituals. In the lodge of a keeper it is also the area where the sacred bundle hangs from a rafter, and in other lodges it is the location of a family's private altar or shrine. Visitors are seated at the west end of the lodge when one wishes to show them respect.

Further signs of respect are offerings of food and tobacco. Hence, in all Arikara ceremonies, religious and curing, the three standard offerings made to the deities and spirits of the deceased are the smoke offering of tobacco and the two food offerings of corn and meat. Similarly, when an honored guest arrives at a home, the host shows his respect by seating the visitor in the west and giving him tobacco to smoke and having food served to him.

There is, in addition to these standard forms of extending honor, another overt set of symbols denoted by the term 'to clothe someone' that Arikaras extend to the living as well as to spirits. That custom is illustrated in several narratives here. In one (24), a family wishes to honor a she-bear who visits their lodge, and besides seating her at the west end and giving her food, the family paints her face and puts a feather on her head. In another story (54), in which a bear and a buffalo bull fight and kill one another, a party of Arikaras who witness the battle wish to pay honor to the animals' spirits. As in the previous story, they paint the faces of the dead animals and put feathers on them, and because they are males, they offer them smoke.

The same symbols are employed to honor a human and are frequently combined with a magnificent set of clothing that is put on the person. Vividly illustrating this form of honoring someone is a historical account of how its symbolism was employed to end a battle in 1862 between two camps, one of Arikaras and the other of Hunkpapa Sioux, who had been trading with each other until a fight broke out over a horse race. During a lull in the fighting the Arikara chief went forward and called for Sitting Bull, the Sioux leader, who came and was led to the Arikara's tipi:

> Inside the tipi, the Ree chief helped Sitting Bull undress. Then he brought out several bags of fine clothing. . . . He honored Sitting Bull by dressing him in these fine clothes with his own hands. He put on him two fine scarlet trailing breech-cloths, a foot wide, reaching from his belt to the ground, before and behind. He helped him into a pair of handsome leggings of soft, pliant buck-skin, decorated with a broad bead stripe down the leg, and having heavy twisted fringes from the hip to ankle. On his feet he placed moccasins with

stiff rawhide soles and flexible elkskin uppers covered with designs in dyed porcupine quills. Over Sitting Bull's head the Ree chief slipped a shirt of mountain-sheep's skin, with trailing fringes, decorations of quillwork across the shoulders and chest, and tassels of hair in rows on either side. This shirt he laced up the side, and tied the sleeves to fit. . . . Having painted Sitting Bull's face, he then took from a painted cylindrical rawhide case a swagger war-bonnet and put it on his head—a splendid headgear, with an upright crown of glistening plumes from the golden eagle, a beaded brow-band, and a long tail of feathers cascading down the back to his heels. The Ree tied the chin-straps under Sitting Bull's chin, and belted the tail of the bonnet around his waist.

Leading him outside the tent, the Ree made him mount a fine black horse with a bald face. A war-bonnet was tied to the mane of this horse and another tied to the tail, and its back was thick with blankets. When the horse moved, the tails of the war-bonnets dragged the ground. The Ree chief led this horse to the open space between the lines of hostile warriors. [Vestal 1934:22-23].

That symbolic gesture of the Arikara chief ended the hostilities.

Yet another way of conferring honor on someone in Arikara society is through sponsorship of the *piireškáni'*, or child-naming, ceremony. The Arikara name means literally 'many-handed child' and is cognate with the obsolete Pawnee name for the ceremony, *kskári'* 'many hands.' This early twentieth-century ritual appears to have been a development from one or both of two separate ceremonies of the late eighteenth and early nineteenth centuries, one for piercing children's ears and the other for adopting children (Parks in press; Abel 1939:214-16; Will 1934:33-39), the latter a form of the widespread Calumet Ceremony.[29] The *piireškáni'*, at least in its twentieth-century form, is sponsored by parents who wish to honor a child by having him or her named at a public celebration before the entire tribe. In the ceremony the child not only receives a new name but is also painted and reclothed, all honorific symbols representing the new period of life that a candidate is entering—a period marked by new religious and social responsibilities. A child so honored is known thereafter as a beloved, or favored, child *(piiraasštawí'u')*.

Pitifulness. Another pervasive Arikara cultural symbol occurring in narratives is that of pitifulness *(kaapaačíšu')*, denoted by the two synonymous descriptive verbal stems *kaapaačiš* and *takaahuun* 'to be pitiful, poor.' This state is to some extent relative, as illustrated by the Pawnee use of the term 'poor ones' to designate Indians in general, in apparent contrast to white people, who are so richly endowed by their 'power' *(waaRUxtii'u')*, manifested by their technology. In Arikara society, however, the poor person is one

---

29. The Pawnee Calumet Ceremony is best known as the Hako, a term Alice Fletcher gave to it in her classic study (Fletcher 1904).

who has no relatives, the orphan or the widowed who have no kin to help them in the accumulation and social distribution of such valuable commodities as food, hides, and horses. Not able to provide adequately for themselves or to participate in the interchange of goods, they have no social status and are objects of pity. In Arikara lore Bloody Hands and his grandmother embody these traits: they live in a tipi rather than an earth lodge, located by the dung heaps on the outskirts of the village, where they eat the scraps thrown away by more affluent families, and they have only a swaybacked nag for a horse.

The notion of pitifulness is extended to circumstances other than social status. The invalid, the sickly, and the simpleminded, as well as the old person who is no longer able to lead an active life or who is beset by the infirmities or feebleness of advanced age, are all said to be pitiful, too. In contemporary life as well as in traditions, elderly Arikaras, in fact, regularly intersperse their conversations with an appositional *wačéh* 'poor thing; poor me' in reference to their own condition, just as narrators frequently do in stories when describing a person portrayed as pitiful.

Sensibleness. There is, finally, another cultural concept that occurs repeatedly in Arikara stories as well as in ordinary conversation. It is the notion denoted by the verb *asškaxa* 'to have sense, to be sensible.' The term is used most frequently to describe a child who has matured to the stage where he is consciously aware of his surroundings and is able to reflect on them. When he has reached that level of maturity, usually about age six or seven, he is said to be sensible or have sense. The term, however, is also used in its negative form to describe an adult who engages in antisocial behavior—who lies, steals, kills, or violates social custom. People say that such a person "has no sense."[30] He is an object of pity or scorn; they accord him no respect and do not listen to him.

Related to this characterization is another one, 'to be no good,' which is commonly used in Arikara and contrasts with English usage. In English there are many forms of varying negative intensity and social opprobrium to describe a person who transgresses social mores: whose behavior is, for example, insensitive, cruel, terrible, evil, insidious, horrible, or outrageous. In Arikara, in contrast, only the one expression "He is not good" is used to cover this semantic field. No matter how mildly or intensely bad a person's action or behavior is, an Arikara always describes it with this single term, which to an English speaker generally seems a flat understatement.

30. Truteau noted this Arikara expression and its Sioux equivalent 'to have a bad heart' as early as 1796 and described the significance of the characterization (Parks in press).

Kinship. Integral to the Arikaras' world view is their conception of kinship relationships, which are extended not only to a broader group of people than Euro-Americans generally recognize but also to various nonhuman beings with whom the latter recognize no affinity at all. Among Arikaras, as among most Plains Indian peoples, the orientation of individuals to the people in their world is ordered through kin ties, real and fictive. Their social relations are regulated by the behavior prescribed by those ties, and their verbal interactions are marked by terms of address and reference symbolizing them.

In addition to a wide net of consanguineal and affinal kin relationships with the people in their own village and extending to individuals in other Arikara villages, and even among other tribes when such relationships are created through marriage, Arikaras commonly forge kinship ties with nonrelated individuals through ritual adoption. It is not uncommon for a couple who either have no children or who lose their sons in war to adopt a child in another family or perhaps even in another village. That child will not necessarily move into the adoptive couple's lodge, but the parent-child relationship will be established and will henceforth govern interaction between the families of the couple and the child.

During intertribal visits Arikaras frequently establish kin ties that symbolize friendships formed with individuals in the other social group, and those relationships thereafter govern interaction between the two who adopt one another as well as between their families. Similarly, when an outsider enters an Arikara community to live and interact with its members, it is common for an Arikara who is particularly close to that individual to adopt the person and incorporate him into the kinship network. Historically, this adoption was frequently extended to traders and other whites who worked with Arikaras, and today it is still informally practiced. When I began working in the Arikara community, for example, several of the female narrators in this collection took me for a grandson, two of them even giving me an Arikara name, while Mr. Morsette took me for a son. In all cases, appropriate kinship terms have been used and the expected behavior associated with those fictive ties has prevailed.

For Arikaras, however, as for most American Indian peoples, kinship ties extend beyond human society to include animals, trees, and other forces of the universe that have mysterious power, and these ties regulate the manner in which an individual symbolically interacts with the beings in activities like rituals, prayers, and dreams. These relationships are commonly illustrated in Arikara oral traditions, in which, for example, Moon, Corn (as personified by Mother Corn), and sacred bundles are mothers. The cedar tree, in contrast, is grandmother. And so when an Arikara addresses one of these powers in prayer and refers to one in conversation or narrative, the person will use the appropriate kinship term, mother or grandmother, for the culturally understood relationship (e.g., see 11, 108, 109, 146), just as a human relative would be addressed and talked about. Similarly, Sun and the Chief Above are fathers, while the male spirit in a buffalo skull and the spirits in rocks are grandfathers (see 59, 109). In the story of Hidden Man (15), the two holy men who are Hidden Man's benefactors are his fathers, as are benefactors in many spiritual encounters, and Hidden Man's wife is, by extension, the daughter-in-law of these men.

Directions. Illustrating the numerical patterning of four in Arikara culture is directional representation, another set of symbols permeating Arikara religious life that is occasionally reflected in the present collection of oral traditions.

Directional symbolism, which divides both heavenly and earthly space into two primary axes, north-south and east-west, is fundamental to the religious thought of Arikaras as well as most other Plains tribes. The four quarters of the world recognized by Arikaras today are the cardinal directions—north, south, east, and west—but based on a combination of ethnographic data and narratives collected earlier in this century, the testimony of several older people today, as well as historical Pawnee usage, it is clear that formerly the four primary directions were the semicardinal points of the compass (i.e., northeast, southeast, southwest, and northwest, which correspond to east, south, west, and north respectively).[31]

Particular deities are associated with each of these semicardinal world quarters, to whom prayers and offerings of smoke and food are made in all Arikara rituals (G. A. Dorsey 1904a:20, passim). In the earth lodge there are four pillar posts that represent the world quarters, and in ritual gatherings the members of bands seat themselves in the quarter of the directional post in the lodge with which their band is affiliated (Gilmore 1927:344–45). The west side of the lodge *(huNAhtAhtiš),* which is opposite the entryway in the east, is, moreover, the area of the altar in the Medicine Lodge where the leading priests or doctors always sit when conducting ceremonies; and it is the area in the lodges of individuals where a sacred bundle or other holy objects hang and where honored guests are seated.

Colors. In Arikara culture four symbolic colors are distinctive: black, yellow, red, and white. The same set of colors occurs in the religious symbolism of the Pawnee and Siouan tribes, among whom each color is associated

---

31. The semicardinal points are, for example, the symbolic directions in narratives Murie recorded at the turn of the century (G. A. Dorsey 1904a:20, 40, 54, 105; Gilmore 1927:336). For Pawnee usage, see Murie (1981:109–10).

with one of the four directions in rituals. In the literature on the Arikaras there is not sufficient information to determine whether there was ever the same ritual association of colors and directions, but there is a suggestion of it in one narrative in this collection. At the end of Alfred Morsette's story of "The Race between the Horse and the Buffalo" (3), he refers to four colored horses in the heavens, each one having its station among the powers at one of the points of the compass. Here a black horse is in the east, a palomino (yellow) in the south, a sorrel (red) in the west, and a white horse in the north. (Historically these colors were associated with the semicardinal directions as follows: black and northeast; yellow and southeast; red and southwest; white and northwest.) Whether the symbolism in this story reflects an earlier Arikara usage or borrowing from another tribe is not clear.

Nevertheless, the four symbolic colors pervade various aspects of Arikara culture. In oral traditions holy objects, powers, and characters often occur in sets of four, and they are inevitably associated with the same four colors. In the story of Bounding Head (6, 154), for example, there are four spinsters, each of whom grows a certain color of corn—red, black, white, and yellow—after which she is named (thus Red Corn Woman, White Corn Woman, etc.). Similarly, in the legend of the young man who carries a feathered staff (23), the protagonist jumps into a body of water where he encounters four bears, each one of which is one of the four symbolic colors.

In Arikara personal names, which often derive from individual religious experiences, only the four symbolic colors occur as nominal modifiers, so that when a person is named after an animal or other spirit being, the latter will be red, black, white, or yellow if a color is specified. Moreover, some of these colors have symbolic associations. White, for example, when modifying an animal name refers to the favored child of that species.

Blessing. Rubbing or stroking an object or the body of another individual, a symbolic form of blessing, is a gesture that occurs extensively throughout the oral traditions of the Arikaras and their kindred Pawnees, reflecting its prevalence as a cultural symbol among these people. The act is denoted by one of two closely related verb stems *(in...ut...ištawi'a* or *ut...ištawi'at)*, both literally meaning 'to stroke, pass the hands down over in a brushing movement,' and generally is translated in these narratives as 'to stroke in blessing; to stroke in appreciation.'

Arikaras nearly always translate these two verbs into English as 'to bless,' but for them the gesture has a somewhat wider range of meaning. It is a frequent act in rituals, illustrated, for example, during a smoke offering. After being given the pipe, an individual draws in smoke while simultaneously stroking the pipe toward himself; and then as he exhales he first rubs his hands in the smoke and then rubs them over his head, drawing the power of the pipe to himself. Generally, too, the man who leads the smoke offering will conclude the ritual with a "blessing" of the pipe after he has emptied the burned ashes from the bowl, just before returning it to the altar. Here the act is a symbolic form of reverence or thanks that closely approximates the Western religious notion of blessing.

It also symbolizes appreciation, as when, for example, one person grants something to another and the recipient then strokes that person's head and arms in thanksgiving.

Supplication. The custom called "carrying the pipe" to someone is illustrated in several narratives in this collection. This is a formal symbolic gesture to which a person may resort when one individual becomes estranged from another person or from a group and then is reluctant to comply with a request or fulfill some duty. In such a situation, an individual who wishes to persuade the estranged person to reconcile himself to the other party and become consentient will take a pipe filled with tobacco, lay it on the ground in front of him in the prescribed manner, and beseech him to reconsider the situation. Although such a formal supplication generally changes the heart of the disaffected person in real life, in the stories in this collection it does not always accomplish its aim.

An instance of carrying the pipe occurs in the story of Red Dog and the four star men (18), in which a young woman marries the leader of four star men who come to the Arikara village. Later she is unfaithful to her star husband. When he discovers that she has been seduced by Red Dog, he forsakes her, and together with his companions he leaves the Arikara village. As the four men travel off the young woman follows them and entreats her husband to return with her by taking a pipe to him and laying it down in front of him four times. He refuses to accept it, but since a person never steps over a pipe, he steps around it, alternately from each side, creating a winding path that is replicated in the heavens when the stars return there. Other examples of this custom occur in stories 65 and 67. The act of laying the pipe before someone is also illustrated in the Bloody Hands stories (65–67).

Cultural Themes

Most Arikara traditions center on the theme of power acquisition: how a person gains and uses supernatural power. Those experiences, frequently called visions in the written literature, are said by Arikaras to occur during dreams, typically when a person, generally a young man, fasts and puts himself in a pitiable state. Then some animal or other being comes to him and out of compassion confers on him certain power together with a symbol or symbols representing it. This power may be for achieving success in hunting, war, or doctoring, and sometimes for all three of those endeavors, which are the routes open to a man who would achieve prosperity and prominence in Arikara society. War stories that relate an individual's exploits are generally accounts of how that person's power enabled him to achieve his feats, and in a like manner the narratives of doctors who perform miraculously are descriptive attestations of their power.

So dominant is the theme of power acquisition, in fact, that in addition to its being the primary topic of all the legendary and some of the historical stories in this collection, it has been integrated into many of the myths as well. Such a widespread myth as "The Race between the Buffalo and Horse" (3), for example, is not only an explanatory narrative of how humans came to ride horses and hunt buffalo, but in this Arikara version it is set within the context of a dream in which two star beings appear to a young man and tell him what to do to help transform the primordial condition in which buffalos killed and ate human beings. Likewise, in the story of a boy and the hoop and pole game (12), several mythological themes are combined with the familiar one of power bestowal to create a larger drama.

Within the more general context of power acquisition, there are many other contingent or subsidiary themes occurring in legendary narratives that give to each a distinctive significance. A popular theme is the abuse and subsequent loss of power, a theme that occurs in two plot types. One is exemplified in the story of the man with a sharpened leg (8), in which a person who has been given power uses it to kill so many young men of his own tribe that he finally oversteps the bounds of tolerability and causes his supernatural benefactor to kill him. Illustrating the other plot type is the story of Mice Mouth (20, 89, 112), who at first uses his power in the performance of good deeds but then begins to abuse it until he, too, goes beyond the limits of social tolerance.

Another popular subsidiary theme, described above, is that of the poor boy who raises his social status and achieves prominence either through power that he or his grandmother already has or through the acquisition of it by evoking compassion in a supernatural being. Related to this type is yet another theme, also previously described, the vindication of abnormality, in which a reclusive boy who is thought to be unmanly actually possesses power that his passive behavior masks, and, finally, after deciding to demonstrate his abilities, achieves social prominence.

There are other equally common themes intertwined with that of power acquisition, two of which account for power used for social rather than more strictly personal ends. Stories that recount the origin of a cultural tradition, especially dances and rites, exemplify one of the themes. In such narratives an animal or group of animals wishes to convey a tradition to the Arikara people and uses a young man or young woman as the intermediary who brings the dance or rite to the people and who instructs them in it (e.g., 29–32, 70–72). The other theme is relief from starvation; in such stories a young man acquires the power to summon buffalo herds toward the village so that the animals can be killed to provide the hungry village with meat (e.g., 15, 16, 18). A variant of the latter is the story of how on several occasions Mother Corn and Buffalo Woman saved the Arikara people from starvation (11).

Another related popular theme is the abduction of a human being by an animal. Sometimes the victim is a man, but more often it is a woman. When it is a female, the animal usually turns itself into a human and mesmerizes the victim before taking her. In one scenario of this type the animal is hunted down and killed, whereupon the human captive is released (e.g., 22, 119), while in another common version the animal takes the person to its home or into another world, generally underwater, where he or she is forever destined to what is said to be a difficult life but where the person also becomes an intermediary between the animal captor and human beings, conveying to the latter power or good fortune from the animal (e.g., 21, 23, 25). Another variant of this theme is the marriage of an animal to a human. In one example (24), a man has sexual relations with a she-bear that result in a human child, and later, when the father is rearing his son, the bear mother confers power on both father and child. More commonly, though, the human partner is a woman, and again the union results in power bestowal, for example, on the woman's husband (26) or on her brother (29).

Many other narrative themes do not result in power bestowal. One of these types is animal aggression toward human beings, the topic of several myths (e.g., 2, 3). Related to it is aggression resulting from a disrespect for the holy, as when, for example, a husband tries to kill a bear that is having sexual relations with his wife but is actually conferring power on the husband *through* his wife (13, 87); or the story of the two Foolish Ones who kill the beloved snake child (14, 88). Lack of respect for the holy crosscuts other thematic types, too, as when, for instance, the simpleminded boy imprudently eats snake flesh (96), or when the leader of a war party recklessly climbs onto the back of a giant turtle despite a companion's warning (25).

Historicity

Vividly illustrating a difference between Arikara and Western notions of historicity is the type of story that Arikaras consider true and historical: myths and legends, as discussed previously, were as historically real for them as they were unreal for the Euro-Americans who first encountered the Arikaras in the eighteenth century.[32] Also within the Arikara rubric of history, however, are traditions that do correspond closely to what Euro-Americans consider to be true, albeit perhaps skewed, accounts of the past. The narratives of tribal separations (37, 38), for example, and of the Fort Laramie Treaty of 1851 (41) and the Custer campaigns (42), as well as war stories, (e.g., 43–51) correspond closely to the Western notion of history.

There are, nevertheless, differences between what Arikaras and their Euro-American counterparts consider to be the substance of history, and so to appreciate the Arikara perspective it is necessary to recognize the features that are inherent to it.

Timelessness. One fundamental contrast between Arikara and Euro-American traditions is an Arikara indifference to chronology. Dates and historical periods do not occur in Arikara accounts or in their conception of the past. Instead, events take place simply in the past. Myths and legends generally begin with the formulaic time frame marker "long, long ago when our people were moving upriver" or a similar expression that places them in a remote past. Recent historical accounts similarly fix the temporal setting with a general statement like "when our villages were below Fort Clark," although incidents that occurred more recently, when the Arikaras were living in Like-A-Fishhook Village, are said to have occurred, for example, "when our people were living in the old village."

Nondevelopmental. Early Arikara history—the holy period described in myth and legend—is not, moreover, developmental or even sequential. There is no chronological ordering, for example, to the events recounted in myths. Narrators, at least today, tell mythic and legendary traditions in random order and do not perceive them to belong to a recognized historical sequence. Once, for example, in a discussion with Alfred Morsette about the order in which to present his myths and legends, he stated that the best grouping would be according to the type of animal that figures most prominently in each story (so that all stories of bears, for example, would appear together). He also gave a general sequence for narratives, placing what are here grouped as myths in an earlier period and what are legends in a later time frame, but he could not provide a finer succession and did not perceive one event or story to build on another in either mythic or legendary times.

---

32. In his "Description of the Missouri River," Truteau discusses at some length the traditions and beliefs of the Arikaras, to which he gives no historical validity (Parks in press).

Interpersonal topical focus. Another feature distinguishing Arikara historical narratives from those of Euro-Americans is their subject content. In
contrast with the Euro-American tradition, in which there is a focus on events
and their outcomes, in the Arikara tradition there is an emphasis on interpersonal relations, often reduced to either a single putative incident or to a sequence of incidents, which is associated with the outcome of an event even
though it may only be incidental to it. For example, in the two narratives of
tribal fission (Crow-Hidatsa and Arikara-Pawnee), the splits between groups
are attributed to social discord—to a dispute over the division of the parts of
a butchered buffalo in the Crow-Hidatsa story (37) and to recurrent social hostilities in the Arikara-Pawnee account (38)—and not to any other motives or
causes, as though there were no wider historical context to the event beyond
the discord described. In the narrative of the Fort Laramie Treaty (41), as another example, the treaty council on Horse Creek and the trips to and from
there serve to establish a general narrative framework, but the topics that fill
in this outline are again predominantly interpersonal matters: how the Hidatsa
chief Four Bears does not want to go to the treaty council and is said to be a
coward when the delegation of Arikaras, Mandans, and Hidatsas enter enemy
territory; how one member of the Arikara party, Young Fox, becomes ill and
has to return home; how the American soldiers feed the Arikaras splendidly;
how during treaty negotiations the Arikaras, led by Son Of Star, establish the
precedent that is subsequently followed by all the other tribes in attendance;
and how Son Of Star slights Carries Moccasins at a celebration after the treaty
has been concluded. Although the general stipulations of the treaty and its
social aftermath are mentioned, they are not considered to be any more important to the narrative than are the outstanding social topics of the trip.

Oral repetition. Still another characteristic of the Arikara historical tradition that contrasts with the Euro-American is the manner in which it is transmitted and by extension how its authenticity is established. Unlike the written
history of Euro-Americans, the Arikara tradition is oral, and narrative authenticity is based on the presumption of faithful repetition, beginning with what
an eyewitness or participant told and continuing with the words of his story as
repeated by individuals since then. Consequently, these orally transmitted narratives contrast with Euro-American written ones in that the former may be by
their nature more subject to individual reworking, whether purposeful or acci-
dental, whether through misunderstanding or memory lapse, during the transmission process, even though the Arikara tradition insists on exact repetition
(see Performance Evaluation, below). The oral tradition must, of course, rely
on an absolutely faithful repetition from one telling to the next over time, a
process which is obviated by a written tradition in which words, once

committed to paper, achieve a permanence that is altered only by rewriting or by destruction.

Temporal displacement. Another marked contrast between Arikara and Western notions of historicity, at least from the Euro-American perspective, is the displacement back in time, and so the displacement in narrative type, of a character or story—a displacement that apparently results in part from generations of telling. Stories of Scalped Man in Arikara and Pawnee traditions offer an instructive example of how a character diffuses through time and role type (Parks 1982). Scalped men were, of course, historical personages: ones who survived scalping during warfare but who, according to Arikara custom, were not able return to their village or reenter human society because, after scalping or even maiming, they were thought to exist in a transformed state as spirits who were no longer human. Because they were forced to shun human contact but yet necessarily lived on the outskirts of areas populated by Arikaras, where they occasionally came in contact with people, diverse traditions developed about these scalped men. Some are accounts of encounters with them (e.g., 98, 122, 123, 124) and are what from a Euro-American perspective are historical anecdotes; but other traditions go beyond the simple encounter and move toward an association of the scalped man with a spiritual benefactor. Thus, in some transitional stories the scalped man becomes a provider for a lone hunter or some other person whom he meets (G. A. Dorsey 1904a:149–51; Gilmore 1933:39–43), giving him horses, meat, and eagle feathers, for example (e.g., 94–95, 113). In other narratives the scalped man takes on the attributes of a truly legendary figure, becoming a spiritual being who bestows hunting and curing powers on individuals, just as celestial and animal beings do (e.g., 34, 35, 36). Moreover, Scalped Man also appears as a figure in myths (e.g., 1) and even tales (e.g., 81), illustrating his transformation into a mythologized or trickster character.

A similar kind of development is probably exemplified in many stories that appear to have originally been dream, or vision, stories accounting for some individual's power but that through time have become more public and ultimately more mythological. The story of Hidden Man and the two holy men (14) illustrates this apparent development. It is, first of all, an account of a man who is pitied and given the power to bring the buffalo herds toward an Arikara village during times of starvation. Such a story would originally have been the personal account and property of a man who had had the vision in which he was given that power. But over time, as the story was retold by him and perhaps later his children, it would become widely known and retold in turn by many other individuals so that its original significance was finally lost. And so after the episodes of buffalo calling in the Hidden Man story, there is the addition of a long episode embodying the common mythological theme of the triumph over abuse of supernatural power, in which Hidden Man is led by a buffalo bull to an evil man who enslaves him and then subjects him to a series of tests. The latter subplot, certainly not a part of the original story, was combined with it subsequently.

The narrative of Red Dog and the four stars (18) is a similar example in that it, too, is a combination of what were formerly apparently two separate stories. Red Dog also has the power to call the buffalo, a feat he accomplishes during a period of starvation, suggesting again an original vision story; but the beginning of this narrative has another plot—the marriage of a woman to one of four star beings who come to earth—that was apparently added to the story of Red Dog. The two parts of the narrative are connected when Red Dog seduces the young woman after she has married one of the star beings, with the result that, despite her entreaties, her star husband and his three companions return to the sky, where they form a constellation.

That the significance of traditions changes over time through public dissemination and frequent retelling was also noted among the Pawnees by George A. Dorsey (1904b:xxii). After pointing out that each bundle ceremony and each dance had its origin story that was the personal property of the keeper or owner of the bundle or dance, he states:

> Naturally, these myths of the origins of bundles and dances do not always remain the exclusive property of the priesthood; they find their way among the ordinary people, where, when told, they lose much of their original meaning. Thus, by a gradual process of deterioration, they come to be regarded as of no especial religious significance, and are told as tales are told.

Although among the Arikaras origin stories for bundles and dances are no longer owned by individuals or societies, they clearly were formerly, just as vision stories were individually owned. Hence the evolution of religious stories from the secret, individual sphere to the public domain described for the Pawnees undoubtedly occurred among the Arikaras as well and evolved, moreover, with episodic embellishments of the sort illustrated above.

Humor

The stories in this collection that are intended to provoke laughter are tales. In fact, every one of the tales with animal characters is humorous. Some, like the ones about Lumpy Toad (82, 83) and about the war party of insects (132, 150), are told for the amusement of children but still are considered to be cute by adult audiences. Stories of Stuwi, in contrast, are sexual in content and appeal primarily to adult audiences, who generally find them uproariously funny. Among Arikaras, however, it is Coyote tales that epitomize humor. The trickster Coyote is always a comic character, never a serious one, whose name, whenever it is mentioned, invariably brings smiles to the faces of listeners and whose antics always evoke laughter, no matter the age of the audience.

Ordinarily the content of true stories, which tell about the holy and other historical events, is serious and not given to humor. There are, however, occasions when even acts of desecration can be funny—when, it would seem, a satirical episode allows the tensions inherent in ritual seriousness to be released socially as humor. One illustration of such satirization appears in the story of a scalped man and an eagle trapping party (59). When the party of men set up a hunting lodge in which to eat and sleep, their leader makes an altar composed of a buffalo skull and an ear of corn representing Mother Corn. During the day while the men are in their individual traps, a scalped man steals into the empty hunting lodge and paints a face on the Mother Corn and rubs soot over the buffalo skull. After he repeats this desecration for several days in a row, the members of the party determine to catch the culprit; and when they finally surprise him in the act, they cause the scalped man to die of fright. To the narrator, Alfred Morsette, this story—both the scalped man's antics with the sacred objects and the narrative climax—was hilarious.

A different example appears in a narrative of two undisciplined young men who are urged to go on a vision quest when an older man thinks that a religious experience would help them mature and become men (125). They fail in their attempt, however—first by breaking the rule of fasting and finally by running home when they hear strange, frightening sounds near the spot where they are fasting. Their experience, a story of irreverence and cowardice, is also a source of humor.[33]

In contrast to the satirical themes that turn on religious observations, another form of humor frequently occurs in true stories: comic relief. That technique is illustrated repeatedly in the stories of this collection, always by the introduction of Coyote, the supreme comic. In one example, the story of a star boy who comes down to earth to live with human beings and experience their wars (5), the protagonist comes to a village where he encounters Bloody Hands and his grandmother and decides to live with them. After moving into their lodge, the star boy doctors Bloody Hands to cure him of bedwetting. Just as he finishes this serious endeavor, Coyote comes onto the roof of their lodge and urinates on the fire, putting it out as he always does, and so the star boy nocks an arrow and shoots Coyote in the testicles, causing him to run off yelping. This type of brief comical interlude also occurs earlier in the same story in an episode when the village chief seeks to learn the identity of a mysterious young man, in reality the star boy, who is killing the invincible enemies of the village.

33. In a collection of Pawnee narratives, Weltfish (1937:vii) notes two examples of the vision told in humorous parody.

To determine who the young man is, the chief shoots a marked arrowhead into his leg and then has his crier announce through the village that not only can he, the chief, extract it but he will also give his daughter in marriage to the stranger if the latter makes himself known. At that point, Coyote comes onto the scene, dragging one foot as he enters the chief's lodge, and pretends to be the young man. The chief, however, is not fooled by Coyote's deceit, and throws him out. Similar intrusions of Coyote into otherwise serious narratives form a common literary technique of comic relief.

Performance

When the recording of this collection of narratives began in 1970, the Arikara oral tradition as an ongoing feature of tribal life had vanished long ago. Older people no longer told stories among themselves, and they no longer told them to younger people. As Ella Waters commented in describing her naming ritual, "We had sacred ways—all the rituals that the Arikara tribe used to perform. No one knows those ways now. Dust has covered all the old traditions. But now only a little is known" [109]. What remained were memories from a bygone era—the stories that many elders remembered hearing when they were younger, either from parents or grandparents, or perhaps from some other relative or elderly person—while the last generation of participants in that tradition still lived. During the course of my work, some older people, particularly Alfred Morsette and Lillian Brave, remembered numerous stories, often in full detail, and had in fact told many of them to their own children, while other narrators remembered fewer and frequently had forgotten many of the details of most of the ones they knew or, as some lamented, they confused parts of one story with those of another.

In this situation, then, it was no longer possible to observe a living tradition. It was necessary to question people about it and to ask them to tell the stories they remembered.

Performance Settings

Formerly, nearly every social occasion offered a context for telling stories. Whenever people got together and chatted or whenever old men or women visited one another, they generally told stories. When an older couple would visit another family, whether friends or relatives, the older ones would tell stories. Settings were also diverse: in a living room, around the kitchen table, on the front porch or seated on a bench by the house, in a wagon or car, in camp or in a park.[34] Wherever it might be, story telling was an integral part of social interaction among adults and particularly older people, who were purveyors of knowledge and instructors of the young.

Intertribal visits were, and still are today, another popular context for story telling. During the period of intertribal warfare that preceded the 1880s, not only tribes friendly with each other but even enemy villages would sometimes camp together, if only for a short time, to trade and visit. Based on interviews with the Minneconjou Sioux chief White Bull in the 1930s, Stanley Vestal (1934:18-19) describes such occasions when Sioux and Arikaras would declare a truce that permitted economic and social interchange:

> Such a truce was always interesting. In those small nations, every prominent man was well known to his enemies by name and record, and, when there was a truce, the warriors would get together and discuss last season's battles, checking up on any of their own side whose claims to *coups* might require verification, and giving evidence, when asked, as to the deeds of their enemies. Thus, if a Hunkpapa had claimed to have wounded a certain Ree, the Hunkpapa might ask the Ree to show his scar, and thus make sure of it. In this way, warriors and chiefs became well acquainted between fights, just as rival football teams might become acquainted and talk over old games.

Immediately after intertribal warfare ended on the northern Plains in the late nineteenth century, groups of people from tribes that had formerly been at war began visiting each other, intensifying an older tradition of camping, visiting, and dancing for a period of several days, just as groups from friendly—and frequently unfriendly—tribes had done previously (see stories 45-47). In the 1880s, for example, groups of Sioux from reservations like Standing Rock, Cheyenne River, and even Pine Ridge visited Fort Berthold, where men who had been at war with each other only a few years earlier now exchanged stories as an integral part of social interaction, frequently reliving old battles and comparing accounts as they had always done. Arikaras reciprocated with visits to those communities, where the process of narrative interchange continued (see, for example, story 47).

Although story telling was not restricted to any time of the day, the evening was particularly congenial, especially after a meal when people were sitting around in their homes or in camp and could continue into the early hours of morning if so inclined. Evening, too, was a favorite time to tell myths and tales to children, and today many people remember their grandmothers telling them stories at bedtime when they were youngsters. Nevertheless, a

---

34. G. A. Dorsey (1904b:xxii) says that Pawnee men told Coyote tales whenever they assembled during the winter months—at home, on the hunt, and on the warpath. This characterization clearly held for Arikaras, too.

younger person might be told stories by an older person in the household at any time when the opportunity arose, and men certainly would tell stories whenever they were together.

Another setting in which stories were frequently told was when a boy or youth was urged by his mother or grandmother to take some meat or tobacco to a certain old man, frequently an uncle, and ask the older person to tell him stories and sing songs that he might learn. Alfred Morsette's grandmother used to do this when he was young. She would give him food to take to old men like Snowbird to learn songs and hear stories. Often, too, a young boy might be the companion of an older male relative, when each had the responsibility of looking after the other. An Arikara man who passed away recently knew many old songs he had learned in this way as a youth when he used to stay with his uncle, Albert Simpson, for whom he was a companion.

Whenever one approached a person to ask him to tell a story, it was customary to give that person a small gift, generally food, as a form of payment. The present might be a cornball or a small amount of dried meat, or it might be tobacco, but there must be some tangible offering, which then obligated the recipient to tell a story. If a token sacrifice was not made, people used to say that the story was not valued and so there was no reason to tell it since the hearer was not really interested in it and would not remember it. One elderly lady today relates a humorous anecdote that vividly illustrates the seriousness placed on payment for a story. When her grandparents came to visit on one occasion, she and her siblings—all young children—asked the grandparents to tell them stories. For each one they told over the course of the evening, the grandchildren gave the old couple one of the farm animals that their parents owned. The grandparents went home that night but returned the next day, pretending to claim the animals and thereby leave the family without any for food and work. Feigning surprise, the parents scolded the children to impress on them the gravity of this custom. The children should have presented the grandparents with actual gifts, even if only tokens.

Another custom associated with the oral tradition was a restriction on the season when certain stories could be told. The Arikara narrators represented in this collection of narratives agreed that in former times myths and tales were to be told only during the winter months. Some affirmed that if a person told a story during the summer, when snakes were not hibernating, he or she would be bitten by one. Two individuals, Alfred Morsette and Lillian Brave, insisted on observing the custom and generalized it to include a prohibition on all storytelling during the nonwinter months. For Mr. Morsette the story-telling period was approximately bounded by the first snow in the fall and the breakup of the ice on the Missouri River in early spring. For Mrs. Brave the timing was similar, but she insisted that the end of the winter period was actually marked in the February sky by the appearance of a constellation whose Arikara name is *NAsaahaanu' šiniinaáhNA* 'invalid being carried.' No one can identify it any longer.[35]

Mr. Morsette adhered to yet another custom: once he told a story he would not retell it during the same season. His reticence to repeat a story arose several times during the course of our work together when, after telling a story, we discovered that the tape recorder had malfunctioned. In every instance he insisted that we wait until the next winter to record it again.

Performance Interaction

Public performance of oral tradition was predominately a male activity, in part because men had the leading roles in ritual and social contexts. During social gatherings, as Ella Waters once remarked, women were usually engaged in cooking or other domestic duties that minimized their opportunities to listen when men were exchanging stories. Nevertheless women did learn and tell traditional narratives. They heard them in the home from family and visitors, in rituals when spectators were allowed, and in formal situations when, for example, a doctor imparted his knowledge to a man whose wife assisted him in learning the secrets. Women also exchanged stories among themselves and told them to children, frequently at bedtime.

The story-telling situation, no matter its setting, was a performance in which there apparently was fairly constant interaction between narrator and audience. When a man began a story, he frequently would name his source for it and listeners would voice a grunting sound to indicate their acknowledgement or agreement, and then throughout the narration listeners would periodically utter *híni'*, which has no exact translation but is the equivalent of 'Go on!' serving as a signal to the narrator that his audience is listening attentively and wants him to continue with the story.

---

35. This constellation is perhaps the same as the one known to the Skiri Pawnees as *raaruka'iitu'* 'Stretcher,' also referred to as *raarukitkucu'* 'Big Stretcher' to distinguish it from a smaller constellation named *raarukitkiripahki* 'Little Stretcher.' The former has been identified as Ursa Major, the latter as Ursa Minor (Murie 1981:41; Parks 1991).

The Skiri had a similar restriction on telling tales in the summer and associated it with the appearance of a star. According to George A. Dorsey (1904b:xxii–xxiii):

Such tales are not told during the summer months, or rather during those months when the snakes are visible; for it is supposed that the tutelary god or star of the snakes is in direct communication with the star of Coyote, for during these months the Coyote-Star is early visible in the eastern horizon, and, not liking to be talked about, directs the Snake-Star to tell the snakes of those who talk about him that they may bite him.

When men were gathered telling stories, there was also an ongoing interaction among them as narrators in which, for example, after one man told a story another might tell a different version of it. Or the interaction might reflect the interrelatedness of many stories and their episodic structure. In reminiscences today, elderly men have commented how in the past one man would begin a story and tell only so many episodes—perhaps all he knew— and then another person would take up the narrative with other episodes and still another man might continue with it, leading the narrative thread into another story. Sometimes an incident mentioned but not described in one story might serve as an opening point for another man who knew that story. In William Deane's version of the buffalo wife (148), for example, the buffalo woman's husband and his son escape from the buffalo by climbing onto a rock that rises upward, taking the two of them out of the reach of the buffalo. At that point Mr. Deane says, "There is a story about when they sat there on the rock," and then continues with a subsequent episode. Formerly, another man knowing that story would have taken the cue to tell it after Mr. Deane had finished.[36]

Older people today still remember several formulaic statements that were used when tales were told. If the narrator wished to conclude his story telling, he would say *wetAhneesí'it* 'Now I am letting go of the gut' at the end of his last story, thereby signaling that he was finished and that it was now another's turn.[37] At the end of the last story of the evening, the one telling stories would say *wetireskaá'At* 'Now the gut has gone in.' If a listener wanted the teller to continue with another story, however, he would say *wetatuhneesáhUt* 'I am holding onto the gut' before the narrator said *wetAhneesí'it* or *wetireskaá'At*, thereby forcing him to tell another story. A similar expression was *wetatuhneesuuníkUt* 'I have caught the gut,' which a listener could also say at the end of a story if he wanted the narrator to tell another. The original significance of these expressions is no longer known.

Although there rarely was an audience during the recording of most of the stories in this collection, there were small ones on the first two occasions when I began recording stories in 1970. That winter, in particular, the situation was a relaxed, intimate one, in which Mr. and Mrs. Howling Wolf, Mr. and Mrs.

36. For discussions of the interrelatedness of narratives among other tribes, see Wissler and Duvall (1908:5) for the Blackfeet, and Beckwith (1937:268) and Bowers (1965:290–304) for the Mandans and Hidatsas.

37. Dorsey (1904a:xxii) notes a similar term used by the Pawnees and explains its origin: "As the tale is finished it is the custom for the teller to say, '*We na netsu ut*' (Now the gut passes), referring to the custom of an individual passing his dried fat buffalo entrail to the one next to him after he has satiated his hunger by chewing upon it, when upon the march."

White Bear, and I were staying at the home of Mrs. Fanny Whiteman. Over a period of several days the two men told stories, first one man relating one or two stories, then the other man picking up with a story that he remembered, while the women were either sitting close by listening or were engaged in sewing or cooking and partially listening. In this situation, while each man recited a story, the other one or one of the women would occasionally say *hini'* to encourage the teller to continue. Similarly, the women would respond to actions in the story, laughing when a line was funny or gasping when it was frightful. Beyond that, Fanny would often tell one of the two men to say *wetireskaá'At* at the end of a story as a conclusion to it, even though the expression was more correctly reserved for the last story of the evening.

During the recitation of stories, narrators varied in the amount of dramatic voice modulation and gesture they employed. Men consistently gesticulated more dramatically to act out certain aspects of a story, but they did not accompany the oral narrative with a running version in signs. Although women used their hands to gesture, too, they employed them less for dramatic effect and more for explanation. Men would, for example, use their fingers to indicate the number of times something happened, perhaps pointing one finger forward at the first occurrence of a sequence, then two fingers at the second occurrence, and so on. At dramatic moments they would typically punctuate a statement with a clap of the hands. When size was being specified, however, all of the narrators usually indicated it with the hand brought to the appropriate height above either the floor or a table, which served as a base line, or with one hand opposed to the other. Direction was indicated gesturally in a similar manner, particularly when two or more contrasting reference points were being described.

Performance Evaluation

It is not possible to specify precisely all the criteria an Arikara employs for evaluating a narrative performance. Throughout the period during which these stories were recorded and translated, I posed the question many times to elderly speakers of the language, but it was never satisfactorily answered, in part because they were loathe to evaluate critically the aesthetics of another person's performance. But today at least, when so few individuals know traditional stories, what seems to concern Arikaras most, older and younger alike, is a familiarity with narrative details, while stylistic elegance is clearly of secondary importance.

A comment frequently made by any older person listening to a story told by someone else, particularly a younger person, is that some of the details are not exactly as he or she heard them—sometimes simply noting that this version differs somewhat from the one he or she knows, but more often suggesting that the teller has not recounted the story correctly. Although such an evaluative statement serves to reinforce the authority of elders, the perspective also reflects a fundamental Arikara concern for reproducing a tradition in exactly the form in which it was learned. When Mrs. Waters talked about ritual performances, for example, she never neglected to state emphatically that the old people had always admonished her to do *exactly* as one was taught and neither add to nor neglect any part of it. Hers was a cultural concern for exact reproduction, reiterated by other contemporary Arikara elders as well, which applied to myths, songs, and chant recitations as well as to other ritual acts. For that reason she refused to record stories that she could only remember in part or that she felt she had confused with other stories.[38] Alfred Morsette reiterated the same concern when he used to assert that he had recounted a certain story precisely as he had heard it—that he had not elaborated on it or added to any of its details. Thus it can be said that one primary criterion for evaluating a good Arikara narrator is his or her ability to reproduce a traditional account precisely as it was heard.

In many American Indian cultures, and perhaps nowhere more so than on the Plains, a raconteur's creativity—his or her ability to utilize culturally patterned techniques of expression in novel and aesthetically pleasing ways—is highly valued.[39] Among Arikaras it is not clear exactly what role the creative aspect of performance played in story telling since the tradition is no longer a living one and the language is no longer actively used. Myths, legends, and other true stories were at least in principle patently more subject to the criterion of exactness in verbal performance, while Coyote stories and other tales, which were told for pleasure and laughter, were undoubtedly less stringently held to it. But whatever the story type, linguistic creativity apparently did play an important role in defining an outstanding raconteur; on numerous occasions one elderly man stressed that the sign of a proficient Arikara speaker is the ability to create and use new, compositionally complex words. Earlier in the century Gene Weltfish (1937:vi) noted a similar value placed on word creation among older Pawnees:

> The dominant tendency of classic Pawnee to compound and integrate ideas into one complex is also falling into disuse. Conversations with older people

---

38. Radin (1915:35–36), for example, notes this same concern among the Winnebagos: "The Indian has a firm belief in the existence of a 'correct' version for each myth, which seems to evidence itself in his refusal to tell a myth unless he knows it perfectly."

39. During the early part of this century Robert Lowie studied Crow culture when its oral tradition was vibrantly alive and later wrote about the value of linguistic creativity in it as well as what distinguished a good raconteur (Lowie 1935:104–13).

indicate that this type of integration has a very real aesthetic value for speakers of the older language. On a number of occasions verbal complexes which were compounded of many involved ideas were enjoyed by informants as "beautiful words."

Thus it seems reasonable to conclude that linguistic creativity was another significant criterion for distinguishing a good narrator.

Beyond those two criteria, however, only social status has been observed to influence the evaluation of verbal performance. Elderly people, particularly those descended from prominent families—ones in which members were chiefs, priests, doctors, warriors or others with valued social roles in the nineteenth century—who themselves have carried on Arikara traditions and who have led exemplary lives are today recognized as important repositories of the tribal past and are highly valued in this role.

Conclusion

Although a people's oral traditions have various functions, fulfilling artistic as well as recreational needs, their fundamental purpose is to answer the human quest for knowledge about the world in which people live: how one's physical environment took its present shape, how one's cultural world came to have its present form, where one's social group came from, and what and who were eventful in its past. For a preliterate society, oral traditions contextualize the individual's existence in this world, giving it meaning and temporal as well as spatial orientation.

The oral traditions presented here are representative of the Arikaras' literary heritage. The narratives span its full range, from sacred traditions of a mythical past, through legendary stories of prominent figures and their deeds, to relatively recent historical accounts set in the late nineteenth century. They include ritual descriptions as well as short anecdotes telling about mysterious occurrences, both of which, like the historical traditions, are intended to be instructive. They also include tales illustrating the stories Arikaras told to make one another laugh and the stories parents and grandparents told to entertain their children.

The Arikara historical tradition, composed of its sacred myths and legends as well as other more recent narrative accounts, is not finely sequenced, with each story having its acknowledged position in a temporal order, nor is it developmental, except in the loosest sense. The myths of the earliest period in human history tell about a primordial world in which humans were helpless and had no control over the elements in their environment—when animals hunted and killed people, in a time before humans had learned horticulture. With the intervention of star beings, however, this order was changed so that man became the hunter rather than the prey, and later humans received corn as well as mysterious powers for curing and summoning the buffalo—events that created the order found in eighteenth- and nineteenth-century Arikara life. But beyond those two important developments, Arikara history is primarily an aggregate of timeless narratives, set in a period "when our people were moving upriver," which describe the accretion of rituals and social customs as well as recount the exploits of heroes and malefactors.

A relatively small number of themes predominate throughout Arikara historical traditions. The fundamental one is the belief in a mysterious power (*waaRUxtii'u*) that pervades the universe and is capable of doing both good and harm. This power, which resides in a host of celestial and earthly beings, must be respected and propitiated. One must not be skeptical of it or tamper with the beings—the animals, natural objects, or celestial beings—possessing it since they can do people irreparable harm. These beings can, however, bestow some of their power on humans and thereby give them good fortune: the ability to cure and to achieve success in hunting and war as well as to control such natural phenomena as rainfall. If a person wishes to prosper and succeed in life, he or she must seek a "blessing" from a spirit being, which imparts some of its powers on the individual and remains his or her spiritual guardian throughout life. Thus the central theme of the Arikara historical tradition, extending through the centuries when they were gradually moving northwestward up the Missouri River, is human interaction with spirit beings and the resultant power bestowal. Most of the traditions, then, are either accounts of men and women who were blessed with certain powers because they were pitiful or in some other way were deemed worthy, or are accounts of those who refused to accord respect to the holy and suffered the consequences.

That pervasive theme is, of course, also characteristic of the oral traditions of other Plains tribes. In fact, Arikara traditions, like those of other tribes in the region, include stories that have passed back and forth between tribes during the friendship visits and trading fairs that have been a part of their lives for centuries past and that have continued up to the present. For the Arikaras, stories represented here have come from the Pawnees, Sioux, Hidatsas, Mandans, Cheyennes, Crows, Assiniboines—indeed, from all the surrounding peoples with whom they have had contact over the past two hundred years or longer, maintaining a pattern of story exchange that over millennia diffused myths throughout both North and South America.

What distinguishes Arikara traditions is not so much their basic themes but rather the particular cultural symbols that permeate the expression of those themes in combination with the personalities—the individual characters—appearing in them and the linguistic features of style that create an Arikara narrative form. The latter compositional elements, built into more widespread themes that have been adapted to specific cultural context, to a large extent give Arikara stories their distinctive texture and identity.

This collection of narratives represents the end of the Arikara oral tradition in the native language. The individuals who contributed the stories here belong to the last generation who grew up speaking Arikara as their first language and were privileged to hear tribal traditions recounted as they always had been. During their lifetimes they have seen the use of their language overwhelmed by an ever-growing use of English and simultaneously have witnessed interest in Arikara traditions dissipate as the acculturative processes begun over a century ago have continued unabated. In this changing world, where most of the outward forms of Arikara culture have been almost completely replaced by that of a dominant Euro-American society, they have retained only in their memories what survives of Arikara oral traditions, since the generations below them neither speak the language nor maintain a distinctively Arikara lifestyle. Consequently, when this collection was recorded, some narrators remembered a larger number of stories than others, and some recalled structural details in them more closely than others.

Yet despite its adverse context, this collection clearly represents the content and quality of Arikara oral traditions as they existed throughout this century. The earliest, and only other, comparable collection is the one compiled by James R. Murie and published by George A. Dorsey (1904a) at the beginning of the twentieth century, nearly eighty years preceding the recording of this one. The range of story types and narrative diversity in the two collections are quite similar. In fact, twenty-four of the stories in Dorsey's monograph appear in the original edition of this collection (Parks 1991) as well, many of them told today by the sons and daughters of the men who recorded them for Murie in 1903. The quality of the narratives in the two collections likewise does not seem to vary significantly. Many here are recounted in almost identical form to what Murie recorded. Alfred Morsette's version of the young woman who married an elk (21) is, in fact, richer in detail than Standing Bull's narrative (G. A. Dorsey 1904a:127-29). Similarly, Ella Waters's version of the star husband myth (85) and Lilly Brave's rendition of one Bloody Hands story (66) are virtually identical to their fathers' versions (G. A. Dorsey 1904a: 45-55, 69-70). In contrast, however, are a few others here that are abridgements of what were formerly much longer stories (compare, for example, story 93 with G. A. Dorsey 1904a:109-14).

Most importantly, though, the renditions here are the first to be recorded in Arikara as well as, rather than solely in, English, and to be presented in a translated form that carefully attempts to preserve the literary devices of the original language. Although the oral traditions of the Arikara are no longer passed down in the native language, this collection, which has been preserved through the efforts of the most knowledgeable elders of the last generation of

Arikara language speakers, preserves for the future an authentic record of the tribal legacy that enables Arikara people to reenter the world of their forebears and allows other people to share in it. For Arikaras, then, it serves as a primary link with their people's past, and through written form many of these traditions may take on new life as they are retold in English and passed on to future generations.

An Opening Prayer

1

A Prayer to Mother Moon and a Midwife's Song for a Newborn Infant

MARY GILLETTE

*In 1972, shortly after I had begun my study of Arikara, I asked
the narrator to record for me on tape a lullaby she was reputed to
know. What she sang is a midwife's medicine song that is a prayer to
Mother Moon asking for good health for a newborn infant.*

*In recording it for me, the narrator was also giving me the right
to have the song. To do that she had to present it in the context of a
ritualized instruction that included a prayer to Mother Moon and the
spirits and was accompanied by a purificatory incensing of ourselves
with the smoke of sweetgrass. It was also necessary to confer an
Arikara name on me so that I could be addressed and referred to in
the ritual, which could be spoken only in Arikara, the sole medium of
communication with spirits. This text presents the song together with
its ritual context. The instructional context in which the song is
embedded is a prayer asking that the spirits and Mother Corn watch
over me and the people in general and gives sanction to my efforts to
document Arikara traditions. It is, according to Mrs. Waters, the
translator, a good example of the prayer style of doctors in the
Medicine Lodge, a style no longer in use today.*

*It is difficult to convey to the reader the depth of feeling that this
ritual text evoked in the narrator as well as several other elderly
Arikaras who later heard the tape-recorded version of it. Reactions
must suffice. While translating the text Mrs. Waters several times
broke into tears. A decade later, after Mrs. Waters had passed away,
one woman told Lilly Brave that Mrs. Gillette had "cheated" me by
not recording the actual midwife's song. To clarify the matter, I
played the narrative for Mrs. Brave, her daughter, and two other
family members. As soon as Mrs. Gillette's voice began, the situation*

immediately took on an uncharacteristic gravity, with everyone listening intently. Like Mrs. Waters, Mrs. Brave wept several times as she listened to the recording. At the end there was silence. I asked whether the song was authentic. Mrs. Brave's daughter nodded and quietly, solemnly replied, "Yes." Nothing more was said. I trust that readers will approach the text with the same respect and seriousness that is appropriate for any profound religious expression.

And now here I sit. I am going to support what you are seeking, Quivering Buffalo. Perhaps it will happen that the spirits will guide you. Surely the buffalo is strong. It knows everything.

Now surely the buffalo must know that it is to be this way—that you are going to get a personal name here. This is what we are going to call you. This is what we are going to call you: Quivering Buffalo.

Now this is what I myself mean. I mean that you want to learn something about how we used to live and the things that used to happen among us Indians who are living—about a custom of we who bear children. Now this is what you want to know in order to protect yourself.[1]

Now surely I am not the one in authority. Mother Moon is the main one, she who has certain days for us. Now truly I am praying that you will live well, that nothing bad will occur, and that nothing evil will accidentally befall you.

Now you yourself are going to imitate that buffalo, Quivering Buffalo.[2] Now that is what I mean.

Now I am going to sing what you want—what used to be the tradition when a newborn baby appeared—when they sang the lullaby.

But this is the custom of Mother here on earth. Mother Corn is the one we are beseeching.

Now I am going to sing what used to be the tradition, the lullaby they sang when a baby appeared.

---

1. A reference to the Arikara belief that during life an individual acquires knowledge—here a doctor's knowledge represented by a song—in order to increase one's power, namely, the ability to protect and provide for oneself and to increase one's good fortune.

2. Historically, an animal name generally represented that individual's guardian spirit. A person who had such a guardian would sometimes manifest the qualities of that animal—what the narrator signifies here when she states "you are going to imitate that buffalo." Doctors, for example, imitated the animals from whom they had received their power. By receiving the name Quivering Buffalo, the editor is acquiring, at least symbolically, the buffalo as a guardian spirit.

But this must be the way when we have our own children. Perhaps I'll be truthful. I, poor thing, used to do things for the spirits [and hence they will grant what I request, and I ask] that you yourself will live well.

Whenever you come up against misfortune, this is what you should do: think of it.

Now I am going to do this: now I am going to sing this. I am praying for this to Mother Moon herself.[3]

> Here I stand,
> Where he stood.
>> It is the main place, too.
>> It is the main place, too.
>
> And whatever will be,
> She is the cause.
>> It is the main place, too.
>> It is the main place, too.
>
> They must be thankful,
> When I stand here.
>> It is the main place, too.
>> It is the main place, too.

I am not the one in authority, Quivering Buffalo, when I ask of the spirits and this Mother Corn to let it be that to the end of your days you will live well and do well in whatever you undertake.

Look, Mother watches over us! She watches over us. However negligent we are—what we want of her, let it be provided, no matter what it might be!

Perhaps this is what will happen, Quivering Buffalo—what the spirits will do for you. Whatever burden you encounter, let it be that things will be lighter for you. This is what I mean.

3. The structure of this song text is identical in form to those of Arikara and Pawnee doctors (see Murie 1981). The song is divided into stanzas, here three, each of which comprises two lines followed by a two-line chorus (indented) that is the same in each stanza. The lyrics recapitulate in abbreviated form the vision on which the song is based.

The initial stanza typically relates the doctor who is singing the song to the original visionary, on whom it was originally bestowed: the doctor announces that he (or she) is standing in the Medicine Lodge, performing where the original visionary did. Subsequent lines usually refer to the vision itself, but in this song the lyrics of the second stanza attest that Mother Moon is the cause of whatever happens to the newborn infant, while those of the third stanza seem to declare that the family (or perhaps people in general) should be thankful for the midwife's power to bring good fortune on the newborn.

You must not have ill feelings toward anything. Believe in it!
You are doing well by helping us, poor things. We are pitiful here. There is plenty that we don't know about the ways of Mother Corn that used to exist and that you yourself are now reviving here.[4]

This is what I wanted to say. Now.

4. A reference to the impoverished state of the Arikara people, who are forgetting or do not know their traditions. The narrator is sanctioning the editor's efforts to record those traditions that are still remembered and to preserve them in the hope that contemporary Arikaras might revive them.

Narratives of the Past

Of Ancient Times

2

How Summer Came to the North Country

ALFRED MORSETTE, SR.

*This story is an Arikara version of the widespread Promethean
myth, which, in variant forms throughout North America, accounts for
the origin of daylight or fire on earth. Here it accounts for the origin
of summer on the northern Plains. Distinctive of this version is the
incorporation of Scalped Man, usually a legendary or historical
character in Arikara stories but who here joins the ordinary cast of
animals in stealing the Sun's son. The narrator heard this story twice,
once from his grandfather Short Bear and once from Harry Gillette
(White Shield).*

Long, long ago when we people were not yet living on this earth, when the
ways on this earth were holy, there was no summer here in this country. It was
always cold then, always winter. Oh, it is not known how long the time was
when it never got warm, when it was always very wintry.

Well, now Raven came along, wherever he came from. It is not known
where Raven came from. And Coyote, wherever he came from. Coyote. And
this Scalped Man I talk about. Now Scalped Man was one. Now there were
three of them.

Then one of them said, "Say, everything sure is difficult for us when it is
winter like this all the time, never getting warm, just winter, winter." It is not
known how long it had been that way. "It sure would be nice if it were warm
and green grass were to come up for these buffalo and the other creatures
roaming around here to eat, instead of its just being winter. It makes things
difficult." That is what these three were talking about.

Then this Raven said, "Say, there surely is a being living who controls
things where it is summer. [It is Sun.] If we were to steal Sun's child and bring
him here, Sun will come looking for his child. He'll come pursuing us."

Then one of the others asked, "Well, now how will we do that?"

Then Raven said, "Now, we'll go south to where he lives. Truly I know where he lives—where Sun's lodge is. I know."

Well, then they went. Then they went as a war party. They went after summer so that it would be warm some of the time here where we live. Then Raven took them to the place, wherever it was.

"This lodge here is the one. This is Sun's lodge, and here is where his child lives. Now this one—this Scalped Man is the one who is going to go inside. Then he'll bring the child while his father is sleeping. The child is a hoop that is hanging there. Sometimes the hoop is round there where Sun hangs. Then we say it's wintry when Sun is making summer."

"And you, Scalped Man, will take the hoop. And after you get out, they're going to chase you. Ah, they're watching. They're watching over him. You'll go in, and as soon as you come out, I'll be right there. You'll put the hoop around my neck and I'll come flying north, ah, for as long as my strength lasts.

"Now this one here, Coyote—when I arrive where it's winter, then Coyote will be the one to take the hoop. Then Coyote will be the one to take it. Now he'll carry it for as long as his strength lasts, and then Scalped Man will be the one to take it. Now meanwhile the heat is going to follow us, so that summer will come while they are chasing us."

And so that is what they did. Then Scalped Man entered the lodge. Since he could see well at night, he looked all around. He found the hoop. He took it. He took it around the inside of the lodge and went out. Now he gave it to Raven; he put it around his neck.

Then Raven flew up into the air. Now he fled with the boy as the tribe of beings—whoever they were I surely do not know—were yelling back there. This is what they used to say.

They began chasing after Raven, and meanwhile this Scalped Man was the one holding the pursuers back. He was the one holding them back so that they would not shoot Raven. He was holding them back while Raven came north.

Finally Raven said, "Well, my strength is gone now," and, oh, then he arrived where Coyote sat. Then the ring was put around the head of Coyote.

Then Coyote said, "Truly no one ever overtakes me," saying this over and over. Then Coyote ran off as fast as he could, coming, coming, coming [here to the north where we live].

Now, after four days his strength left him. Four. Then Coyote tired. Then he sat down. "I'll sleep for just a little while and then I'll regain my strength."

After he lay down and fell asleep, some birds came flying up to Coyote, whatever kind they were. Whatever kind of bird it was, it picked Sun's child up and turned back with him.

《　　》

Now, there, that is where the boundary of winter is, here where we are living today. It isn't known how things would be if Coyote had kept his strength up. But he tired and lay down to sleep a little while. "I think I'll just sleep a little while!" Had he gone still farther north, it isn't known what things would be like.

Now this is what happened when summer first arrived here. It became winter again, and then it became summer. Now this is the reason things came to be as they are now.

That is what I myself heard. The old-timers who used to tell stories, the ones who were storytellers, have all died.

This is the reason things came to be as they are now. This is what happened.

Comparative references: ASSINIBOINE Kennedy 1961:3-7; Lowie 1909:101-5; CROW Simms 1903:282-84; KIOWA Marriott and Rachlin 1975:57-60; Parsons 1929: 11-14; KIOWA APACHE McAllister 1949:22-26; TONKAWA Hoijer 1972:46-48.

3

The Holy Boy Who Stopped Animals from Killing Humans

ALFRED MORSETTE, SR.

The setting for this myth is the earth at a time when large animals and birds were the aggressors and human beings were the victims. To change this primordial relationship, a holy boy, actually a star, comes down to earth to punish the animals and birds. After subduing them and insuring that they will no longer molest humans, he returns to the heavens, where he is one of the stars visible even to this day in the night sky. The narrator heard this story from his grandmother Squash Blossom.

Now I am going to tell a story. It isn't a long story.

Long, long ago when mysterious things occurred during the holy period, the different kinds of animals that roam around today used to hate us human beings. When they would see a human, the stags, buffalo, or whatever they were, would burn him. And these birds that fly around—geese and cranes—would fly in a circle over a human whenever they saw him. Then while he was looking for food for himself, the poor thing—whether a man or a youth—he would become dizzy as he watched them and be knocked to the ground, as he went about wherever he was going, seeking to find food for himself. Things were not good for human beings during the holy period. I don't know when that time was.

Well, then a boy came down from up there in the sky. Before he came down here, he said, "I don't like what these animals are doing down there, molesting human beings, the poor things. Now I am coming. I'm going to hurt them." Well, then he came down to earth.

Then as he traveled around, he would nock an arrow in his bow and shoot it into the brush. In this way he felled stags, elks, bears, and other ferocious animals when he shot at them. He would also fell a buffalo whenever he released an arrow and let it fly somewhere. Likewise, whenever he shot an arrow up into the air, it would land and then there would be a flock of dead geese or cranes lying there.

Then the living powers became angry. "Eh, he has killed a multitude of us, this holy boy who goes around shooting us. Now let him die of thirst!"

Then all the water disappeared. There was no more water. Wherever the creek and river valleys were, the water disappeared entirely. And the boy would go to different places looking for water while he just wandered all around. When he came to a bank there would be only mud there.

One day while he was looking at things along a dry bank, he saw what is called a spring peeper, the one that makes sounds in the evening at the edge of a creek or spring.

Then this boy sang:

> Tell me where the water is, and I shan't jab you.
> Tell me where the water is, and I shan't jab you.
> Tell me where the water is!
> Tell me where the water is, and I shan't jab you.
> Tell me where the water is!

Now the spring peeper, poor thing, became very frightened since the boy was kicking it around, molesting it. Then it stood up and thought, "I might save myself."

And so the spring peeper went to a mud flat where the ground was damp.

The spring peeper put its two forelegs into the mud and then backed off. Oh my, then water emerged. And as the water came out, it grew in volume. Why, now this boy began to drink his fill!

Then the boy said, "Now, you creatures who did this to me, my vengeance will fall upon you."

And after he nocked an arrow, he felled an elk or whatever kind of animal it might be, as he was killing different ones. "Now do not do it again!" he warned. "If I return, the consequences will be even worse." When he shot an arrow into the air, he brought down geese and cranes, killing them, too. "Let that also be all of your killing of these human beings of mine, the poor things! If I must come again, it will be even worse."

Then the boy returned to the sky.

Now that is why animals no longer molest us poor human beings like they used to do long, long ago. When the different kinds of wild animals used to oppose us in those times, they must have been ferocious. When the stags bellowed, they burned a person up. The stags and elk and other such animals were fierce and attacked human beings. [Then this boy came and] here they were the ones that became frightened! The boy said, "It's no longer the way it used to be. It's not going to be that way again."

And then this boy went back up into the sky to wherever he had come from.

Comparative references: ASSINIBOINE Kennedy 1961:3-7; Lowie 1909:101-5; CROW Simms 1903:282-84; KIOWA Marriott and Rachlin 1975:57-60; Parsons 1929: 11-14; KIOWA APACHE McAllister 1949:22-26; TONKAWA Hoijer 1972:46-48.

4

The Race between the Horse and the Buffalo

ALFRED MORSETTE, SR.

This story, like the preceding one, is set in the period when animals preyed on human beings. Here the primary aggressors are buffalo. In a dream two star beings appear in human form to a young man. They instruct him to teach his people to make bows and arrows and then arrange for a meeting among all animal kind to determine whether animals will continue to kill humans or humans will hunt animals. In a race between a horse (representing this breed as well as wolves, coyotes, bears, and eagles) and a buffalo (representing his species as well as various types of wild cats), the horse wins, establishing a new order in which humans hunt buffalo and ride and care for horses.

Unlike versions of the mythic animal race found among surrounding tribes, this Arikara narrative has the typical form of a vision story and concludes with an explanation for the origin of horse medicine, a doctoring power that many individuals among Plains tribes possessed to cure horses of maladies. The ending is significant, moreover, because it integrates four horses, each of them one of the four sacred directional colors—red, black, white, and yellow—into Arikara religious symbolism, where the horses assume their stations in the Heavens together with the powers of the four directions.

Our people used to tell about how things were when we were moving upriver. Long, long ago things were not good. The buffalo used to come to a village whenever they smelled humans. That is what they used to say. Then the buffalo attacked the people. They did away with us, killing many people when they attacked, and tore the village down where it stood. The buffalo killed lots of people and ate the bodies they obtained, eating the dead human beings. That is how the buffalo were. They used to do that.

[After they had attacked a village,] they moved off. And after they had departed, those people who had survived came back to the village and then put the remains of the dead, the poor things, on scaffolds after the buffalo had torn up the bodies and eaten them.

Now there once was a boy going around who was sixteen winters old. He was pitiful after his father and mother had been killed. The boy would go to the scaffold on which one of his parents lay and would cry. Then one time he lay down after he had been crying and became tired. Then he dreamed of two men.

One of the men said, "Now you are strong as you go around crying, here where you have been crying. Now we have come here to do something for you because of what the buffalo are doing, because of their eating you people. Now you people are going to be saved. Those who have been killed will become alive again. You'll see your father again, and you'll see your mother again.

"Now in the morning you are to go to your village there in the woods, and you'll tell the men and young men." Then these two men instructed him: "This is what bows are like. This is how you'll make a bow. And you'll make arrowheads and arrows. You'll tell the men, 'This is the kind you should make.'

"Now you'll go to the different bodies lying on scaffolds there. <The flesh has not spoiled yet. It is still good.> Then you'll touch the body and say, 'Wake up quickly! Fix yourself up!' Then they will get up and come back to the village. 'Now all of you must get yourselves ready!'

"After you people have finished making the bows and arrows, after you have finished doing it <we are going to a different world>. The different kinds of animals, the different kinds of us creatures, are all going to gather together. They're going to talk about different things. Now this is what will be the main topic: what is going to happen—whether or not the buffalo will continue to eat you humans. Now that is what they're going to discuss. And we'll tell you what is decided, what is going to happen."

Then this boy went off.

Now when the different animals—the buffalo, elks, coyotes, bears, the different ones—gathered together to plan how things on this earth would be, the horse said, "Now I'll be the one who is first to say something."

Then this horse said, "I don't like what this buffalo is doing. After you abuse some pitiful human being, a weak human being, you kill him. Then you eat him. But here is grass, the thing which was intended for you to eat as you roam around. The human being is helpless now that you have cut his life short."

Then the buffalo said, "No one is telling me what to do as I roam around. Now we'll race. If you beat me, you'll win. But if I beat you, it will be the way it is now. Things will remain the way they are now. I'll eat human beings. I like eating human flesh." That is what he said. "I'll have my way, as I think it should be."

Then the horse said, "Now I'm in agreement. Let's race!"

There was one buffalo standing out in front. He said to the other buffalo, "Now who is going to be the one to run?"

Then one put his fore hoof out. He was the one, a bull, a young one who was four winters old. "Now I'll be the one. I'm the fastest. No one can equal me."

Then everyone became fearful.

Now a horse, a palomino, one four winters old, said, "Now I'll be the one to race him. I'm fast. I can run four days straight. That is the strength I have to run. Now I'll be the one. We'll race. On the land passing by here, on this bare land, is where we are going to race. Oh, the goal will be the edge of the water—the edge of the water. Now if you beat me, you'll win. But if I reach the edge of the water first, I'll beat you."

Now the two of them planned it. Then these horses, the poor things, became fearful. The buffalo was *so* strong.

Then the two raced. When they went, this horse was *really* fast when he ran on the course they took. And then this horse got in the lead. Then he got in the lead. The buffalo fell behind and then swerved to one side.

Now when the buffalo did that, the humans yelled out. Then they mounted the horses and chased the buffalo, shooting them, too.

Now the horse who was racing went on. Then he arrived at the goal. But this buffalo ran off, running away after he was beaten—after he had been saying, "No one can outdo me."

Now this is the reason we ride horses: to chase the buffalo as they roam. That is what the plan of the horse was. That was what he planned for himself.

Well, then the horse said, "I have saved you. And now I want you to keep me, poor me, and I'm going to take care of you, seeking out things for you. Wherever you want to go, I'll take you there. Meanwhile you are going to keep medicine for me here, too."

This was the horse's plan. That must be the reason we rode horses when our people traveled around long ago. We are still doing it, riding horses.

The horse said, "Now I am standing here. I'm the black horse." In the east here on this earth is where he stands. A palomino stands over there in the south; a sorrel horse, in the west; a white horse, on the bare land in the north. Now there is where they have their stations among the powers in the sky when we pray for things to the Chief Above, the one who looks after us who are living here on this earth.

Now this is how the story goes. This is what I used to hear from my grandmother when she told it. And my father used to tell the story, too.

Comparative references: ARAPAHO Dorsey and Kroeber 1903:321-29; ARIKARA Cf. G. A. Dorsey 1904a:40-44; CHEYENNE Grinnell 1926:252-54; Kroeber 1900: 161-62.

5

Bloody Hands and the Star Boy

ALFRED MORSETTE, SR.

This is the story of a star boy, the son of Morning Star, who lives in a celestial world. During the mythological period he comes down to earth to live among humans and participate in their wars. His visit is filled with a series of adventures. First he encounters an evil man who can transform himself into a whirlwind. Later he goes to live in a village of people, and there one by one he overcomes the four enemies who are harassing the village. Incorporated into the story is the popular mythological character Bloody Hands, a poor boy who lives with his grandmother on the outskirts of the village. Here, however, Bloody Hands lacks the mysterious power that he possesses in most Arikara and Pawnee stories. Nevertheless Bloody Hands triumphs when the star boy raises him and his grandmother from their poverty, enabling them to live with the chief's family. The story also explains the origin of the contemporary woman's name Sage Woman.

Now I am going to tell another story that my relatives—my grandmother and my aunt—used to tell me. My mother died when I was a baby, but I used to listen when they told stories, when my grandmother would tell one.

Now, there are beings who live in a world up in the heavens beyond the sky. I surely don't know about it, but this is the story as it was told.

A boy there said, "Father, I like it. I want to be among the people living in the world down below. I like their wars. I want to be among them and do what they do in that other land."

And then his father said, "You're a man now. It will be as you wish. You can go. And after you are satisfied, you can come back here again. You'll come back after you're satisfied with what you're going to do in that place there where you're going to live."

And so this boy descended. I don't know what he did or what happened when he dropped down, but he reached here where we were living on this earth.

Now after this boy had come here from above, he was going along, just wandering all around looking all over the land. As he was going, he noticed smoke coming up in the direction he was headed. There was smoke there. Then that is where he went.

This boy came to it. There were earth lodges there. They were well built. The lodges were sturdy.

Then he went up to them. As he approached a man just came out of one.

Then the man asked, "Where did you come from?"

"Myself, I'm just wandering around. I'm looking for some place to live for a while."

And then this man—he was a heavyset man—said, "Say, it's sure good that you came here. I'd like you to stay here awhile to do some work for me, to do some things for me that I need to have done."

And then he said, "Alright, I'll certainly do that. I'll watch over things for you." Now this boy was going to work for this man.

Well, then morning came and the man said, "Now you're going to gather up things for me. But that lodge close by, where the door is facing us—don't go there. Don't ever open the door!

(Now right here I wanted to find out from my grandmother when she was still living—I asked, "Why did he give him keys? Surely there weren't any keys around at that time.")[5]

"Don't open that door! But you can look around the other lodges. And you can enter those where I have my things. But I don't want you to lay a hand on that lodge."

And then that morning the man was just not around. He must have gone somewhere.

The man had a horse, a white horse. Oh, it was nice looking! It had a chunk of meat. That is what the horse was eating. When the boy came up to it, it stopped.

And the man had a bear that was tied up. Oh, a big black bear! It was large. It had hay. It was tied up, too. The bear was eating the hay, and the horse was eating that meat. That is what this man was doing with the two animals he had, forcing them to eat what he gave them.

And then this man went off somewhere while the boy was working for him, while he went all around working for him, getting meat for the horse and

---

5. This parenthetical remark was intended to follow a statement—which the narrator neglected to make in this rendition—that the man had a set of keys to open the earth lodge doors.

cutting hay for the bear.

After the boy had been up on a hill, he came down. The lodge must have been at the base of the hill where he had been going around.

Then the boy thought, "I wonder why he doesn't want me to look in that lodge. I wonder what's inside it."

Then this boy went there and tried out the keys. Now he must have gone to the place where the keys were kept. Then he opened the door and when he peeked inside he saw them. Oh, dead people! There were many dead human bodies piled up inside, human beings whom the man had apparently killed. But the boy certainly did not know what tribes the different kinds of humans were.

<"Oh, so that's where he gets the meat that he gives to the horse! The horse is eating human flesh.">

Now when he wanted to lock the door, it would not lock easily. Oh, it was with great difficulty that he locked it. Then the key got bloody as blood dripped down all over the door.

Then the boy went over to the man's lodge. As soon as he entered it, the horse over there said, "Now hurry! You've made a mistake. Now quickly!" And it said, "Give me that hay over there! And you can give this piece of meat to that one over there."

And so that is what the boy did. He picked up the meat. Then he gave it to the bear. And then he gave the hay to the horse.

Then the horse began eating the hay. It said, "Let me fill myself up! We're going to go far, far off."

Then the horse said, "But first go into that pond!"

Then the boy went into it [to wash off the smell of dead human flesh]. Oh, he had nice looking hair on his head! His hair was golden.

Then the horse said, "Put those things hanging up over there on yourself!"

Oh, they were nice clothes [armor], and a wooden sword. Then the boy got himself ready.

And then the horse said, "Put one of those saddles on my back! Now you're going to ride me. You and I are going to run away. He'll do something evil when he comes back. The three of us here will be dead if we stay. [The man is a whirlwind.] Now let's go quickly!"

Meanwhile the bear had already run off.

Then this boy mounted the white horse. Then the two of them went off.

Then the horse said, "Now we'll head south there [where he can't go]. Now whip me! Our flight is going to be very difficult! He'll be fast when he comes after us."

Then he mounted it. Then he made the horse run fast. It ran exceedingly fast as it went.

"Now keep looking back! He must be coming."

He looked back. Oh, black clouds were rolling toward them as a big storm came, coming, as hail beat down and the whirlwind came forcefully. Meanwhile this young man whipped the horse.

It said, "He's coming exceedingly fast, but you and I will leave him behind."

They went on, went on, until, oh, it was morning. Then this horse said, "My speed is slackening. Now bark like a coyote does when it yelps!"

Then that is what the boy did, yelping the way a coyote does, the way a big white wolf does. And then this horse regained its strength.[6]

Then it said, "Now he's going to turn back."

Then, after they went on, the sky cleared up. "Now we've beat him. He's turned back. He's gone back there."

So they went on, with the boy riding the horse.

Now at last the horse said, "Now, my brother, there's a village over there, one like you want for the life you wish to lead and the things you want to do. It's a village of human beings. Oh, it's a big village!

"Now this is where I'll stay. This is where I'll roam. Now then, when you get down, you'll take off the things you are wearing. You'll tie them onto the saddle I have on myself. And then you'll kill me. You'll strike me on the head with the wooden sword you have. Then I'll be dead.

"But when the enemy comes to attack, you'll come here. This is what you'll say: 'Black horse of mine, come! Now we've found each other.' Or 'Yellow horse of mine' or 'Sorrel horse of mine' or 'Now white horse of mine'—however many times it may be that the enemy comes, and whatever your strength may be. Now this is what I have planned for you: you are going to go around on the warpath and I'm going to watch over you while you accomplish different things for yourself."

It said, "Now disguise yourself [since you are from a different world]! I know where you came from."

Then that is what this boy did. He took off the armor that he was wearing. He tied it to the saddle. He struck the horse on the head. It fell over. It disappeared.

《   》

6. The motif of a man barking like a coyote or wolf to reinvigorate the horse on which he escapes is a recurrent one (cf. Parks 1991, 4:608–10).

Then the boy went on. As he was coming along he climbed up a hill. As he looked all around, he saw a line of smoke over yonder. Then that is where he headed as he went on. Then he went to the edge of the village. There at the end of the village, oh, there at the end of the village, was where the smoke was coming out. Then he went on.

There was a boy there playing around. The little boy was not very old. He had an old buckskin horse picketed there. Oh, he and his grandmother had a lodge there.

This boy got there. "Hey, I have come!"

Then the little boy said, "Where did you come from?"

Then he answered, "Myself, I'm just wandering around." He had his head covered with a honeycomb tripe.[7] It made his head appear as if it had sores when someone looked at him. Then he said, "I want to play with you—for us to be companions."

"Let me tell my grandmother first!"

Then he ran off.

"Grandma, a boy has come here, and he says, 'I want to play with you.'"

"Oh, they always do that. They always beat you up. Don't do it. Don't pay any attention to him."

He ran off. Then this Bloody Hands said, "Uh, my grandma said, 'They always beat you up. Don't pay any attention to him.'"

This one said, "I certainly wouldn't do that. I'm poor like you are. I wander around because I don't have any relatives."

Then this Bloody Hands swung back around. He said, "Grandma, he says, 'I don't have any relatives. Poor me, I just wander around. I'm poor like you are. And I want us to be companions, and I want to live with you, where you and your grandmother live.'"

"Alright, let him come in!"

Then he said, "My grandma said, 'You can come in.'"

Then the two of them went inside. When this old woman saw him, she thought, "He's different. He isn't a human like we are who live here."

"Now sit down, sonny, you who are just wandering around!"

Then she fed them and they ate. Meanwhile the boy told Bloody Hands's grandmother various stories while she scrutinized him, thinking, "Here you are different! And here you've come from far, far off!"

She said to Bloody Hands, "When you two are sleeping together, don't pee on him. You're a bed wetter."

---

7. Tissue forming the wall of the reticulum, part of a ruminant's stomach. After putting the tripe on his head, the boy is known as Sore Head.

The boy said, "Oh, there's nothing to that. There's nothing to it." Then he doctored Bloody Hands for what she had said he did by rubbing ashes over his crotch.

Now as he always had been doing, Coyote came onto the top of the lodge to urinate, to urinate on their fire from the top of the lodge and put the fire out.

This time this boy Sore Head nocked an arrow in his bow. Then he shot him. He shot him in the testicles, and Coyote went running off into the distance yelping.

A long time passed now, and when each morning came, Bloody Hands had not wet the bed.

While they were telling stories, Bloody Hands said, "In the evening I always go swimming. Our chief has four daughters. Oh, they're fond of me when we play, and they push me under the water when we're swimming. You'll see them."

Then the two of them went off. He took Sore Head around.

In the evening Bloody Hands said, "Now the girls have gone there."

Then these two went there. Then Sore Head sat down on a bluff, but Bloody Hands went down to the stream. These four young women—the maidens—were happy to see him and began to play with him.

"And over there Sore Head is sitting."

And then they said, "Oh, his head must smell bad." They began calling him names, but the youngest one began to take a liking to this Sore Head. She liked him. She looked at him, unable to take her mind off him. He was really quiet while the other young women called him names.

Then the young women went home.

Then Bloody Hands asked, "Did you see them?"

Sore Head said, "Yes."

"Don't pay attention to what they say when they are looking for something to say!"

"I know what they were saying."

Once when they were going back to the river bank, however many times they went there, the crier announced, "The enemy is coming to attack! Hey, we are going to have a battle! And this is what our chief has said: 'Iron Shirt is among the enemy. Whoever kills him will be the one to marry my daughters.'" This is what the crier was announcing as the men went off to fight. I don't know how many times he did this.

And then this Sore Head said, "Ah, my friend, let me mount the old buckskin gelding! I'll go there. I want to see the action—to see what happens where the fighting is."

Then Bloody Hands said, "Grandma, he says he wants to go to where the fighting is."

"Ah, grandson, don't go close to it! They might wound you. Oh, it's not good! They aren't careful where they shoot."

"Oh, I'll go anyway. I just want to watch them. I'll peep over the hills here and there."

The boy mounted the old buckskin horse and rode on while men passed by him, going to fight in the battle. Everyone passed ahead of him.

<"Where are you going?" they asked. "You should go home. You might get killed.">

Then he got off the old buckskin and left it. Then he quickly climbed the hill where his horse had been. Then he said, "I have come. I want to ride a black horse."

Then there was a loud rumble and a cloud of dust. There stood a black horse. Oh, it shone!

Then he put the armor on himself. Then he charged up the hill, too.

Then, in the fighting between the enemy and the villagers, he killed the warrior who wore the metal shirt. He scalped him. He ran off with the scalp. Then he hid.

Then he made the black horse disappear as he had done previously. After he made the horse he had disappear, he took the scalp. Then he mounted the old buckskin gelding and began to shoot here and there <at prairie chickens> as he came along slowly.

Men were passing him by while the battle raged. "Hey, this one isn't going to be the one who killed Iron Shirt." That is what they were saying [ridiculing him because he was going so slowly on the old horse].

Later this boy Bloody Hands arrived at the creek where the maidens were.
"Hey, Bloody Hands, did you see it?"
"Eh, I saw the battle."
"Did they kill him?"
"Say, I don't know. I don't know what happened. I don't know if they killed him."

He did not reveal it when one of them pried to see if he had been the one who killed Iron Shirt. That is what the maidens were asking him over and over.

Finally the youngest one lost her patience. She couldn't take her mind off this boy [Sore Head] she liked. Finally she began to come to the lodge of Bloody Hands and his grandmother.

Then the young woman came. "I just brought moccasins for the boys, your grandsons, who live here with you."

"Oh, these boys will be *so* thankful!"

This boy Sore Head was the real reason the young woman came to play with them.

Finally the boy began to sleep with her. Meanwhile she persisted in coming and bringing things.

But her sisters did not approve of what she did. "Whatever does she want to do with someone who has a sore head—whose head smells rotten!"

But this young woman did not care when they said those things. She could not take her mind off him.

Now there were other battles. Then Sore Head killed Iron Ear. And Iron Hand. And Iron Hair. There he killed the fourth one. That was the number of those who were the major enemies of this village. Those were the bravest warriors who came to fight the people in this village.

When the village crier announced, "The enemy is coming! There is going to be a battle!" this Sore Head mounted up. "I think I'll go watch!" Then he mounted the old buckskin gelding. The men, when they were passing by him on their faster horses, said, "Why, this one won't be the one to kill Iron Hand!" And all of them went up the hill to the battle.

And then the boy ran to the spot. Then he said, "Yellow horse of mine, come!"

Oh, then there was a buckskin horse, a fine-looking horse!

Then he put on himself the things that were hanging from the horse. He hurried to join the fighters where the battle was. Then he killed Iron Hand. Then the Sioux ran away.[8]

Then this young man slipped off unnoticed after he killed Iron Hand. He made the buckskin horse stand there and tied onto it the things he wore. Then the buckskin disappeared.

Then he mounted the clubfooted old buckskin. While he was coming through the valley shooting arrows here and there, men said, "Why, you going through the valley here, you aren't going to be the one to do it. You should be like the one who killed Iron Hand!" They said things like that. Everyone went on.

Then Sore Head returned home. Then he said, "Grandmother, here are some prairie chickens."

8. In Arikara oral traditions the term Sioux frequently has, as here, the more generalized meaning of enemy.

She plucked them.

Then Last Child,[9] that young woman he was sleeping with, arrived. After they all went to bed and he lay with her, she forgot the holy things she had said.[10]

Now when Iron Ear was the one who led the enemy when they came to fight, the young man rode a white steed.

"Whoever kills Iron Ear will be the one to marry this daughter! Whoever he is who has been killing these enemies—the one who is the brave warrior—we don't know him."

And so the chief, the father of these young women, made an arrowhead and an arrow. He made a groove around the end of the arrow, where the arrowhead is. Then he joined the fighters to spy on the unknown warrior.

Then the white horse the young man was riding suddenly appeared as he got to the front line. The young man charged this Iron Ear. He yanked him off his horse. He scalped him. Then he swung around and rode along at the edge of the fighting.

Meanwhile the chief shot the arrow somewhere into one of his legs, whichever leg it was. I don't know.

This young man continued on, though. Then he quickly rode down the hillside. He hid from them. He put his things on the white horse.

His leg was aching where he had been struck. So he broke off the arrow shaft, realizing that someone would recognize him as the one killing the enemy warriors.

Then he returned to where he was living. After they had boiled some meat and, oh, as they were eating, the young woman Last Child walked around inside the lodge. His grandmother watched the young woman.

Then this Sore Head said, "Hey, my wife, my leg hurts me terrifically. Your father is the cause of it. He shot me in the leg with an arrow, and the arrowhead is in it and now my leg is swollen. It's really paining me."

Meanwhile, there in the main part of the village, the crier was calling out, "The chief says, 'I grooved my own arrowhead. I want the man to come. I'll doctor him. I'll take it out. And he'll be the one to be my son-in-law.'"

Now Coyote came into the chief's lodge, wanting to be the one to marry these young women. Coyote dragged his leg inside.

This chief: "Hey, he's different. Take him outside!"

9. A name for the youngest child in a family. Here it refers to the chief's youngest daughter.
10. An obscure reference.

They threw him out, Coyote, Mischievous Coyote, as he underhandedly tried to marry these young women.

And then this young woman ran up to her father's lodge. She said, "Father, I have come. My husband wants you to doctor him. You shot an arrowhead into his leg. Now his leg is paining him. His leg has swollen up."

"Eh, what are you doing? Bring him over here!"

Then they took this young man up there. They laid him down. Then this man the chief extracted the arrowhead with a stick. He pulled his arms. Then the wound healed.

"And here he's the one who killed all of them—who counted coups on the ones molesting us! Now he is my son-in-law. Now he's my son-in-law. Now, you people of this village, this son-in-law of mine owns the village."[11]

Then this Sore Head said to the daughter, "Let things be as they were. You and I are together. That's good enough. Nothing else matters. Your father has the village. Meanwhile we are now all together. And it wouldn't be good if I moved my grandmother's things away. Nothing else matters, just that we're together."

Then she told her father what he said. "This is what he says."

"Well, it doesn't make any difference. You two are together."

Now the other sisters of this Last Child, when they brought moccasins and war shirts to him, they would be told, "Ah, he doesn't need it. He has one of those. You were always calling him names."

When she said that, the three maidens left. They said, "Ah, we made a mistake when we did that, calling him names."

And here he must have been a handsome young man all along! For then he did it: he took the covering off from his head. Here he was a handsome man!

Well, then he married this young woman. Well, then she had a baby for him. It was a girl that they had.

Then he said, "Now, my wife, now my spirit wants to go home. My father is calling me. I'm not one of you people living here on earth. There in the sky is where I came from, where my father is, where you see the star that comes up just before daybreak. The big star [Morning Star]—that one is my father. Now he's calling me. He wants to see this child of mine."

Well, then the young woman cried as she mourned, not wanting him to do it.

11. The expression 'to own the village' is a metaphor designating the position of village chief.

He said, "It doesn't matter. You don't need to feel bad. My father and I will watch over you. But I must take this girl. But you will have another one. She'll look like this one. Now I want you, Last Child, and her to be together. And I want her to look like me."

Now they made a sweat lodge. They went inside. They went inside the sweat lodge.

When this young man called out in prayer—after he and his father had spoken—then he said, "Now, grandmother, I want you to say how old you would like to be so that you can be young again."

Then his grandmother said, "Now, my grandson, you have taken care of me. You have taken care of us and what we have been doing. Now we feel bad that you are going to leave us.

"Well, I want to be as old as a young woman who has had four children, one who is thirty winters old. I'll be that age."

"Now, my brother, how old do you want to be?"

Then the boy said, "I want to be as old as you—a man like you are."

"Well, that's good. It's going to be that way."

Then he began to splash water on the hot rocks.

"Now, Last Child, open the door!"

Then she opened the door. There she sat: there sat his grandmother. She was a young girl. And the other one, his brother Bloody Hands, sat there. The two of them [Bloody Hands and Star Boy] looked like twins.

Then they all went out.

Then they ate after Last Child cooked a meal. Oh, they ate!

Then this young man said, "Now the night has passed. Let's go up on the hill! Let's go up!"

Then he and his wife took the baby girl. They were dipping water while they talked. "This is how you people here are going to fare. You are going to be thus" [foretelling their future].

"Now, bring me a bunch of sage! White sage!"

Then she brought it. She wrapped the sage up into a bundle. It looked like a baby.

"Now, this bundle will be like this girl. Now I'm going to go. My father is calling me—my father, the one there looking down on you. My father sees you.

"Now turn that way to face the west!"

Then the young woman stood up there. Then he put the bundle of sage on her back. He put a robe over her shoulders, so that the sage was wrapped like a baby.

Then he said, "Now you're going to go back."

He turned her around.

"You're going to go back to where you live. Now this baby will begin to cry; when she gets lonesome, she'll cry. Don't pay any attention to her, but watch over her.

"As soon as she begins to hang down, hanging down over your shoulder, take her in your arms. You'll nurse her. The white sage is going to be like mine. Put her on your back. Nurse her. Now this one will be just like the child we have.

"You'll know that my grandmother is waiting for you where she lives, and my brother Bloody Hands. You three will be together. And if my brother wants to be chief of the village, that is how it will be."

And it happened that way for this young woman, just as he said it would. When morning came and the baby cried, the young woman thought, "Now it's time, just as he said."

She took the bundle. "Why, here this sage is mine!" Then she took it. Then she nursed it.

Then she and the baby went on. They arrived where she, the old woman, and Bloody Hands lived, and they all mourned there.

Then she told them, "Now we're all going to move to my father's lodge."

Then they gathered their possessions and went up to the lodge in which the young woman's father lived.

"Now my husband has left. Here this boy had come from a great distance away, from another world! The star that comes up in the morning, the bright one, the big bright one—that one is his father."

Now, this young man Bloody Hands became a great warrior. Bloody Hands became chief of the village. And this young woman raised that girl, Sage Woman.

Now this is what happened. These young women and older women who today are named after the sage, who are named Sage Woman, get the name from this incident. But there is no man among us who is named Sage.

Comparative reference: SIOUX Beckwith 1930:391-95.

6

The Man with the Sharpened Leg

ALFRED MORSETTE, SR.

*This myth is an Arikara version of the widespread northern
Plains story of the man who sharpened the end of his leg to use as a
weapon to kill people. Among tribes like the Arapahos, Assiniboines,
and Crows, it is a young man who sharpens his leg and then kills his
companion and frequently other people as well, whereas in this Arikara account the antagonist is a man with a beautiful daughter whom
he uses to lure young men to his winter camp and there kill them.
This narrative also exemplifies a common Arikara mythic theme: an
evil old man, generally a father-in-law, who abuses power that he has
been given and so is in turn killed, usually by or with the assistance
of his benefactor, after he oversteps the bounds of tolerability.*

Now I am going to tell the story of a man who used to sharpen the end of
his leg. After he would sharpen his leg, he would call his son-in-law and tell
him, "Now we are going to kick each other." And that is what he did. Then
when it was becoming spring, this man would come back to the villages of
whichever tribe it was, whether the Arikaras, Hidatsas, or Mandans. This is
what they used to tell.

Now there was a village, and when it was becoming spring that man came
there. He had a young daughter. Oh, she was beautiful, a nice-looking young
woman. She would mingle among the people during the summer, and then
when autumn came her father would say, "Now we are going to go back to
where we always stay during the winter. I hunt there, where there are plenty
of antelope, deer, and buffalo. But, poor us, we're the ones who are full."
Oh, there were young men who liked the daughter of this man, and every
year one of them would follow her when she and her family left for the winter.
There had been many of them who had done this, following after the young
woman.

Well, so one young man went. And then he said, "Hey, surely there have
been many young men whom this young woman has led off. Then when spring
comes, the young man does not come back. Then he disappears. I just want to
find out about it. I wonder what's happening?"

And so that was what happened when that man went off, leaving with his wife and daughter. "And now we are going where we usually go for the winter." And then this young man followed along with the young woman, going with her family to the badlands.

There was an earth lodge there in which they used to stay. And then the father-in-law said, "Now this other one will be your lodge, son-in-law." There were two earth lodges. "This other one is the one where my daughter always lives. That is her lodge."

The two of them lived there, and this young man would go out hunting and bring back deer, antelope, and buffalo. Whenever an animal was killed, he brought back the meat. Oh, there was plenty of meat. Meanwhile the man stayed around his lodge. Oh, there was plenty of dried meat for them to eat during the winter when it was cold! Oh, they lived in a nice meadow at the base of a hill! Oh, it was nice land!

[After there was a sufficient supply of meat stored to last through the winter,] this man said, "Now, son-in-law, get ready! We are going to kick each other. We'll kick each other. And if you beat me, my daughter is yours. You're going to have the one you are living with."

Then he did that: then there was a pounding sound in the lodge where the man and his wife lived. Then there was a pounding sound.

Then the young man thought, "I wonder what that is?" Then he went to the other lodge where his father-in-law lived. Then he opened the door, and there went the man's wife off into the brush at a distance where her gardens were.

Then he asked, "Are you ready?"

After that sound began inside, the young woman said, "Now he's doing what he always does. This is what my father always does. Oh, there have been many young men he has killed—ones I was going to marry. This is what he does."

After the young man opened the door, he peeked inside and saw his father-in-law sharpening the end of one of his legs. Then the leg came to a point.

"Now I'm ready. I'll charge outside. Now be ready! We'll kick each other."

And then this young man hurried outside.

Then the young woman told him, "You won't be able to kill him even if you shoot him. You aren't going to be able to kill him. Run away! He's really fast."

This young man ran outside with the bow and arrows he had. Then he ran onto a flat.

Then the father-in-law came charging out. When he saw the young man his leg was sharpened. "Hey, where do you think you can go? Now I'll kick you." Then he ran after him. Now the man was extremely swift: he would hook his leg into the ground and then spring forward. Now he was gaining on the young man.

And there there was a tree. Oh, it was a big tree! Then it said to the young man, "Hey, come closer! Surely that man who's coming has gone too far. Come closer!"

The boy quickly came up close to the tree, and then he climbed up it. He got to the top. Then the tree got higher.

Then the man rushed to the base of it. Then he sprang up. He said, "I'll stick you in the ribs and then bring you down." That is what he was saying.

When he sprang up he stuck his leg into the trunk of the tree. The leg stuck straight out. Then he was not able to get down. Now he was hanging there.

And then this tree said to the young man, "Now go on! He can't get down. He'll hang from here. He won't live. We blessed him previously, but now he's gone beyond the limit with these things that he's been doing.

"Now go on home! You'll go back to the lodge and then you'll go home to your village. But meanwhile he'll hang here until he dies."

Then the man said, "Now by all means take me off! You're making a mistake. I surely was just teasing you." That is what he was saying over and over.

But the young man went to his lodge. Then he arrived there. Then he, the young woman his wife, and his mother-in-law got themselves ready.

Then the old woman said, "Yes, he's gone beyond his limit doing the things he's been doing here. But now you have beaten him. Now let's flee! Now let's go home quickly!"

Then they did it: they arrived at the village. Then they told about it: "This is what happened. So this is what the man who used to come here has been doing."

Comparative references: ARAPAHO Dorsey and Kroeber 1903:257–58; ASSINI-BOINE Lowie 1909:184–86; BLACKFOOT Wissler and Duvall 1908:153; CROW Lowie 1918:212–14; GROS VENTRE Kroeber 1907:87–88.

7

The Young Woman Who Became a Bear

ALFRED MORSETTE, SR.

One of the most spectacular geographical features on the northern Plains is Devils Tower, a large, solitary butte that rises dramatically 865 feet from its base on the Wyoming plains northwest of the Black Hills. Because of its symmetry, geological uniqueness, and prominence—it can be seen from nearly a hundred miles in some directions—it inspired awe among the many tribes who lived near or visited it. To most northern Plains peoples, Devils Tower was a sacred site where men went to fast and pray when seeking power or a supernatural blessing. So deep was the impression created by it that early in this century Kiowas still remembered the landmark in tradition, even though sometime before 1800 the tribe had moved to the southern Plains from their homeland in and west of the Black Hills.

The Arikaras and Kiowas have nearly identical myths about the origin of Devils Tower. Both tribes tell how a girl and her brothers escaped from their sister, who had turned into a bear, by standing on a rock that rose into the sky to become Devils Tower, and how they then became the stars of the Pleiades. Other tribes tell similar variants (but sometimes lack the star transformation ending). The version recounted here, told to the narrator by his grandmother Squash Blossom, is a fine example of what is one of the most widely known stories among contemporary Arikaras. Today there is no Arikara name remembered for Devils Tower, but to Arapahos, Crows, Cheyennes, and Sioux it is known as Bear Lodge. The origin of the English name Devils Tower *is uncertain.*

Now I will tell an old story. It happened a long time ago, long ago when the people were migrating this way. It is what I used to hear when my grandmother told the story. It is a holy story.

When the people were wandering around as a group long, long ago, traveling somewhere, wherever it was, in the land to the south, it happened while the children were playing, when the chokecherries and plums were coming on but were not yet ripe.

The children were playing. There were many of them playing. Among them was one girl who was a little older than the others; she was fourteen winters old. Then they told her, "Now it's your turn to be a bear." They were imitating a bear as it charges out of the brush, and the children would run away. "A bear is charging!" they would say as they played. And then they told that girl, "Now it's your turn to be a bear."

The young girl, however, did not want to do it. "I don't want to. Leave me alone! Ask someone else!"

But they continued to ask her.

Finally she gave in and said, "Now it will be that way."

The girl's sister was younger. She was ten winters old. Then the girl told her sister, "Now go on! Hide somewhere in a dog's den, where she has had her puppies. Go in it and hide there! When I arrive, you'll come out. Now what is going to happen is not going to be a good thing."

Then the young girl went into the woods.

She was fourteen winters old when she turned into a bear. And the children moved toward the woods where the plum bushes were. Then the young girl charged out of the brush, and here she was a bear! She chased the children, knocking them down as they yelled, "A bear is charging!" They began shooting at her, but they were not able to do anything to stop her. She killed various ones. Then she even included those who were her relatives. Then she killed her brother. And she did away with her sister, her mother, and her grandmother. Oh, finally she must have satisfied herself, for she came back after everyone else had run away.

The village was now empty except for the bodies of the dead lying all around after she had killed them.

Then she went around and said, "Magpie Woman, wherever you are, I have arrived."

This girl came out of the den there where a dog had had her puppies.

Then the young woman said to her sister, "Now let's go up into the hills somewhere! Let my wounds heal where they shot me and where they cut me! Now I was afraid this would happen. I didn't want to play, but they insisted on it."

When the girl mourned after she saw the dead bodies of her mother and father, her older sister said to her, "Cease your crying! I'll kill you if you continue doing it."

Then the girl followed her sister as they went up a hill, up a high hill.

Then this bear woman began to dig a hole in the woods, wherever it was. Then she said, "Here is where we'll stay."

And when they finished their digging, the two went into the hole.

Then the bear woman told her sister, "Now make a fire! And bring dried meat from our village. There must be dried meat there. Bring some of it!"

Then this girl went back to the village, and then she began picking up the dried meat that people had stored. She brought it back, and then they cooked it.

While they were eating the bear sister said, "When you go outside, you must look all around. Our brothers went on the warpath. When you see them coming back, you must tell me. I'll kill them, too. I don't like what has been done to me, the way I am. I didn't want it."

The girl now went out early the next morning and climbed up where she could look all around while she was digging Indian turnips here and there. This incident must have occurred when summer was beginning, since the turnips were still in the ground for her to dig up to bring back to her bear sister.

Then the girl said, "It's terrible back in our village. Flesh and other things are rotting. It's not good."

Then her bear sister said, "Let it be! Don't go there. Go somewhere else!"

Then the girl said, "There aren't any turnips growing close by. I must go far off."

The bear sister said, "The chokecherries and plums must be ripe now. Those are what we'll eat."

So the girl went out and went up on a high hill where she could look all around and pick chokecherries, Juneberries, and whatever else was growing on the trees.

Then she saw her brothers. There they came. There were four of them. So the girl went. Then she went to meet them.

Then she said, "Something bad has happened. Our sister is a bear now. I'm living with her. She's killed our father, our mother, and our grandmother. She killed them. No one is living there in our village now. They've gone off in different directions. They've apparently taken their possessions secretly. They must have been coming back for the things they left behind."

Then the young men said, "Now we'll stay here awhile."

Then they helped her pick plums.

"You should go find out things from your bear sister. You must say to her, 'We're living here alone. It might happen that the enemy will find us. You say, "They cannot kill me. No one can kill me." However, what will happen if they do kill you? Where can you be wounded?'" The brother continued, "She will tell you. That's what you should say."

Then the girl went back to where she and her sister lived. Then she entered the den. Then the bear sister said, "You have the strong odor of a human. Have our brothers returned? You must tell me. I must kill them."

Then the girl said, "Surely no one is around. I went to where our father and mother lie, because I'm lonesome now that we are living alone."

The bear woman calmed down after having become angry.

The next morning the girl went out. "I think I'll go off for a while! I think I'll look around!" She went up into the hills wandering around, and then went to where her brothers were.

Then they told her, "Now you must eat!" They had killed a deer. Then she finished eating.

After she had eaten, one brother asked, "Now what did she say?"

She said, "I asked her. Now this is what she said: 'They cannot kill me, even if they were to shoot me. But if they wound me here on my little toe, either of my two little toes, that's when I'll die. Then they'll kill me. But if it should happen that any blood spurts out, I'll come back. Then it will not be good if I come back. I'll be different.'" And so this girl related to her brothers what she had been told.

Then one brother said, "We'll make preparations now. You stay here awhile! Wander around here on the sides of the hills close by! There are enemies around and they might see you."

And then these young men went and picked a cactus and the branches of a thorn apple bush. Then they broke the thorns off and brought them to the girl.

One said, "Now lay these around outside the hole in the ground where you two live. The sharpest ones, the cactus thorns, you must lay closest to it. Now, after you have done this, you'll come tell us."

Then that is what the girl did: she laid them around while the bear sister, who was a deep sleeper, slept inside. The girl's hands moved around rapidly as she set the thorns of the thorn apple bush and cactus all around in the ground. She prepared everything in front of the entrance.

Then she came to where her brothers were. Then she said, "I'm finished doing it."

Then one young man said, "Now go there! Rush inside and say, 'The enemy is chasing me!' When you run out, go over there to the left. You must run up the hill. Your sister is going to head straight to the entrance. She's not going to see you. Now we're going to rush her. We'll kill her and then burn her."

And then that is what this girl did: she ran there. Then she ran inside where her sister was. Then she said, "The enemy is coming! They're chasing me!" Then she swung around and ran out.

And now the bear sister manifested her mysterious power as she jumped up angrily and ran outside. She ran on the cactus and apple thorns. Then as she rolled over growling, the young men cut off her toes. Then she lay still after they had killed her.

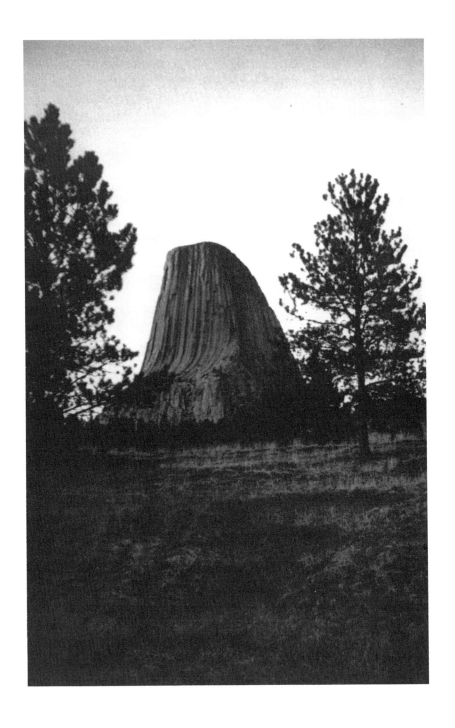

Plate 15. Devils Tower, Crook County, Wyoming. Photograph by Raymond J. DeMallie, 1973.

Then he said, "Quickly!"

Now they gathered wood which they brought. Then they set it on fire. Then they put her on top of the fire. And then they burned all around the spot while her body flopped around. They burned everything.

"Now let's flee! Let's go quickly! She's going to come."

Then they ran off. Then these young men put the girl in the lead. She led as they told her where to go: "You go there!"

Now they must have gone far. It was a long time later.

Then they said, "Now there she comes."

And there she came. Now there was no telling what had happened: some blood must have splashed onto the ground; wherever it was that the blood lay on the ground, it must not have burned. Then she chased them.

The bear woman was fast as she pursued them, especially because she was angry. Now she was gaining on them.

The eldest brother then said, "I'll do something to slow her up. She's catching up with us."

Now he threw an awl. And when he threw it where they had just come from, there was a thicket of thorn apple bushes. Oh, there was indeed a multitude of them! And as the bear woman came up against them, she started to look for a place to go through the thicket. She was barely able to pass through.

Now she came on. "There's no place where you're going to run to. I'm going to kill all of you."

Now the second brother threw a knife. Then it cut the ground open; it made cracks in the ground. And where the ground was cut open, the crack was very wide.

The bear woman nearly reached the top of the precipice. When she was about to climb up over the edge of it, she fell back. She fell to the bottom. She began to jump around.

Then she came up. Again she ran after them.

Why, now another brother threw something: a comb. And there there was a large cactus patch! When the bear woman reached it, she began jumping around as she went into it. She barely crossed it, too, as the thorns pricked her paws. Then she ran after them again.

While they were going, the youngest brother said, "Now we are dead."

Now he took a grooved stone, a black stone, the kind one would have to sharpen knives, and he said to it, "Now, grandfather, do something! Quickly! She's tired now, and I can't do anything with her."

And there there was a stone. It was so big around. Then they all stood on it. Then this stone grew upward. Then it expanded higher and higher.

Now after it was high up the bear arrived. She began jumping up, throwing herself against it so that she might knock it over. At first her claws reached the top of the stone, where they stood on top. But the stone got higher. Then the stone said, "Don't be afraid. She isn't going to harm you, for the land slopes downward where we are standing. She isn't going to be able to knock it over."

Then the bear woman said, "Now you've outdone me. Now you are safe. Now I shall never see you again. But now I'll go in the other direction. I shall roam around over there, in the land over there in the west. You've outdone me."

Then the stone reached up against the sky there.

Now when people roamed around in that barren country they used to see it over there. The butte was the way it was when the bear woman jumped against it: there were claw marks on it. They used to say that one could not see the top of the butte.

Today, when airplanes fly over and people look down at it, there is something on top. It is white, whatever it is. But these [the girl and her brothers] went up into the sky. They are the five stars that are bunched up.

Now this is what I used to hear when they used to tell the story.

Comparative references: ARAPAHO Dorsey and Kroeber 1903:152-53; Salzmann and Salzmann 1950:82-85; Voth 1912:44,49; ARIKARA Parks 1991, 4:590-95, 733-36, 775-77; ASSINIBOINE Lowie 1909:179-80; BLACKFOOT Michelson 1911:244-46; Uhlenbeck 1912:101-12; Wissler and Duvall 1908:68-70; CHEYENNE Curtis 1907-30, 19:143-44; Marriott and Rachlin 1975:99-110; CROW Lowie 1918:205-11, 1960a:100-116; GROS VENTRE Curtis 1907-30, 5:123-27; Kroeber 1907:105-8; HIDATSA Lowie 1939:220-27; IOWA Skinner 1925:465-68; KIOWA Parsons 1929: 9-10; PLAINS CREE Bloomfield 1930:61-65; PONCA J. O. Dorsey 1890:287-93; SARSI Simms 1904:181-82; WICHITA G. A. Dorsey 1904c:69-74.

8

Corn Woman and Buffalo Woman

ALFRED MORSETTE, SR.

Arikaras believe that corn originated among them and that it subsequently spread to other tribes. Such peoples as the Teton Sioux and Omahas, who tell similar stories of its origin, support this tradition.[1] Indeed, corn was so integral to the life of the Arikaras that in the Plains sign language they were known as corn shellers. Certainly the cultivation of corn thoroughly permeated Arikara life, providing not only a major part of their subsistence but forming the most important symbolic element in their ritual life as well. Among the Arikaras and Pawnees, the veneration of corn culminated in the personification of the plant as Mother Corn, a spiritual manifestation of corn sent to earth as a woman by the Great Holy One, or Chief Above, to give the people food and assistance in times of distress.

There are two major mythic accounts of Mother Corn's role in Arikara history. In one, the origin story, she led the people out of the underworld and along their path of flight, after which she gave them their cultural institutions and moral teachings. In the other, exemplified in the account presented here, she revisited the people at a later time. The present narrative, however, is actually a concatenation of three separate stories: how the corn plant first came to the Arikaras; how Mother Corn, a personification of the plant, came to the tribe to save them during a period of starvation; and how Buffalo Woman, a human manifestation of the buffalo people, came to save the tribe during another period of starvation. The narrative thus presents a neatly balanced description of how in the past representatives of the two primary sources of subsistence—corn and buffalo—have come in human form to the Arikaras in times of need to give them aid.

Now I am going to tell a story that I used to hear when they told stories. They are all dead now. I was interested in the old stories that they told—of what had happened when the people came this way from wherever it was that

---

1. An Omaha account recorded at the turn of the century, said to be of Arikara origin, is remarkably close to the first part of Mr. Morsette's version presented here (Fletcher and La Flesche 1911:76-78).

the villages used to be clustered when they were migrating this way upriver. There were many Arikaras then.

Now one time when a young man went hunting, when he was wandering around hunting, why, all at once he saw a buffalo! It stood far off on the prairie, on the level prairie. As he watched it, it stood there facing the east. Then, after searching for a way to get nearer, this boy thought, "Why, there is nowhere to hide so that I can get closer to where you are standing to shoot you!" Oh, then he gave up. Then he returned home. Then he arrived at the village, where the villages were clustered.

When morning came he went out again. Then he arrived where he had seen the buffalo standing. Now it was facing south. Oh, while he sought a way to get closer to where it stood, it was still too difficult for him! When it was sunset he came home.

Now again morning came and he went out. When he saw this buffalo, it was facing the other way: west. Oh, it was big! Then he thought, "How can I sneak up on you?" Then he gave up when it was too difficult for him. Then he came home.

Once again it was morning, and then he went out. He arrived there, and now it stood over there facing north. It seemed to see this young man as he ran furtively about, trying to sneak up on it to shoot it. He gave up. "Why, it's impossible for me." He came home; he arrived where he lived.

Then he thought, "Why don't I go to where I have been seeing the buffalo!"

It was no longer standing there. Then he arrived there. Now he looked all around. There were tracks where it had stood. Something was growing there. There was a clump of stalks growing here, and also over there, and also in the middle. After he looked at them, he came home.

Then he told people, "Something has happened. I tried to sneak around a buffalo that was standing there. Oh, the land was level where it stood. It was impossible for me to get close to where it stood. Now, look, I just now went there, and a clump of stalks is growing there, whatever they are. These things that are growing, whatever they are, are puzzling."

Then he gathered the holy men, the leading priests, the ones who had the holy ways. Then they went there to look at them. "Say, they are something. We don't know what these growing things are, these stalks growing in a clump."

Then they drove sticks into the ground to fence them off so that the buffalo and antelope roaming around would not eat them. "Let them grow! Let them grow up so that we can find out what they are going to be," they said as they watched over them.

《   》

Now in midsummer something strange was there: ears of corn were growing on the stalks standing there. When they looked at them they did not know what they were. And one man said, "I'll try it. Let me eat one of them! Let's see what happens to me. I'll cook it, since it appears that one must cook it."

Then they made a fire. Then this man began to roast it. Here it was green corn. "Surely it's cooked now." Then he took a bite as he sat there and ate it. "Why, say, it tastes good!" Then he gave one of them another ear; then he gave each one of them an ear.

"Why, say, this is something! It's edible. Now let it grow up!"

Then as they watched over it, the corn got fully ripe. I do not know what happened when they discovered that it was corn, but then they divided it up among the people. After they shelled it, they divided it up. "In the spring you shall plant it as it was; you shall do it thus, the way it was when it was growing. Then put soil over it."

Now then that is what they did: when spring came, when the green grass came up, he said, "Plant what I gave you!" And then that is what they did.

Now it was not a long time before clumps grew here and there, sprouting as they had seen them do before. Then ears hung grew the stalks.

Now that is where the corn increased. After people gave it to one another and after they planted it, the corn increased as the people migrated this way upriver. They had corn. Oh, it tasted good!

Now I don't know how they happened to acquire squash and beans, and what are called ground beans.[2] But the ground bean is different. Now what I have told here is the limit of my knowledge.

《 《 《   》 》 》

Now, sometime after corn had appeared among us, while this one man, one who was holy, was sitting there examining this ear of corn, he said to his wife, "Say, make a dress, a woman's dress! Then put the dress on this ear of corn! I just have a notion that she is holy. It just appears that I'm seeing a woman."

---

2. Ground beans (*Amphicarpa bracteata*), also called hog peanuts, are both aerial and underground beanlike seeds that were gathered and used as a food item, especially during the winter, by Arikaras and other Plains tribes.

Then this woman, his wife, made a dress. Then she clothed it. Then she put a shawl on it, and wrapped it around the ear.

Then he took it to the Missouri River and said, "Now I'm going to name you as a relative. Now you are my Mother. Now make haste! Come back quickly!" Then he threw her into the water. She floated downstream.

Now sometime later they saw a woman. They did not know who she was as she went among the people. She just came. They did not know who she was.

Now the priests sought her out. "Call this young woman who is going around so that we can see who she is and where she came from!"

Now they got things ready. Then they called her. The young woman came into the lodge. Then she sat down. They did not recognize her.

Now, wherever the man who had dressed the ear of corn had been, he entered. Why, he said, "Hah, my wife made the dress for this young woman and I put it on her. And I called out to her, 'I want you to be among us so that we may know you. We shall call you Mother from now on, since from my observation you are a woman.' Now this is the one."

Then this young woman said, "Now you are right. You are the one who sent me floating downstream. What you have said is the way it is—I have come here. Now I have come back so that you may know: now I am the one, your Mother. You have found me. Here on earth different things will appear: the green grass coming up, and the corn when it has been planted. Now I am the one who has come onto this earth. You see the Big Holy One in the sky. He is the one. All these different things are what He put here. This one whom you call your Father is the one: He is your Father. But you are mine. I am the one, your Mother."[3]

Now this is the end of the story of this young woman when she was going among the people.

It was sometime later, a long time later. It was one of those years when there is no rain, when everything is dry, when the grass barely comes up because there is no rain.

Then this young woman said—after she prayed to the powers, she said, "I will do something for you. Before morning comes, when the sun has not yet risen, at dawn, then you will have things ready. Open your cache pits! Clean the ground! Clean the interior of the pits! Now I am going to pass by them.

---

3. Corn Woman is telling the Arikara people that the Big Holy One (also called the Chief Above), the creator of everything on earth, is their father, while she, who comes to their aid on earth, is their mother, Mother Corn.

Now you are going to tell me where you store your corn. You must tell me which ones are the kinds of corn you value most among the ones you plant.[4]

"Now this is what I am going to do: I will pass by there. Early in the morning, before the sun has risen, when the crier calls out, when he announces it, you will know that I am going to start out as I said. You women who are heads of households, stand where your cache pits are, telling me where your cellars are. That is why I am going."

Then that is what this young woman did. "Now what do you have in your cache pit here?" she would ask.

"This is where I store my white corn, yellow corn, blue corn, red corn, and squash."

"Now cover it!"

Then she would cover it over. Then the young woman would pass by.

After the young woman finished, she entered the Medicine Lodge. Then she said to the crier, "Now after four days have passed you can announce, 'Open up your storage pits to see what I have done for you.' Now that is what you will do!"

Well, then this man called out, "You now know that in the morning each of you will go to where you have your storage pit. Open it up! Now this is what is yours."

Then they were very anxious, so they got up. Then each woman went to her cache pit, and there there were plenty of different kinds of corn, just as the crier had said. Oh, they all became reinvigorated, and then they planted again. Then they all became reinvigorated again when the ears of corn were whole and the corn could be shelled.

Now this is what she said: "I am the corn that you are going to shell. Wherever there is a stalk with an ear of corn on it, I am that corn. Now I am Mother, the one who leads us. That is why I hurried when I returned, just as this man, the one who clothed me, planned for me to do."

《 《 《   》 》 》

Now while they were migrating this way, the people began seeing a young woman. They did not know her, either. Now this is what she did: she did not eat meat, or dried meat; but she ate corn, squash, plums, chokecherries, and wild artichokes. She did not eat meat. Now the other one, Corn Woman— Mother Corn—did not eat corn. This was the difference between them.

Now things became difficult when the buffalo did not come near the village, when they did not roam close by—when, alas, a famine occurred.

4. Will and Hyde (1917:299-300) give a provisional list of eleven varieties of corn grown by Arikaras.

Then this young woman said, "Now I am the one who came in the herd. I like being among you people, eating this corn, eating this green corn. I prize it. I do know that you are getting short on meat, which you value most. Now I want you to make me four pairs of moccasins so that I may do something for you."

Now a woman who knew how to make moccasins sat down. She finished them. "Now here are the moccasins." Also another pair.

Then they went into the Medicine Lodge. After they had prayed to the powers and had offered smoke, then she said, "Now I am going. I am starting out."

There where the four upright lodge posts were, there on the left on the other side, she started out, going and going. Then she arrived at the post there, where she took her moccasins off. The ones she had worn were worn out.

Then she put another pair on her feet. Now again she did the same thing: she also did it, going to that post there. She got to it and took her moccasins off. The moccasins were worn out.

Then she put on another pair. Well, then she did it: she got to the other post and, as she had been doing, she arrived there with ragged moccasins.

She put a different pair on her feet and then she did it: she arrived [at the post] where she had started from. She sat down. They offered smoke.

She said, "Now I have gone all over this world.[5] The buffalo have gone far, far off in different directions. I have seen my grandfather and grandmother. Now I did beg them, the poor things, to cause the buffalo to move closer toward here where we are living. Here where I am going among you people I appreciate being able to eat fresh corn, corn balls,[6] and squash.

"Now, after four days have passed, pick out four young men, four who know how to hunt. Before the sun has yet risen, they should run up that long hill and look all around to see if the buffalo have come.

"Now listen. Now I am tired. I have been all over the land."

Four days passed; then they picked them. "Now, we have faith in this one. This one is dependable." Also another, and another. "Now you are going to go up the long hill, this long hill. You can see whatever is going on in the village."

---

5. Although the spectators see Buffalo Woman walk only from post to post, her spirit actually travels throughout the world searching for the buffalo. Her spirit's travels are represented by the four pairs of worn-out moccasins.

6. Corn balls were made from coursely ground dried corn mixed with fat and shaped into oblong balls. After hardening, the balls were carried by men when traveling on the warpath or hunting to serve as high-energy food. Today, sugar is added to the corn mixture and the balls are eaten as a treat.

Well, then they ran up the hill. Oh my, the buffalo had drawn near! Then they began to call out, shouting, "Now there's a multitude of them! There's a large herd of them!"

Then the men mounted, then they rode up the hill, and then they attacked them. They killed the buffalo, and then they ate their fill of the meat.

So this Corn Woman, when she ate, her favorite food was meat, and dried meat—that is what she herself liked. But this other one ate corn and corn balls.

Now this Buffalo Woman said: "I face the west as I travel. That land over there is my favorite." This one used to come from the west. That is where she came from. "I face that way. No matter how long it takes, we will continue to go that way. If you turn me around, if you face me the other way, toward the east, it will not last a long time—the village will not last after I die."[7]

Now, this is the end of what the old timers used to tell. Now what I have told is what I used to hear. There is no one living who knows—who knows the story. I was interested in things, in what I heard when they used to tell stories.

Comparative references: ARIKARA G. A. Dorsey 1904a:35–37, 124–25; HIDATSA Beckwith 1937:63–66; MANDAN Beckwith 1937:166–70; OMAHA Fletcher and La Flesche 1911:76–78; Gilmore 1929:167–72.

9

The Man Married to Buffalo Woman

WILLIAM DEANE

This narrative is a concatenation of two seemingly separate stories only tacitly related here. In the first part, a young man, after pitying a strange old woman by carrying her on his back, cannot rid himself of her and has to resort to different animals and people with

---

7. Here Buffalo Woman ordains that the Arikara people, if they are to survive, must always travel in a northwestward direction and that the buffalo skull in the Medicine Lodge must face the west, the direction from which the buffalo come.

medicine for help. In the second part, the young man follows his wife and child, who are in reality buffalo, on their journey to rejoin the buffalo people. Throughout the journey and after reaching the buffalo, the young man is subjected to ordeals, in all of which he triumphs. At the end he and his son escape and return to the Arikara people with the power to summon the buffalo during times of starvation.

In 1907 Edward Curtis recorded a similar version of this narrative, which he said was told in slightly modified form by Mandans and Hidatsas as well. In Curtis's version the protagonist is named Lucky Man, the common Arikara mythological character, whereas in the version here, as occurs frequently in other Arikara tales told today, he is called Stays In The Lodge Dressed In Finery, the Hidatsa counterpart. The substitution of the Hidatsa character for the Arikara Lucky Man illustrates just how thoroughly mythological borrowing has progressed among the three tribes. The Curtis version, moreover, makes explicit the relationship between the clinging old woman, who is burned to death, and the later buffalo wife, a connection not made here. The buffalo woman is said to have taken the form of the ugly old woman when she first came to the people—a mistake later acknowledged to account for the treatment she received—and subsequently she changed her form to a young woman when she reappeared in the illuminated tipi on the very spot where she had been burned to death. In the Curtis version there is also the explanation that the buffalo woman had come to the village of humans in order to obtain feathers and shells for the buffalo to use in their medicine.

There was a young man who always stayed in his lodge. He was named Stays Inside Dressed In Finery. He would never go anywhere. He did not know the lay of the land. The farthest he would go was the outskirts of the village. People said, "If he were to go off somewhere, he would get lost."

Then one time he left the village. Then he went off.

Then he thought, "I think I'll go swimming!"

There was a stream over there. And so he went over the rise to it. Then he began swimming. When he finished doing it, an old woman came along.

The old woman said, "My, here it's you, Stays Inside! I wish you'd carry me across the water. You could put me down over there."

"Alright. Let me carry you on my back!"

Then the old woman came up as she was walking around. Then she came and climbed up so he could carry her. Then Stays Inside carried her into the water. And so he took her across over there.

"Now get down!"

Why, now she would not get down!

She said, "Take me over it," there where a hill was, "and then I'll get down."

Then he took her there. Now this young man resented it, but then he took her to the place she meant.

Then she would not get off. And so he shook himself to get her off. And then he hit her on the head over and over. "Get down!" When he threw himself around she still would not get off.

Then he went on.

The old woman said, "Hey, you have a very pretty wife!"

It was now late afternoon. Finally he turned around and came back. Then she covered her face, and then he came into the village. It was now dark at his lodge, and then he went inside.

This old woman had a bushy head of hair. Her eyes shone.

He said, "Now, father, something strange has happened. I went over there, and this old woman got stuck on me. She said, 'Take me across!' Then when I took her—after I took her where she asked to go—she wouldn't get down. Now I can't do anything to get her off."

Then the old man got up and went outside. Then he told the village crier, "Cry out, 'Is there someone who has medicine to get the old woman off? An old woman is stuck to this young man.'"

Then the man called out.

Ho! A coyote went charging by, and a kit fox. "We'll be the ones to take the old woman off."

The old woman said, "Heh, you two standing there are ugly! You can't take anyone off no matter what you do!"

Then it was impossible for them to do it.

Then a magpie and a woodpecker tried it. It was impossible for them, too.

And then several spinsters had their turn. And then the spinsters took ropes and went for her after they went into the lodge. Then the old woman became frightened when she saw them.

Then the spinsters set the boy down. The oldest one swung a rope around. Then she caught the old woman's arm. When she pulled the rope she took the arm off.

Shortly afterward, another spinster also did the same thing: then she also caught a leg. When she pulled on it, she took half the old woman off.

"And now you're going to take the rest of her off."

And the other one caught the old woman's other arm, and the youngest one yanked her off. Then they took her outside.

Coyote soldiers took it upon themselves to kill the old woman. Then they piled wood up. Then they burned her. She burned up.

《 《 《   》 》 》

After it had become dark the young man got up from his bed. It was sometime late in the night when he went outside to urinate.

There was a lodge over there. The tipi was completely lit up since there was a fire inside. She was talking there. It was a woman. There was also a baby there crying.

Then this man went over there. Then he looked. He peeped inside. There sat a woman. Oh, she was really nice looking! She had long hair. She was doing something that could not be seen.

Then the young man turned around, then he went home, and then he picked up the things that belonged to him: his bow, arrows, and knife.

Now when he came back out, the woman and her baby were going off there in the distance. And so he followed behind them at a distance as they went on and on.

Then it was morning, and it continued the same way as they went on and on. Then the young man tired. Then they stopped.

Then the woman said, "Don't come near! You didn't treat me well."

As the tale goes, it suddenly happened that the child had grown up. Then he became a boy.

While they were going along, the boy came back to the young man and said, "Father, are you hungry?"

"Oh, I am hungry!"

Then this calf stood up and humped his back to defecate. Then he dropped chips that were round.

He said, "Now pick them up! They're for you to eat."

And so the young man picked them up. Then he did it: he took a bite, and, why, here they were pemmican! Also as he ate and ate, the quantity did not diminish. He got full.

After they had gone on, however far it was, the boy came back again. Then he asked, "Father, are you thirsty?"

He said, "Yes, I'm thirsty."

It was this way there: there was a muddy spot where water was under the ground. The boy put his hoof into the mud there and made a hole. Then water came out. It was clear water. Then the young man drank. After he drank, he regained his strength.

Then they went on.

Then the boy came back and said, "My mother says, 'There sits your grandfather.' She said to him, 'There comes a human being. I've brought a human being. Now your hoof will taste him.'"[1]

Then the boy said, "Father, this is what my mother said. He must be my grandfather. That's what she said."

Then the young man put his hand into a bundle and took out an eagle plume. Then he gave it to the boy. Then he swung around. Then he said, "This is where you'll put it on him."

Then the boy did that: then he put the plume on his grandfather.[2]

Then as they were going on, there sat two buffalo bulls. Then the woman said the same thing again to them.

Then the boy swung around again. He said, "Father, two of them are sitting over there. They must be my grandfathers. This is what my mother said."

Then the young man took out two plumes.

Then the bulls were thankful when they were given them.

Then they went on. As they were going along, they came close to where a vast herd of buffalo was ranging.

Then the boy came and said, "My mother says, 'They're ranging close by here.'"

Then the buffalo bulls began planning how to kill the young man.[3] Then they chose ten calves that looked alike. Then they put the boy calf in among them. "If he doesn't find his son, we'll kill him."

Then this boy swung around. He arrived over there where the young man waited.

Then he said, "Father, they have selected ten calves. They're putting me among them. We apparently resemble each other. Now you're going to have to choose me." Then he continued, "When you come to the end of the line and get in front of me, I'll flap my ear down. And then you'll know and you'll say, 'This is my son.'"

Then that is what they did: then they stood the calves there. There were ten of them. The calves looked alike.

Then they told the young man, "Now you must come. You must pick out your son."

1. An expression meaning 'Now you can kill him.'
2. The plume is a symbol of honor that the boy puts on the head of the bull.
3. The young man is now staying among the buffalo in their territory.

Then he came. Then he started there on the end. Then he came in front of the calf. When he got there, he recognized him. Then the calf bent his ear down.

And so he said, "This one is my son."

Oh, the buffalo bulls did not like it! And so they made another plan: this time it would be ten cows. They all looked alike.

The boy came, and then he said, "Now you'll have to choose my mother. You'll start there in the front. I'll go over there to the end. I'll put a burr on my mother's tail."

And then the boy did that: then he put a burr on her tail.

When the cows stood up, the young man went and started there in the front. When he came to the end, he said, "Here is my wife."

Oh, they did not like it! He was *very* holy! One old bull said, "Now quickly kill him! Surely you can't do anything to him!"

Then the boy went to him and said, "Now, father, they're going to kill you. They have become angry."

Then the young man said, "Let's go over there! Let's go over there!"

There was a nice spot over yonder. It was a knoll. Then the two went up it. Then they sat down. Then the boy took a stone out. It was a light-colored one. It was round. Then he set it down, and then they stood up.

The boy said, "Now hurry! It won't be long before they come."

Then this stone spread out, whichever way it was going. Then it also began rising. Then the young man and his son sat down in the middle of it. Then it went up and up as it was rising.

Then the buffalo said, "He must be doing something mysterious. Look!"

They looked: the two bodies were visible upon it.

Then the buffalo went at it. They began rubbing against the rock as they were going around it. But they weren't able to do anything.

Then this young man began shooting them with arrows, shooting them and shooting them. He killed a huge number indeed!

Meanwhile, over there in the village things were not well, since there was hunger.

The buffalo said, "Why, they've killed a huge number of us indeed! Let's let them go!"

Then the buffalo ran off.

This is what the young man and the boy did. There is a story about when they sat there on the rock.[4]

Then they started back for home.

---

4. No version of this story has been recorded.

Meanwhile, over there in the village people were saying, "He must have gone off somewhere. The young man must have felt ashamed. He must have gone off somewhere." Then those people in the village began to starve. There was nothing for them to eat. The buffalo must have been ranging far off indeed!

Then [after returning] this young man said to the boy, "Now you're going to call the buffalo." And so they stood that boy in the lead. He was given a pipe. He was the one who was going to call them.

After so many days—after four days passed—one man awoke in the morning and then he told everyone, "The buffalo are ranging close by here." Oh, they killed a huge number of them indeed! They began bringing meat back—bringing meat back and making dried meat.

And then this young man and the boy became chiefs.

Now this is what happened.

Comparative references: ARAPAHO Dorsey and Kroeber 1903:388-418; Salzmann 1957:28-31; ARIKARA Curtis 1907-30, 5:93-100; G. A. Dorsey 1904a:94-101; ASSINIBOINE Lowie 1909:180-81, 195-200; BLACKFOOT Josselin de Jong 1914: 52-59; Uhlenbeck 1911:18-23; CHEYENNE Grinnell 1926:87-104; Kroeber 1900: 186-87; CROW Linderman 1931:169-94; Lowie 1918:107-19; Simms 1903:289-90; HIDATSA Beckwith 1937:66-76; MANDAN Bowers 1950:276-81; Curtis 1907-30, 5:50-55; Libby 1910:694-707; OMAHA J. O. Dorsey 1890:131-47; PAWNEE G. A. Dorsey 1904b:284-93, 302-3; 1906a:62-68, 72-82, 104-5, 109-14, 202-3; Weltfish 1937:203-23; PLAINS CREE Bloomfield 1930:208-9; PONCA J. O. Dorsey 1890: 147-62; SIOUX Beckwith 1930:399-400; Deloria 1932:184-90; McLaughlin 1916: 170-78; Walker 1917:183-90; TONKAWA Hoijer 1972:49-53; WICHITA G. A. Dorsey 1904c:187-91, 199-206.

10

The Boy and the Hoop Game
of the Buffalo

ALFRED MORSETTE, SR.

*In Arikara and Pawnee mythology the hoop and pole game is
derived from buffalo. In some stories two young bulls turned into the
first set of poles, or javelins, and a buffalo cow turned herself into the
first hoop; in others a man was directed in a dream to wrap two poles
with strips of tanned buffalo hide and to cover a hoop with skin from
a buffalo cow's vulva. The hoop and poles, moreover, are frequently
associated with buffalo calling rituals.*

*In this Arikara story there is the same association of the game
with buffalo, but the game is already in existence, and the symbolism
is somewhat different. A chief's son wants a hoop with which to play
the hoop and pole game, and so a male buffalo—the chief's spiritual
benefactor—changes himself into one to become the boy's companion. In the ensuing drama several widespread mythological themes
are combined to develop the plot. One is the motif of the stealing of
light, in which a hoop usually represents the sun (cf. Parks 1991,
3:129–31). In this story first Coyote and then mice steal the hoop and
take it to another world below this one. Three animals—Mole, Shrew,
and Badger—enable the chief's son to get to that underground world
by boring a passage through the earth, a motif found in the Arikara
origin story. Once in the other world, Bloody Hands and his grandmother appear as characters to aid the chief's son to regain his hoop.
In its conclusion the story becomes one of power bestowal, the theme
of most Arikara stories, in which here the buffalo resumes his animal
form but promises to watch over the boy and help him achieve
whatever he might wish in the future.*

*The narrator learned this story from his father, John Morsette,
who in turn had learned it from Red Corn Woman. Mr. Morsette
noted that he had never witnessed the game, and from his description
of it here it is unclear which of the two variants that were found
among the Arikara—one using a hoop and poles, another employing
a ring and barbed darts or arrows (Culin 1907:420–41, 461–69)—is
referred to in this story. The narrator calls the projectiles "arrows."*

It was many winters long, long ago when the old man, my father, told this story to us when he would come to our home to stay for a few days. He had many stories that he told—ones that he had heard—including this one that I am going to tell.

One man had a boy who wanted a hoop—who kept asking him for a hoop. "Father, make a hoop for me! I want to have a hoop."

And so the man went out. Then he went to look for a hoop since his son wanted to have one. It was the kind of hoop used in the hoop and pole game. I don't know whether it was a large or small one.

Now this man had been blessed by a buffalo, one that was four winters old. Now it said to him, "I'll be the one. I'll be friends with your son. We'll play the hoop and pole game. I'm like he is: I like the game very much. That's what I want: that the boy I'm going to be friends with and I win prizes."

Now this buffalo turned itself into a hoop. It was a buffalo, a male buffalo four winters old.

Then the man brought it home. Then he said, "Now, my son, it's good for you to have this hoop. The two of you are to be friends. This hoop is holy. The hoop is holy. When you play hoop and pole and have had enough of the game, bring it home. Then set it down nicely. And don't just throw it around."

And so that is what the boy did, taking good care of the hoop when he played the hoop and pole game. Then he took prizes whenever he played.

Now there were people who were jealous when this boy won prizes. Mischievous Coyote was one. During one game he lay down near the point where the hoop was always thrown and would come to a stop.

After the hoop was thrown, two men, one on each side, would throw an arrow, trying to send it through the hoop. When the hoop stopped, the arrow that lay closest to it was the winner.

But now Coyote Chief, the one who always plays pranks, lay there close by the goal watching the boy win various prizes for himself. Coyote lay there close to the spot where the hoop stopped after it had rolled. Then he put it over his head. Then he ran off with it while the players looked for it. Oh, it had disappeared.

Coyote—Mischievous Coyote—ran off with it. Oh, after he had gone so far, Coyote, being tired, lay down on the side of a hill. He had the hoop around his neck while he slept.

Well, then some mice stole the hoop that Coyote had around his neck. The mice stole the hoop. Then they took it under the ground. There must have been another country down below.

Coyote awoke. He did not have the hoop around his neck. Now he darted around anxiously as he looked for it. "Oh, where could I have dropped it? Oh, I certainly had it around my neck when I lay down." That was what he thought.

Meanwhile the boy began to search for his hoop, standing on different hills crying as he mourned for his lost hoop. Well, then he went up one hill, and, oh, as he cried someone said, "Why don't you come in? Whoever you are, you're causing dirt to drop down all over."

Then the boy went down the hill, and as he was looking all around a door just opened into the ground. There was a lodge there. He entered it. There sat a woman.

"Why, grandson, you who have come from far away, now sit down!" Then she cooked dried meat for him. "Why, my grandson is hungry!"

Then she said, "Ah, grandson, you have come from such a *long* way off! I know the reason. Now, we'll do it for you—we'll give you a blessing. We'll help you achieve what you want. Now, farther on your grandmother has her home. She is going to be eager to help. I'll go right over there."

And then she told the boy, "Now go! If you cry like you were doing, she'll call you."

Then the young man went out. Then he went to a hill over there. Then he went up it and cried like she had said.

"Oh, why don't you come inside? You're causing dirt to drop down on us. I have some meat boiling." That is what she was saying over and over.

Then the boy went down the hill. As he was looking all around for the door, there it was. "Over here!" Then the two women took him inside.

"Hey, grandson, you who have come from far away, now sit down! You must eat."

Then they fed him while they, too, ate.

"Grandson, I know what you're after. Now, your grandmother has a home over there. You go over there to her! Now meanwhile we'll go over there, too." The first grandmother whom the boy had visited previously had already arrived. "She and I will go right over there, too. We'll follow behind you. Over there you'll learn the truth. We're going to reveal what you want to know— where your friend is. He feels the same way you do: he's tired in spirit and he's hungry. We must hurry!"

Well, then he went there. Then he arrived.

Then she said, "Hey, whoever you are who is a visitor, you're causing dirt to drop down all over. Come in quickly!"

Then the door opened. Then she led him inside. Oh, there sat a woman. She said, "Ah, grandson, you have come from such a long way off!"

Meanwhile the two women whom he had previously visited had already arrived. Now there were three of them as well as the boy.

Then this third woman said, "We'll do it right away, here where my home is. We'll start from here. Your friend is near here."

Now there were three of them: Mole, Shrew, and Badger. Now these sitting here were the grandmothers of this boy.

Then Badger said, "Now I'll be the first one." Then she went into the ground, boring a hole and going in and in. The others followed behind her as she tunneled her way.

Then she said, "Now one of *you* go on! You do this, too! Let me rest for a while!"

Then another one, Mole, took her turn.

Oh, and then the other one, Shrew, did the same thing, too, boring through the earth as she went.

And then it was the boy's turn to bore through the earth.

Now each of the four had had a turn. Then one of the grandmothers said, "Grandson, we have gone through to the village. Now be smart! That one [the hoop] will quickly calm down when he's told what's happening."

When the boy emerged he changed his form. (I have forgotten what he turned into.)

And there they were playing the hoop and pole game. The hoop they were throwing was the one: it was the hoop he was looking for.

When the hoop came to where he was, he said, "My brother, I have come here."

Then that hoop said, "Yes, I know. I know that you have come. Oh, I'm starving to death! I haven't eaten anything yet. When they take me inside, they hang me up. I'm not able to eat anything. I'm hungry. Now hurry!"

Then the game ended. Then they set the hoop down. Now they watched over it.

Meanwhile the boy watched where they took it. Oh, there he stood on a hill with the entire village extending in sight over there. And there at the end of the village smoke was coming out. The smoke was wafting upward.

Then the boy went over there. He went onto a knoll. There was a boy there. He was playing. Then he went to where the boy was, and then he said, "Ah, I've been watching you here."

And then this boy asked, "Who are you?"

The one who had just come there said, "I'm just wandering around. Let's play."

Then this short boy, Bloody Hands, said, "Let me tell my grandmother first!"

He ran inside. He said, "Grandma, there's a boy wandering around who wants me to play with him."

And then his grandmother said, "Hey, they always fool you. Then they whip you. Then they make you cry. Be careful!"

Then Bloody Hands went back and said, "My grandma said, 'They always whip you after they fool you.'"

The other boy said, "I certainly won't do that. I'm just wandering around. I had no place to go when I came here. We'll be companions. I want us to be brothers."

Then Bloody Hands ran inside. Then he said, "Grandma, he says, 'I don't have any place to go to stay overnight, and I came here. I want us to be brothers—for us to be together with your grandma, for all of us to live together. I'll help you two in various ways.'"

"Well, now that's fine. Bring him inside!"

Then they all lived together.

Now the old woman, whoever she was, was holy.

Then she said, "Hey, you two eat!" Then she set boiled dried sweet corn down for them.

And then they all lay down to sleep.

Then Bloody Hands said, "Grandma, he wants us to sleep together."

"Hey, you are a bed wetter. Don't urinate on him!"

Then he said, "My grandmother says, 'You're a bed wetter. Don't urinate on the brother you have now!'"

Then he said, "That doesn't matter." Why, now this boy was also holy.

After they had told various stories, Bloody Hands said, "I have to urinate."

The boy then said, "Now wait! You'll get cured of this bed wetting."

Then he went and took some ashes. Then he rubbed the ashes on Bloody Hands's abdomen. "Now you'll get over it."

Then he did not wet the bed.

It was morning. "Well, I suppose you wet the bed, Bloody Hands."

"Grandma, this boy doctored me. I didn't wet the bed."

Oh, his grandmother was thankful. "Why, it's certainly a good thing!"

He [the chief's son] said, "Nothing must ever happen here where you people live."

Then Bloody Hands replied, "Yes, I'll tell you. Our chief has a young son. He wanted a hoop. And Coyote brought one—one that he stole. He brought it here. Then it was taken from him. He had wanted them to buy it, but they just took it from him. They stole it. Now our chief has it."

They had brought it here for him—the ones who lived above [in the other world] are the ones who had brought that hoop. This boy was the one. He was the one—this one looking for it.

Then he said, "Say, the story you have told is good." He asked, "Where is the lodge where they keep it?"

Then Bloody Hands answered, "There in the middle of the village is where they keep it. It's hanging there where the medicines [i.e., the sacred bundle] hang.[5] Oh, they watch it carefully."

Now the boy decided to tell him. So he said, "That hoop you told about is what I have come for. Now that's what I came for. I'm the owner of the hoop." That is what he told Bloody Hands.

Then he said, "Grandma, this boy has come from where they live at the end of the sky, and he has come for the hoop that they have here. That's the reason he came here. He wants us to get it so that he can take it home."

Now the old woman said, "Hey, grandson, I'll do something for you now myself, since you cured my grandson when you doctored him for his bed wetting. You made him well. Now I'll do something for you in turn. Now I'll take the hoop from them. Now I'll get it."

Then she said, "Now, you two here, be ready! When I bring it back, you two are going to run away with it. If they catch up with us, all of us will die. They'll kill all of us here. Now to the best of my ability I'm going to try to bring it back."

Then she continued, "I'll go there first. I'll observe everything. I'll observe things where they always keep the hoop hanging. And then when I go back there a second time, I'll pick it up. Now you two be ready!"

Then this old woman, their grandmother, went there. She went to visit at the lodge of their chief. Oh, the family was happy to see her, but meanwhile she was observing everything. There the chief had the hoop hanging. She looked all around the area where it hung in order to determine what to do when she returned to get it. She took note of everything. Then she came home.

Bloody Hands said, "Grandma, what did you learn?"

She said, "I'll get it. I now know what to do when I get there where it's hanging. Now, you two be ready! You two will take it from here. You two are going to go where you came from. You'll change yourselves back into little boys." They were both young men now.

Then, after everyone had gone to bed, the old woman went there. While the family had told stories [on her earlier visit], she had observed everything. Now she changed herself into a mouse. Then she ran along the wall to where it hung.

"Now, my grandson came after you."

_____

5. A reference to the chief's lodge in the center of the village, in which the sacred bundle hung.

The old woman ran out with it into the dark. She took it to where her two grandsons were waiting.

Then they took the hoop, and then the old woman went to her lodge.

[At the chief's lodge they discovered what had happened.] "Oh, the hoop has disappeared! It's been stolen!"

Then they set out to search for it in the morning. But Bloody Hands and the boy had already run away with it.

Then Bloody Hands turned back. "Now, my brother, go on! When everything dies down, I'll be a handsome young man like you are."

Now, meanwhile, as the searchers went through the village, they said, "There was a boy living here. Where did he go?"

"Oh, I don't know where he went. He just wanders around."

Then Bloody Hands returned.

"Where did your friend go?"

"Say, I don't know where he went. Why, I'm not friends with anyone. When I'm together with anyone, I always get whipped." Now he was acting pitifully.

They gave up their search.

Now the young man passed beyond the boundary of that country back there [as he brought the hoop back to where his three grandmothers were].

"Now, grandmas, you have pleased me by doing all that you have done for me. Now my brother [the hoop] and I are going back."

Then he came back up to this earth.

"Now, brother, go back to your range!"

He threw the hoop. And then a male buffalo jumped up. It was lean from hunger.

While it began grazing, it said, "Brother, you have saved me. When I get full, I'll go to where my uncles, my father, and my mother roam. But I'll watch over you. Whatever you desire will come to pass."

Then the boy went on. Then he went home. Then he went inside.

Then he said, "Mother, make a fire! I've returned."

Then she said, "Oh, why, they're making fun of me!"

The father of the boy said, "Ah, you have nothing now, old woman. Get up! Make a fire! Our son died. We had only the one."

Then the woman rose. Then she made a fire, and there sat the young man, her son.

Then he said, "Father, mother, I was looking for my brother, the poor thing, after my hoop disappeared. And I've found him. This is what happened.

"And now he's gone back to his range, where he roams. Now he's gone back. He who was mine must have been starving to death while he was in the form of the hoop. But he told me that he would watch over me wherever I go, and whatever I desire will come to pass."

Now, this is the end of the story.

Narratives of the Past

Of Power Bestowed

11

When the Bears Attacked the Arikaras

ALFRED MORSETTE, SR.

Several times early in their history, according to tradition, the Arikara villages were attacked by hordes of a particular animal species—buffalo, bear, and snake—just as at an even earlier period humans were the victims of the animal world at large. In two accounts of such attacks—one by bears and another by snakes—the animals' aggression was precipitated by human passion and a lack of judicious restraint. In the story presented here, a young man discovers that his wife is meeting another young man in her garden and having sexual intercourse with him. When the outraged husband shoots the young man, his wife's paramour turns out to be a bear—in fact, the favored child of the bear people. Although the Arikaras are able to repulse the subsequent attack on their village by a horde of bears seeking revenge, the husband is doomed never to find power or have good fortune in war. For Arikaras the irony of this incident lies in the fact that the bear, by having intercourse with the young man's wife, is thereby giving the husband power; but because he shoots the bear out of jealousy, the man never again is able to obtain it. The story illustrates a general Plains Indian belief in the transmission of power from one man (or animal) to another through sexual inter- course with the recipient's wife.

Now I am going to tell another story. It is not really a long one. It is what I used to hear from my grandmother, who was the one who told us the story.

It occurred long, long ago, somewhere along the way when the Arikaras— the ones I am telling about—were migrating this way upriver.

There was a nice-looking young woman who had a garden in the brush. That is where the women used to have their gardens—in the brush. It is not known whether this incident occurred near where we are living today [or whether it happened when we were farther downriver].

Now this young woman would be in her garden planting corn, squash, and beans. There were no potatoes at that time when they used to hoe their gardens. Her husband would wait for her return from the garden, and it would be late at night before she at last came back to the lodge.

"Ah, you sure must have a big garden!" The man did not like what the woman was doing. When the women and young women would come up from their gardens in the brush, the sun would already have set when they returned home, but this man's wife would not have started to come back. Oh, it got dark. Then at last she would appear. That is what she was doing all the time.

Meanwhile this young man did not like it. He thought, "I wonder what you're doing."

Then this young woman would get up really early in the morning again. She would go off into the brush to her garden.

And this young man did not like what his wife must be doing. So one day he took his bow and arrows and lay in wait for her.

As soon as the young woman got up, she did as she always did: she got up really early in the morning, and then she went out. She went off. Then her husband jumped up from bed. Then he sneaked after his wife as she went along. Then she went down into the bottomlands, oh, as he secretly followed her and watched her.

Oh, then someone came out of the brush by the garden. There at a distance in the garden sat a young man. Then this young woman went there, and, oh, they embraced each other where this young man sat in the garden. Then the two of them went off. They went into the brush.

Meanwhile the real husband of this young woman followed at a distance when the two went into the brush. Now the young man lay on top of the young woman and was having intercourse with her. And then the husband came out of the brush with his bow and arrows. He shot this bear several times. And here the young man having intercourse with the young woman was a bear when he jumped up screaming!

Then her husband said, "And here this is what you are doing when you come here! I'm going to punish that one." Then he shot the bear repeatedly until the arrows were sticking out of him as he ran in the brush.

And then the young man drove the young woman ahead of him as he was whipping her and whipping her. Then he drove her out of the brush.

Then he said, "You are not going to come back to where I live. You can go wherever you want to go. You have not treated me well after I have been supporting you. And here this is what you have been doing!"

Now when he was shooting it, why, here he discovered it was a bear! It had turned into a white bear—a white bear, a bear that was white all over. He must not have killed it. He must only have wounded it in various spots when he was shooting it with arrows. But now, the bear was holy! Then it just disappeared.

《   》

Then sometime later it became foggy. Then this young man, as he was going around, was warned by a bird, whatever kind it was. It said, "They have sent me to tell you what you did when you wounded the bear. He is the beloved child [of the bear people]. Now from all over the entire country the bears are coming here to your village. They're going to kill all of you. But now I have told you. You are numerous! There certainly are many of you people. Get all of yourselves together! Put up a palisade! Put a palisade up around your village! Make it strong! The bears are coming. There's a horde of them. Now get your arrows ready! You're going to battle the bears."

Well, then that is what this young man did. Then he came home. Then he told his father. Then he began to call out from the top of his lodge.

Then the people of this village were willing to do what he said. Then they put up a palisade. It had four rows of posts. Now this village—the entire village—was ready. The young men and the older men made arrows in order to be ready. "Use them freely when the bears come!"

Then it became foggy. There were two days of fogginess. Everyone was uneasy. It was getting dark. And here it was the breathing of the bears when they were coming! Here the bears were the ones causing it to be foggy by their breathing!

Then the people said, "They must have arrived."

Oh, a large horde of bears arrived and came against the palisade while the people in the village were shooting them and, oh, killing the bears. <They kept shooting and shooting; they kept killing them and killing them. And the bears knocked down the outer row of the palisade and then the second one.>

Now only one row of the palisade remained to be knocked down. But there were many bears killed and wounded by the shooting.

Finally one bear said, "There are certainly a lot of us, but we haven't accomplished anything, the way we thought we would! They have beat us. Now, those of us who remain, let's withdraw!"

And then the bears retreated. But now there were carcasses lying all around.

And then this young man said to his father, "Now announce this: they can butcher these bears. They're the ones who took my wife away. They took my woman."

And so that is what he did. "Butcher them! These bears lying here are meat."

Now this is what happened.

Well, then misfortune befell this young man whenever he thought that he would do something. And so he had no success on the warpath. He was not able to find anything for himself. Everything that he attempted was a failure for him as his life progressed. Well, he never was able to get married again, either.

That woman—and, through her, the bear—was the cause when she brought on misfortune for him. The bear took his wife in order to bless him, but this young man did not allow it. He did not like what was being done. Whether he killed the bear, I don't know. And then this woman died from grief. She did not feel right about what had happened to the bear.

Now this that I have told is the story.

Comparative references: ARAPAHO Dorsey and Kroeber 1903:227; ARIKARA Parks 1991, 4: 596-97; G. A. Dorsey 1904a:126-27; KIOWA Parsons 1929:9-11; SARSI Simms 1904:181-82.

12

The Foolish Ones Who Killed
the Beloved Snake Child

ALFRED MORSETTE, SR.

Most Plains tribes had a society or group of men who acted by doing the opposite of what they were bidden. This contrary behavior was found, for example, in the Children of the Iruska Society of the Pawnees, the Heyoka of the Sioux, the Fool dancers of the Assiniboines, and the Contrary (or Bowstring) warriors of the Cheyennes.

> *Among the Arikaras these men were known as Foolish Ones* (sak-
> huúnu'), *a term that connotes reckless, crazy, or foolish behavior—
> behavior, that is not socially normal or acceptable. At any one time
> there were never more than two men who were* sakhuúnu'. *Besides
> being fearless, Foolish Ones were reputed to have strong medicine
> and thus to be good doctors.*
>   *This story continues the theme of animal aggression from the
> preceding narrative. Here its cause is a lack of respect for what is
> holy. Arikaras feared snakes, believing them to have mysterious
> power, and consequently avoided them. In this incident, however, a
> pair of Foolish Ones recklessly kills a small snake that all the other
> members of a returning hunting party have encountered on the trail
> and cautiously bypassed. This snake, like the bear in the preceding
> story, is the favored, or beloved, child of the snake people—a chief's
> son. As a result of the killing, the Arikara village is attacked by a
> horde of snakes. Although the two Foolish Ones are able to fight them
> off, the story illustrates the consequences of antisocial behavior,
> particularly a disregard for the holy. This story was told to the
> narrator by his grandfather Short Bear. In 1910 Robert Lowie
> recorded a nearly identical version from Bear's Teeth.*

Now I am going to tell a story that happened long, long ago when
mysterious things used to occur. I surely don't know that it happened; it is
what I used to hear when someone told it. Now my grandfather [Short Bear]—
the one who reared me—was the one I heard it from when he told this story
that I am going to relate.

It happened somewhere long, long ago when our people were moving up
the Missouri River. I do not know the location, but I will relate the story as I
heard it.

Now it happened when all the people were out on a communal buffalo
hunt, wherever it was that they were roving about after the buffalo had
withdrawn from the vicinity of the village. The people were still doing that
long ago, going on communal buffalo hunts. Now it occurred this way: they
had traveled around camping here and there until they had got enough meat.
[Then they said,] "Now let's go back to our village!" Meanwhile there were
people living alone in the village, ones who had been left behind and remained
living there alone.

Then they returned <toward the middle of summer>. Then they were
coming back as a group. Now they had just about reached the outskirts of the
village, and there lay a snake coiled up in the middle of the trail, guarding it.
That is what I used to hear.

Now we are afraid of snakes. So the party was bypassing it, going around it so that they would not disturb it where it lay coiled as they traveled by. They were going into the village there.

Now there were two young men who were what they used to call Foolish Ones. They did things differently whenever they did anything. If someone said, "Get angry!" they would not get angry. But when someone said, "Don't get angry!" then they would get angry. They would start charging about after turning around to fight, just as if it were the enemy who used to count coups on us long ago when there were intertribal battles all over. Both of these young men were fierce.

When the two of them were coming along, there that snake was, lying coiled on the trail. "I don't see why they're afraid of it. There's nothing to fear." Then they killed the snake. And here it was the favored child of the snakes, the one that they killed!

Then they went on into the village.

Now sometime later when the young men were out watching the horses, there on the surrounding hills everything was shining brightly. When the sun came up the surrounding hills shone.

"Now whatever might it be?"

And then those two Foolish Ones said, "Now, all of you here in the village, hurry! Make a palisade with four rows of poles. Get things prepared really well! What you see there shining on the ground are snakes. I think something mysterious must be happening." These two were the ones who were the cause, but they were not telling about it. "Now those are snakes that are shining on the ground. They're coming to attack."

Ah, then everyone in this village became excited as they went about erecting the palisade and tightening the posts so that no snake might crawl through. Ah, they got things prepared!

"Now get yourselves ready! Have some sticks ready to hit on the head the ones that are going to come through the palisade. The snakes aren't going to be careful."

But these two Foolish Ones themselves were fierce when they began killing the snakes outside the palisade, shooting them with arrows from their bows.

Now over there the same thing was occurring. There were many snakes, a multitude of them. Then they started coming over the palisade where the poles were crossed. Whenever someone was bitten by a snake, he was killed.

And then the snakes started coming into the earth lodges where people were inside, coming through the smokeholes and crawling through any cracks in the walls. Now innumerable people were killed!

Meanwhile these two Foolish Ones were going back and forth doing away with many of the snakes, killing the ones that were biting them, that were biting their legs.

And then the two went. Then they went into the Medicine Lodge, where the sacred objects were inside. Then they restored the flesh to their legs, the way they had been before, and then they went back out and killed a huge number of snakes again. <After they had killed many of them, ones that bit the flesh off their legs, they went back into the Medicine Lodge, where their flesh was again restored. I don't know how many times they did that, whether four times or more.>

Then many people, the poor things, died as each one was crying. Their sounds ceased after they died, when the snakes did away with our people.

Now these two Foolish Ones climbed up onto a drying scaffold.[1] Then they sat down back to back. They faced in opposite directions, each young man hitting a snake on the head as it came up. The snakes dropped down, one after another. Then they killed a multitude of them, killing them and killing them. Then the dead bodies of the snakes were piled up.

Now the snakes became frightened. "Why, we can't do anything to these two boys! They are exceedingly holy! We haven't hurt them at all. Now let's retreat far away from here!"

Now whatever snakes were remaining, they withdrew. They crawled away.

Now these two Foolish Ones went into the Medicine Lodge, where they sang their holy song; and where the flesh on their legs had been bitten off, there their legs were, restored just as they had been before!

Now, the two Foolish Ones came among the bodies of the dead and injured, the pitiful ones who had been bitten by the snakes. "Now get up! They've gone. The snakes have withdrawn."

The dead people got up, for these two boys were holy. The two made the village alive again. Then they also dug holes for burying the dead snakes.

"Now, you people, get yourselves ready! Let's move to a different location!"

And then that is what they did: all the people in the village got themselves ready. Then they moved off as a group. Now they began to head toward the west, here where we now live.

---

1. Beside each earth lodge there was a drying scaffold, or stage, on which corn and squash was dried after harvesting. See Plates 1 and 2 for illustrations of the scaffolds. For a description of the Hidatsa scaffold, similar to the Arikara structure, see Wilson (1917:98-104).

Now this is what I used to hear when I listened to what they told. Now this
is what happened.

Comparative references: ARIKARA Parks 1991, 4:597-98; G. A. Dorsey 1904a:
125-26; Lowie 1915:674-75.

13

Hidden Man and the Two Holy Men

ALFRED MORSETTE, SR.

*A poor boy living with his grandmother is the protagonist of this
story. Social outcasts, he and his grandmother choose not to accompany the people on their communal winter buffalo hunt but to return
instead to remain alone in the permanent earth lodge village. There
the boy is pitied by two strange men who name him Hidden Man.
These men are in reality stars, but are related to the buffalo on earth.
(Hence they eat only horticultural products—corn and squash—but
not meat; and they remain out of sight during the buffalo slaughter.)
They cure Hidden Man's father-in-law, save the people from starvation, and kill an evil man who has enslaved both Hidden Man and Big
Star, the leader of the buffalo herd that has come to the village. The
story thereby combines the themes of curing, buffalo calling, and
triumph over abuse of supernatural power to explain the name of a
poor boy who acquires celestial benefactors, enabling him to perform
good deeds.*

*This story, like many others told by Arikaras, is nearly identical
to one told by Hidatsas. Both groups claim the story as their own.
Although they have shared a reservation for more than a century and
have increasingly intermarried, Arikaras and Hidatsas have maintained distinct cultures and tribal identities. Yet they have inevitably
borrowed much from one another, especially apparent in oral traditions. In a Hidatsa version of this narrative recorded from Bear's
Arm in 1929 by Martha Beckwith, Hidden Man has the name Unknown One, while the two star fathers are referred to as Two Men but
are identified as Lodge Boy and Spring Boy, the Hidatsa counterparts*

of the Arikara characters Long Teeth and Drinks Brain Soup (see Parks 1991, stories 4, 63, and 155). The exploits of Lodge Boy and Spring Boy, however, are primarily told in other Hidatsa stories, and their association with the two star fathers seems adventitious.

Now I am going to tell a story. It is about a personal name from long, long ago when the people were coming this way. It is what I heard from my grandmother—what she told. Also I heard it from someone else. It was the same story that he told; I think it was Ray Gough. I think it is the same story that my grandmother always used to tell—about when they gave this name Hidden Boy to the boy they found, because the boy and his grandmother were poor. They lived in an earth lodge, living in it by themselves [on the outskirts of the village].

<It was in the fall, when it was getting cold.> Then the chiefs in this village planned it: "Let's go somewhere far off, where the buffalo have gone! The buffalo aren't close by around here now. They must have gone far off. Also the deer are diminishing in number. There aren't any around. They must have gone far off. Now let's all go as a group to a different place! And then we'll come back; we'll return here when spring comes."

And then they got themselves ready. Then they were going to leave the village as a group.

Now this boy and his grandmother, the poor things. . . . <They were getting along. The boy was about fourteen winters old. He would go out to hunt prairie chickens and rabbits, and his grandmother had a supply of corn, squash, beans, and chokecherries. They were getting along.>

Then the hunting trip was organized. There were the marshals, the "forbidders," who enforced the rules. That is what I used to hear. But today they call the ones who watch over things "scouts." Now that was the position for the young men who were fearless, who were brave warriors, when the village traveled.

"Now we are leaving. We are going to go off somewhere. After setting out, if anyone wishes to turn back, these soldiers are the enforcers. They will come and kill your dog, the one you have. Even if you have a bunch, say thirteen, they'll kill all of yours." Now that was the custom.

Then the people left as a group. Meanwhile this old woman—the grandmother—and the boy decided to go. "Well, let's go! There is no choice. We have only our one dog, and they might kill it. A soldier might kill our dog that carries wood for us."

And then they followed behind the group as it went off after the weather was cold in late fall. After leaving the village, they traveled for however many days it was.

Now, but the boy who lived with his grandmother—then he said to her, "Hey, grandma, let's turn back! It's nice where we live in our lodge and I always go around hunting and we eat cottontail rabbits or prairie chickens. But now it's difficult going somewhere far off. I'm just lazy. Now let's go back home!"

Then his grandmother said, "Yes, we should do that. Why, that's just how I feel: I'm just too lazy to go on. Now let's do it! Let's turn back!"

Then the boy said, "Well, I'll go early in the morning, before it's daybreak yet. I'll take this dog of ours. We'll go back there. We'll hide. And when the village starts moving on, I'll come back in the evening. Then we'll go home.

"If the enforcers come, you should say, 'He went after meat. He must have killed a deer. He's the one I'm waiting for. And as soon as he returns, we'll catch up. I'm ready now.' And that's what you'll say."

Early in the morning—*really* early in the morning—this boy got up. Then he ran off with the dog that they had. Then, wherever the place was, he stopped with the dog to wait there.

It got to be daybreak. Then the camp crier began calling out, "Now get yourselves ready! Our camp is moving. We are going on until we reach a nice location, where there are woods and where there is plenty of wood and water. Those are the main concerns. That is the purpose of our going. And when the weather begins to get warm again, we will be coming home." That is what was planned.

Then the group began moving on.

Meanwhile, this old woman, the poor thing, took down the brush shelter she and her grandson had. Then she was ready. Then the young men, the enforcers, came. "You aren't ready."

Then she said, "I'm waiting for my grandson. He went after meat. He must have killed a deer. That is what he went after. As soon as he returns, then we'll catch up."

Then they went on. The young men, the enforcers who were hurrying everyone, left her.

In the evening the boy arrived. Then he and his grandmother loaded their gear onto the travois pulled by the dog. Then they went back to their lodge in the village. They arrived there.

"It's good to be back home safely. It's too much trouble making a camp all the time. One no more than puts up a lodge than one takes it down again." That is what he was saying repeatedly.

He went hunting, shooting cottontails and prairie chickens. And that is what he and his grandmother ate.

Early one morning the boy arose and went up onto a hill to look all around. There was smoke coming out of one earth lodge there in the village. Smoke was coming out of it.

Then he came home. Then he said, "Grandma, I stood on top of that hill over there. In the village there's smoke coming out of one lodge. Someone must be living in it. Maybe someone else turned back, too. Perhaps you should find out! Go there!"

Then his grandmother said, "That family never goes anywhere. They're living there. The man's legs are paralyzed. That's the reason they're not with the village on its trip. I'll go. I'll go to see them. I'll go into the village."

After the boy went hunting for prairie chickens, cottontails, jackrabbits— those kinds of things—his grandmother went through the village to where they lived.

Then this family was happy to see her—that man and the woman who was his wife and the young woman who was their daughter. Oh, she was nice looking, this young girl who was about fourteen or fifteen winters old.

Then the grandmother came home in the evening. There sat her grandson inside the lodge.

Then the boy said, "Grandma, I killed a cottontail. I'm boiling it."

Then she said, "I went through the village where you said, and they're living there. Now they've invited us to their lodge to live with them during the winter."

Well, then he said, "Well, it will be that way, but first I think I'll go somewhere to hunt for a while!"

Then his grandmother took her belongings to where the two of them had been invited.

"Well, my grandson and I are going to come here."

Then the man said, "Where did your grandson go?"

"Oh, my grandson went hunting."

Then he said, "Well, I want my daughter to marry your grandson since I'm not able to go around hunting anything. I want this boy to be my son-in-law to help me."

"Now I'll ask him."

Then the boy arrived. They were calling him. Then they told him.

Then the boy said, "Well, it'll be that way. I'll marry this young woman."

Then that is what he did: then they married. Then they lived together for a while, however long it was.

Meanwhile, nothing was difficult for this young man when he went out hunting and killed various things. Even if it was a deer, he killed it. Then he brought the meat back.

"Oh, son-in-law!" Now his father-in-law was thankful. "Ah, that's what I want: to eat well. I'm just not able to go hunting for anything myself. It's impossible for me."

Then the boy went off one time. While he was out hunting, going all around, he saw two men. Then they found him.

"Ah, Hidden Man! They say he's married now, and we came to see our daughter-in-law. Now that's what we came for. Ah, it's truly good. Now we'll watch over her while you go around."

Then one said, "Now, we want some roasted corn to eat, and some squash, so that, ah, we might eat well; and something to smoke."

Well, then the boy said, "Well, can you possibly come tomorrow?"

Then one said, "Ah, it will be that way. We'll go. Now, Hidden Man, when it gets to be evening, when the sun goes down, you'll tie up the dogs. Oh, this one, my brother, and I are afraid of dogs. We're afraid of dogs, but we'll go there. <Also you must bank the fire in the fireplace so that it burns low—just enough to see one's silhouette, that someone is sitting there. And spread sage where we are going to sit.> When we eat, we want to see our daughter-in-law, the poor thing. Now, we'll come in the evening."

They departed. Then the boy went. Then he arrived. Then he told the young woman his wife, "My fathers are going to come. There are two. They want to eat something and to smoke, to eat corn—roasted corn—and squash, and to smoke something. You must tell your father about them." That is what he told the young woman.[2]

"Yes, it will be that way."

[To her father,] "His fathers are going to come. They're coming to see us. They want to smoke."

"Ah, it will be that way. I'll get things ready."

Then this man, the poor thing, began mixing tobacco. He was not able to get around, but only sit on his bed.

Now they tied the dogs up. Then they spread sage out on the floor. "This is where they'll sit." <And then they fixed the fire so it would burn low.>

Then the boy went outside. It was getting dark now.

Then the two men saw the boy. They were coming. They were talking.

---

2. Traditionally the relationship between an individual and his or her parents-in-law was one of respect. Consequently, most Arikara husbands would not speak directly to their mothers-in-law or fathers-in-law, but used their wives as intermediaries. Reciprocally, fathers-in-law would not speak directly to their daughters-in-law, but would communicate through a child or other intermediary.

Then one said, "Hey, we have arrived. Why, surely it's a good thing. We're going to eat something from our daughter-in-law."

"Now come!" Then he led them inside the lodge. Then they sat down where the sage had been spread. Then they sat down.

Then the women dished out roasted corn and squash for them. They placed the food before them. But first the man filled the pipe. Then after they smoked, they began to eat, eating roasted corn and squash. Oh, they were thankful. They consumed everything.

Then one said, "Now, daughter-in-law, we are full. We've eaten your meal after we smoked your father's tobacco. Now it's good. Now let's go! We're going back over there."

Then they went outside.

Well, after so many days then he saw them again.

"Ah, here we come again, Hidden Man, so that we might eat. Ah, it's certainly good that our daughter-in-law can cook for us. Now we'll come again. But we want to know why your father-in-law doesn't get up."

Then the boy said, "Why, his legs are paralyzed. His legs don't move well. It's too difficult for him."

"Well now, we'll doctor him when we come. He'll get well. He'll start getting around again. It's nothing. We scrutinized him. It was good to smoke his tobacco. We just felt good." This is what they were saying. "Now we're going to come again. You must have things ready and our daughter-in-law will have a meal cooked."

And then the boy came back and told his wife, "My fathers are going to come. They're going to doctor your father to make him well."

Then the young woman was thankful. Then she was glad.

She told her father and mother, "This boy's fathers are going to come again. They're going to doctor you to make you well, so that you'll be able to get all around at last. They're thankful for having smoked your tobacco."

Then this man said, "Ah, hand that to me! I should get ready!"

He began mixing the tobacco. He got everything ready.

Then the boy went outside there. When it was sundown he tied the dogs up as they had done before. Then he went to where they were. They were talking as they came, talking. "Now here we have come. Our daughter-in-law must have everything ready for us to eat roasted corn. And now it's ready. Let's go!"

They went to the lodge. They entered. Now they sat down where the sage was spread out, as they had done before.

Food was set before them. Then they began eating well. They consumed everything. This man then fixed the tobacco for them. Then they also smoked.

Then one told Hidden Man, "Tell your wife, 'You must lay your father here where we're sitting.' We'll doctor him. He'll get well."[3]

Then this boy told the young woman his wife and her mother. They made a bed for him. They laid him down.

Then one said, "Alright, I'm going to be the first one to doctor you."

Then he got up and rubbed his hands in a circular manner <rubbing sage between them>.[4] He took hold of one leg, then the other leg on the right, too. Then he pulled out a snake, a bull snake.

Now this man: "This is the one that crippled you." Then he laid it down. Then he sat down. "Now it's your turn, my brother."

"Ha, now I myself will do it." Then he did just what his brother had done. Then he took out a bull snake, too. Now this one was the female kind.

"These are the cause of your not being able to walk around. And, Hidden Man, you'll wrap the two snakes up and throw them away. Now we're going. Well, sometime later we'll find each other again."

And when it was morning the man who had had the crippled legs walked around inside. Then he was tremendously thankful, being thankful that he was able to walk all around again after they had made him well—after they had taken away his paralysis. "Why, I'm thankful that I'm able to walk all around here again!"

Now while this young man was traveling around, the two men found him.

Then one of them said, "Hidden Man, we have come purposefully." Then they gave him two arrows. They gave him two.

Then the man said, "Now when you travel around, if some difficult situation confronts you, this is what you're going to do: you'll nock one of these arrows and you'll shoot it up into the air. Then we'll come. Whatever the problem is, we're going to take care of it for you. Now this black arrow is going to watch over you. Whenever you travel around, have it with you. Don't forget this quiver you have, and keep the arrow in it together with the other ones."

Now as the young man was traveling around, he saw them again. Then the two men saw him.

Then one said, "Say, the village that's traveling on the hunt is turning back. They're coming. They're hungry. Children have died, starving to death. They're traveling this way. They're coming back home.

---

3. See footnote 2 above.
4. An act of purification.

"Now truly I have come here. Tomorrow I'll take care of things immediately. Your grandmother and your mother-in-law shall make arrows! Oh, you should make many of them! Now we're going to call the buffalo. The buffalo are ranging close by here. They're headed this way toward your village. They're going to come. Now you're going to shoot them. You'll butcher them and take the meat inside all these lodges to be sliced and dried. And you'll place pieces on these scaffolds. There's going to be plenty. Now we'll be shooting them, too. Now, you and the old man your father-in-law, get yourselves ready!"

This boy went home. Then he told his mother-in-law.

"Now, grandma, you'll sharpen the arrowheads."

They did not tell how many days passed [while they prepared]. Now there was a huge number of bundles. There were bundles of arrows all over.

Then they said, "Now tie up the dogs! The buffalo are coming now. There's a multitude of them. They're headed this way toward our village. Now this old man and I are going to shoot them."

When morning came—early in the morning—the ground was rumbling. And here there was a herd of buffalo coming! Oh, there was a multitude of them coming to the edge of the village!

And this man and his son-in-law killed a huge number of them when they were killing them. Then there was a line of carcasses there. And here the other two <star fathers> were shooting the buffalo from out of sight, so that the buffalo did not see them. Then the herd of buffalo passed by. There were carcasses scattered all around here and there.

Then they began butchering them and taking the meat into different lodges, the vacant lodges, and putting the meat on scaffolds. Ah, there was plenty! There was no lack of meat!

And, oh, as the boy was going all around, he saw someone there: there stood a man. He was barely able to walk. He was staggering as he came.

Then this boy Hidden Man went to meet him. Then he said, "Hey, hello!"

Then this man said, "Everyone traveling in our party is *so* pitiful. Children have died, starving to death. And everyone among us is hungry. Now the group is returning. But we came ahead. Everything was ruined for them. They're tired, but they're coming on anyway. Oh my, I'm so tired! I'm so tired, too!"

Then the other one said, "Now be strong for a while! Our village is close by. You must come there! We're living there with the man who is now my father-in-law"—whatever his name was. "I'm with the young woman who is his child." Then he said, "Be strong! You'll make it."

Then this boy quickly turned back. Then he arrived.

Then he said to his wife, "Tell your mother, 'Boil meat!' Now they're coming. There are four men. The group that went on the hunt is returning. They turned back half way out. Children have died, starving to death. Now there are three others following the one coming ahead. They're tired and hungry. But this one coming close by is going to come here. Let him drink only soup first! Then later you can set meat before him. You'll get everything ready for him. As soon as he has eaten, then he'll turn around. You'll give him some dried meat. Then he'll take it to the three who are coming. They'll eat some. Then he'll take meat farther on to the others who are coming. This is what my fathers told me."

So now that is what she did: then she boiled ribs. Then they also roasted ribs over the fire.

Then the man who was coming appeared. Oh, he was barely able to walk, and when he looked, oh my, in this village here there was meat hanging from the scaffolds! There was a huge quantity of meat there. Then he hurried along, coming faster.

Then Hidden Man led him to the lodge where his wife was. Then she dipped up soup for him. He calmed down. Then they placed meat before him. He ate.

Now the boy said, "Now turn around again! You are strong now. You are sturdy now. There are two bundles of dried meat here. You'll give some dried meat to those three men who are coming. But then you'll take the rest of it to the group that is coming. As soon as you arrive there with it, you'll tell the people, 'Make a fire, a big fire!' And then you'll throw the dried meat onto the flames. You'll become lively after having been sick and hungry. You'll pass the meat around. You'll place it before them. You'll distribute this dried meat. One pile will go around evenly! <It will increase and there will be enough for everyone>."

And then that is what he did, just as I said.

The boy came back. Then he ate. Then this man went and took the dried meat, as he had told him, just as I said.

Oh, later the group arrived in the village. This Hidden Man had made everyone lively again, and now the women were making dried meat [out of what was in their lodges].

Now that is what he did.

《 《 《   》 》 》

Once when he was traveling around, when he was going around hunting, well, wherever he was going, he crossed the water, wherever it was, to the other side when the ice was floating on the river.

Now he sat on a hill. While he was looking all around, he saw a single buffalo. There it came, oh, as it grazed on grass. Oh, as he looked all around he saw that there was one stand of trees nearby and just beyond there was another one. The two stands were facing each other [forming a sort of corridor].

Then this boy thought, "Oh, before that buffalo comes through, I'll go down there. I'll wait over there. And as soon as I eye it between the two stands of trees, I'll shoot it."

Then that is what he did: he waited over there. That buffalo came into the open space between the two stands of trees. As soon as it got there, this boy shot it. The arrow glanced off. As he chased it, shooting at it again and again, he was unable to bring it down and kill it. And here it led him far, far off as he chased it!

Then there was a lodge. That is where the buffalo was going inside. Now the boy caught up with it.

Once it was there inside the lodge, it said, "I have led Hidden Man here. I'm barely alive. He has wounded me all over."

And there inside someone said, "Now sit down! Now that's nothing at all. You'll get well."

A man was inside. He called out, "Come in!"

Then this Hidden Man entered. There sitting against the wall was the one he had chased and had been shooting, <a bull named Big Star>. Also sitting there was something, whatever it was. It had sharp bumps; it also had arms and a mouth. It had long teeth. <There was also a man sitting there, and there was a heart hanging there.>

The man said, "Aaah, Hidden Man, you have come now, but you never think, 'My uncle lives over there.' It's good that you have come. Now sit down over there!"

Then he was seated. Food was placed before him. Then he began to eat.

Then the man said, "Hidden Man, I called you purposefully since we who live here are always hungry. On this earth you are outstanding in the ways of hunting. And I am hungry as I sit here wanting something to eat. You never think, 'My uncle lives over there,' and you never come." That is what this man was saying.

And here the man was evil, doing different kinds of evil things and killing various ones. Whoever had holy power would lose it to him.

"Now you lie right here. This boy, the poor thing, is mine for running around to perform errands."

A little boy went in front of them as he scurried around. He was about so tall.

Then the man said, "Say!"

After they had lain down to sleep, this boy Hidden Man thought, "I wonder why I came. I don't like being around this place."

Now it was morning, and this man—I don't know what his name was, only that they just say "this man"—he said, "Now you're going to hunt for a white bighorn sheep. Ah, it'll be conspicuous among them. Ah, the horns—I want one of those horns for a horn spoon so I can drink water with it. I want you to bring that."

Meanwhile this young man would go around hunting, killing deer because the man wanted to eat something. "But don't eat any! You'll spoil the taste of mine!" [he admonished Hidden Man].

Then Hidden Man would bring the meat to him. Then he would set it down for him. "Now throw it away! The meat might be spoiled." That is what he was doing.

First the man wanted it; then he did not want it. Now this Hidden Man, the poor thing, was rather hungry. He was left out [when they were eating].

Meanwhile his in-laws were looking for him while they were waiting. "He must have been killed by the enemy." His two star fathers also looked for him, but they did not see him anywhere.

"Now, you are going to bring this white bighorn sheep to me. Oh, it's difficult to find one, but I believe they say that nothing is difficult for you when you hunt things. That's the reason I want you to kill that white bighorn sheep for me."

Well, this one, the poor thing, set out to go off. But he was *so* weak when he went, since he was so hungry!

As he was going along he found one. Why, he was barely about to kill it and then he slit its legs behind the knees. He wanted to carry it on his back.

Then it became too difficult for him. He was *so* weak! It was too difficult for him to get up.

Then he heard something there, up above where he was going. "Heeey, heeey, Hidden Man, where are you?"

Then he thought, "Why, here they're looking for me!"

Then he arose. Then he was barely able to take out the black arrow, and then shot it up into the air. There was a thud on the ground. There stood his fathers.

"Ah, you have erred. We have searched everywhere on this earth looking for you. And here this is where you have come! This is where you must like living."

He said, "Why, this is how it is. This is what happened."

Then they said, "Yes, well, we know that man."

Now one of them made a fire. He took a rib. Then he placed it over the fire.

He made Hidden Man vomit after they gave him medicine to drink [as they doctored him]. Then they made him strong again.

"Now eat!"

Then the boy began eating. They made him strong again.

"Now leave this sheep here! I'll kill a different one" [one of the men said].

Then they went on. Then they killed a different bighorn sheep. The other one put it on his back and then they went on.

"This is the place. That's the lodge."

"Now take the meat inside!"

Hidden Man said, "As soon as I go inside, he'll say right away, 'Bring me some water!' That's what he's going to say."

Then he entered, but the two men stayed outside.

There inside the lodge the man said, "Hey, Hidden Man, whatever were you doing! I'm starving to death, and I'm dying of thirst. Whatever were you doing!"

Then the boy Hidden Man said, "Why, it's certainly difficult to find a sheep of this kind. One can't just bump into one easily. I had to look for it. That's the reason it took a long time."

"Ah, now bring me some water! I'm dying of thirst."

Now that he had been made a slave, this Hidden Man picked up a pail, an empty pail. He went out. After he had gone outside there where the two men were, one of them snatched the pail [and got the water for Hidden Man].

Then he said, "This time when he does it—after he drinks a little water and says, 'Throw it away!'—you throw the water in his face! [Say,] 'This is what you have been doing, tiring me out.' You aren't going to do it anymore."

He took the water inside. The man drank a little.

"Now throw the water away!"

Hidden Man said, "Hey, this is what you always do." Then he threw the water on him.

Then his two fathers who were standing outside came running inside. When this man saw them, he was afraid of them.

"Now this is how Hidden Man treats me," he whined.

Where he sat on top, there the heart was hanging. <One of the men threw it onto the fire. After it burned the man died. He was killed.>

And that thing in the corner—one of the fathers kicked it. It slid across the lodge. It was the one that had long teeth. Then they pierced it with its teeth. Then they killed it. They threw it into the fire.

Then this buffalo Big Star said, "Oh, I want to live! Poor things, this is how it was when we lived here as slaves."

"Now you go on quickly! We heeded you when you called us to come help you, when the human beings were starving. We heeded you when we came, when the humans who had been traveling around looking for buffalo were coming back to their village.[5] Now go on quickly! Don't turn around at all! We might kill you, too."

Then this buffalo bull went out. Then he went off.

Then one of the star fathers said, "Now go on quickly! Don't ever turn around!"

Then this bull said, "There may be a day when I [a buffalo] may be among you people, and I'll kill someone."

"Oh, go on quickly!" They scolded the bull.

Meanwhile there were carcasses lying around. The men destroyed the holy things that this evil man had there.

"Now let's go on quickly!"

Then they flew off to the village. "Your in-laws are weary, and your wife has a child for you. She's weary from having waited for you."

Then Hidden Man went to his home.

Then they cried when they saw him. His grandmother was living yet.

Ah, his little boy was growing up; the little boy, the one he had of his own, was growing up.

Now this man was named Hidden Man. The meaning of it is 'not to be going around plainly.' It signifies that he is around, but he is not obviously there. But he is around, but people do not know his ways, the good ideas that he has. What he does is good, always doing good deeds for others. Now this is the meaning of the name Hidden Man. He is around, but he cannot be prominent.

Now this is what I used to hear when my grandmother told the story—when they talked about Hidden Man.

Comparative references: ARAPAHO Dorsey and Kroeber 1903:294-98; CHEYENNE Grinnell 1926:193-200; HIDATSA Beckwith 1937:43-52, cf. 103-6; Bowers 1965: 306-8.

5. One of the star fathers reminds Big Star, the buffalo bull, that they had come to his aid when he had wanted to help the starving people by bringing the buffalo herd to the village, where Hidden Man and his father-in-law could slaughter them. Subsequently, after the evil man had enslaved Big Star, the bull helped the man enslave Hidden Man, the star fathers' adopted son.

14

The Young Man Pitied by
the Spotted Buffalos

ALFRED MORSETTE, SR.

The plot of this myth is the familiar vanquishment of an evil
father-in-law, here a man who uses his daughter to lure young men
to his winter encampment, where he sets them impossible tasks, then
kills them when they fail. After one young man, the protagonist of the
story, is determined to learn why previous youths who followed the
girl have never returned, he is aided first by five animals that impart
their powers to him, enabling him to overcome the hurdles put up by
the evil father-in-law. Then the story continues a theme from previous
narratives of associating buffalos on earth with stars. When the son-
in-law is given impossible tasks, the young man is aided first by a
buffalo cow in human form and then by seven spotted buffalos who
are in fact stars that have come down to earth in animal form. It was
these buffalo stars that had endowed the father-in-law with his power,
represented by a black rock, and now they are the ones who must
overcome him for his abuse of it. The story was told to the narrator
by his grandfather Short Bear.

It was a long, long time ago when our people lived there <toward the
southeast> where we migrated from, long, long ago. And they told this story
when they were coming up the river. They told the story.

Now our grandfather used to tell stories. He had stories. My grandmother
was that way, too.

Now there once was a village, a big village, in which Arikaras lived. And
there was a man—it was a man—who lived alone in the badlands, who lived
alone with his wife and daughter. The young woman, his daughter, was pretty.

He lived there in the badlands during the winter. He had lodges there: he
had two big earth lodges, and another one that was small. The large one was
their dwelling.

And when summer came the family would return to our villages along the
Missouri to live among the people, and the man's daughter would be courted
by various young men.

And when it began to get cold in late fall, he would go back to where "I **always go for the winter. I have a nice place where I live. I'm not in want of things like wood and water, and there's plenty of game so that I eat well.**"[6] And then the family moved back there.

Then a young man who liked the daughter and who had been courting her would follow the family. The family would return to where they lived in the badlands with this boy following the young woman he was courting.

But then the young man would be given difficult tasks by this man. And finally he would be killed. The man would kill him.

This man must have been doing that many times. He would come to the village in the summertime, and then he and his family would return to the badlands as they always did.

And then one time a certain young man said, "Now I must find out. I wonder why none of the boys who follows her ever returns here. Anyone who has courted this young woman has not returned. And when his parents look for him, he's dead."

And this man [who was the father of the young woman] would say, "Ah, the enemy must have found him. They must have killed him. We looked for him, but he didn't come back." And this is what he always said when he was explaining things.

It began to get wintry now, just about wintertime. "Now we're going where we always go for the winter." Then he went off. Then the family moved back there.

And then this young man followed them. The family must have left two days earlier; then the young man went afterward.

As he was running along he went up a hill. When he looked out over the land there, he saw the trail where they had gone. Then this young man went on.

As he was going along, there they sat over yonder. There sat over yonder a bear, a mountain lion, an eagle, a rabbit, and an ant. There was a dead buffalo lying there [in front of them]. Oh, the buffalo was big!

Then the young man passed by them. Then he turned around. "Say, what's going on?"

As he went to where they were, this bear got up. Then it said, "Yes. Now it's good that you have come. We want someone to butcher the buffalo we have here and to distribute the meat evenly to us. That's what we're sitting here waiting for."

---

6. The narrator switches here to a first person perspective, in which the man himself describes his winter quarters.

Then this young man said, "I'll do it for you. It isn't difficult for me to butcher it."

Then the young man began butchering the buffalo. He finished doing it. "Well, now, what's going to happen?"

Then the bear said, "You'll give me one hind leg and a foreleg. And you can also do the same for this other one, the mountain lion. Give him a hind leg and a foreleg. But now I don't know what these others are going to say."

Then the eagle said, "Now you can give me the back, and I'll eat it. I'll peck on it."

And the rabbit: "Now you can give me the ribs. I'll eat them. I'll nibble on the ribs. They're what I always eat."

Now the ant said, "Now this head is what you'll give me. It'll be my home. That's where I myself will live inside."

Then the young man divided things evenly as he laid them down.

Then the bear said, "We're indeed thankful for what you have done for us here. Now we'll bless you. We know why you've come here. The man who has the young daughter has already gone by. We blessed him previously, but now he's gone too far. His actions are bad. <He doesn't want anyone to marry his daughter.> He's killed all the young men who have followed him. Each one has died after the man has had him killed.

"But now we're going to bless you. Whatever you desire is going to happen. What you have done for us is good."

Now this mountain lion: "And from me here you'll have the gift of bravery over the enemy as you travel about. The ways of the warpath are not going to be difficult for you."

And now the eagle said, "Now I'm giving you the power of hunting. I'm going to watch over you. I'm going to be hunting for things for myself, too. I'm thankful for what you've done for me."

Then the rabbit said, "I feel the same way, too. I'm thankful for what you did. Now you'll be fast. No one will be able to overtake you when you run. Now whatever you chase will not be hard for you to catch. And you'll be able to do whatever you want."

Then the ant said, "Now I, too, am thankful for what you have done. Now no matter what it is that has been hidden, it won't be difficult for you to find, just as I find it as I travel about. That is my power. Even though something is well hidden, I arrive there and find it. I'm the one to get there first. And I'm giving you that power. I'm going to watch over you. I'm going to make the trails for you that you and I are going to travel. Now make haste! Quickly!"

Then the bear said, "Now when you go on and reach the man's lodge, when you arrive there, this is what he's going to do. Oh, there are two big white wolves sitting outside. They're tied up. They'll start to attack you when

you arrive, but he's going to come out. He'll stop them. The wolves are the
ones eating up each of the boys. Whenever he gives a task to a boy and the boy
doesn't accomplish it, then he tells the wolves. Then they kill him. And then
this man butchers him, and [whenever anyone comes to the lodge] he feeds the
person human flesh. [He says to the visitor,] 'Now this will be the food that
will be cooked first. And you and I will eat it. We'll eat it up.'

"Now whatever task he gives you that he wants done, tell me, and I'll take
up the task myself."

And now this mountain lion said, "Now whatever task he gives you, you
must go to do it, and it won't take me long to go wherever one must go to
accomplish it."

Now this ant: "Now you and I are going to marry the daughter of this man
who is preventing her marriage. Now we're going to marry her. It won't be
hard to accomplish. Now go quickly!"

Then this young man went off.

And he arrived there. There were earth lodges. There were three lodges.
They lived in the large one.

Then the young man went to the door. The big white wolves were sitting
outside by the doorway. Then they started growling when they saw him.

Then the man came charging out of the lodge. "Why, it's my son-in-law!
The wolves are barking." [To the wolves:] "Sit down! Be calm!

"Now, son-in-law, come inside!"

Then he took the young man inside. "Now sit down!"

Then the young man sat down.

Then the man brought out a pot, a black pot. Then it began dancing. It was
dancing around. Then his wife came and she picked it up. Then she took it
outside and after making a fire out there she began to boil meat in it. Here it
was human flesh! Then she brought the pot of meat inside.

Then the ant told the young man, "Holler! Those two [your animal
guardians] will then eat up the flesh."

Oh, this bear and the mountain lion [who were now invisible spirits,] ate
up everything. They drank up all the soup.

Now that holy man watched the young man. [But he could not see the bear
or the mountain lion.]

The young man said, "Now I have eaten."

After a little while the daughter brought dried meat and corn balls inside
for the young man. Then this young man ate well.

Then the father-in-law told him, "Now you can sleep right here."
Something was sitting there in the corner [where he was to sleep]. It was blue.
It had warts. It resembled a toad. Then it began to get angry.

The young woman slept on a bed high off the ground on the other side of the lodge, while her father and mother slept on a lower level. So it was impossible to reach her bed.

Then the ant told him, "Sleep awhile! It isn't difficult. We'll get there where she sleeps."

Then the thing sitting in the corner began to move around. Then it began to croak. It sat there with its mouth wide open as it croaked.

Then the bear said, "Now wait! Bring that! Give me the stick that's lying there!"

Then the young man gave it the stick, whatever kind it was.

Now when the creature sitting in the corner opened its mouth, the bear thrust the stick into its mouth. Then it was impossible for the thing in the corner—the one making the croaking sounds—to close its mouth.

Then the man got up from bed [because the creature was making so much noise] and made a fire. "What did you do to it?"

He said, "I didn't do anything. I don't know what that thing is, the one making the noise, with the stick in its mouth."

The man took the stick out. "Why don't you behave, you who are moving around angrily!"

And then the young man said, "If it starts to get mad again, I'll cut its throat."

Then this man became frightened. He was becoming fearful of his son-in-law.

After everyone was asleep, the ant said to the young man, "Now you and I are going to go over to where the young woman is sleeping."

Then the two of them went to her bed. Then the young man got into bed with this young woman, the one whose parents opposed her getting married and who made it difficult for suitors. <But before daylight the young man got down from her bed and went back to his own.>

Now sometime later this man said to the young man, "Now, my son-in-law, I want to eat elk. I want the hide of a white one. My old woman will tan it and I'll wear it when it gets cold."

This young man said, "I've never seen a white elk, but I'll look for one. As long as I've been hunting, I've never seen a white elk going around."

Then the young man went out. Then he went up onto a hill. And then the eagle flew up into the air above him and looked all around. Then a white elk was found. The young man killed it. He brought the meat, and those two who were always together—the bear and the mountain lion—helped him carry the meat back. They were getting near the man's lodge as the two animals packed the meat on their backs. The young man took it on inside the lodge by himself.

"Now here's what you wanted."

Then the man stared at it. Oh, he stared at it! The elk was white. "Now here it is. And it's big! This fur and the hide are what I wanted." Then the man began to butcher it.

It was sometime later, and then the man gave the young man another task. It was wintry now, in the dead of winter. Then this man said to him, "Now, son-in-law, I want to eat some plums. Go after some for me! Let me have some plums to eat!"

Then the young man said, "There aren't any plums growing on bushes in the winter. When it's in the middle of winter—I've never seen any plums on bushes in the middle of winter."

"You talk too much! Go on quickly!" Then the young man was given a sack.

Then he went off. There was snow on the ground as he traveled along the coulees which had wooded slopes.

Then he cried as he fasted. There was a clump of plum bushes there. It was a big stand of bushes.

Then a boy came out of the bushes. He said, "My mother is calling you. Follow me!"

Then he followed the boy. The two of them went into the brush. There there was an earth lodge in the brush. It was a big lodge. The two went into it. There sat a woman. She was cooking a meal. She was boiling dried meat.

"Sonny, you who are traveling around, now sit down! Why, you must eat something!"

Then this young man sat down. Food was set down for him and the boy, and they ate.

"Ah, now what's the matter?"

Then he said, "The man who is my father-in-law wants plums. Now where indeed are plums growing during the winter!"

And then the woman said, "Why, he's gone too far this time. He's going beyond his limit with the things he's requesting. We're the ones who blessed him. [We gave him power.] He was pitiful when he stood alone on top of different hills crying. Now he's going too far. What he's doing isn't good.

"Now I'll do something for you. Spread out the robe you're wearing! And then go outside and bring back a plum bush. Take it up there where the smokehole is [and hold it over the opening]. As soon as I begin singing, you'll shake the bush."

Then that is what this young man did. Then he took the bush up onto the roof of the lodge, and then this woman began to sing. He shook the bush over the smokehole.

Oh, there were thuds as the plums fell down through the smokehole.

And then the woman said, "Now surely there are plenty of them. Now put the bush back into the hole where you dug it up and set it upright!"

And then that is what this young man did.

Then he went back into the lodge and gathered the plums lying there on the robe.

"Now go quickly! He might discover what you're doing. I don't want him to know about it. Now go! You shouldn't say anything. Say only, 'They were there on a bush. They must not have frozen.'"

This young man was very swift indeed. He arrived back at his father-in-law's lodge. Then it was not long before he entered it. The wolves meanwhile were calm as they sat there. He took the plums inside. Then he laid them down.

Then he said, "Here are the plums. They must not have frozen. They were on a bush. I picked them hurriedly. There aren't any plums on bushes in the winter!"

"Yes, yes," the man was saying. Then he began to eat.

Then the young man said, "Eat them up! Don't leave any!"

Oh, this man gorged himself. Now he was barely able to eat up the plums.

Now it was not long before the father-in-law said again, "Hey, I wish I might eat some Juneberries. Say, son-in-law, go find some!" Then this young man said, "There aren't any Juneberries growing on bushes in the winter! Why, you're just making it difficult!"

"You talk too much, son-in-law! You must go look around for them. You won't lose anything by it."

And so this young man went off. He went to where his mother lived [she who had helped him previously], and then he put the matter before her. "This is what he wants now."

And then she told him they would do as they had done before.

After he brought a Juneberry bush to the smokehole on top of the lodge, he shook it. And hanging there on the bush were Juneberries! Then he began to pick them off the bush [and dropped them down through the smokehole onto the robe below].

"Now take them quickly! Don't divulge anything!"

Then he went off. Then he arrived [at his father-in-law's lodge].

"Now here they are. You must eat them all up! Don't leave any!"

Now this man was becoming rather fearful of his son-in-law. He was barely able to consume all the Juneberries when he ate them.

And then sometime later the father-in-law said, "Say, it's getting warm now. The time is approaching for us to return to our village. Now look for a spotted buffalo for me! And when you bring the hide back, this old woman will tan it. Then we'll go back to our village, and I'll wear the spotted buffalo robe when I go around."

And then the young man said, "Why, there aren't any spotted buffalos among the ones I've ever seen! The only kind I've ever seen among buffalo is a white one, but I've never seen a spotted one. But I'll look around anyway."

Then the young man went back to where his mother lived. Then he told her, "Now this task is too difficult for me."

"But it isn't difficult," she said. "Go over there to the east! They'll be there in a valley. There are seven of them. They are spotted buffalos. If they start to run off, you should yell out, 'My mother Red Bear Woman sent me and this is what she said: "You will comply."'"

Then this young man went off. While he was running along, he climbed up a hill. There they were in the valley below: they were all nice looking; they were spotted. Then they began to run off. "A human being is coming!"

Then the young man called out, "I didn't come of my own accord. My mother Red Bear Woman sent me. This is what she told me to say when I came."

"Yes. Alright." Then they stopped. Then they came back to him and sat down.

And then one of them asked, "Now what has happened?"

Then he said, "My father-in-law made this request. [He wants a spotted buffalo like you.]"

"Hah, he is surely going too far now. That man is the one we blessed. He was pitiful when he would cry all night long until morning. But now his actions are wrong. This is the end of the blessings that we have given him.

"Now this is a difficult matter, but we'll do whatever we are capable of doing. <We're not from this earth. We really live in the sky. But we knew what you were doing and so we came down here to help you. Every so often we come down to this earth as we have done now. Your situation is a difficult one, but we'll try to get rid of this man.>

"Now go <over there into the hills and> bring back a black rock. If we succeed in splitting the rock, we are going to be able to kill him."

Then this young man went up a hill. Then he found the rock and brought it back.

Then he said, "Now here it is."

Then one of the spotted buffalos said, "Now we're going to hit it. If we split it we're going to be able to kill the man. But if we fail we'll all be dead. <He has power just like this rock.>"

Now these seven buffalos began butting it with their heads to see which one would hurt its neck [attempting to split it].

Then the oldest one—he was an old buffalo bull—said, "I thought that one of you young ones would be the one to split it. Now I don't know what my strength is, but I'm not really strong like I used to be. Now I don't know what I'm going to be able to do. Maybe I'll strike it. Maybe I'll do the job right."

And then he did that: hurting his neck, he split the black rock.

Then he said, "Now there's no obstacle. Now we have overcome him. Now we have got ahead of him."

[To the young man:] "Now you should take one of these other buffalos with you. The eldest one [is strong, but he] is not really fast. But the next oldest one is the fast one. He runs swiftly. Now you two will be the ones to go.

"Now when the two of you arrive close by the man's lodge, you'll twist the arrows that you have and stick them into the buffalo's fur where it is thick. This buffalo will tell you then what he's going to do."

Then this spotted buffalo [turned into a man, and he] and the young man came running. When they got close to the lodge, the one turned back into a buffalo—oh, one that was spotted! Then it said to the young man, "Stick the arrows that you have into my fur where it's heavy. I'll hemorrhage from my mouth. And you go up to the lodge and holler. Say, 'I've driven the buffalo here that you wanted. I found it. And now I don't have any arrows. Perhaps you can help somehow. Maybe you can do something.' As soon as he comes hurrying out and gets close, I'm going to hook him with my horns."

So that is what this young man did. Then the two of them came on. Ah, then this buffalo was staggering around as they went up to the lodge! Then the young man began calling out, "Hey, what are you doing? You must hurry out to help me! Here's what you wanted! I have no more arrows!"

Then this man rushed out of the lodge. Then he was laughing when he looked at the spotted buffalo. [He went back inside and] then brought his arrows out. Then he went close to the buffalo, which knelt on its forelegs. It appeared to be dying.

When that man came up close to it, the buffalo jumped up and knocked him down. Then it began goring him. Then it hooked him in the stomach. It yanked his arms off and then his legs. It tore out all his intestines.

<Then the young woman and her mother came outside. They began helping the young man.>

Then the buffalo said, "Now quickly burn him! Now let those two wolves go quickly! Let them run off!"

Then the wolves went off running. They had been captives.

"And now I'll go on since I have a long distance to travel. Now burn the ground where his blood is! If you don't burn all his blood, he'll come back to life. He won't be good then. He won't be afraid of us. Now do everything I have told you!"

Then this buffalo departed quickly. Then it ran off.

Then these people burned the man's body, oh, after the young woman his wife and the old woman his mother-in-law piled up wood. Oh, they burned him! They burned everything up where he lay after he had been gored to death—they burned his intestines and everything.

"Now let things here be as they are!"

Then the young woman and her mother took the various robes and things they wore, and then they all returned to where our villages were.

Then the people said, "They've come!"

Then the young man said, "We've done away with that man. Here this is what he was doing! He did away with the young men, killing them. He was the one mistreating them."

This woman [who had been his wife] said, "Oh, poor me, I was a slave. He kept us as slaves. He said, 'If you don't do as I tell you, these two wolves will eat you up.' Now that's the reason we were living there doing what he told us to do."

Comparative references: ARAPAHO Dorsey and Kroeber 1903:294-98; CHEYENNE Kroeber 1900:177-79; CROW Lowie 1918:149-51; GROS VENTRE Kroeber 1907: 88-90; HIDATSA Beckwith 1937:79-80.

15

The Young Man Who Became a Snake and

Carries The Antelope

ALFRED MORSETTE, SR.

This narrative is a conjoining of two stories now common to the Arikaras, Hidatsas, and Mandans as well as many other Plains tribes. In the first story a young man breaks a cultural taboo against eating snake flesh and subsequently becomes a snake himself. A companion puts him in the Missouri River, where he stretches from Eagle Nose Butte to the Killdeer Mountains. Herein is the explanation for why hunting parties made offerings to this snake in order to cross the Missouri safely. This story has a ritual significance for Hidatsas not found among Arikaras (Bowers 1965:359–60).

The second story is an account of supernatural powers bestowed on Carries The Antelope, a young man so named in recognition of his hunting prowess and habit of carrying antelopes into the village on his back. After thunderbirds take him up onto one of the Thunder Buttes, he saves their children by killing a gigantic two-headed snake in the water below. In gratitude the thunderbirds give him their powers and he becomes a bird himself. But the snake in the Missouri River from the previous story takes from him all his bird ways except the powers to flash lightning from his eyes and to control rainfall. Reputedly of Hidatsa origin, this myth exemplifies the widespread motif of cosmic conflict between thunderbirds and underwater beings. For Hidatsas it explains certain rituals as well as the origin of their Low Cap clan (Bowers 1965:360–62). It has no ritual significance for Arikaras.

Now I am going to relate an old story that they used to tell—what I used to hear about things that happened when we were migrating upriver. I do not know where the village was when this story occurred. I do not know where it was.

Two young men went out hunting and were going all over hunting for game. They say that after they had hunted, they started for home. They had not found anything. Now they were hungry as they were coming back.

Then they came to a certain place where there had been a prairie fire. The land was burned off. And there lay a snake. It stretched a long way. Its body was high.

"Now, say, let's go around it over there where its head is."

But they could not reach the end of it.

Now they went along the side of it. Then they walked the other way toward the end of its tail. <They were going and going. But there was no end to it.>

Then one said, "I'm tired. Also I'm hungry. Let's stay here overnight! And in the morning we'll go looking for our people."

And then the other boy said, "Say, surely I'm starving to death. It sure smells good. I'm hungry. This one is a fish. It smells like a fish does when it's cooked. Why, I'll eat it."

Then he cut it. Then he sliced the meat. Then he began to eat the snake meat.

But his friend said, "We certainly don't eat snake. Why, even if we're hungry, what you have done is not good."

"Hey, I'm truly starving," he said as he ate.

Now they lay down to sleep. One lay on one side of the fire and the other lay on the other side of it.

Now when it was morning the young man got up. His feet were spotted all over, and his hands were also spotted all over.

Then the other young man said, "Now, look! After I told you not to do it, after I didn't want you to eat the snake, this is what has happened to you."

"Hey, it's certainly nice. When we reach our village and I roll my leggings up, my legs will be spotted when I go around the village. The young women will admire me when they see my spotted hands."

Then as they were coming along, the young man said, "Say, I'm tired." He felt heavy as he came.

Then he said, "Let's stay overnight here!"

Then they lay down to sleep again. The one could not do anything when he was becoming spotted. The other one was the one who was now making their fires.

"Surely I told you not to do it—that you should not eat the snake. You didn't listen to me. Now look! What has happened to you is not good."

Then they came on again. Then the young man became worse. His entire body was spotted that way. Now his legs were barely able to step forward. Then they stayed overnight again. Wherever they had gone, it must have been far off.

Now in the morning the young man said, "Now, brother, I can't get up. I am whole: I don't have any legs; I also don't have any arms. Only my head remains separate. But I want to tell you, don't be afraid of me. You must drag me close to the edge of the Missouri River. Lay my head facing there to the east. And the end of my tail will be there by the Killdeer Mountains, and my head will be there at Eagle Nose Butte.[7]

"Now you people will be coming across the river to this side. Whenever you come to cross the river, you must give me a corn ball. And then I'll

7. This hill is located on the west side of the Missouri River, south of the present city of Mandan, North Dakota (see map 1).

surface and make a bridge for you, and then you'll cross on top of me. But you must give me a corn ball; and then all of you will cross. Also when you come from the other way, you should do the same thing.

"Now I am half Mandan and half Hidatsa. Now I want you to do this for me. Whatever you ask of me will come to pass."

Now this young man cried as he mourned for his friend while dragging him. He dragged him to the edge of the water. "Now this is what you said, brother." Then he rolled him into the water. The young snake man went into the water.

Then the young man came up the bank and returned home.

Then he told the people about it: "This is what happened. My brother became a snake, a water monster. He ate snake flesh. I warned him against it. He didn't listen. This is the way it was. Now he has disappeared. He is no more.

"But this is what he said: 'When you people cross the river, give me corn balls, and I'll take you across. Corn balls are what I liked the taste of when I was living among you.'"

《 《 《   》 》 》

Now here is where the story of Carries The Antelope commences. This young man must have been one who had good fortune whenever he went hunting, whenever he hunted for various things.

And one time he was led farther west, over there to the area around what we now call Mandaree.[8] That is the place there. A tall hill was there—the hill that was there.[9] That is where Carries The Antelope stopped to camp overnight. Then Carries The Antelope made a fire. "I'll stay overnight here, and then I'll begin to hunt." He spent the night there.

Then it became daylight, and when he awoke he was in a different place. When he sat upright, here he discovered that he had been carried up to the top of a butte by thunderbirds!

There they were, two of them. Here they were young ones! When they looked around, lightning flashed. And when they flapped their wings, sparks flew out from under the wings while he watched them.

8. A community established in 1955 in the Western Segment of the Fort Berthold Reservation after construction of the Garrison Dam. Many residents of Elbowoods, which was flooded by the dam, settled here.

9. It is generally identified as one of the Thunder Buttes west of the Missouri River southwest of Sanish, North Dakota (see map 4).

Plate 16. Thunder Buttes, McKenzie County, North Dakota. Photograph from the early twentieth century, courtesy State Historical Society of North Dakota.

"Ah, I wonder what happened for me to be lying here on top of this butte."

And then one young thunderbird said, "Now!" Then the rain came. Then drops of rain fell while it thundered.

Then one—here it was a young male—said, "My father has given me permission to tell you that you won't die. You'll go back to your village.

"But this is the reason you were brought here where we are living. My father here has been saying, 'We're depending on you. Nothing is going to be difficult for you as you go around, as you kill different things when you're hunting. Now we're depending on you. That's the reason we brought you here where you are now.'

"Now that's my sister there. She's a young female and I'm a young male. Now my mother and my father and my uncle are all coming. They're coming here to see you where we are now.

"Now whenever it's time for us to leave the nest and begin flying, our downy feathers drop on the water of the lake down below to the west. There's a snake in the water. It has two heads. One comes up over there in the west, and the other comes up over there in the east. There are two of them. Then the one here eats us up <just when we are big enough to provide good meat>. I don't know how many times this has happened.

"Now this is the reason that you have come here—that our parents brought you here. Now you are going to kill this snake. Now if it does happen that you do this, you're going to have done a thankful thing. The powers will look favorably upon you.

"Now this is what is going to happen. We'll prepare you. Our parents will give you two arrows which you're going to use."

Then it got dark again while he waited. Then it was morning and it rained again as it thundered.

Then the thunderbird boy talked; he said, "Come closer! Now I'm going to tell you."

Then this man sat down by him.

"Here are the two arrows that you're going to use." Oh, they were sharp arrows! "These are the ones you're going to use. Now everything is ready. Early in the morning, when it begins to dawn, it's usually foggy. My father says, 'The air is not clear.' But now you're going to watch over there in the east: that is the place. There is where the first one comes up. When the head comes up, it's a really large one. Right underneath its jaw, below the base of the throat, there is a black spot. That is where you are to shoot it.

"And when the other head comes up, you should do the same thing.

"Meanwhile we are going to help you. The other thunderbirds up above will weaken the snake by shooting bolts of lightning. And then you'll shoot the arrow accurately."

And then this young man got ready. Then he strung the bow. Now he sat beside a stone by the ledge, on the side where it usually came up.

Then the <big yellow> head appeared where the thunderbird boy had said. Now it opened its mouth as it went angrily at the two young thunderbirds. The young man shot it where he had been told. The arrow went straight to that spot. The arrow disappeared.

Then the head fell back. Then it made thumping sounds as it rolled down the side of the cliff.

Then the young man went over there to the west side. Now the head came up there. He did the same thing again: he felled this head, too, while the thunderbirds above were also hurling lightning bolts at it.

Then, after it rained, the sky became clear. Then the sun came out. There it lay on the prairie in the distance: there was a long body; there were two heads.

Now the thunderbird boy said, "My sister and I are going to take you. You'll hang onto us and we'll take you to the base of the hill. Now you are to butcher the thing lying there, cut it up, and spread its flesh around. Now birds from all over this earth are going to come and eat it. They're going to eat a meal.

"Now my father, my mother, my uncle, my grandmother, and my grandfather are going to talk to you. Now grab onto us. Our wings are close together."

Then they brought him to the base of the hill. They set his feet on the ground. Meanwhile the relatives of the thunderbird boy and girl flew down. They swooped low. After he was set down by them, this young man Carries The Antelope butchered the snake. Oh, he cut up chunks of meat and then laid them on the prairie. Then, oh, all different kinds of birds flew down here and there. Then they ate.

It clouded up again. Then he saw them. There lay what they call flat wood, paddles to whip things as when lightning strikes. One strikes [an enemy, for example] with it, and then one has done something. Then one has performed a great deed. These were the ones.[10]

Then the thunderbird boy said, "Now there are seven of them. Now all of them are new except the last one, which is old. You'll take that one. You'll use that one! That one is really the strongest one. It's already old. It's been there a long time. They've had it a long time. Those others are all new. They aren't really strong. They aren't as swift."

---

10. "Flat wood" designates a paddle-shaped coup stick, approximately two and a half feet long. Such sticks were attached to the outer part of village sacred bundles.

Well, then he asked, "Do you want to return to your village or would you rather be among us here? We want you to come be among us for a while. Now there remains one more thing that we want you to kill for us. It's there in the water. Its tail is here close by, but its head is far off down the river. Now you should attack it at its head! Kill it for us, too! Oh, we'll be thankful if you do that for us. Then you can go to your village. We'll take you.

"Now things won't be difficult for you whenever you want to go against the enemy. You'll have the powers to get everything you want, no matter what the powers may be."

Now when the rain came the young man and the thunderbirds flew over the valley yonder as they were looking for the water monster lying in the river—the one who had been put into the river after he ate the snake meat that I told about previously.[11]

But the one lying there in the river knew what was happening when it was being spied upon by Carries The Antelope. It knew it. Then the one there in the river surfaced. It thought, "Approach close to me! Then I'll grab you." Then that is what it did when the water always rose—when the water rose and got deep. That is how it was when the water rose.

And then Carries The Antelope, as he was flying overhead and looking all around watching for it, saw it. There its head was, close to the river bank. Then he landed. Meantime the thunderbirds were flying around in circles, watching Carries The Antelope. He landed and lurked about, wanting to trick it.

But the one in the river was watching Carries The Antelope. When Carries The Antelope went toward it, it smacked him with its tail. It snagged him in the mouth. It took him underwater. Ah, the ones up above were shooting lightning bolts at it as he was taken underwater.

Now the snake there under the water was the young man who had previously eaten the snake meat. And then he said, "Now, brother, you have done wrong to lurk about, looking for me. I know what you have done. You are holy, and I am that way, too: I am holy. Now I have overcome you by catching you. Now I beseech you: let things be as they are! Don't do this again! Now I'm going to take your powers away from you."

Then the two of them went into a sweat lodge. Then the snake man began making this Carries The Antelope vomit things up—whatever his powers were, whatever the powers were that he possessed. Then he changed him.

---

11. Carries The Antelope has now been transformed into a thunderbird, one of the powers conferred on him.

Then the snake man said, "Now you are going to go to our village. Now don't do it again! I'll know. Things won't be difficult for you. But now I have deprived you. But there remains one thing that is too difficult for me to do: you still have the power to shoot lightning bolts with your vision, of having lightning in your eyes when you look around. But I'll give you the power of shed buffalo hair. You'll tie it over your forehead, and it won't lightning when you look around.

"Now go back to our village!"

Then he brought him to the surface and doctored him. And then Carries The Antelope went. He returned home to his village, wherever the Hidatsa, Mandan, and our own Arikara villages were.

Now that is what that man used to be able to do. Whenever he looked around, his eyes flashed lightning. And that shed buffalo hair is what he had tied on his forehead. Now people feared him. Whatever he said would happen always happened. And when there was no rain, the people filled a pipe when they wanted rain to moisten the gardens. Then he would do it: he called the rain, and then it rained.

Now the people took good care of him. He was accorded high social status. Things were not difficult for him: he had the power for success in stealing horses and hunting for the enemy. It was natural for him to be a leader, to be a chief. Now Carries The Antelope was the one, the one I have told you about.

When they used to tell this story, they would not tell it in the summer when the thunder was coming.

It is not known where this man went after he died. He said, "Now I'm dying. But I'm going to be coming back to do what I'm supposed to do. Remember to give me the pipe sometimes. Oh, I'll be thankful <and give you rain>. Offer me the pipe <when you want it to rain>!" Now that is what the old people used to do when there were spirits around.

Now today we do not have those powers. We are negligent. I know a little of what they used to tell me. I usually do what I should and He[12] always grants me what I beseech of Him, what I want.

Comparative references: ARAPAHO Dorsey and Kroeber 1903:145–46, 150–51; Voth 1912:47–48; ARIKARA Parks 1991, 4:605–7, 620–23, 711–14, 731–33; G. A. Dorsey 1904a:73–78; ASSINIBOINE Lowie 1909:181–83; CHEYENNE Grinnell 1923, 2:97;

---

12. The Chief Above *(neešaánu' t^{i}načitákUx)*.

1926:154–57; CROW Lowie 1918:144–49, cf. 152–56, 169–71, 214–16; Simms 1903: 295–97; GROS VENTRE Kroeber 1907:115–16; HIDATSA Beckwith 1937:92–95; Bowers 1965:360–62; Maximilian 1843, 2:380–82; KIOWA APACHE McAllister 1949:101–4; MANDAN Bowers 1950:198–200; Maximilian 1843, 2:338–39; PAWNEE G. A. Dorsey 1904b:57–59, 167–68, 293–94; Grinnell 1889:171–81; PONCA J. O. Dorsey 1890:317–23; SIOUX Beckwith 1930:417–18; Deloria 1932:235–38; McLaughlin 1916:23–28; WICHITA Curtis 1907–30, 19:104.

16

Mice Mouth, the Boy Blessed by the Mice

ALFRED MORSETTE, SR.

The Arikaras, like surrounding tribes, saw the mouse as a potential source of power, particularly the ability to slip furtively and quickly into and out of difficult situations. A historical observer of this attitude toward mice was the fur trader Henry A. Boller, who recounted that in 1858 Sioux visitors at Fort Berthold were so troubled by the many mice running over them at night "they got up, lit their pipes, and declared they could not sleep because the mice were Great Spirits" (1959:171–72). The following story tells of a young man rewarded with their power after he saves a mouse couple's children. Like many such legends, this one is also a narrative about the abuse of power; the recipient uses it for evil and the people are ultimately driven to put him to death.

They used to call this river the Heart River. That is where the villages once were when our people were migrating this way from down below in the south, they used to say. Now it is not known how long they lived there after coming to its banks, but they stayed a long time.

Then there were no deer in the vicinity of the villages, after they became scarce because of so many boys going around hunting.

Well, then the chiefs, the ones who made the rules, said, "Surely it's difficult here. Let's move farther on to where there is game! Let's go there!"

It was some time in the spring, when the weather usually gets warm. Then the people moved off. When they were migrating closer up this way, they came up onto the top of a ridge.

Now one young man had remained behind in the village, where he was going around among the lodges. "Later I'll go where the people have gone."

While he was going around he heard a woman crying inside an earth lodge. A woman was crying. This young man went there. Then he entered the lodge and there sat a woman crying.

And then the young man said, "Ah, what's the matter? Did they leave you behind? What happened that they left you?"

Then this woman said, "No. They didn't leave me. But they took my children, who are with the group that has gone. They took mine. They are the ones I'm crying for. Now is it possible for you to bring my children back?"

Then this one said, "I'll go. I'll do it. If it isn't too difficult, I'll do it."

Then the woman said, "Fine. The men who are in the lead have a white buffalo robe and in it are my children. Now is it possible for you to bring my children back?"

Then this one said, "I'll go. It's difficult, but I'll do it if they're willing to unfold the white buffalo robe." Inside it is where the medicines were kept. That must have been how they kept their medicine long, long ago. "I'll return if it isn't too difficult for me."

And then this young man came after them. He came up onto the hills there. Then the people were on top of one in the distance. Then he arrived where they were. They had turned the horses loose to graze. "It's far where we're going." <And the horses needed food and rest.>

Now this young man arrived there. Then he said, "You chiefs who are sitting here, I want you to unfold that robe. I want to see it. I want to pray to the medicines in it."

"Yes. Now do that!"

Then that is what he did. Then he untied it, and there were four mice. There were four mice lying there in it. Then he furtively took them up and put them under the robe he wore. Now he retied the medicine robe. Then he quickly left the group and went back to where he had been. He vanished all at once.

Before long he came quickly into the deserted village. And then he went to the lodge where the woman had been inside. Then he entered and there she sat. Also there sat a man. There were now two inside the lodge.

"Now here they are. Are they the ones?"

Then she said, "Yes. They're the ones. Oh, now we're so thankful to you. This is the one who is my husband. These are our children."

Now those two talked to the young man. "Now the ways of the warpath are not going to be difficult for you, nor will whatever you may want, no matter what it may be. You aren't going to have it hard."

Now the other one, the man, jumped up. He just flew against the young man on one side. On the young man's cheek there was now the image of a mouse. The other one, the woman, did the same thing on his other cheek.

"Now we're thankful to you. You aren't going to have it difficult. Whatever you want you'll find it. And you'll take it and you'll have it. <And when somebody talks about you, you're going to hear it. You'll know.>"

Well, then the young man came after them. Then he caught up with the people as they were moving on. And, wherever it was, they camped there. And the ways of the warpath—horse stealing and striking the enemy—were not hard for him. <His relatives were proud of him.> Perhaps he married. They never mentioned that matter.

Well, then he began to do bad things. He was a bad person when he was stealing the wives of other men. After some man would marry a woman, here he would steal her. Then he would elope with her. Then as he was doing these things, people began to dislike him.

And whenever a baby would cry, its mother would say, "Stop crying! Mice Mouth will come." When Mice Mouth discovered it, he would snatch the baby and bash its head on the ground. He killed it, just as he was killing many of them. His actions were evil.

Now there was one man who was violent. He was strong. He was confident of his strength. Then one day he said, "I've just been hoping that Mice Mouth and I might encounter one another and that I could work him over." That is what the man was saying.

That man went off somewhere one time. Then he began trapping. Now they used to dig a pit. It would be a deep pit in a trail habitually traveled by deer. <The pit was covered so that the trap could not be seen.> And then when a deer passed over it, it would fall into the pit, and then it would die after it was trapped inside. Now sometimes, too, a coyote or some other animal would fall into it and be killed.

That is what this man was doing: then he began digging a pit. While he was busy doing it, he looked up and there standing above was the man called Mice Mouth. He had an antelope skin cap over his head.

Then the man in the pit said, "Ah, you're the one I have been looking for. It's certainly good that you've found me here." Then the man got out. "Your actions—the things you're doing—are bad. You've hurt the feelings of many people in this village of our tribe. Now we're going to fight."

Then Mice Mouth said, "If it has to be that way, let it be. If you want it that way, we'll fight."

And then this man put his bow and arrows down. The other one put his bow and arrows down, too.

Now they fought there, each struggling with the other. Now when this man who had been trapping was pushed backward, he kicked Mice Mouth's bow and arrows away so that he could not snatch them up. And it was the same way with the other one: when Mice Mouth was pushed back, he did the same thing, kicking the man's bow and arrows away.

But after they had been struggling with one another for a while, they calmed down. Now neither one of them was beaten.

This man, after Mice Mouth caused his eyes to swell, was barely able to see. Then he went off. Then he went back toward the village. As he was going along he called out for someone to help him.

People came for him. "What's the matter?"

Then he said, "Mice Mouth and I found each other. He must be as strong as I am."

Then they took him into the village.

Now this Mice Mouth was tough. No one was able to do anything with him. Whenever they talked about him, why, he would hear it! "Now we'll spy on him. We'll kill him." Why, he would know it!

Now a group prepared to go on the warpath. "Let's go on the warpath!" Then they set out. There were many of them.

Now they always had corn balls made of ground corn flour. Oh, that is what the man Mice Mouth liked, ground corn flour. They had it.

As they were going along, they saw Mice Mouth. He was running by in the distance. Then he went into the water. There he crossed to the other side. It was a lake.

"There goes Mice Mouth."

Then they began to call him. He came running.

"Hey, it's certainly good to see you. You must just be wandering around."

Then he said, "Yes. Why, I usually just wander around. I don't live in your village anymore. You people don't like me." That is what he was saying.

"Now we've brought this for you. It's what you like to eat."

He was overjoyed when he ate it. Then he gulped a mouthful.

"Now!" Then they grabbed him and tickled him. Then he choked. He fell over unconscious. Then they killed him.

Then they went on, and after they had traveled around they started back for home. "Now let's go to where we killed Mice Mouth. Let's see if he's there yet."

Then they arrived there at the lake that he had gone into. But he was not lying there. The mice must have come. They must have picked him up. They must have hidden him.

Then the party came back home. After they returned, they said, "We killed Mice Mouth, who has been bothering us. We left his body. He was lying there. He was dead. But when we came back, we said, 'Let's go see him!' And then he wasn't lying there! We don't know what happened. We don't know where he went."

He had died. They had killed Mice Mouth. His actions—the things that he did—were not good. Then the people hated him.

Comparative references: ARIKARA Parks 1991, 4: 599-605, 657-60; G. A. Dorsey 1904a:80-83; CHEYENNE Grinnell 1926:138-41; PAWNEE G. A. Dorsey 1904b: 101-3.

17

The Young Woman Who Married an Elk

ALFRED MORSETTE, SR.

This story exemplifies the power of elk to charm women and to lure them from their husbands. At the same time it is a story of power bestowed on a man who makes himself pitiful—here the aggrieved husband mourning the loss of his wife—and who is given war and hunting powers that enable him to achieve chiefly status through successful exploits.

Now it is not known exactly where this story occurred, but it was when the people were migrating this way from the east. I do not know whether these people coming from the east were Hidatsas, Arikaras, or Mandans, but I do know the story of what happened.

Now after a young man married and he and his wife were living together, the young man's father told him, "It certainly would be good if you were to go out hunting, if you were to go on a hunt." That is what they used to say.

Then this couple—the young man and young woman who had recently married—got ready to go. Now they must not have had horses. But they had eight dogs.[1] Then they packed their gear on what they used to call a travois, which the dogs pulled. They had various things, all of them light in weight.

Then they set out toward the west. "Over the hill" is where they used to say it was—that is where they used to live.[2] Then they went west, over there where the land was wooded and where buffalo, elk, and antelope roamed, not where people lived.[3] Game must have liked the wooded country there.

Now this couple made camp where water was close by. Then they built what they used to call a hunting lodge[4] and picketed their dogs. And in the morning the young man would go out hunting, wandering off somewhere, and bring back a deer or antelope after he had killed one. When he would come back to the camp, the dogs would get up, happy to know that he was returning.

Shortly after he returned with meat, the young man and his wife would eat some of it after it was cooked. Then the young woman would begin drying the rest of the meat, and the young man would go off again.

The dogs watched. They watched over this couple. At night they were untied so that they could bark at coyotes coming up close to the camp.

Now finally the couple had a large supply of dried meat. Then the young woman told her husband, "I feel like going home now. We have been here a long time, and now there is plenty of dried meat."

Then the young man replied, "I think I'll get just a little more! Make some more dried meat, and then we'll go." Then the young man went off hunting. He wouldn't come back all day since he went far off searching for game.

So the young woman took one hide and staked it out. Now she was scraping it to take the hair off. They did not tell whether it was a deer or buffalo hide. Then the wind came up and brought a nice odor. Then the young woman began to look around.

1. In another version of this story, told in English, the narrator says that the couple had seven dogs.
2. The expression 'over the hill' is a reference to the Arikara village at Fort Clark, occupied by the tribe between 1838 and 1861. It is also used sometimes to refer to the former villages along the Missouri River south of Fort Clark, when the tribe lived farther downstream (see p. 81).
3. Here and in other Arikara stories the expression designating 'wooded country out west' refers to the badlands country of western North Dakota.
4. This lodge, termed *akanaanuútu'*, was a conical shelter built on a foundation of four forked poles covered first with branches, then with a layer of grass, and finally with earth. The semipermanent earth-covered lodge was built by a hunting party when it planned to be camped in one place for an extended period. (See Wilson 1934:411–15.)

There in the distance stood a young man. She looked at him, but did not know him. Oh, there was a nice odor brought by the wind.

Then the young woman picked up her things and went into the lodge. After a while she came out. He was not there. He must have gone.

Now the dogs began to growl when they saw the strange young man. Now the young man kept doing this, coming to the spot for however many times it was.

That night the young woman told her husband, "I want us to go home. I don't like it: I've been seeing a strange person. He might be an enemy. Maybe he'll kill me or make me a slave."

Then the young man replied, "There certainly is no one around here. I certainly know the country here, and no one is around. But now we'll go home. I think I'll just go out once more! Let me go hunting once more and then tomorrow we'll go back home." It was the next day that they planned to return home, and when the young man left to go hunting again for the last time, he said, "Now we'll truly go home."

Later the strange young man whom the young woman had been seeing came to the door of the lodge. Then he said, "I've come after you. Hurry! Let's go!"

Then the young woman jumped up. He must have mesmerized her [with medicine]. Then she began to follow him. The dogs meanwhile were growling. Then he took her off, eloping with her. Then the two went off, with her following him.

Later the husband of the young woman returned to their camp, and when he looked for his wife, she was not there. There lay the things that she had been sewing, or whatever she had been doing. The dogs were whining.

Then the young man said, "You dogs are holy. Now tell me where she went!"

Then he untied them. Then the dogs jumped up and followed the trail of the young woman and the strange young man.

The husband went up onto a high hill, and there in the distance went the two, the strange young man and the young woman who was his wife.

Then he told the dogs, "Now go home from here! I don't know what I'm going to do, but I might bring her back."

Then the dogs stopped, but the young man went on in pursuit. He caught up with the couple. Then he got ahead of them. And here to his surprise it was an elk!

Then he thought, "I'll shoot it." But when he shot at it, the arrow glanced off. It did not penetrate the hide. It would not pierce it.

222 Myths and Traditions of the Arikara Indians

He followed and followed the couple, shooting at the elk until he used up all his arrows. Then the couple went up a hill. There was a valley below, and in it was a lake. That was where they were headed.

Now no matter what the young man did, when he approached his wife she paid no attention to him. She followed the one ahead of her, and here it was an elk!

Then the elk went into the water. Then the young woman went into the water, too. They both went underwater.

Then the young man [who was her husband] cried and cried while he was at the edge of the water. Oh, then it became dark.

Just before morning the young woman came to the surface. Then she said, "You must go home now. We can't be together again. It's difficult where I live now. And now you must go! When I was anxious for us to go home, you didn't heed me. Now what I didn't want to happen has happened. And you yourself are the cause. Now go!

"But if there is anything that you want—good fortune on the warpath or in hunting—you should come right here. You should tell us what you want.

"Now after winter has passed and the weather begins to get warm, bring me a dress, a belt, and a pair of moccasins. You'll lay them here. Bring them for me!

"Now you are going to marry another young woman. She will look just like I do. It isn't going to be a long time off.

"Now go! Make haste! Go!"

Then the young man hastened to go back to gather his things. Then he returned to their camp. He arrived back at their camp. He gathered everything up. The dogs were there, and then he loaded the gear onto them and led them back.

He arrived there, wherever our village was, wherever it was. Then he arrived at night. He entered the lodge. Then he lay down to sleep. Everyone was already sleeping. No one knew when he returned.

In the morning when his father, mother, and sisters arose, there the young man lay.

"All of you get up quickly! Look! Here's a pile of dried meat. He must have brought it. Our daughter-in-law must have gone somewhere else. She must have gone to her mother's lodge." That is what they were each saying.

Then the young man arose. Then he said, "The daughter-in-law you're looking for is not here. This is what happened. She and another eloped. An elk is the cause, when he took my woman. And then this is what she said to me: 'You yourself are the cause.' She had wanted us to hurry back home, but I didn't do it. My hunting delayed me. I was having no difficulty in killing all kinds of game. I liked that. I was enjoying it.

"Now that's what happened. She lives there now. She lives in the water there where the hills are clustered." He told them the place. "That's where she is living.

"And this is what she said: 'Bring me a dress, a pair of moccasins, and a belt. After the weather usually gets warm, when it usually gets hot, that will be the time.

"'But now you will marry another woman. She will look just like I do. It isn't going to be a long time off.'"

Now it happened that way: then he and a young woman began living together. She looked like his former wife.

Now after the weather usually gets warm, after the earth usually gets warm and the green grass comes up, when it was hot, the young man led a party on the warpath, and he took a dress, a pair of moccasins, and a belt, just as his former wife had said. They went on, and then they arrived right there near the lake.

Then the young man left the party. "And now I'll go off for a while. I'll look all around." Then he went over to where the lake was.

Then he said, "Here are the things you asked for."

Then she surfaced. Then she said, "You have pleased me. And now, what you have wished for will happen. Nothing is going to be difficult for you. Whatever you seek you will find."

Well, then this young woman went underwater, and the young man went back to where his companions were.

Now he subsequently did as she had said, counting many coups on the enemy. Then he became a chief. After he had everything—after he and his father had many horses—he began to own the village.[5]

Now this is where it was. This is what happened. I do not know whether the story belongs to the Arikaras, or Hidatsas, or Mandans. I never found out.

Comparative reference: ARIKARA G. A. Dorsey 1904a:127-28.

5. The expression 'to own the village' means to be its chief and have social and political control of it.

18

The Young Man Who Was
Given Elk Power

ALFRED MORSETTE, SR.

Several themes are combined in this story. Two of the most common are the abduction of a young woman by an animal and the ability of animals and humans to transform themselves into one another. Here a bear assumes human form and mesmerizes a young woman whom he takes away. While mourning the loss, her husband is pitied by the spirit of a dead elk, which endows him with the power to transform himself into that animal, known for its strength and virility. It also instructs him how to charm women with a whistle that imitates the call of an elk, illustrating once again the elk's sexual power over women. The drama culminates in a test of strength among the three most ferocious animals: the bear pitted against the young elk man and his brother, who has the power to transform himself into a young buffalo bull.

Now I am going to tell a story. This one that I will tell is a true story.

Now a young man got married to a young woman after they had been going together.

"Now let's go on a hunting trip out west!"

I don't know where the village was.

Now they gathered their gear together. They had dogs to carry their belongings. And then they went off.

Oh, then they camped somewhere in wooded country. They had a lodge, either a wall tent or a tipi, whichever kind of lodge it was.

And then the young man would go out hunting and bring back deer, buffalo, or antelope, and the young woman would make dried meat and also tan the hides, while they were preparing for winter. That is what they used to say one did in the fall.

Now one day while the young woman was in their lodge, a man just came up to it. Then he said, "Now come! I've come after you."

This young woman just sat there. Whatever it was that he did, the man made her forget everything.[1] Then she followed him. They went off, wherever it was that they went.

There were three dogs there. They were growling angrily. They were tied up.

And then the young man came back to the camp late in the afternoon. He brought back meat, but his wife was not there.

"I wonder where she is? Maybe she went after wood." As he was looking all around, he thought, "Maybe she went after water." She was nowhere around.

Then he untied the dogs. "What is it? Where did the one who looks after us go?"

Now those dogs were whining. They headed over there toward the west. When they got to the edge of the woods, they stopped.

Then this young man said, "Now I know. Now here's the way she went!"

Then the young man took the dogs back and tied them up, and then he went all around, crying as he looked in vain for his wife.

While he was searching around, there lay something on the ground! It was the remains of an elk that had apparently been there a long time. Its bones were there. Its bones were there. The skull was there with the horns still on it.

Then he thought, "They always say, 'Elk, you are holy.' Perhaps you might pity me."

Then he began crying out there where the elk's bones lay, going around them and crying.

Oh, finally he was satisfied. Then he lay down and slept.

A man touched him. "Now, I've come to tell you. I know what you are seeking. You're seeking your wife. Your wife is not lost. This is what he's been doing. Why, now he's overstepped his limits. A black bear is the one. He took your woman. But he hasn't laid a hand on her yet. He's the one responsible for taking her away. He lives over there. His den is far away. This is what he's been doing. He has a large number of women whom he has taken.

"Now tomorrow gather up some provisions! But make your pack light for yourself! In the meantime, go! Go home! When you get there, you should ask your father to make you an elk whistle, one that imitates the sound of an elk. Your father knows how. It'll take two days.

"After four days have passed, you'll come with your brother. Your brother is exceedingly powerful. You'll come with him.

---

1. That is, he mesmerized her.

"Oh, the one who has your woman is extremely holy. But we are going to help you, too.

"Now do these things quickly! Hurry!"

Then this young man started out. Then he went back to his lodge. Then he untied the dogs. He packed some moccasins. Then he came on. Then he arrived at the village after dark.

Then he lay down to sleep. While he lay there, it became daylight.

When his father arose he said to his mother, "Get up now! Our son has come back. Our daughter-in-law isn't with him."

And then this woman, his mother, got up. She began cooking.

The young man was awakened by them.

"Why, hello! What's the matter?"

He replied, "Well, this is what happened. A bear stole my woman. This is what happened.

"Now, father, hurry! Make me an elk whistle! They call it a double whistle, don't they?"

That one, the father, began making it.

Later he said, "My son, I have finished. Here it is. Oh, it sure has a good sound."

"Now my brother and I are going to go."

Then his brother said, "Yes, we'll go. My brother and I will go. We'll go looking for her, wherever she is."

And then they went off; these two brothers, who were still young men, went off.

Then they arrived where the camp was. Everything was the same as it had been. Then they began cooking dried meat over the fire.

Then this young man started to leave. He said, "Brother, let me go for a while to the elk there in the woods!"

Then he went. Then he arrived there and cried all night. When dawn came, there sat the elk spirit in the form of a man.

Then he said, "What you have done is certainly good. There's nothing preventing us now. It's good that your brother has come, and that you are together. Now, it isn't going to be difficult.

"You and your brother are going to go. You'll go to the west this way! There will be a creek on level ground, where the land is nice. You'll tell your brother to wait for you there in a coulee. Then you'll go on, into the middle of that country, and then you'll blow your whistle. It's a wooded area there. You'll blow the whistle. You'll do it again. Blow it three times! Then after the last time, the fourth one, you'll go to the edge of a creek where she is, where the den is in the woods.

"Now the young women will come out. Your wife will be in the lead when they come. Then you and she will come here. But you'll tell the others to go to their villages.

"Meanwhile that bear is going to come. He's going to chase after you. Oh, your wife is the one he's after! That one is his favorite.

"Now you two come! Hurry to where your brother is, where he's waiting for you! Both of you are going to fight the black bear."

Then the young man went back to his camp. Then he told his brother, "Now come! We're going to look for my wife now."

And so they went there, wherever it was, wherever the creek went through the level land.

Then the young man said, "Now, brother, you stay here for a while! Let me look!"

Then he went on. And now he had the elk whistle, just like the elk had said. He blew on it. Oh, he did it again. Then he moved closer. He did that once again. As he moved closer, he blew on it a fourth time.

Within a short time the women and young women came running out of the woods. His wife was the one in the lead.

"Oh, I lost heart waiting for you. But you have finally come! Now back there in camp, my mind went blank. When I came to my senses, here I was, here!"

"Now quickly, let's go!"

Then he and his wife came back, running as they came. The young man looked back. There in the distance came the big black bear.

Meanwhile, the other young women had scattered, each one going in a different direction to her village.

But the black bear chased only this one, chasing after the couple.

Then the young man said, "Now go on ahead! Go on!"

While the young man and his wife were coming, the bear caught up with them. Oh, the bear was huge! He gained on them by jumping through the air.

Then they arrived where the young man's brother was.

Then he said to his wife, "Now quickly, go down the bank! Go down the bank! Now the bear and I are going to do it."

Then the young man swung around. They used to say that 'one flung himself down onto the ground.' Now when he flung himself down, he transformed himself. There stood an elk, after he had transformed himself. Oh, the elk was huge! The bear was that way, too: he was a gigantic bear.

[Then he and the bear went at each other.] When this elk lowered his horns, he pierced the bear's neck. Then he stuck his horns into the ground and went round and round, trying to extract them, while the bear was digging his claws into him. When he was scratching him, the bear tore some of his hide off as they fought and fought.

Then this elk jumped up. And then he threw the bear down onto the ground.

Now he was tiring. This elk who was a young man said, "Now brother, I'm tired." Then he went charging at the bear. Again he stuck his horns into the ground when he pierced the bear in his neck and pinned him down.

Then his brother said, "Now that's what I wanted you to say, what you just said." And then the other one flung himself onto the ground. Then he became a buffalo, what they call a calf. This one was a four-winter-old buffalo.

He ran into the bear. He gored his stomach. He continued going on, and there in the distance swung around. Then he came charging back. Then he began hooking him.

Then the bear said, "You two have at last beat me. Why, you're both exceedingly strong! I thought I would overcome you, but you've beat me. Well, now you've beat me. Take the woman! Ah, I prized that woman. But you've beat me. And you've killed me. It won't be long before I am dead. Now, all of you, go on!"

Then the young men brought the young woman back to the camp. They gathered things up and then returned home. They arrived there at the village.

Then they told about it: "This is what happened. A bear eloped with this woman. But these young men brought her back."

Now this is how the story goes. It is one my grandmother used to tell me. The story, as I told it, was told to me three times.

Comparative reference: ARIKARA G. A. Dorsey 1904a:84–90.

19

The Young Men and the Snapping Turtle

ALFRED MORSETTE, SR.

Another story widely distributed on the Plains tells of a party of young men who climb onto the back of a gigantic snapping turtle and, unable to get off, are taken underwater. This Arikara version illus-

trates the fate of skeptics who do not respect, and so do not fear, the
mysterious or holy. After the young men are taken underwater, where
they are henceforth destined to live, the lake becomes a holy site and
thus a source of potential power and good fortune for anyone who
prays and makes offerings there, just as it is for the boy in the
original party who out of respect refuses to join his companions and
later mourns them on its bank.

This story that I am telling, which occurred long, long ago, is what I heard from someone—one of the stories they used to tell. He told about a snapping turtle that was really big; it's not known how big around it was.

When a party was out going around on the warpath, however many there were in the party, they just did not find anything. Then they started back home. "Let's go home! We haven't found anything."

As they were returning, they came up a hill. The land was nice. There sat something. It resembled a rock; it was big and grayish white.

The party went up close to look at it; among them was a young man, as there always is someone in a group, who was a skeptic, one who does not believe in things.

And here this object was a gigantic snapping turtle! Then it moved around, and then it started off after it put out its arms. Here it had arms and legs. Then it went off.

Then the young men, however many there were, followed it. Then one [climbed onto it and] stood on top of it.

Then he said, "It's sure nice here. Come up on top!"

Then the others climbed on it, too, except for one who became frightened by it. He said, "Certainly this turtle is holy. You're going to do something to yourselves."

"Oh, what does he know! You should stand here on top. Anyway it's nice. It's carrying us."

It was moving while they stood on top. And here this thing was a turtle.

Meanwhile the young man went alongside it as it went on.

Now the turtle went a long distance after they got on top of it. Over there on the flat prairie was a lake there in the distance. It was a big lake. That is where the turtle was headed.

Now the lake got to be closer.

Then the young man going alongside the turtle said, "Now see what I was saying! It's headed toward the water!"

Then one young man started to get down, but then his foot was stuck. No matter what he did, when he tried to move his foot, his foot was stuck. Then it became impossible for the others, too, when they wanted to get off. Then it became impossible for them. The turtle had a hold on them.

Then this turtle went to the bank of the lake, and then it began to go into the water while the young men on it tried to jump off. They were not able to do it, however, and then it took them underwater while the other young man who had not got on top of it went along the bank there crying and crying into the night.

When morning came, one of the young men came to the surface.

Then he said, "Brother, go home now! We're unable to do anything to come up out of the water. It's holding us, and it's difficult where we are now. It's impossible to turn back again. It has taken us. But it's good for you: whenever you go on the warpath, come to this spot where we are in the water, and tell us whatever you want. Now we'll watch over you as you go around. Now do this! Go home! We can't turn back. And tell them in our village what has happened and that we ourselves are the cause of it. It's no one else's fault."

Well, then that young man who was talking—the one they had had as their leader—went underwater.

Then this young man came home. Then he returned to wherever our villages were.

Then he told about it: "This is what happened. Their feet got stuck to it when they stood on top of its back there. And when they tried to get off it, their feet were stuck to it. Now they live in the water. There's a lake there. It's a big lake there where I was together with my brothers [i.e., companions].

"Now this is what they told me: 'Whatever you desire, come here and tell us. Now it's difficult; we can't turn back.' Now this is what they said. And here I have come back alone."

"Now the lake where I used to go was holy."[2] And if one had anything to offer, he set it down as he prayed to them where they were in the water. And what happened afterward was good; they were granted whatever they desired.

Then our people migrated this way, closer toward this country here. Then they began to stop going there. Then this was the end of this tradition, [of going to the place where] the young men, however many there were, had stood on top of the turtle.

Comparative references: BLACKFOOT Josselin de Jong 1914:108; CHEYENNE Kroeber 1900:184; CROW Lowie 1918:220-22; Simms 1903:314-15; PAWNEE G. A. Dorsey 1904b:273-74, 1906a:426-27; SIOUX J. O. Dorsey 1889b:136; McLaughlin 1916:23-28.

2. Here the narrator is repeating the words of the person who told him this story.

20

Young Hawk and the Power He Lost

ALFRED MORSETTE, SR.

The theme of this story is how power, once given, can be with-
drawn if the recipient does not use it. The protagonist is once again
an indolent young man, upon whom a hawk mysteriously bestows the
power of fleetness. On his first and only war party, the young man
appears to be foolishly slow, then miraculously fast, vanishing only
to appear suddenly elsewhere, thereby securing the party's success.
Once back home, however, he reverts to his indolent habits and sub-
sequently the hawk takes his power away because he is content to be
lazy.

Now I will tell a story that I heard—what I used to hear when they told
stories. Maybe others heard it from the old men I used to listen to when they
told stories. There were many stories that have been lost.

Now the story I am going to tell is about a boy who was fourteen or
fifteen winters old when this occurred. He was not interested in anything: in
going along with a war party or even going hunting—not even in going
hunting. He was not interested in manly things. When the young men went
around, he was just silent when he was told, "This is what one does. This is the
way we men do things. You are becoming a man and you yourself should get
some power while you're growing up." But this boy didn't pay any attention.

Now one time something happened, whatever it was, and the boy said,
"I'll go on the warpath."
A party had already gone off.
"I'll follow behind."
His father said, "Now that is really good. Don't let them get the best of
you. Whatever they do, you do it, too."
<Then his father gave him a bow and arrows and a knife. But the boy
refused them. "Oh, I don't need them. They'll be in the way too much if I have
to carry them around.">
Then the war party left the village. After they had gone off, this boy went
off following them.

And as was his custom, he just wouldn't do anything. Whenever the party stopped, he would eat. He would sit there way off somewhere on the prairie. He would walk around on the prairie at a distance, looking all around. That is what he would do.

But, oh, this boy was fleet!

Then scouts were picked out. When the scouts went out early in the morning and were scouting around in advance, they saw something. Then it came toward them. When it came closer to them, they saw it was the boy. Then the scouts said, "Surely we left him behind in camp. He was still lying there in bed, a left-behind, when we came scouting."

This is also what he did again when they went out. The boy was sleeping when the scouts went out, when the four young men went out to go scouting and to look all around. And then someone was coming, coming toward them. And there it was he, that boy. They were bewildered when they saw him.

Now he said, "It's located close by. There's a big village here. Oh, it's a big village!"

Now that was what he told them, but these scouts did not see the village.

Then they came back to the camp.

One of them told the leader, "There's a big village here."

Now they did not know it for a fact. It is what this boy had told them.

Then this boy said, "There's a big village here. Oh, it's a big village! But these scouts didn't see it. They were lying when I heard them saying it here just now."

Then this boy said, "When you stop to camp, hurry if you wish to steal horses. Now, hurry!"

Then this boy suddenly vanished. They no longer saw him.

Then the party went on. They got up and went.

The village was close by.

Then the boy said, "There's the village there. Oh, it's a big village!"

Now they selected the horse stealers who were held in highest esteem. "He will be the one to pick out some horses."

Now they selected them. Now they were ready.

"Drive them here!" [they told the horse stealers.] "Then we'll help."

Then that boy said, "Now everything is ready. When you go [you don't have to go into the village]; there are horses close by over there [just outside the village]. Drive those horses here! Then we'll drive them off. When you two groups get together here, then we'll go on."

When the group drove the horses off, oh, there were many of them! They herded them together to where the rest of the party waited for them and then each caught a nice-looking horse to ride.

Then one of the men asked the boy, "Aren't you going to ride one yourself?"

Then the boy said, "No. <I'll go on foot. I don't know how to ride.> You all go on quickly! Go over there to the west! Don't go north! Go over there to the west! They're going to chase us. There will be a lot of them when they come."

The party ran the horses off.

As the party was coming along, it began to get light.

Then this boy said, "There's a lake over there. It's a big lake. Scatter the horses in among the bulrushes! The bulrushes are tall. The horses will be hidden in among them. The enemy will come, but I'll lead them in another direction."

Now they stared at him.

Now there was the lake. Oh, it was a big lake! That is where they drove the horses. They drove the horses down into the bulrushes along the shore. The men sat down in different places there among the plants.

Then, on the ground there was the sound of the enemy coming. Oh, when they were going around on the land above the lake, they did not see anything. But those men were there among the bulrushes.

Then there were two riders coming toward a rock, and by it is where this boy sat. Then the two Sioux came up to this rock while they were talking and making signs. Meanwhile the boy sat behind the rock and watched their faces. They did not see him.

They moved off. The two of them went over there in another direction. The boy waited. As soon as it became dark [he jumped up and called to the party], "Now drive the horses off quickly! They are still chasing us. They'll catch up with us."

The men came out. They drove the horses out as they came.

Before long it was getting light, and the enemy was overtaking them.

Then the boy said, "Hurry! Whip the horses!"

Then that boy was coming in the rear. His horse was trotting along.

Then those Sioux who were coming up hollered, "Hey, we're going to kill that one. He must not know how to ride." That is what they were saying.

Meanwhile the party whipped those horses as they were running.

And then the boy rode over there in another direction on the prairie. He was looking back repeatedly.

Then the enemy was chasing after him and shooting at him. They could not wound him as they pursued him.

Then he rode down the hill while those riders pursuing him were on top. There in the distance on the other side of the creek valley, there he went up the hillside.

Once again they ran after him. Now when they were about to overtake him, he rode down the hill and disappeared.

"He must surely be around here. When he goes up the hill there, we'll run him down."

There, on the hill on the other side of the coulee, there in the distance, he went up and over it again.

Finally the horses the Sioux rode became tired. "Ah, something is strange. He certainly must be extraordinarily fast!" Then they turned around.

Meanwhile the party with the horses ran on with them.

Then the Sioux gave up. Then they turned back.

As the party with the horses came, there was a tree line. They drove the horses into the woods.

And then they said, "Ah, they must have killed the boy, the poor thing. He shouldn't have gone that other way. He went over there, poor thing, and they must have run him down. They must have killed him."

Then suddenly the boy came out of the brush.

"They were running me down, but they tired their horses out."

Then they fed him.

Then he said, "While I'm eating, you fellows will go on. You'll go on quickly. You'll run at the same speed when you're going in the morning. But I'll come on later, as soon as I've eaten."

Well, then the party mounted their horses. Then they whipped them.

But this boy was still eating. He ate everything. Then he came on. He arrived back at the village first. But the ones who were driving the horses were still coming.

The boy entered his lodge. He lay down on his bed.

Then his mother said, "Hey, old man, someone has entered. He's entered. He's gone over there to the boy's bed. Make a fire to see who it is!"

"Ha, poor thing, he must be tired. They don't know how to go out on the warpath. Maybe our boy is tired."

Then the old man made a fire.

Ah, there lay the boy, lying on his bed.

"Hey! Here you've come back! Now what happened?"

Then the boy said, "The party is bringing some horses, but I came on ahead. They'll arrive here. They're bringing horses."

"Don't you have any?"

Well, later Young Hawk said, "Now this is what happened to me. That's what happened to me. I myself am the cause." That is what he used to tell.

This is a Pawnee story. It is not one of our Arikara stories.
Now this boy never did have good fortune again. He never married; and then many years later he died of old age.

21

The Origin of the Arikara
Crazy Dog Society

ALFRED MORSETTE, SR.

A popular organization among young Arikara and Hidatsa men was the Crazy Dog Society, notable during the past century of reservation life for its Doorway songs. Groups of young men would go from door to door in the village or camp serenading young women with these songs, whose lyrics told of love. The origin of the Arikara society is recounted here. Its source was an animal lodge of dogs said to be located at Dog Den Butte in McLean County, North Dakota. The society derived from a dog chief's son who married a human being.

Now I am going to tell another story that I used to hear. It occurred when our villages were there in the country to the east. It occurred in the winter, in the winter when it is very cold, in midwinter.

There was a village and in it was a family that had a young daughter. They loved her. She never went anywhere, but just remained at home, where she was always sewing.

At night when the family was ready to go to bed, when they said, "Let's all go to bed," after they had piled up the wood they would burn during the night, a dog would come into the lodge. Oh, it had the mange. The dog was ugly. And it sat on top of the young woman's bed. In the morning they opened the door, and then they whipped it as they drove it out. It was doing that for some time, however long it was.

Then the young woman became pregnant. Then she was going to have the baby. It was getting to be the time to have it.

Then her family asked her, "Oh, were you talking with anyone?"[1]

Then she said, "No. I don't know why I'm this way, pregnant as I am." She was telling about herself, "I know that I didn't talk to anyone."

And when summer usually begins, when the ground gets warm, the young woman began to have pains, and then she bore puppies. There were four of them. Oh, they were cute, and they were spotted.

Now her mother said to her brother who was ten winters old, a boy of ten winters, "Ah, throw these dogs away! Let them freeze over there! Why do they ridicule her?" That is what the mother of the young woman was asking over and over.

Then the boy picked the dogs up; then he took them out. When he was taking them, he took a liking to two of them. Oh, they were spotted. He wanted to keep them.

Then he fixed a place and put the two puppies inside it. And the ugly dog—the one that was their father—would be inside keeping them warm.

In the morning the boy would gather together scraps of food and leftover soup from the family's meals. Then he sneaked them outside. And here he was going there to feed the puppies.

Then, after winter, it became summer—when it becomes summer, when the green grass comes up. This young woman thought, "I wonder what my brother is doing when he takes the meat and other leftovers outside? Where is he taking them?"

Then she followed him. There the little puppies were. Oh, they were cute! They were spotted. There, too, was the mangy dog they had been throwing outside. Then he put the food down for them, and then he came back.

And then the young woman saw him. Then she said, "Why, here my brother is feeding the dogs that I bore! He's keeping them over there. But he must have thrown two of them away."

Now one day, early in the morning, she heard someone singing at the end of the village, where he was singing. Then the young woman went outside. Then she went there, and there they stood: a young man and two boys beside him.[2]

Then the young woman came back. Then she picked up a shawl, and her bag, whatever it was. Then she went over there. And there they were going in

---

1. An idiom for having sexual intercourse.
2. The dog father and the two puppies in human form.

the distance. Then she followed them, walking behind them as they traveled <to the northeast>.

Sometime during the evening the two boys ran back toward her. Then one of them said, "Mother, you should turn back. My father says, 'Let her turn back! She certainly didn't treat you well, the way she treated you.'"

Then the young woman said, "Now it was that way, it is true. But I certainly didn't know that you were the ones. If I had known it, it wouldn't have been that way."

Well, then the two swung around. Then they became dogs when they ran behind their father as he went on.

Then the two came back after two days. One then said, "Mother, are you hungry?"

She said, "Yes, I'm hungry."

Then he said, "Now, my father has killed a deer over there. You can take whatever parts of it you want—whatever you will eat. My father has made a fire. When you get over there, you'll feed yourself. We'll all be going slowly. We won't leave you."

Then the young woman went, and there lay the deer. It was just as he had said: there was a fire there, too. Then the young woman began to roast the meat. Oh, she got full, and then she took meat for herself. Then she went on again.

While she was going, following them at night, the two little boys came running up to her. One said, "Tomorrow we'll arrive where our mothers and fathers, our grandfathers and grandmothers, and our uncles live. We're getting near there." It was now close by.

Then this one went there. Both the dogs ran there where they lived.

Morning came. Then the two came back. Then one of them said, "Now, mother, when we go up this rise, you'll see a hill, a hill way over there standing alone on the prairie. That's where we're going. That's where the village is. That's where my grandmothers, grandfathers, and uncles live. That's where we're going."

Then they all kept going. Then the two ran off to it again. The young woman went up a rise. There in the distance was a hill.

Then they all kept going.

Now when they were close to the hill, the boys came up. Then one said, "Mother, we are arriving there. Now, mother, be ready! When we go inside, when you enter with us, sit over there on the left side. You must sit by the doorway. <That's where my grandmothers, grandfathers, mothers, and uncles sit.> Don't sit on the other side, on the right! You must sit on the left side!

"Now they are going to talk first. We'll tell you whatever they're going to have planned."

《   》

Then they arrived where they lived in the hill. There was a doorway, and then they went inside. Then she sat down where they had told her.

Well, then they began their meeting when they saw the young man, who walked ahead of the two boys. Now he reached the west side of the interior. Then he was handed a pipe, which he smoked and smoked.

Then one said, "Now you are going to explain why this young woman has followed you here."

He said, "Yes. I chose to marry this young woman. Now here is what happened. Now her brother—the brother of this young woman—saved these two boys of mine. Now you are going to decide what is to happen to her."

Then the ones on the right side said, "Surely the young woman should be dead—she should be killed. What she did to the two offspring that she bore for this chief's child sitting here with the two boys was wrong."

The other ones sitting on the left said, "That surely cannot be. She certainly did not know what happened. This one himself erred. This young man erred when he did not present himself clearly as the dog he is, just as this young woman is clearly a human.

"Now she shouldn't be killed. It won't happen. We will side with the young woman so that she won't die, but so that she may turn around and go back to her village.

"But now we are going to bless the boy who is her brother. We are going to bless her brother."

Then they called the young woman. Then she sat down by her two sons.

And then one said, "Now it happened that way: he himself erred."

The young man said to the young woman, "It is my own fault that I didn't tell you what I had done. I myself erred. I myself am the cause. But now you are going to turn back and return to your village.

"Now we are going to bless your brother. We are going to give him powers so that he won't be poor—so that your brother won't be poor. Whatever your brother wants will come to pass. Whatever he undertakes is not going to be difficult for him. We'll go with him. We'll watch over him. When he sets out on the warpath, he'll have no difficulty achieving what he desires. It will come to pass.

"Now your brother will take these powers from us. He is going to learn these songs. These songs will come to him mysteriously."

Well, then that is what he did.

He said, "They are going to take you back home. These four will return you there. And this is what you'll tell your brother."

Then all day, from morning until into the night, they were bringing the young woman back, and then all night until just before morning. It did not take long.

《   》

There the chiefs were meeting inside.

Then her mother said, "Old man, our daughter has returned."

It was morning now. Now she said, "Now this is what happened. We erred; and the one who chose to be my husband himself erred. He himself erred. For whatever reason, he didn't make his identity clear when he came, and consequently we lost two children.

"Now they're going to bless only my brother here. Now things won't be difficult for him. Now he's going to have these songs, which are to be sung at night so that the enemy won't come close—to be sung at night so that the enemy won't attack us. Now he'll keep these songs."

Now the boy achieved those things after he became older. He had all sorts of valuable things since he was a brave for whom nothing was difficult. When he went on the warpath, too, horse stealing was not difficult for him after he had been blessed by the dogs.

Now this occurred there near Devils Lake. The hill stands there prominently. The hill stands on the prairie when we arrive there [Dog Den Butte]. That is where the dogs were meeting and where they lived.

Those sitting on the right side were coyotes with strings plaited in their braids. Those sitting on the right were the ones who had strings of otter skin plaited in their braids. Now they were the ones who were mean—the ones who had otter skin strings plaited in their braids.

And those over on the other side of the coyotes were kit foxes, the ones who had defended the young woman and had led her back home.

Now the songs they used to sing were the foremost ones. And we called the songs Whipping the Door. They used to call the members of the society Crazy Dogs.[3]

The Hidatsas had a Hidatsa Crazy Dog Society, too. That is what I used to hear. The Hidatsas still sing the songs.

And I know the Doorway songs—the Crazy Dog songs—because my grandfather, old man Short Bear, used to sing them. He gave me the right to know the songs.

---

3. In published sources this name has also been translated as Crazy Horse (Lowie 1915:670) and Foolish Dog (Curtis 1907–30, 5:150).

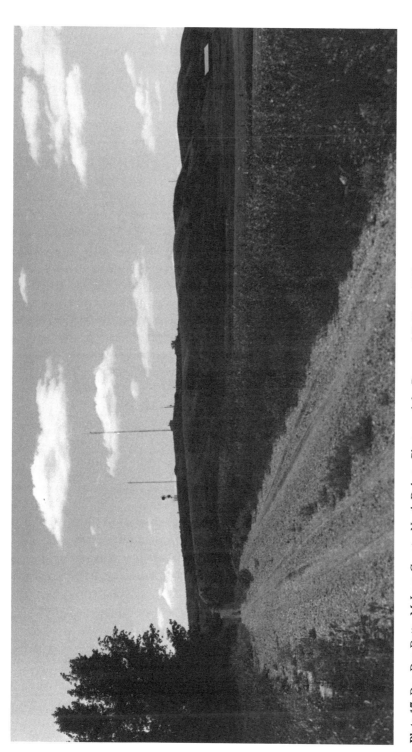

Plate 17. Dog Den Butte, McLean County, North Dakota. Photograph by Raymond T. Haas, 1990.

Comparative references: ARAPAHO Dorsey and Kroeber 1903:205–26; ARIKARA Parks 1991, 4: 536–39; CHEYENNE Kroeber 1900:181–82; HIDATSA Beckwith 1937: 142–43; MANDAN Maximilian 1843, 2:343.

22

The Pawnee Woman and the Scalped Man

Alfred Morsette, Sr.

This is one of many stories about scalped men, individuals who had fallen in warfare but later revived, only to find themselves permanently scarred and destined to live thereafter in isolation in the opaque world of spirits because the scar represented their transformation into spirit beings called tshunúxu'. *One folkloric portrayal of the scalped man is a character who is a potential source of miraculous power. This role is illustrated here, where a scalped man discovers a young woman who has fled her village during an enemy attack. He marries her and subsequently endows her brother with power for success in war and hunting.*

Now I am going to tell a Pawnee story that is also an Arikara story. We understand Pawnee when we are talking. When the Pawnees say something, we understand it. And it is the same way for them, too: when we say something they understand it.[1]

It happened somewhere, I do not know where, long, long ago. There was a Pawnee village, and the enemy came to fight. During the battle the attackers made it rugged for them.

Then one young woman ran off. Then she ran off from the group when the enemy was counting coups on them and killing them, and half the people in the village ran off in all directions. This young woman carried a small boy on her back. Then she ran into a ravine.

---

1. Because Arikaras and Pawnees recognize a close relationship between their tribes, they assert that they can understand one another's language. Today, however, the two languages are mutually unintelligible.

While she was hiding in different places, it became night. As she went on, there was a cut bank over there. Then she went into a recess in it. Then she sat down after she was in it.

Where the village was the enemy had scattered out and were around fires that they had made here and there as they remained overnight. There were fires here and there when the young woman looked.

Then she thought, "I'll stay inside here for a while. Then when the enemy goes off, I'll get out. I don't know where I'm going to go." That is what the young woman thought over and over.

Now there was a sound on the ground that came her way. Oh, it passed by. Then it came back. Once again it passed. Then it stopped right here over where she was in the recess.

Then someone sat down. Then his legs hung down; his feet hung down. Now she saw his feet from where she was there inside.

And then the one who sat on the edge of the bank said, "Now I am the one they call Sees Him Everywhere.[2] I'm the one named Sees Him Everywhere. Whoever you are who is inside here, get out." That is what he was saying over and over.

Then he got up, and then he quickly disappeared.

It was not long before he quickly came back. He came back again. Then he sat down where he had been sitting just as he had done when his feet were hanging down. "Now here I am. I'm the one Sees Him Everywhere." That is what he was saying.

Then this young woman thought, "Now surely I wonder who you might be, you who are coming here. I am hungry."

Then the boy cried. The little boy, however old he was, cried since he was hungry.

Then this young woman said, "Now whoever you are, Sees Him Everywhere, my son and I are hungry."

Then the one sitting on the edge of the cut bank, Sees Him Everywhere, jumped up. There was the sound of footsteps as he went off. The young woman who was in the recess heard him.

After a while there was the sound on the ground of him coming again. He sat down. Then he said, "Now here I am. I'm the one Sees Him Everywhere. Now come! Here's some food for you to eat."

The young woman was afraid of him. "Now it doesn't make any difference if we starve to death. He might pity me," she thought. Then she came out.

---

2. The narrator translated this name as Looking At Himself, but the translator felt that Sees Him Everywhere was a better translation. The latter is the one used here.

There sat a man. He was a very young man. Oh, this young man sitting here was dressed nicely! Then he said, "Now eat!"

Then the baby boy and she began to eat since he was hungry. Oh, they ate the roasted ribs and dried meat that he brought for them, eating everything!

Then he said, "Now follow me! It isn't far to where I live."

Then that is what the young woman did: then she followed him. Oh, this scalped man led her to where his dwelling was. <There was a disguised door on the hillside that opened into his lodge.>

He said, "This is where I live."

Then they went inside. Oh, it was *very* nice indeed there with a fire! It was warm.

"Now sit down right there! Now none of your people are close by. The people of your tribe have gone far off. They have gone *far* off indeed, after what happened when many of them were killed.

<"Now you must know me."

"Yes, I knew you when you were still young. You were a little boy yet," she said.

"Yes, it happened the same way to me. I was captured, and then I ran away. They captured me, and I got away, and then they killed me. They didn't notice, but I wasn't really killed. I didn't die. Someone came and picked me up—revived me.

"But now I'm not supposed to be among people, not able to go back to our people. I'm different. I have a different way of life.[3]>

"Now if you want, I'll take you. We'll go. Your father, mother, and family are still alive. They are looking for you."

Then the young woman remained there overnight after she and the boy had eaten well. Now the young man must have been good.

Then he said, "You and I will go. We'll all three go. But I want to be together with you, to marry you. And whenever you want something, you must go off—you must leave the village and we'll meet and go off. And you'll tell me whatever it is that you want, whatever you desire."

Now he must have married her. Then he must have taken her back to wherever her band of Pawnees had made their new village. Then the young woman went there to rejoin her people.

Then the scalped man said, "Now this is your home here. Here is where your father and mother live. They survived. They were not struck. The ones who were battling were the ones who were killed, but those living here now are the ones who separated and fled."

---

3. For a discussion of the scalped man in Pawnee and Arikara folklore, see pp. 53-54, 304 herein and Parks 1981:47-58.

And this woman arrived at the lodge of her family. "Why, mother, father, I have come!"

But the scalped man had warned her in the meantime, "Don't tell on me. Don't say, 'Sees Him Everywhere and I are together.' "

Oh, her father and mother were glad. They were all thankful and happy when they saw her.

Then she said, "I went off there and I hid. I was inside a recess in a cut bank. We were hungry and so we got out and came on. We ate Juneberries and chokecherries. Those are what we ate. We were just starving to death."

Then her family cooked for her and the boy, oh, who now ate!

Now for a long time this young woman would do this: when the men went out on war parties and her brother went off with them—whenever he would do that and go off—then this young woman went far off from the village. She and her husband met.

"Now my brother is going on a war party. You must watch over his movements. Let him find something for himself."

And then she came back, while her brother was going on the warpath.

Ah, no matter what he did, nothing was difficult for her brother. Then he had a great reputation after people talked about his deeds and his being a brave warrior.

Now, it is not known how long this young woman and the scalped man named Sees Him Everywhere were married.

Now what I have told here is a Pawnee story. My grandmother used to tell the story when she reared me.

Comparative reference: ARIKARA Parks 1991, 4:623–25.

23

The Young Man with the Broken Leg
and the Scalped Man

ALFRED MORSETTE, SR.

*This story illustrates once again the scalped man as a potential
source of power that can be conferred on someone who is pitiful.
What is unusual here, however, is the teasing, jocular manner char-
acterizing the scalped man's exercise of his power. His humor is
manifested through irony and suggestive illusion, both of which are
subtly depicted in the narrative. In a nearly identical Pawnee story
the scalped man has the power of ventriloquism, which he uses to
create the scenes that are here achieved by suggestive illusion.*

Now I am going to tell a story. It is a true story that occurred when our
people were migrating upriver. I don't know exactly where it occurred—
whether it was here on this river [the Missouri] or whether it was on another
river in the country to the north, where they used to go on the warpath.

One time a group of young men, however many there were, went out,
going on a war party. And here another war party had gone in the same
direction earlier. Now I don't know how many days they had been out going
around, but then they reached a certain spot. There was a river valley there. It
was nice land with trees all over. The land was rolling.
"Now let's camp here for a while! And then we'll go on. Let's go look
around for something that we can eat!"
Then that is what they did: then they made a hunting lodge of willow
saplings and got their camp ready. Then they completed the lodge. It was a big
one since there were many young men. After they had gathered wood, they
built a fire. Oh, after it was dark they remained awake telling stories. There
was a fine rain outside. It was raining.
Then the leader said, "Isn't there any water?"
Then the errand boy said, "Say, there isn't any water. It's all gone. Let me
go! I might be able to go to the bank of the river in this valley."
And then the errand boy went down to the bank. Then on his way he
picked up stones. Then he was throwing them ahead of himself since it was

dark. He did not know where the water was. Then there was a splash as a stone struck the water. That is where he went. There the river was flowing.

This boy was about to dip water over there at the edge of the bank when someone said, "Don't dip water there! Go a ways over there to the west! There the water is better. There is blood in the water there where you're standing. They killed us here. Dead bodies are lying all around where they killed many of us."

Now this boy who had gone after water just stood there. Then he went toward the one who had spoken.

Then the voice said, "Why, say, we came here on the warpath long ago. While we were going home they found us and then we had a battle. But I broke my leg. They didn't scalp me. I broke my leg. That's the reason I'm sitting here in the water. I hid here where I'm sitting."

"Ah, now I'll lift you onto my back. I'll take you to where our party is."

"I knew when you all came. You began talking. Then I knew when you came here for water. I thought that if you were to go there to dip water, I'd call to you to go to another spot. I can hear you men when you're talking."

Then the errand boy said, "Now let's go!"

Then he put the wounded man on his back. He lifted him onto his back. Then they went to the lodge where the men were inside.

The errand boy said, "You sit here awhile! Let me go inside and tell them! They might shoot us thinking that you must be some enemy. Let me tell those inside!"

Then he took the water inside. Each of the men drank. They were roasting ribs over the fire.

Then this errand boy said, "I want to ask something of you men here. I just want to find out something. Now tell me, are you brave men?"

"Yes. We wouldn't be going around here if we weren't brave. That's the reason we're traveling here, because we're brave. Why do you ask?"

"Alright, that's what I wanted to know."

Then he hurried outside again. Then he came back inside carrying on his back the man with the broken leg.

"Now this one is one of our people."

Then they tied the man's leg to a wooden splint while the leader of the party doctored him by applying medicine to his leg.

Well, now he roasted a rib for them to eat. Now they began eating. Then this man with the broken leg began to tell the story. "We were returning to our village when we encountered Sioux. We battled. Then there were dead bodies lying all around in this valley where we battled. My leg was broken, and then I ran into the water. I hid there. There are three men there in the water—three,

I think. When one jumped into the water, they killed him. Now those are the ones whose blood is mixed in with the water in the river."

Now it was morning. Then the leader—the one who was the main leader—said, "They'll leave wood for you. There is plenty of dried meat. And fresh meat. They'll leave water for you. Now we are going on, and when we arrive back at our village we'll tell your relatives—your mother and father. Then they'll come after you."

Well, then those were the things they put down for him: wood, water, meat, and dried meat. "Well, we are going now." Then they started out. They went off.

Then a long time passed and no one came there. One morning when he awoke, his supply of wood had mysteriously diminished; so also had the water and the dried meat hanging there. All his supplies were nearly exhausted.

Oh, there now was only one piece of dried meat left. Then he took it down. Then he began to roast it. His supply of wood was also nearly gone.

After eating at the dried meat, he left a piece of it. "Now in the morning I'll eat it." Then he put this piece of dried meat under his pillow.

"Now in the morning I'll eat it. But if no one arrives before long, I'm going to starve," he said as he sat there in the evening. Now it was getting dark. He sat inside his lodge. He cried.

While he was crying for himself, a person just came inside. "Hey, why are you crying? What's wrong?"

"Oh, I'm crying for myself since I'm not able to do anything. My leg is broken. A party left things for me, and now all the things are gone, wherever they went. My stack of wood is gone. The water is gone. And the meat—the dried meat—now it's gone."

Today was the day to eat the dried meat that he had saved under his pillow, but when he got up there was no dried meat there. Now this was the day when he cried for himself. This was also the day when the scalped man came in, wondering, "What's wrong?"

"Hey, now go fetch water!"

Then the young man said, "I don't have any water. My leg is broken. I can't go."

"Let me see where your leg is broken!"

Then he felt the leg all over. "It certainly isn't broken anywhere. Go bring some water!"

Then that man with the broken leg got up. Then he went and, oh, he picked up a pail. He went down the hill over there in the distance. He dipped water. Then he came back.

Now as he was about to return, his leg broke again. He fell over, spilling the water.

Then the scalped man began to laugh. Then he said, "Hey, get up quickly! I'm dying of thirst."

"No. My leg broke."

Then the scalped man came down. "Let me see your leg." Then he turned the leg in the other direction from which it was broken. Then he was laughing again, too.

"Go on now!" He had healed him.

Then they went on. Then they entered the lodge.

Then this scalped man said, "Say, at least make a fire!"

Then that one with the broken leg said, "Why, I don't have any wood."

"Well, let's go to my lodge for a while! You know where my lodge is."

"I don't know, and here you have your lodge close by!"

"You were certainly in there," he hollered.

Then they went there. They arrived at the scalped man's lodge. There was a fire there. Oh, there also was a rib cooking over the fire.

The scalped man said, "You must stay! Let's tell stories!" That is what the scalped man was saying.

Then this man with the broken leg was looking all around.

The scalped man said, "You said, 'I'll bring you some wood at last.' There it is."

There it lay against the wall in the scalped man's dwelling, and there on a line hung dried meat. Here he had been the one stealing the things!

The scalped man said, "Bring it for me at last! But I brought it." He was teasing the man as they sat there and he doctored the one with the broken leg.

Well, then this scalped man said, "I think I'll go to our village for a while. And don't go outside! Don't walk around outside! But stay inside. There is a hole to look through, to peep out. Now, I think I'll go to our village for a while. I'll tell them, 'He must be well.'"

Then the scalped man vanished.

Oh, after awhile he returned. Then he came inside his dwelling. He had corn and moccasins.

"Your father gave these to you. He said, 'Take them! And he'll put the moccasins on.' And your mother had this corn. Then she said, 'He'll get well where you live when he eats some fresh corn with you.'" This is the way the scalped man told it to the young man sitting there with the broken leg.

The scalped man began to roast the corn, and they ate.

Then the scalped man said, "I think I'll go to our village for a while! Do you want anything? What shall I tell your father?" He was saying these things to him.

Then the young man with the broken leg said, "Surely they haven't said anything."

"You have certainly been away a long time. They must have thought that you were dead. Truly I told them that we are living together. They know that we're living together." The scalped man was telling him these things.

Then he vanished.

Then in the morning he entered the dwelling. "Now, hello. We had a meeting. And then I arose. I said—I think that a village is coming here to where we are. They will camp here where you and I are in this valley. I told them, 'It is alright—that it would be good if you people were to do that, to camp here. There is water.' I told them, 'My brother and I live there.'" This is what he was saying as he was fibbing.

The boy with the broken leg said, "Hey, it will certainly be good if the village comes here and we see my father and mother."

"I have certainly told them that you're living here. They know." This is what the scalped man was saying.

Oh, sometime later, after however many days it was, the scalped man said, "Why, say, look! There's the camp. They must have arrived. Surely they said, 'We'll go there.'"

Then this young man with the broken leg arose. When he looked out, there was a village there, with men watering horses and standing around fires here and there. The scalped man and the young man with the broken leg surveyed the scene.

Then the scalped man said, "Let's go!" Then the two of them went there.

There was a man crying there. He was crying. Then the scalped man said, "The one crying is your father. He's your father. Your mother comes once in awhile."

The village was sleeping. Then his mother came into sight, and they were all glad to see one another.

Then his father said, "Are you returning?"

Then the one with the broken leg said, "I'm going to go back over there for a while, and when I'm ready to return, I'll tell both of you."

Well, then his parents were thankful to see their son.

Then he vanished. He was now like the scalped man. Then he arrived back at the scalped man's dwelling.

Then the scalped man said, "Did you go to where your father was crying?"

The one with the broken leg said, "Why, I did go, and there was no one there."

Oh, the scalped man began laughing. "Yes, that is what always happens," he was saying over and over. He knew how to say things.[1]

After so many days the scalped man got ready to take the young man home.

Then the scalped man said, "Now you are going to go. Now you'll get ready to go home. Now it's good. Let the village come back awhile! When they camp there, you'll go there."

Now the one with the broken leg was waiting.

Then the scalped man said, "Now it's true this time. It isn't the way it was before. The village is the way you used to see it. It wasn't true before. Now this time it is true that the village is coming here. They're going to camp here where we are. Don't do anything! Don't talk about me when we go to your father and mother's lodge.

"But now you have already seen them. You dreamed an image of them. Now this time their coming here as a group is real. The way you saw things before [in your dream] is the way they're going to be when you see them now."

Then they both went. There was his father crying.

The scalped man said, "Now speak to your father!"

Then the young man went, and there was his father. His father was happy to see him. "Now let's go over there! See your mother!"

Then the two of them went to the lodge. All of them were glad to see the young man. His sisters were happy when they saw him.

Then he said, "I'm not going to come home for a while. Later on I'll come back. Now, I want to go back for a while to the dwelling of the one who pitied me."

Then his father said, "Now surely that is a good thing. Do that!" Then he said, "My friend wants a knife and a black rope"—whatever a black rope is.[2]

Then they gave him the rope, and the knife and tobacco.

Then the young man went off. Then the one who had had the broken leg vanished. Then he entered the dwelling of the scalped man.

Then the scalped man said, "Ah, I was watching over you. What you were doing was good. You have brought me some kinnikinnick to smoke. Now I

1. That is, he knew how to create illusions.
2. Pawnees, and presumably Arikaras as well, braided black ropes from buffalo hair. Among their many uses, men wore them tied around the waist over a buffalo robe (G. A. Dorsey 1904a:352; Weltfish 1965:362–66).

have what I have wanted. I have the rope for horse stealing. Well, in the morning you're going to go home.

"But now I'm going to impart something to you. The way I have treated you is the way of my medicine. It is my power to do things in a joking way. But now take care of yourself! Live well! Don't do the things I've been telling you and showing you! Don't do them! You'll take care of yourself."

And then this is what he did: when it got dark again, the two of them came there. Then they arrived at the lodge of the parents of the young man with the broken leg.

Then the scalped man said, "But whenever you go on the warpath, you must come to where I live. It won't be long now before your village is moving."

And then that is what they did: after a certain period—it was not very long—after time passed, then they went on. The group proceeded to move.

Then this young man who had had the broken leg married.

Meanwhile he had the power to doctor people. When someone broke an arm, then he doctored him. Then the person got well after having gotten hurt. He had good medicines. So people depended on him.

The scalped man said, "Don't talk about it! Don't say anything like, 'He lives here.' Meanwhile I have blessed you, after Night gave me the power.[3] And now you're going to live well. You have grown up. Now you'll rear your own children."

And that is what he did.

Now whenever it was, he died, the poor thing. When that one who had the broken leg was dying, he said, "Now a scalped man was the one who blessed me. He blessed me. And he said, 'When you die, we'll die together.' Now it must be that way. Now he must have died, too."

Now this is how the story goes.

Comparative references: ARAPAHO Dorsey and Kroeber 1903:259–60; ARIKARA Parks 1991, 4:625–26; PAWNEE G. A. Dorsey 1906a:390–94

3. Night is a spirit of the northeast direction in Arikara religious symbolism. This spirit brings rest, and restores and refreshes all things (Gilmore 1929:95–120). Night is the spirit who generally revived and blessed scalped men.

24

The Seven Scalped Men and the Hunter

Alfred Morsette, Sr.

To become a scalped man, a person need not have lost his scalp. When falling unconscious in battle, the loss of any body part, as this story illustrates, was sufficient to transform the victim into a spirit being, should he revive. Any disfigurement received in war rendered him "no good" and thus unfit for human association. Also demonstrated here is an important characteristic of the spirit world: the lack of tobacco there and the spirits' desire for it to smoke. Spirits frequently beseeched a pitiful young man for tobacco and in return conferred power on him. This theme recurs throughout Arikara traditions and in part explains why the smoke offering was integral to all ritual activity in which spirits were invoked.

Long, long ago when our villages were there in the south, a group of young men was out hunting. They were going through rolling country. It was wooded land. They had each killed a deer, and this one young man who was with them drifted off from the others when he killed a buck, and then he butchered it. Afterward when he looked around he discovered that here the others in the party had left long ago! Now they had left him.

Then this young man packed the meat on his back. As he was going along he lost track of wherever it was that the party had gone. He then forgot where the village was. This must have been the first time he had gone out hunting. He did not know the lay of the land yet as he went out hunting for the first time.

As he was going along late in the evening it became dark. As he went along he thought, "There's no point to going on any farther. I might wander off to some distant place. I might as well spend the night right here, and then in the morning I'll start looking for the village, wherever it is."

And so that is what he did.

Then as he proceeded he began imagining things. "Surely someone is talking." Then he stopped. Then he lay the meat down on the ground.

Then a man came running up beside him. Now the man stared at him. Then he went around and around the young man, looking at different parts of his body. When he was going around him, he said, "Ah, surely I'm just imagining that this one is a human."

Then he hollered, "Hey, One Leg, where are you?"

Then another one came, too. Then there were two of them.

After he stood there awhile, then he hollered, "Hey, No Hand, you must be coming. Look, this one is something else!"[1]

Then another one came. Then there were three of them.

Now again: "Hey, No Ear, where are you?"

Then he came. Then there were four of them.

And then he hollered, "Hey, No Nose, where are you?"

Now they numbered five.

Once again he hollered, "Where are you, No Leg?"

Then he came running up beside him. There he had one leg! He was hopping all around.

Now he called out again, "Where are you, No Fingers?"

Then he came running up to him. Now there were seven of them standing there.

As this man gazed at them, he hollered, "Hey, all of you going around, why is it that you aren't going back to our village?"

Now the ones who were standing there ran off. They vanished. Oh, then they went off. And here one of the men took the meat.

And when the young man wanted to pick up his meat, it was not there. "Now, you who were here, you took my meat. Something is wrong!"

One had no ear. Two of them had a leg cut off. One had an arm cut off. Another did not have a foot. Another had no fingers. Another had a nose cut off. Each one was disfigured.

<"I'll follow them to see where they have gone. I'll find them."> Then he went where they had gone.

After he had gone a ways there was a river there. As he went on, as he got close to it, there was a cut bank there. Then there was singing, the sound of it coming from the edge of the water.

This young man stopped, and then he went down the bank. As he was looking all around, there was something protruding. A root was sticking out. Then he pulled it. Then a door opened, and there they were singing.

He gazed at them as they sat there singing.

And then one said, "This song will be yours, No Leg."

Now the one with one leg jumped up and began hopping around.

"Now this song will be yours, No Hand."

Then they sang again. Then they were dancing.

Meanwhile the one sitting there singing—the one with no nose—was the one singing. When they looked up and saw the young man, they said, "Hey, he's come inside again." They all piled up on the one who was singing.

---

1. That is, "this one is a strange being who is not one of us."

Then this young man went inside. Then he sat down by the fire. There was a fire in the middle of the room. There lay the meat he had had. A rib was roasting over the fire.

Then one of them got up and sat down again. And also another one. And then they all got up and sat around. Then the one who had been singing, the one with no nose, sat upright. <"You boys, don't do that! You almost killed me again.">

Then No Nose said, "Now you have found us. It was planned that we should find you. We're the ones. You lost your way after your companions went off. Your village is close by. But we're the ones who have called you. We've arranged it.

"And here you are a warrior! And here you are brave! You're not afraid of us. And yet we're all deformed, we who are sitting here. We were going around on the warpath, and we were killed. And then Night pitied us who were living. Now here is where we're living.

"And now that we've called you here, this is what you're going to do for us. Why, we want to smoke tobacco. It's hard to obtain.

"Other things aren't difficult. Now these are the powers we'll give you. Now you're going to doctor anyone who aches. This medicine is the one you're going to use. <If someone breaks a leg, you'll use this medicine. If someone can't stop bleeding, you'll be able to stop it. If he has a fever or freezes his hands, you'll be able to cure it.>

"And the ways of warfare aren't going to be difficult for you. You'll have those powers on the warpath and over the enemy; you're going to know how to do everything. And we'll be around. We'll be watching over you. Wherever you go we'll be around and we'll be seeing you.

"Now this is what I want you to do for us: we want to smoke some tobacco. It's pitiful for us here. Things are indeed difficult for us.

"We brought this meat for you. Here it is. Now you're going to eat."

And so that is what happened. <The one who had no ear was the cook and the one who cut the meat up.> Then they set food in front of the young man. Then they dipped water for him.

"Why, you would have smoked our tobacco. But it's impossible; we don't have tobacco. And that's the reason we brought you here, for you to do something for us so that we might smoke. Now they're going to take you to your village."

Then the young man ate.

Then they began to sing the song of each one of the men. <When they sang the song of No Ear, he got up and danced around. Then they sang One Leg's song and he got up and danced. And No Feet. Each had his song and his

medicine. No Hand had lost his hand when it froze, and now he had a song and medicine for that.>

"Now you know these doctoring songs. Now things aren't going to be difficult for you. Whatever you want you'll be able to do. It won't be hard.

"Now after you have eaten, these two young men will take you to where you came from, to where your village is. Now you must not divulge anything after you arrive back at our village. Don't say, 'I saw them.' We surely are not good now. We are disfigured.

"But Night must have thought that we should live awhile yet. This is his plan, what we have done for you. But you must not mention it to anyone. These young men will hear you if you start to say anything. Then if you do it, that will be all: you'll lose the powers we have given you. And it can't be repeated.

"Now do what we beseech of you—tobacco! After they have taken you home and you have arrived there, and when you are ready to return after four days have passed, you'll bring it and you'll come alone. Don't come with anyone else. This is what you'll bring. Bring the tobacco here. Now whatever remains to be learned of the power we have, we'll give it to you."

Then the two took this young man outside. It was not long before they had taken him to the village. They carried the meat for him.

Meanwhile his companions were fearful that the enemy had found him and killed him. "Perhaps he's lying dead somewhere. He must be dead. They must have killed him."

Then he just walked into the earth lodge. "Say, I lost my way after you left me. Now I have finally come back. I've finally found you."

Now sometime later he said, "Father, I want tobacco."

Well, then his father mixed it for him, whatever kind of tobacco we used to have among us. Today we have this kinnikinnick, but I do not know what kinds they used to mix together when they mixed kinnikinnick then.

Then this young man took it. <Then he met No Hand and No Fingers, who took him back.> Then he went to where his adopted fathers, the ones who had blessed him, were. He arrived crying. Then they embraced him.

"Now come in!"

They took him inside.

"Now here is the tobacco you said you wanted."

Oh, they were glad! Then they began to sing and dance out of thankfulness after they smoked. <They offered the pipe to the east, to the south, to the west, to the north, to the earth, and up above. "Now we have tobacco for our ceremonies. We have ceremonies in the spring in order to have rain and good weather during the summer.">

Now they continued to give him powers. "This is what you'll do. This is what you're going to do when you're doctoring. This is what you'll have to say."

Now the blessing they gave him was a great thing. And this is the end of the story, of what they used to tell me.

And then they took the young man back. He arrived back at his village. And then this young man became a great warrior who performed many deeds and who married. Now things were not difficult for him: stealing horses, counting coups on the enemy when on the warpath, and doctoring. When someone was ill, he was called and then it was not long before the person got well. When someone broke a leg, it was not long before he got well.

Now that young man lived among us and traveled all around for a long time, and then he reached old age.

《   》

Now this is where the story as I used to hear it ends. Some say the Pawnees tell the same story.[2]

Comparative references: PAWNEE G. A. Dorsey 1904b:74–78; Weltfish 1937:238–40.

25

Wakes Up The Hills and
Red Shield, the Scalped Man

ALFRED MORSETTE, SR.

Another role in which the scalped man character appears is that of the provider—not the bestower of power, but the supplier of culturally valuable items (horses, scalps, and eagle feathers) that increased the social standing of the beneficiary. In this story a scalped man named Red Shield from time to time furnishes a young man named

2. A Pawnee version of this story was recorded by Weltfish (1937:238–40).

Wakes Up The Hills with these articles, which the latter portrays to people in his village as booty that he himself has captured on the warpath. In this way he rises to the status of chief.

I'm going to tell a story that occurred when we used to travel around long ago, when the Arikaras used to travel around on the hunt over the open plains where buffalo, deer, and antelope roamed, where different kinds of wildlife were plentiful.

One time after banding together, a group of young men went off. Then they went far off. Then they stopped to camp. Then they built a lodge and prepared things by going out hunting and bringing back game. They knew how to make dried meat while they were camped.

After they had rested, the young men went on. I don't know where they were going. Wherever it was they were traveling, as they were coming along, one young man separated from the party while they were hunting early in the morning. There weren't any deer roaming around. And so he went over there to a hill, a big hill. It was a high hill.

Then the young man went up the hill. While he lay on top looking all around at the wooded hillsides, he saw a clearing. There were trees here and there in it, but otherwise it was clear land. Standing off there in the distance were three deer grazing. Then he looked the situation over. "I'll go around this way. If I get up close, I might kill one."

While he was watching them they became frightened. One fell over. It fell down. Before long a person appeared. Then that person went over to where the deer lay. Then he stopped to look. He looked over this way where the young man was lying on top of the hill.

The one I am talking about—the one I am telling about lying on the hill watching this person—was named Wakes Up The Hills.

The person was rapidly turning this way and that. He had something on his head. Then he was looking at this young man: it was as though he knew where he was lying. He watched the young man. Then he picked the deer up quickly. Then he ran off after packing it on his back.

Meanwhile the young man lying on the hill was watching him. The person appeared here and there among the trees on the hillsides. In the distance was a hill with a cut bank, and then he went up it carrying the deer. Then he disappeared.

Then this young man who was lying on the hill ran down. Then he went to where the man he had watched—the scalped man—had gone up the hillside.

Then he got there. There were stones lying around, the stones he had stepped on, one above the other, so that no one would know where he went. And there was a tree root sticking out of the side of the hill. Then he did it: then he pulled it, and a door opened.

Then he went inside. There was an entryway, and then this young man went inside. I don't know whether he alerted him, but then he went on, going down an incline. Then there was the smell of smoke. When he got to the end, there was a fire there. And there sat the man butchering the deer he had killed.

Then the young man said, "Now I have come. Are you one of our tribe?"

The man sitting there did not say anything. He was startled while he was butchering.

Then the young man said, "Now I have come here. Are you one of us? I'll shoot you if you don't answer me."

The man who sat there said, "Yes, I am one of our tribe. Now I sort of had a premonition that you were coming. And yet I doubted it. And now you have arrived, and it is good. It's good that you're not with someone. Now sit down! We will eat together."

Then they began to butcher together. Then they piled the meat around. Then he said, "Here is this pile for you."

There was a rib over the fire. Now Wakes Up The Hills was hungry.

And then he said, "Now I recognize you when I see you."

He said, "Now that must be it. I am named Red Shield. I died long ago. I was killed. But Night had compassion on me so that I could go around here. I know that you and your party are staying nearby. I know it. And I always go to our village, to go around to see you all. But you don't ever see me because I come as a spirit. And now you have found me, and I am thankful. Now stay!

"After it gets dark, we'll go to the valley. Now your party must hurry. You all must go! The enemy has arrived. They're coming this way. Oh, I want to tell you so that you'll know that there are many of the enemy! They're coming this way, here where you're staying. And the enemy camps are following behind the warriors. Now you and your party must leave quickly! Otherwise they'll find you and count coups on you."

Well, then they ate, and he was happy.

"Now let's go to where your party is camped! When you arrive there, you must say, 'They're chasing me. Quickly, let's run away! They might find us. The enemy is coming near.'"

And then they ran toward the camp.

Then they arrived there. Then Wakes Up The Hills said, "Now quickly, let's run away! Hurry! The enemy is chasing me. They saw me. Let's go quickly!"

Then the others who were camped there got up and left their things behind, whatever they had, such as dried meat. Then they ran off, and no one remained. Then the scalped man was alone now that he had fooled them, thinking "They mustn't find me."

Then the party ran back to where our villages were and told about it. "This is what happened."

Now sometime later the young man Wakes Up The Hills said, "Now I think I'll go! I think I'll go on the warpath alone!"

Then he did that: then he went out alone when he went on the warpath. He headed toward where Red Shield, the one he had befriended, lived. Then he arrived there.

Now Red Shield said, "I knew that you were coming. Now that's good. Now sit down! Now tonight I'll go out by myself. The enemy camps are close by."

Then Wakes Up The Hills said, "Yes, I want a horse—perhaps even four."

"Now I'll do for you what you want. In the meantime don't go out! Don't go outside! You must stay inside here!"

Then they ate a meal. They ate.

This young man Wakes Up The Hills asked, "Will it be tomorrow night when we go—when we go home?"

Then this Red Shield said, "It'll surely take two days at least; two days, and then you can go. But now you're here, and you want me to return right away. If I did, the people in the village might find out that you were really only close by. You haven't been gone from the village long enough on the warpath. But you'll stay two days and then you can finally go back. In the meantime I'll get things ready."

Then this scalped man Red Shield went out.

Then just before morning he entered. He made a fire and then he said, "Now get up! There are horses for you over there. The ones you wanted are standing over there in the brush. I have put the four horses there for you.

"But I want you to take the black pinto to my son and my wife so that it can perform deeds for them.[1] This black pinto is nice looking. Now this is what I want you to do for me."

Then this Wakes Up The Hills said, "Now truly it will be that way. I'll do it."

And two days later Red Shield said, "Now go!"

---

1. In former times, spotted or pinto horses were rare and consequently highly valued. They were thought to have unusual or mysterious power.

Then the two of them returned together. They led the horses back to wherever the village was. When they arrived there, Red Shield, the scalped man, turned back and Wakes Up The Hills took the horses into the village.

Now he told of his own bravery. "This is what I did. The Sioux must have gone on a hunt. They were camped there. This is what I did: I ran off with the horses."

And while he was telling about it he said, "But this boy is pitiful. He no longer has a father. He and his mother can only look at the horses belonging to you people. Now I am going to pity them by giving them this black pinto to work for them."

Shortly afterward he did it: then he gave the horse to them.

Meanwhile the other one, Red Shield, was making plans.

And subsequently there were many occasions when Wakes Up The Hills gained good fortune by visiting Red Shield's dwelling.

Then Wakes Up The Hills became ill.

Now, years later, after Wakes Up The Hills had become a man, after he had become an old man, he said, "Now I'm telling it to you, my relatives, and you tribesmen here. You all know it: I have found all kinds of nice things. Nothing was difficult for me. Now I'll tell you. It was not on my account. It was not my own doing. You all know that Red Shield died. It was long ago. Now I found him. I found him. That is where I used to go whenever I went away, when I went out to look for things. He was the one who found the things for me. Now the black pinto that I gave this woman had belonged to this boy's father. He gave the boy the horse, but I pretended to be the one giving it to him because his father had told me to do it; he told me not to betray him.

"But he must now be an old man like I am. Now you all know it: Red Shield is the one who did those things, the things that I did when I became a chief among you. Now I'm leaving you. But this is where he lives; this is where I found Red Shield."

And now the woman who had been his wife said, "Let us go to see Red Shield."

Then they went there after Wakes Up The Hills told where he lived. Then they arrived there. The door was wide open. He must have gone somewhere else long ago. He had left. He had built another dwelling. And then he had left everything just as Wakes Up The Hills had said: "This is how it is. This is how the land lies. This is how the door is situated."

Now that is what happened: they did not find him. After they mourned they came back home.

Meanwhile this man Wakes Up The Hills died. He died. But the scalped man lived. He was holy, and things were not difficult for him.

Now this is the end of the story.

Comparative references: ARIKARA Parks 1991, 4:614–16, 660–65; G. A. Dorsey 1904a:149–51

26

The Boy Who Had Coyote Power

JOE FOX

The protagonist here is once again a solitary, withdrawn young man who, although he has never accompanied other men to war or on the hunt, in fact has been pitied by a coyote or wolf. Once, when his older brother joins a war expedition, the young man leaves the village surreptitiously, travels ahead of the party, and uses his powers to ensure its success in a raid on a Sioux village. This tale of the incident, apparently a fuller version of story 115 in Parks (1991, 4:668–70), explains the young man's reclusive behavior, vindicating his conduct, which had appeared to people to be unmanly but in reality was dictated by the animal spirit within him.

I am telling about a boy who was pitied by a coyote. And here he imitated its sounds when a party went on the warpath.

Now he had an older brother, and this one would go with war parties, but this other young man would never go himself. He would stay in the lodge where his mother and father lived. He never traveled around looking for something, to find some fortune. His brother was the only one to follow along with a party when it went off.

Then one time they did that: a party gathered together to go on the warpath. Then they went off, going on a hunt and looking for some horses to steal and some Sioux to scalp if there was a battle. And then they went off, wherever they went.

Well, after they had wandered around for so many days—perhaps four— then they camped overnight, wherever it was, wherever the spot was. Wherever it was. Then they made a fire. It was a high fire.

While they were around the fire telling stories, why, then they heard a coyote. "Uuuh, uuuh!" That is what it was saying when they heard it.

"Listen! Haa, listen!"

And then this boy said, "It's my brother. It's my brother. He's saying, 'I'll go.'"

Why, these men said, "Well now, talk about someone else! That one who always lies asleep in his lodge doesn't know anything about that. Your younger brother certainly isn't a man."

And so they paid no attention to him.

It was a while later when they were still telling stories. Then that is what the boy said again when the coyote howled. It was a little closer. The boy said again, "It's my brother. He has moved closer."

And then again the men told him the same thing, "Hey, talk about someone else, since he's at home sound asleep!"

They doubted him.

But when they heard it, it was close by when it spoke.

And then the boy said, "Now I'll go. My brother is calling me. He says, 'When the sound is close, you must come.' And I'm to take the bone I was burning. It belongs to my brother. He says, 'You'll burn a bone and I'll smell it.' And that's where I'll go, and this is what I'll take."

And so that is what the boy did: then he picked up the bone and went off.

It must have been close by, and there stood his brother when he arrived there.

"Why, here you are!"

And then his brother said, "Well, now I'm in a hurry. But this is what I said: 'I'll see you.' Now we have seen each other. But I'm in a hurry. There in the direction that your party is heading—there to the east—if you go to the east there's a village at the base of a hill. Oh, it's a huge village!

"And I've finished doing everything. I charged into the first lodge there. I cut all their bowstrings. In all the lodges I cut their bowstrings. Now they don't have any bows to fight with. And I've taken a herd of horses. The herd is close by over there.

"Now quickly! As long as it's still dark, you and your party must go. Don't hesitate. Go right into the village. They don't have any bows to use."

Ah, then the two brothers separated. Then the boy went back to the camp. Then he arrived.

And then he told them. He said, "Now, each of you I'm related to, we're traveling around. We're looking for things like this. Now you doubted me when I said, 'He's my brother.' Now I'm telling you. My brother imitates the sounds of a coyote. That is the reason he doesn't go among people. But now I really know it. He said, 'There's a village close by at the base of a hill. I've got everything ready. I've taken apart all the bows they have. I've cut all the strings. Now they have none. And I've placed a herd of horses there.' He's told me where the horses are. Now we'll go there just as soon as it gets daylight."

Well, when he finished talking, it was just getting to be daybreak. Now they were hurrying to get ready. And then they charged off.

When they went onto the hill as it was becoming daylight, the village was there at its base. But no one in it had arisen yet.

Now they charged first into that lodge in front. The people were just getting up and they picked up their bows and arrows. In the lodge beyond they did that, too: when they picked up a bow, there was no bowstring after the coyote had done that—after he had gone inside the various lodges and ruined their things for them.

Then the party charged into that village and began striking the Sioux after they killed them.

Well, and then they went to where he had said the horses were. There there was a herd! And then they drove them off. They drove the horses home.

《　》

Now this is what his helpless brother did. And here he was a coyote! Here he imitated its voice!

Now this is what happened: one of the many things that happened among our people as time came on—things like this when one would imitate an animal's voice. Now it was that way.

Well, now this is the end of the story I have told.

Comparative references: ARIKARA G. A. Dorsey 1904a:106-9; CROW Lowie 1918: 133-36; HIDATSA Curtis 1907-30, 4:165-71.

Narratives of the Past

Of Historical Events

27

The Killing of White Horse's Son

ALFRED MORSETTE, SR.

During the first quarter of the nineteenth century, Arikara contact with white men was primarily limited to fur traders, who exchanged European goods for peltries trapped by Indians. Relations between the white traders and Arikaras at this time were often tense and sometimes resulted in open hostilities. The most sensational incident occurred during the second expedition of William Ashley up the Missouri River in 1823, when Arikaras attacked the party. After the fight, Colonel Henry Leavenworth led a combined force of soldiers and Sioux against the Arikara villages, which were shelled by Leavenworth's artillery. Accounts of the conflict from fur traders and soldiers are part of the historical record, but nowhere in the record is there an explanation from Arikaras. The following narrative, one of many versions still current a century and a half later, offers a traditional Arikara perspective on this historical event, but is apparently a conflation of separate episodes occurring nearly a decade apart. The shelling of the Arikara village described here can only be a reference to the Leavenworth assault in 1823, whereas the murder and cremation of the chief's son (see also Parks 1991, 4:638– 39) would seem to be an incident reported in 1833 by Catlin.[1]

Now I think I'll tell a story for a while. It is a short story that they used to tell and that I heard.

Long ago when the Arikaras were moving upriver—I am telling an Arikara story—they would build a village somewhere and live there for a

1. Catlin (1848, 2:182) wrote: "But a few weeks before I left the mouth of Yellow Stone, the news arrived at that place, that a party of trappers and traders had burnt two Riccarees to death, on the prairies. . . ."

length of time. After so many years they moved this way [upriver to a new location].

Now there once was a man who was chief of them. He was named White Horse. White Horse is what he was named. White Horse.[2] Now he owned a store. He must have been married to a white woman. She must have been his wife. They traded for ammunition and food with the whites who brought freight up the river on the steamboats, buying supplies to trade with the Indians who brought in the hides of buffalo, deer, coyote, and beaver.

Now one time there was a group of young men, very young men, who must have gone out hunting. They were coming along, wherever it was, and there was a log cabin [by the river]. And here there were white men living there, however many of them there were.

[The party stopped and] then one of them said, "We don't have any tobacco and our village is still far away. Now the white men know your father. Go over there! You also speak a little English since your mother is a white woman. Now go on! Beg for some tobacco!"

So two of them went, the son of White Horse and another young man. Then they went. There went the two of them.

They were going and when they arrived at the cabin a white man came out angrily. He had a gun. "Don't come nearer! Stay there where you are!"

This young man called out, "I came for some tobacco, if you have any for us. Here are [beaver] hides."

The white man paid no heed to his words. Then he shot the young man and killed him.

Then the other young man ran away. Then he arrived running where his companions were.

He said, "They have killed him. They have shot White Horse's son."

Then these men, however many there were, became angry. "Now let us all die, too! Let him not die alone!"

They went for them. Then the white men were killed, but one of them must have hidden somewhere. He is the one who must have taken word, wherever he took it, to the soldiers, wherever they were garrisoned. Then he told about the incident: "The Indians killed all of us. I survived to come here."

Then the soldiers came on the steamboat to fight, bringing cannon with them. They arrived. Then they began shelling the Arikaras. Then they leveled

---

2. Here the narrator gives a different, interchangeable form of the name *xaačiišawatá*. Elsewhere the form is *xaataaká*. Both forms have the same meaning.

the village, killing and wounding many people. And then there was a battle, but the Indians did not want them to kill us.

Now a young woman was running away [from the fighting]. Then something landed where she was headed as she ran. It was not large. It was a ball. A string stuck out of it. The string was burning. Then this young woman took it off [the ball]. Then she removed the string. Then the flame went out.

Then she told the young men who were in the battle. Then, when one of the large balls landed by them, they snatched it up. Then they threw it at the boat of the white men on the water. Then the boat moved on, and then it went over there on the other side of the river. That is where it landed on the water while they were shooting at it.

Then it got dark. Then the white men ran away. But these Indians buried on scaffolds the ones who had been killed after being shot. Then they began to rebuild the village.

Sometime later the ones [who had been in the hunting party] told the head chief of the Arikaras, "This is what they did to us. They killed one of us."

Now when White Horse told the government representative of the president [what had really happened], then he became angry. Then he reprimanded the soldiers for what they had done.

Then the white traders said, "Surely they killed the white men in the cabin."

Then the Arikaras said, "It's not true. You yourselves were the ones. That boy came after tobacco, and then they shot him. Then they killed him. That is the reason we avenged ourselves. We were feeling hurt on account of what you did to the one who has our village, the one who is our chief."

Comparative reference: ARIKARA, Parks 1991, 4:638–39.

28

The Fort Laramie Treaty of 1851

ALFRED MORSETTE, SR.

In 1851 the U.S. government brought together representatives of many northern Plains tribes for a treaty council at Horse Creek, near

Fort Laramie, Wyoming. The purpose of the council was to establish
peace among tribes and between tribes and the United States, and to
establish tribal territorial boundaries. Although never formally
ratified by the Senate, the document signed there came to be known
as the Fort Laramie Treaty. This narrative, which is a description of
Arikara participation in the proceedings, is in fact a conflation of
events and personages from the 1851 treaty council and later negotia-
tions with the government in which Arikaras took part.

Now I am going to tell you about the things that happened when a
representative of the president came here where we were living. This time I am
telling about the years when we Arikaras, Hidatsas, and Mandans were already
living together and when peace treaties were made, when the white man
wanted the Indians to put their heads together and cease their warring—their
killing one another, their stealing horses from each other, and all those things
that happened long ago. Now the white man's president had taken over the
governing of the entire country.

Now here at Bismarck where troops were garrisoned[3]—that is where I am
talking about—they brought a letter. There were no such things among us as
cars or trains in those times. The letter was brought up on the steamboat when
it came up the river to this country here. They brought the letter to where we
were living, where we were in the village together.

And my grandmother's father was a white man. <He had a trading post
there.> He took the letter and he told about it. Then the chiefs summoned
another man. They used to call him Stone.[4] He spoke Arikara and English, and
he translated what the letter said for the Arikaras. This happened when that
white man was living with my great-grandmother Eagle Woman.

Then Stone translated it. He said, "All the different tribes that are living
in this country are going to assemble there [at Fort Laramie] on the Platte
River. The president wants you three tribes who live here to send delegates
there."[5]

Now the one they used to call Son Of Star—his father was named White
Shield—said, "Surely that's good. We'll do that. We'll go. Now no one knows

---

3. An anachronism. The military post that became Fort Abraham Lincoln, south of
Mandan, North Dakota was not founded until 1871.

4. His English name was Peter Beauchamp, Sr.

5. For a photographic reproduction of the circular to Indian agents and traders sent
out by D. D. Mitchell, Superintendent of Indian Affairs in St. Louis, on 4 April 1851,
requesting that all tribes on the northern Plains come to the Fort Laramie treaty council,
see Killoren (1994:107). It is apparently this document to which the narrator refers here.

the country there where the Platte River is. We've never gone to that place there. That's enemy country."

And the one named Carries Moccasins said, "But I always go there. My sister is married to a Cheyenne. It usually takes eight days to get there. I know the place where all the different enemy tribes are going to gather. Well, I'll tell you how to go there."

Then they called the Hidatsa named Four Bears, the Hidatsa who was half Assiniboine,[6] and the other Four Bears, who was a Mandan.

And the Mandan said, "Surely that's good. I'll be at the side of the Arikara. We'll go."

But the Hidatsa did not want to go. Then he made excuses. He said, "The enemy tribes we aren't friendly with roam around there. And if they should find us, they'll wipe us out. Just let it be, whatever it is that you wanted to do."

Then the one named Son Of Star said, "It doesn't matter. We're now all the same. But we'll go. I'll go."

Then they selected a particular day. Then they traveled by horse, riding horseback.

They always tell that when they reached the confluence of the Heart River and the Missouri, they camped there on the prairie. Then one young man in the party became sick. He was named Young Fox. He and his wife were together.

And then Son Of Star of the Arikaras said, "Both of you turn back! Go home! He might get worse. But we'll go on."

It took the party ten days to get there. And after ten days they arrived there where the camps were clustered on the Platte River.

And that Hidatsa Four Bears was coming along in the rear, not wanting to go and making excuses.

And then they reached the Black Hills. Then the one named Carries Moccasins said, "Now this is where there are enemies, here in this country. If they see us, they'll kill us."

Now they must have told Four Bears, for he then became frightened. Then he traveled in the middle of the party, and when it became dark he went into the middle of them. He had traveled in the rear, the last one, not wanting to go; but after they frightened him he traveled in the middle of the party as it went along. And when the party camped overnight, he slept in the middle of them. He lay in the middle of the party when they slept.

---

6. When Four Bears was a baby his Assiniboine mother died and no one knew who the father was. He was adopted by a Hidatsa couple who had no children. That couple reared him as a Hidatsa.

As they were going along that man Carries Moccasins—he must have still been young—said, "When we reach the Blue Hills over yonder, we'll see the village on the Platte River. That must be the post."

It was evening when they reached the top of the Blue Hills. Then the fort was there in the distance. Then Carries Moccasins said, "Now this is the place."

When the party reached the post, soldiers came riding out at a gallop. Then they said, "Be ready! These men who are coming are going to kill us. They are soldiers."

<But Carries Moccasins said, "No. They're coming to meet us, to welcome us.">

When they came to meet us they said, "Here are your tents. This is where you'll stay overnight. We'll take the horses."

The horses must have been tired. There was a corral, and then the soldiers herded them into it.

There were wall tents here in which they were to stay. Then food was brought for them. Oh, there was plenty of food—meat and all the good foods that the soldiers ate!

And while the party was cooking and eating, there was another tribal delegation camped beside them. And here they were Pawnees![7] Then two of them came over.

Then the two Pawnees said, "We are alike. Now tomorrow the representative of the president is going to speak. And we'll be the first ones to respond. We Pawnees here are going to talk to the president's representative first. <I'm going to be the interpreter.>"

The young man who was speaking was named Young Wolf. His father was a Pawnee and his mother was an Arikara. They used to call him Young Wolf.

Now in the morning they were called at eight o'clock. They went. There was a huge crowd of people there. And the Pawnees were the first ones to speak to the government commissioner during the negotiations when they were making the terms of the treaty.

"This is how you'll live. But we are going to take care of you. The government is going to take care of you for as long as you live."

Now today they deceive us, but at that time he spoke well, with good words.

---

7. There were no Pawnee participants in the 1851 treaty council.

Well, then Young Wolf said, "Now we are finished. Now, you Arikaras, come! Son Of Star, lead the Arikaras! Now it's your turn."

And then that is what Son Of Star did. Then he began speaking when they were negotiating. And the government commissioner said, "But I want us, poor things, to help each other. The president is the one who sent me to call all you Indians together and to provide for your children to learn to speak English like I do, so that we can understand each other. For however long it may be, the president[8] will be giving you rations. Whatever you want, he will give it to you. And he will fence off reservations for you Indians to live within. The country you Indians now live in will be established as the land for your reservations. Each individual will be allotted a piece of land to live on and to build a house on."

Now these were his words: "For as long as you Arikaras live, the president is going to help you. And your children will grow up learning English so that we will understand each other. The way it is now, we can only understand each other through English. Now this is the way it is. The old ways are past.

"Now I want you to give me your young men to be enlisted in the army in case a war arises, and the Indians will be enlisted so that we can help each other."

Now that is the way things went when they met to negotiate the treaty. Then they shook hands.

Then Young Wolf said, "We have done it. It's now the other tribes' turn to negotiate."

Then the Crows went up onto the negotiating platform. They were the first ones.

Then they said, "This young Indian [Young Wolf] who has been speaking and negotiating—we'll follow his road, too. It will be the same way [for us as it was for him]. It isn't going to be any different. We want to live there where we now live. We are used to living where we are, in the land we know."

And the other different tribes felt the same way. "Now it will be just as the Arikaras who came from the north have agreed. Now the terms of the agreement they made with the government are the ones we want, too. Now there won't be any difference."

Now the council ended.

Then all the tribes had a big dance.

8. The Arikara term *atípa'*, which is used here, means 'president' and by extension 'U.S. Government.' It is derived from the kinship term *atípAt* 'my grandfather.'

Plate 18. Views of Eagle Nose Butte, Morton County, North Dakota. *Above,* Aerial view looking southwest. Photograph dated 1966, courtesy State Historical Society of North Dakota. *Below,* View looking north. Photograph by Raymond T. Haas, 1990.

Then this one they call Son Of Star—he was also called Comes Last—said to Carries Moccasins, "Now they are glad that you brought me. If I am given something, even if it's a single eagle feather, it will be yours."

And while all the different enemy tribes were dancing and having a good time and feeling thankful, various persons gave their best-looking horses to Son Of Star since they were thankful to him [for what he had done during the treaty negotiations]. When they were giving them to him, this Carries Moccasins thought to himself, "You surely don't have anything, since you promised to give me what you received, just as you said."

Now here is where this Comes Last made a mistake: he did not give anything to him, and Carries Moccasins became angry. Then Carries Moccasins said, "Now you people can go on your own! But I'm going to do this: I'll go to visit my sister, who lives in Cheyenne country."

After Carries Moccasins went off, the return trip was difficult for the party. They got lost as they were coming back. Then they were just wandering all around on the prairie and they were barely able to make it back here where our village was.

Now after the party had returned things happened the way they had agreed. The young men enlisted with the soldiers as scouts, Bloody Knife being among them when these who were formerly the old scouts were enlisted in the army. This is the reason for those graves.[9]

And when the time came children went to school there at Fort Stevenson, and they also went to the school of Reverend Charles Hall.[10] Then it was our turn to learn English. That is the reason they made a treaty of friendship there on the Platte River in 1851.

9. The Scout Cemetery west of the community of White Shield.
10. The Congregational missionary at Fort Berthold who established a day school in 1876.

29

The Custer Expedition

ALFRED MORSETTE, SR.

During the 1860s and 1870s, Arikara men enlisted in the U.S.
Army as scouts at military posts established to secure peace on the
northern Plains. Their service was felt by the chiefs to be an impor-
tant demonstration of Arikara loyalty to the U.S. government as well
as providing protection for themselves from their enemies, the Sioux.
Although Arikara scouts served at different times at Forts Stevenson,
Buford, and Abraham Lincoln, their most memorable assignments
were with the two expeditions led by Lieutenant Colonel George
Armstrong Custer, who was known to the Arikaras as Long Hair. On
the first one, the 1874 exploring expedition to the Black Hills, tribal
tradition asserts that it was an Arikara who discovered gold in the
Black Hills and that Custer promised the tribe a share in the find, the
government to act as custodian of the profits accruing from it. The
second was the ill-fated 1876 military expedition against the Sioux.
In the ensuing battle at the Little Big Horn River, which took the lives
of Custer and some 250 of his men, three Arikaras were also among
the casualties.

Subsequently, stories about these expeditions have figured pro-
minently in Arikara oral traditions. Nine of the surviving scouts told
their versions in 1912 to O. G. Libby, who published them as The
Arikara Narrative, *and today older tribal members still recount the*
events and sing the songs of Long Hair and the three Arikara scouts
killed at the Little Big Horn: Bloody Knife, Bear's Trail, and
Bobtailed Bull. The following narrative, the most complete rendition
currently remembered, is a conflation of events on the two expedi-
tions, treating them as a single campaign.

I will now talk awhile about the soldiers stationed here at Bismarck. Over
there on the other side of the river opposite Bismarck, [southeast of] the town
of Mandan, is where the former military post is, where Custer and his troops
started out when he led his soldiers. There at Eagle Nose Butte is where the

soldiers were stationed.[1] That is where they started out. That is where Custer led them out to war, wanting to pacify the Sioux who were killing white men in the country to the south.

There were Arikara scouts serving with the soldiers. When they went with the troops, there were many of them. There were thirty.

They started out in the country south of Mandan, and after they went up there to the north, then they [moved south and] went into the Black Hills. At the edge of the Black Hills, they said, "This is where the country is rough. Let's go farther away! It's not good here. The land is rugged. We can't cut through. Let's start heading over there to the west!"

And now this is what I used to hear when the Arikara scouts who were with the troops used to tell about it—when they told stories and I was listening.

Then they arrived there in the Black Hills. While the soldiers were camped there, for however long a period it was, there was a young man called Crazy Red Bear with them.[2] He had another name, too, but I do not know it. He was watering his horse early in the morning. Then he saw that the water was shining brightly where it was coming out of the ground. There were objects sparkling where the spring water came out.

Then he began picking them up. They were pretty rocks when he looked at them. Then he put one on his hat, and another one on his bridle. There they shone brightly.

Then he came galloping back, and then he arrived where the soldiers were camped. And then the officers on guard saw him. As he came galloping his saddle and bridle glittered. Also the hat he wore sparkled.

Then a group came up to him. Then they asked, "What are these?"

And the one we are talking about, the one named Bloody Knife, spoke English. He was half Sioux and half Arikara. He was truly a half breed. Then he said, "Where did you find these?"

Then Crazy Red Bear said, "There's water over there. It's a spring. There, way up on top of the hill—that's where the water is coming down. They're lying in the water. That's where I picked them up."

Then Bloody Knife said, "These are the valuable metal. This white man [Lt. Col. Custer] wants to see where you picked them up."

And then they went there, however many soldiers there were. Then they arrived at the spring where this young man Crazy Red Bear had watered his horse. And there they lay in the water.

---

1. A prominent butte along the Missouri River several miles south of Fort Abraham Lincoln (see plate 8). The landmark is identified with the fort by Arikaras.

2. His nickname.

Then they began picking them up. Then they went up onto the top of the hill. That is where the water was coming out of the ground.

Then the white man Custer said, "These are valuable. They are money. Ah, these nuggets you have found are valuable! Now you are the ones who will share in it, you Arikara tribe, and the government will take care of it for you."

Now there was one Indian and one white man. He said to them, "Now you two take these to Bismarck, there where the tall building is,[3] where the commanding officers are." And then he wrote a letter.

And then these two came. The Arikara, who was named Fortunate One, and the other one, a white officer, then brought those valuable metals. Then they brought them to Bismarck.

Now it is not known what happened from there. I don't know.

But now these soldiers went on. But they put up stakes at the site where the metal had been found. Then they went to the Little Big Horn River. Then that is where they went.

Here where they camped the enemy had gathered! Here they had gathered! There were nine tribes where their camps were clustered. It was one big village where the Sioux waited for these soldiers to arrive. The plan was for them to kill all the soldiers. That is what the two main ones, the two leaders called Crazy Horse and Rain In The Face had planned—and Sitting Bull.

And when the soldiers went there they had everything—cannon and good guns—and there were plenty of cartridges. They drove horses and oxen, but the troops went ahead. There were 125 soldiers who went ahead—the cavalry that Custer led. That is what they used to say: they went ahead of those who had the cartridges and those who had the guns—and those who had the food. Well, then the soldiers in the lead made camp.

And there was one scout named Red Star. I saw him. He and another young man were companions. But he had been out hunting alone.

Then he said to Bloody Knife, "I killed a deer. While I butchered it, some men passed by. They were four Sioux. They had horses that were packing meat. They must have killed deer, too. I think they saw me—that they might have seen me. Then they rode on by. They went the other way. I don't know where they came from."

3. An anachronism. This is a reference to the current seventeen-story state capitol in Bismarck, North Dakota, construction of which began in 1932 after the old capitol burned in 1930.

Plate 19. Bloody Knife kneeling by the right side of Lt. Col. George Armstrong Custer, with two unidentified Arikara scouts and a soldier, on the 1874 Black Hills Expedition. Photograph by William H. Illingworth, courtesy Custer Battlefield National Monument.

After he returned from hunting, Red Star told what had happened. While he was telling about it, Bloody Knife told Custer.

Now they took him to Custer where he told his story again. Red Star said, "I don't like having to tell the story again—to have to repeat it. I saw them!"[4]

And then Custer said, "Six of you will go. Red Star, you'll go with them to see if you are being truthful."

Then that is what they did early in the morning. It was not yet daylight when this Red Star jumped up out of bed. Then he mounted and went off. Then he rode up one of the highest hills. There in the Little Big Horn valley were the camps. It was indeed a huge village, with the camps extending in a long line. It was smoky along that valley.

Then he turned back quickly. Now he arrived back at the camp, and now the six officers went. Bloody Knife was among them. Then he said, "I truly went where the camps of lots of people are clustered! I don't know what we're going to do. When they come, they'll kill all of us."

Then this Custer said, "What is he saying?" [asking Bloody Knife to translate Red Star's words].

Then Bloody Knife said, "This is what he has said: 'When they come for us, they'll wipe us out. <There are too many of them—too many people.>'"

Then Custer and his men turned around. He said, "We'll certainly go on. We'll battle them. We'll take them captive."

Then Bloody Knife said, "You surely can't do it! There are too many. They'll massacre us. It's a large village, the one he told you about when he saw them."

Then Custer said, "Whatever I say, it will be that way." That is what this Custer said: "Whatever I say, it will happen that way."

Now these 125 men were the ones to strike when Custer wanted to take the Sioux captive.

But here the Sioux over there had already seen them long ago! Here they were ready when the soldiers went up the hill and showed themselves. Then after peeping over the hill they started coming over the top. Some of the soldiers were now lying on the ground, another group behind them was kneeling, and another group behind them was standing. Then Custer said, "Now you're going to shoot them."

Then Bloody Knife said—then he told the Arikaras; he said, "You go down that hill over there! Don't do anything! But I'll stay here. I've been

---

4. Because they make him repeat his story, Red Star thinks the soldiers doubt his words.

arguing with Custer. I didn't want it to be this way, but he's obstinate. Now we're going to be killed when they come for us. There are too many of them.

"One Sioux there is calling out. He's saying, 'Go to one side, like Sitting Bull said! There are young Indian men among the soldiers. Don't lay a hand on them! Don't kill them! But only those white soldiers.'" That is what he was saying.

It was not long before the Sioux came up the hill for the soldiers. They were not careful where they were shooting at them. They were running over those who were lying and kneeling on the ground. Then they killed them. Now they killed the commander, and half the soldiers ran off. Then they hid. Half were not killed, and half were killed. Now they killed Custer. Then Bloody Knife died. And Bear's Trail—he must have been named Little Soldier then—and that other one, Bobtailed Bull. Right there now, they were the ones who died on the Elk River [the Yellowstone],[5] where the battle was. And now it was over.

« »

But afterward the main column arrived—the supply train and the main body of soldiers who followed and had the guns.

Now there is where Custer erred. This was the plan: there were those coming from the south [under Major Marcus A. Reno], and there was also a large troop of soldiers coming from the west [under Captain Frederick W. Benteen]. They were to rendezvous. My grandfather Chippewa Child [John Morsette] was there among them [General Alfred Terry's column], who came from over there to the north afterward. They arrived after the battle had ended.

They cut down the soldier Custer, the one who was bullheaded. Well, then those Sioux started off. Then they scattered. Then they went back to where they had come from, going in groups up the hillsides, traveling off with their gear after the battle was over.

Now afterward the scouts who were enlisted arrived back among our people, too. Now one among them was Running Wolf. Boy Chief and Red Bear, Bear's Belly—there were many of them. Now they were the ones who were with the troops there where the battle was. Now half the Arikaras survived to come home. When their commanding officer arrived, he said, "Now you go home! But I'll chase after them [the hostile Sioux], wherever the groups have scattered. I might head them off."

---

5. The Little Big Horn flows into the Big Horn River, which is a tributary of the Yellowstone River, the latter called Elk River in Arikara.

And then they began burying the soldiers who had been killed and had died. Then they began burying them, all of them working.

And then our Arikaras came back home on horseback.

Now Bloody Knife had died. Bear's Trail died. Bobtailed Bull.

Now the pinto horse that Bear's Trail had ridden came back. It came back. Bear's Trail did not return, though. It is not known how many days it took that horse to come here by itself. That is the one they found. They learned that it was the horse that Bear's Trail had ridden.

Now this is what I used to hear when they talked about it. But some person will have a little different story. Now another one will have yet a slightly different story. This is the one I used to hear from Nice-Voiced Elk. This is the story that Running Wolf used to tell, too, this one that I have told.

Comparative reference: ARIKARA See Libby 1920:37-160.

30

The Eagle Trappers

ALFRED MORSETTE, SR.

Eagle trapping was an important activity for Arikara men, second only to war as a means of gaining honor. After the Arikaras had moved into Like-A-Fishhook Village, eagle-trapping parties would travel south and west of the Missouri River to favored locations, where members built their individual trapping pits as well as a hunting lodge in which they all slept. The events described in this story occurred sometime after 1863, when the Sioux were still at war with the Arikaras and small parties leaving Like-A-Fishhook Village traveled the prairies at their own peril. Although the narrator heard this story both from his father and from his uncle Snowbird, this telling follows Snowbird's version.

Now I am going to tell a story that occurred when there was still the combined village, when there were many Arikaras, Hidatsas, and Mandans there in the village. It was the combined village there across the Missouri

River. It cannot be seen today. Everything is now under water. It is no longer visible the way things were where the lodges were.[1]

That was where he lived, there on the other side of the river, "where the old village was." That is what they used to say.

Now a group of young men set out. They went eagle trapping. Then they crossed the river to the other side, to the land on the south side, here where I live.[2] Where they went was far off.

Then they said, "This is the land of good fortune, here where eagles always fly around."[3]

Then they prepared a site. Then they made an eagle-trapping lodge sufficiently big for all of them to be inside.[4] "Here is where we'll camp for a while."

Then they built traps by digging holes in the ground. Then they laid poles on top. And they finished doing it, getting everything ready as they were preparing the traps that each one would be in.

And then one man, the leader—he was named Bear Charges In The Woods, and he was also called Scabby—said, "Now get things ready for us to sit downwind. Get everything ready!"

Well, then they went off. Each one would say, "This must be a good location." Each one went off in a different direction. Then each of them prepared the hole in which he would sit. The traps extended in a line, each one being quite a distance from the others. They could not just be bunched up.

1. The reference here is to Like-A-Fishhook village, jointly occupied by the Arikaras with the Mandans and Hidatsas from 1863 to 1886, and today under Lake Sakakawea. There was no single, specific name in Arikara for Like-A-Fishhook village. Instead, Arikaras later referred to it by descriptive verbal forms such as 'where the old village was,' 'where the village on the river bank was,' and 'where the combined village was.' After moving onto allotments, some referred to it as 'in the village.' A translation of its English name (čišwátU 'fishhook') is also used.

2. The narrator lived in what remains of the old Beaver Creek district on the Fort Berthold Reservation. It was on the south side of the Missouri River. Today most of it is under the waters of Lake Sakakawea as a result of the construction of Garrison Dam and the subsequent flooding of the Missouri River valley on the reservation.

3. In the English version of this story the narrator identified this location as south of the present town of Hebron, North Dakota.

4. In the English version of this story the narrator described the hunting or eagle-trapping lodge as a semisubterranean lodge with four walls and a roof, covered by a layer of posts and then pumice rocks. Grass and finally dirt were layered over the posts and rocks. Compare G. Wilson's description of the Hidatsa hunting lodge (1928:134–35). For a description of Hidatsa eagle trapping, see Wilson (1928).

Now each of the young men did it: he stayed in the trap. I don't know how many days passed while they remained there; no one told how many days they stayed there when they were trapping eagles.

And there were those in the group who caught perhaps two eagles, and there were some who caught only one. But among them was one young man who was just having a difficult time. None flew to where he was. He had not caught any eagles in his trap.

Then the one who was their leader said, "It's time to go home now. Let's get ready!"

The next morning the one who had not caught any eagles said, "Now I'll remain here a while longer. Perhaps I might catch one. It wouldn't be right for me to go home. I promised my grandfather I would bring an eagle back for him. And now I've had no success. But I'll stay. Go home! Go on! If I don't have any good luck after four days, I'll go back home and arrive there. I'll stay here alone for four nights and days!"

Well, then they left him. Then the others came back home, but this young man did not come with them.

Then he moved from the trap he had been in, making a different one for himself.[5] He finished it. After the young man had been in it for some time, it got dark. He must have got out of it to go back to the trapping lodge.

And here Sioux were waiting for him! They were blocking his path. Then they began to fight him. Then they killed him. The young man was killed.

But the others returned home. They arrived there.

Now the young man's brother was named Only Brave. "Where's my brother?" he asked when he looked for his brother.

"Well, he didn't return. He remained there alone. He said, 'I'll go home after four days.' He didn't catch an eagle. It was difficult for him, and he decided to stay four more days. 'And then I'll go home.' "

But he did not come back later. And now four days had passed.

And then this man said, "It has been a really long time now. Perhaps something is wrong. Let's go."

And then the young men gathered together, however many there were, and then they set out again. Then they arrived there.

And then it was apparent where he had been. But they did not see anyone when they looked for him. They did not find him.

"Now he must have been killed."

---

5. The young man considered the first trap unlucky and made another one, thinking it would bring him better luck.

And then they came back again. They returned.

"Young Fox must be dead. He must have been killed."

And then his brother said, "Now let's wait! When it becomes summer again, we'll go there. We'll look for him. We'll find out what happened to him."

And after winter passed, it became summer again. It was sometime later. "Let's go! Let's go eagle trapping! Let's look for the boy! Let's see what happened."

And then they went. Again they arrived there where they had camped. They fixed everything up again.

And then his brother Only Brave said, "I'll stay in my brother's trap. I'll sit in it."

After they fixed up the traps in which they had caught eagles before, this boy Only Brave went into his brother's eagle-catching trap. He set the trap.

Now after however many days had passed—after two or three days—when the boy Only Brave was returning to the eagle-trapping lodge, when he was coming along, he saw him. His brother was just walking over there.

As Only Brave watched him, he thought, "You are my brother." Then he went out of sight in a depression.

Then this Only Brave ran. Then he ran onto the knoll. He did not see anything.

There in the distance was a stand of trees. Then he went there. There a skeleton lay in the brush. There his brother lay in the brush. "Now here is where they must have killed you!"

It was rough terrain where the horses had circled round and round. He must have gone into the woods. They must have attacked him in the woods.

Now he picked up his brother's skull. He brought it. Then he said, "Now, my brother, I have found you. And here you are dead."

Then he brought it back. He brought it to the eagle trapping lodge where they were staying. Then he said, "Now I've found my brother. Here he is. They must have killed him. They must have attacked him in the brush."

It was rugged there where they had attacked him in the trees and had gone around in a circle fighting.

Now they offered smoke to the skull. They put food before it to feed his spirit.

Now two days passed. The party caught eagles after this spirit blessed them. Now his brother Only Brave stood there. The one who was their leader was Bear Goes Into The Woods, or Bear Turns Around; and then Bear Goes Into The Woods said, "Say, this morning we won't go anywhere. We'll stay here in the lodge for a while. It's not windy. It's good when it's windy: the eagles fly around when it's windy. But it's not windy now."[6]

And then one young man went up a hill. "I think I'll look around awhile! Perhaps I might kill a deer." Then he went up on foot. They must have been in a valley.

There were trees all around where they had their lodge. The land was rugged.

He stopped on top. Then he ran down the hill. Then he said, "Say, there's something going on. There appears to be a moving column, and the ones in the lead aren't buffalo. These are different. I think they're enemies."

As soon as he had said that, they hollered. The enemy were circling around. Then they began to attack them.

Then one Sioux called out to the ones inside the lodge. He asked, "Who are you? Are you Hidatsas, or might you be Mandans, or might you be Arikaras? We want to know."

And there was one young man among the Arikaras who spoke Sioux. Then he said, "Now we are Arikaras. We are Arikaras who are camping here. We came here to look for a young man. You must have killed him, and now we've found him."

Then the other one, the Sioux, called out, "Are you a Sioux? You're talking Sioux."

Then he said, "No. I'm an Arikara. But my brother-in-law—they called him Lump Face—the man Lump Face was my brother-in-law. He's the reason I speak Sioux. He's the one who taught me to talk in Sioux."

Then the other one, the Sioux who was calling out, said, "Now come! Join us where we are! Let's kill the ones in there! How many are there?"

Then he said, "That certainly can't happen! There are fifteen of us. I won't leave them. These are all my relatives inside here. But now you must be brave men. Now I want you to do whatever you are going to do right now! We're not afraid of you."

Then the Sioux who had been calling out said, "Now that's what I wanted to find out. Today is your last day. You won't see another day. Now when morning comes again, you'll be dead."

And then the one inside who spoke Sioux said, "Now that's how it will be. But I'm not going to die alone. But I'll do that, too: you all will die, too. I'm holding the hands of the young men here. I'll lead them myself. You aren't the only one who is brave."

6. Arikaras trapped eagles only when the west wind was blowing (Curtis 1907–30, 5:88).

Now it was at this time that the Sioux ran around the lodge where they were inside, shooting at the lodge thinking that they would knock it down and flush the Arikaras out. But its roof was sturdily constructed. There were rocks—pumice—on the roof.

Then they decided to burn the lodge down. But the lodge would not burn.

Meanwhile Bear Charges In The Woods, that young man inside the lodge, said, "Now each of you fourteen men load a gun for me! Now from here where I'm sitting I'm going to shoot one gun after another. I'll kill those who are running around the lodge."

And then that is what the Arikaras did: then they began loading their guns. As soon as an enemy would appear, he picked him off when he shot at him.

And here came the main body of the group with their camping gear. Then they formed into a camp circle when they put their lodges up, while their men attacked the Arikaras inside the lodge among the trees.

Then one man began to call out. He said, "They have killed a large number of us. Let's stop awhile and let them stay inside there! They'll starve. They'll remain in there where they are. Let them starve to death! When they get hungry, they'll come out." That is what he was saying.

But the man inside understood. "He is saying, the one who is talking is saying, 'Let them stay inside there! They'll starve. When they get hungry, they'll come out and then we'll kill them easily.' That's what the one who was talking said. But it isn't going to be that way!"

Now the enemy camp was set up, and the Arikaras remained inside their lodge dug into the ground. The enemies were walking around watching the lodge they were in.

Then it got dark.

<Now they prayed to that skull. "We need your help. This is what those people did to you: they shot you; they killed you. Now we need your help today. You are holy.">

After it had become night, one young man said, "I looked. Where we get our water there is an open space. It appears there's a crossing over the creek there where one goes down to it. There's brush on the hillside. One can go up the draw through the trees, get on top of the hill, and then sit down to wait. Let's do that! Then we'll get out of this situation."

Then he said, "Now I'll be the one to go in advance! I'll go. I'll go on ahead first. If they see me, they can shoot at me. They can try to kill me. But that isn't going to happen."

Oh, it was really dark, but there were fires all around, where the Sioux had made fires in their camp. <At the same time it was raining lightly, and the rain would put the fires out and get the wood wet.>

Now this young man clearly found his way. <I don't know what his name was.> Then he got out. Then he crawled down the incline. Then he got to the bottom of the coulee there. Then he dipped water. Then he crawled back.

He entered the lodge. "Here is water. The route is a good one. Now that's what we'll do. Now I think I'll go again! Oh, then I'll cross the water. When you reach the edge of the water, go west there along the bank. The water is narrow there <where I have put a stake in the ground>. You'll cross there. Then go up the hill in that draw there where I said there is brush on the hillside over yonder. Get on top of the hill and then sit down. I'll sit there. I'll wait for you. You'll go there one at a time."

Then Only Brave said, "But my brother and I will be last. You all go first! And my brother and I will go afterward."

After they were going and going, after they had gone down the incline, only he remained. Then he said, "Now, brother, now you and I are going to go, too."

Now they had all taken their eagles, after they had tucked them under their arms. All of them had got out. Meanwhile the Sioux were standing by the fires that were all around, watching.

Now the young man Only Brave picked up his brother's skull. Then he said, "Now, my brother, we'll go. When we arrive at our village, we'll put you in a special place. Our mother and father will see you."

Then he himself got out, too. Then he went down the incline. Then the others were on top of the hill waiting for him. Now he got there. "Now, let's flee! Let's go quickly!"

Then they ran off. Then they traveled all night. Now it was getting to be daylight. They came to the bank of the river here where the village was on the bank, where the old village we used to live in was. They crossed the river.

Then Only Brave said, "Now, father and mother, here is my brother. Here he had been killed! I found him. He's the one who is the cause of our coming home. The Sioux began to attack us in the brush again, but it didn't turn out the way they had intended it to."

But now that same morning the Sioux attacked the lodge at the base of the hill. There were no shots coming back from it. Then one man charged into it. Here there was no one inside! The Arikaras had gone out long before!

Then he came out and said, "They must have gone somewhere long ago. There is no one inside."

Then they broke camp. I don't know where they went.

But our men, the Arikaras, came back. They brought back that young man who had been killed after the party had trapped eagles.

31

An Assiniboine Raid

ALFRED MORSETTE, SR.

Historically, Assiniboines had an ambivalent relationship with Hidatsas. They frequently visited Hidatsa villages to barter for garden produce, but at other times they raided them for horses and scalps. In this story, a large Assiniboine war party came to Like-A-Fishhook Village to raid Hidatsas but instead encountered a group of Arikaras, who routed the party after inflicting heavy losses on it. The success of the Arikara warriors is attributed to the animal powers they possessed, especially one man's rabbit power. The powers mentioned here—jackrabbit, bear, shedding buffalo, and buck elk—reflect the doctors' societies in the Arikara Medicine Lodge.

A notable feature of the narrative style used in this story and appearing here for the first time in this collection, is its first person perspective. Many years after the Assiniboine raid had occurred, in the course of intertribal visiting after warfare among the Plains tribes had ceased, the leader of the Assiniboine party told his story to Snowbird, who subsequently repeated the story just as he had heard it from that Assiniboine, maintaining the latter's perspective, and Alfred Morsette in turn has repeated it here just as Snowbird told it to him.

Long, long ago things used to happen when our tribe was migrating up this way and the village was moving. When they were traveling, they would build a village where wood was plentiful and where antelope, deer, and buffalo were numerous and roamed near by so that they could go out hunting for them.

Now I am going to repeat the words of my uncle Snowbird again. The story occurred there when our people were living in the combined village— what they used to call the old village.

Oh, it is not known how long ago it was, but it was probably in the fall when the hunters used to go out, when they used to go around hunting in the country that stretches out near where the town of White Shield is now.

Then they saw them: there were humans coming. It looked like a herd of buffalo coming. And here the ones I am referring to were on foot. They were Assiniboines.

I am repeating the words of Nice-Voiced Elk [Snowbird]. Now, in turn I'm repeating the words of the Assiniboine leader—what he told when he told about what happened to himself.

And then this Assiniboine said, "Say, I wasn't afraid of things. When I went out on the warpath, I'd charge across the water; even when the ice was floating, I'd charge into the river whenever I saw anything. I considered myself brave when I used to travel around when I was young." That is what that man said.

He said, "This one time we came here on the warpath. There were many of us. I don't know exactly how many of us there were, perhaps a hundred. There were many of us when we came to fight you people living here where your village (Like-A-Fishhook) was. We arrived ready to fight here where they used to talk about where the Hidatsas lived.

"Now here they saw us! We ran off. There were so many of us that things were not good when we went there. Oh, there was a valley! Oh, it was wide! There also were trees here and there. It was rolling terrain. We ran to the brush, those of us Assiniboines who went in the war party.

"Oh, then there were bunches of us here and there in the brush, and different ones were performing the things they say to become holy [to become filled with whatever animal power they had].

"Meanwhile, after the enemy arrived they were peeping up over the rises. They were the ones; they must have been Arikaras—the ones who have corn.

"One Assiniboine called out. He spoke in Sioux.

"Whoever it was on your side answered, 'What tribe are you?' Here he must have been saying that: 'Are you Blackfeet or Assiniboines? What are you?'

"Then they said, 'We are Assiniboines. We have come on the warpath.'

"Now the one on the other side: 'Now, Assiniboine, know this! Today is your last day. Now I am going to kill you.'

"He answered, 'Now it will be that way. And when I die, I'll hold the hand of some young Arikara man who is good.'"[1] That is what this Assiniboine was saying.

"Then he called back, 'That won't be.'

"Now they picked off the Assiniboine who was talking. They killed him.

"'Don't any of you say anything!' And here it was quiet.

"And here one Arikara came up over the end of a hill <in the north-west>!" There was a group of young men sitting on the side of it. There was a shot. "He killed one of us. Then they killed two of our party over there.

---

1. An idiom meaning "If I am killed I'll take an Arikara with me.'

Also one came charging over the hill in another direction and killed another one of us Assiniboines.

"'Now something is happening!' An Arikara came darting over the hill. He was just like a jackrabbit sitting down here and there. He was watching us. Now here where we were sitting on the bank, this jackrabbit was *so* holy as he sat there. He turned to face the east. Then as he sat there his ears began doing it: he was moving his ears.

"Then he jumped around. He began to face this other way, toward the south. He sat there facing that way. We couldn't do anything to him.

"Then he jumped around and began to face there toward the west.

"Now again he jumped around. He went over the hill. As soon as he went over it, they came up over the hill and scattered us all around. Now in the valley they killed another one of us. They killed one of us. Now those of us who were fast were the ones in the lead as we fled.

"The Arikaras were now singing praising songs as they turned back.

"There were now thirty-one of us who were left, poor things, and there had been a great number of us in the beginning. Poor things, we stood there crying for the bodies of those in our party who were lying there dead.

"'Now we ourselves are to blame. Let's go home!'

"We were barely about to get back. Ah, now right there is the place where they nearly killed all of us. They were Arikaras.

"Now the one we saw turn into a jackrabbit was the one who depleted our shells. No matter how different ones were doing it—becoming holy— they used up our shells. Now he must have gone over the hill. Then they came charging up over the hill. It wasn't possible to defend ourselves when we didn't have any shells. Then there was nothing to do but run. Then an Arikara would strike one of us on the head with an ax.

"Now this is how they treated us. They were Arikaras. They were not Hidatsas.

"When we returned, the older people said, 'It's your own rotten fault that those young men are lying dead over there! Those Arikaras are holy.' That is what they said when they used to talk about them. 'When you saw him he must have been a jackrabbit when he made you use up all your shells. And they also have a bear. He does the same thing. And they have a buffalo, a shedding bull. That's what he does, too. And also a buck elk— that's what he does, too. When you use up all your shells, then he chases you and kills you. Be careful! Don't go over there.'

"Now we used to be afraid to just come anywhere near this area. But then when we used to go against those tribes like the Crows [and Hidatsas], they were tough. Then they would begin counting coups on us."

32

Two Kettles and the Assiniboine
Horse Raiders

Alfred Morsette, Sr.

*This story was told in response to a query whether there was a
specific Arikara name for the Assiniboines who live on the western
part of the Fort Peck Reservation in Montana. Although some
Arikaras know those Assiniboines as* watópA, *a borrowing of their
own band name (Assiniboine* watóp'a *or* watóp'ana), *others have
known them by the name of the young man whose exploit is recounted
here, one that gained him the name Two Kettles. Thus some Arikaras
called those Assiniboines Two Kettles or Two Kettles' Village. Naming a band or village after its chief in this manner was a common
practice among Plains Indians.*

Now I am telling a story that occurred long, long ago when there was
intertribal warfare here where the village was—where there were three villages
combined into one for the three tribes they call Arikara, Hidatsa, and Mandan—and where the different enemy tribes used to come on the warpath. And
the ones I am telling about now are Assiniboines, who lived in the west.

Now I am repeating the words of my uncle Nice-Voiced Elk. He is the one
whose words I am repeating. He used to tell stories at his home. I used to go
there when I went around and he told me different stories. Now I am repeating
his words.

After these Assiniboines who live there in the west had gone on raids to
the villages of the Crows and Blackfeet and wherever else they had gone, <a
group of them got together in the chief's tipi and were talking about different
things>. Then one of the Assiniboines said, "We never go over there to the
villages in the east where the people of those tribes have corn. Let's go there.
Let's go to their villages, even if they should kill us. They are valorous men.
They are brave. They will kill us if they should find us. But we'll go anyway."

Now there were thirty-two of them. Then the party came during the
winter. It must not have been really cold yet. There was a little snow on the
ground. It was snowing a little. Then they came. They came near the river bank
here where our villages were, where the combined village was on the bank.

Oh, they were on top of a hill, wherever it was, and were looking all around. Then they said, "That must be the village, there where the smoke is in the distance. We've come a long way from where our village is."

There was a thicket of plum bushes there—I used to see them when I traveled around—and then they went into that thicket during the cold. They fixed up a place there. Oh, it was sheltered. It was warm there. Then they made fires [after dark].

Then one of them said, "Now we sure have come a long way. Now maybe we'll take a horse back."

Then they picked out some men they considered able. "You, you'll be the one to find some."

"You are the ones to go into the village over there. The horses are the purpose of our coming here."

Now one boy went with those young men when they went off. I don't know how many of them there were. Then they got to the outskirts of the village. Then it was difficult: there were no horses in sight.

But this Assiniboine whose story I'm telling—the one who told this story about himself—then he separated from them. Then he saw a group of people. There was an earth lodge there, and then people were coming out as different ones came outside [to urinate]. When they were going back inside, he walked in among them. Then he hid so that they would not see him.

The horses were standing along the wall of the lodge interior. They were nice looking.

Then the door was secured.

When they lifted it up, they used to prop a log under it. Two hides were placed on either side of a pole frame. Now this was a door [which was suspended from a rafter over the inner entrance of the entry passage]. It was heavy. When people went outside, they lifted the door up and set a log under it. And later they let it back down. To lock the door one pole was laid horizontally over two other poles that protruded on the inside. Now the door was fastened. It could not be opened.[1]

But now this Assiniboine was sitting inside the lodge where the horses were standing by the wall. The people were sitting around the fire eating and talking. Then one at a time they got up and went to bed. Why, it was not long before they all began snoring! Meanwhile there were two kettles of food on the fire.

---

1. A brief description of the Arikara earth lodge door is given by John Bradbury (1817:114). Alexander Henry and David Thompson (Henry 1897, 1:339) describe the Mandan door, which resembles that of the Arikaras. For a detailed account of the Hidatsa door, similar to the one described here, see G. Wilson (1934:369-72).

Then from where the horses were—they were nice looking, however many there were—he went to the door. Then he took off the crosspiece that fastened it. Well, then he lifted the door up, just as he had seen the people in the lodge do. He lifted the door up. Then he opened the door. <Then after bracing the door open he went back to the horses and removed the rail that held them in.> Then he slapped the horses. They went out. And then he picked up the two kettles of food. Then he went. He went out.

Then he shut the door for the people inside. And then he went over to the horses. They were tied together in a line after he tied them. And then he went into the brush, as he went there in the brush.

Then he had the horses tied together. Oh, the black horse that he led [the one at the head of the line] was nice looking!

He arrived back where his party was camped in the brush. "Now here I have two kettles of food, whatever kind it is. I don't know whether it's dried meat or whether it's ribs."

Then the group of men [who had gone to the village earlier] returned. They had not accomplished anything.

"And what did you accomplish?"

"Why, there aren't any horses there! We had things worked out. We searched everywhere in the village. There are no horses around. They must not have horses!"

That boy said, "Now here are the ones that I myself captured. This is what I did: [the people from one lodge] came outside to urinate and when they went back in, I went inside among them. Then I hid. They did not see me. Then they locked me inside. After everyone went to sleep, I opened the door. I slapped the horses with the cleaning rod for my rifle. I then laid it on top of the bed of a man and woman who were sleeping close to the door. I laid the cleaning rod on top. Then I closed the door. After I brought out two kettles of food, I closed the door. Then I tied the horses and came on. Here they are. I don't know how many there are."

Then one Assiniboine said, "Now we are really *far* away from home. Now let's go back quickly! They're going to chase us. They're going to come. You know now that their horses must be inside their lodges. That's why you didn't find any. These are the only ones we're going to get."

Then they each mounted a horse. Then they ran off toward the river. Then after they reached the bottomland, they headed west.

Meanwhile the one who had gone into the village—the one I am telling about—said, **"We did it. Just before morning we were hungry. And here the two kettles of food that I had stolen were filled with squash. We got into the brush again. [The leader said,] 'Let's rest for a while! We're far off now.'"**

Then that is what they did: they let the horses loose to graze, and then they began to eat. Now the members of the party talked about that boy. He was the one who singlehandedly had saved them. That one was a brave person.

Then one of them said [later, when he related the story], **"But we went on. [Our leader said to the boy,] 'When we arrive back at our village, these horses are yours. You stole them. You captured them. But we're riding yours while we're coming back.'**[2]

"Now as we were going back it was morning."

Then the party went on to the Assiniboine village. They arrived there, and then they began calling that young man Two Kettles. That boy had found a name for himself. Now that happened there in the country where the Assiniboines live.

Now after peace was established and intertribal warfare had ended, the Assiniboines came one time to Fort Berthold for a visit—to tell stories of what they had done and to dance—and then they told about this exploit.

And an Assiniboine man told this story. **"It happened long ago when I was a very young man. That is when we came. Now my father is the one who used to tell the story of it. This is what my father did here at your village.**

"Now I don't know who the people in that lodge were or even which tribe it was when he stole their horses and picked up the two kettles of food, but you must know which tribe it was."

They said, **"Now the ones whose kettles you took were Arikaras. Now they were the ones who tracked you. They would have overtaken you when you were in the brush, but it got stormy when you were fleeing, and then they turned back. They didn't run after you. The storm covered your flight. Then they turned back. They were Arikaras, the ones whose lodge you entered by going among them. You wouldn't have survived if they had seen you."**

Now this is what they used to say. This is what that Assiniboine man did. This is why they tell about Two Kettles, the Two Kettles of that Assiniboine village. But on the reservation on the east side (the Fort Peck Reservation) the people are Assiniboine-Sioux. They are half Assiniboine and half Sioux. And

---

2. On horse-raiding parties the leader was always the owner of all the horses stolen, even though certain men in the party were chosen to be the ones to go into a village to take the horses. Here, by giving the horses to the boy who actually took them from the Arikara lodge, the leader is recognizing the boy's deed.

the people living farther west are the real Assiniboines—the "chief Assiniboines," as they used to call them.[3]

This is what they used to say. That is what they used to call these people, Two Kettles, Two Kettles' Village, after he accomplished his deed and became chief.

Well, now this is the end of the story that I have told about Two Kettles.

33

War Story of Wet Moccasin and Old Bull

ALFRED MORSETTE, SR.

This war story tells of a Sioux party that came to attack the Arikaras one time when the latter were in their winter village in the Missouri River bottoms west of Like-A-Fishhook Village. It is foremost a story about ironies, of two incidents incongruous with the goals of warfare. One of the tragic outcomes of the routing of the Sioux raiders is the fate of two young companions, Wet Moccasin and Old Bull, who were among the Arikaras besieging them. Both young men were shot by their fellow tribesmen: one was caught in the crossfire and the other was killed by two Arikaras who mistook him for a Sioux. The second irony is the fate of two more fortunate men, one Arikara and the other Sioux: each was the sole survivor of his war party, the Sioux the survivor of the raid recounted in this story and the Arikara the survivor of a simultaneous raid some Arikaras had made into Sioux country. As they are returning to their respective homes, they encounter one another and share their experiences.

Now I am going to tell a story that I heard from the ones who used to have stories that they told while they were still living. And the one who told me the story I'm telling here was Nice-Voiced Elk, who I have been talking about. He was my uncle. My father and he were cousins. We were relatives.

3. A reference to the Assiniboines on the Fort Belknap Reservation.

Now when the village was there—when it was the combined village of the three tribes here—the people used to move into the woods in the bottomlands in the winter, when it began to get cold. They built a village here to the west, where there was plenty of wood in the timber extending westward.

They would live there during the winter, when the land gets cold, when the ice freezes the river over, and when it snows; and on this occasion the snow on the ground had got deeper again.

Well, and there were seven Sioux who came there in a war party. It isn't known where they came from when they came to the village, where the old village was. The country is not the same now: the land is underwater. Their purpose for coming on the warpath was to steal some horses.

There was no one living there in the village on the edge of the bank [Like-A-Fishhook Village].

"Ha, I wonder where the people went." That is what one Sioux was saying. That is what the Sioux later told Nice-Voiced Elk.

Now they went on. Then they found the trail; and, oh, there there was a wide trail where the village had passed.

Then they said, "Say, they must have camped in the woods where the trees are thick, now that it's becoming winter. Now let's go around the other way! Let's come upon their village from the north! And if they follow our tracks, they'll think, 'You must be Assiniboines who have come here.' They'll blame them."

Then they went around. Then they came to the village in the woods, oh, where there was the sound of the drum while they were singing songs. But then it was difficult for them to get close enough to the village so that they could go into it to steal some horses.

Then they said, "Say, let's cross over the river! Let's come at the village from the other side of the river! And then we'll steal horses. They must certainly be all around there in the brush." That is what they were saying.

Then they were imaging there were horses in the brush. They were also stepping in each other's tracks as they crossed the prairie [to make it appear as though only one person had been there]. Then they went into the brush there in the woods. Then they crossed over the ice at another place to the other side of the river. Then they sat down in some brush.

"After they go to sleep, then we'll go on."

Now one youth from the village saw the track there.

Well, in the morning when the young men in the village mounted their horses and rode onto the prairie, there was one track. It came from over there to the north. There was just a single track. The track had the print of one foot. But on one side of it there were holes in the snow. They were looking at it. "I wonder why there's only this one track and on one side of it there are holes in the snow."

Then they told some older men in the village about it.

Then the older men said, "It sure is puzzling. There must be many of them who came. They must be stepping in each other's tracks. It must be a cane that's making those holes. Now go follow that track! Whoever they are, they must be somewhere in the brush."

Then they followed the track past the village there in the woods. Then it went to the bank of the river; then it went across the ice. That is what the young men were doing[, following the track].

And here in the brush were the Sioux! Then the Sioux emerged from the brush when the young men exclaimed, "We've found them!" Then the young men chased them.

The Sioux went up one of the hills where those twin hills are, off in the distance. One hill stands apart from the other <and is pointed>. That is the one they went up. I saw it. There are rocks scattered all around on top. And there is where they were on top.

Then the young men surrounded it. Now they were attacking them on the hill.

An Assiniboine was killed by the Sioux. There must have been some Assiniboines among the young men from the village. They must have come from over there in the northwest after befriending some Hidatsas. There must have been an Assiniboine among them. The Assiniboine was shot by them. He must have had an inflated notion of himself; he must have sat down somewhere too close to the Sioux on the hill. He was shot.

Well, then the young men said, "They'll come down when they begin to get hungry."

Then they completely surrounded the hill as they watched the Sioux.

Then the young men raised their voices. The Sioux must have come down. They saw one run away from the hill. Then they ran after him. Then they killed him. And there it was one of those who had been on top of the hill!

Now they killed six. They did not know that there were seven of them. Well, they killed all of them, they thought. Then they came back to the village. One was going to go into the woods, and they killed him, too. Now the dead were lying all around.

Then the young men came home and were telling about what had happened. They said, "There was one who lay at the base of the hill, where they descended to the foot of the hill. That one lying there is the one he and I killed." Two men were telling about how they shot one man.

It was not a good situation when they had been firing their guns after it got dark. The Arikaras were also killing each other.

Well, there was one of their young men named Old Bull. They had wounded him. He was now lying inside his lodge. Then he said, "I'm waiting for my brother [Wet Moccasin]."

Then they told him, "We're looking for him, but we can't find him. He'll come back when we find him."

Then that young man Old Bull said, "I want to see him. I'm dying."

Then later he said <after drifting back from unconsciousness>, "And here he has gone first. There he stands. He's waiting for me. And now I'll go."

Then that young man Old Bull died. He died.

《   》

Then some men said, "Say, the one that these two talked about—the one they killed at the foot of the hill—perhaps you ought to go there. Take a look at the bodies! He may be one."

They ran there. Then they arrived there at the hill. And there was the young man lying there, that Wet Moccasin, the one in the story these two men were telling: "We killed one where they descended, when they came down the hill. The man lying at the foot of the hill is the one we killed."

And here these two were the ones! "And here we killed our own man, too!"

These two who had killed Wet Moccasin barely escaped getting killed themselves. Now they had killed him, too.

Meanwhile, one of the Sioux who had been on top of the hill had survived after he came down. He now went off alone. He had nothing. After he had gone for some distance, however far it was, he was hungry and cold, since it was wintry when he was traveling. Now this sole survivor was cold and had nothing.

Meanwhile a group of Arikaras had themselves gone on the warpath. There was the same number of them who were killed as there had been in the party of Sioux whom we Arikaras had killed. And here one Arikara survived!

Now the same thing happened to the Arikaras, when they were chased as they drove off some horses. But the one of them who was saved was thrown off by a horse, and then he did not get up. And that was the reason he survived. After the Sioux slaughtered the Arikaras who had gone on the warpath, they thought, "We must have killed them all."

Well, then that man who survived came on back alone. He was an Arikara. He must have had some edible things. He must also have had his weapons.

As he was coming along, there came this Sioux who had survived. Then they found each other. They sat down. Then they told about themselves.

Then one asked, "Who are you?"

Then the other one said, "I'm a Sioux."

"But I'm an Arikara myself. We went over there where your village is. They killed us. But a horse threw me off. I didn't get up. I just lay there. And after all of them went off, I got up. Then I came on. They killed all the rest of our party."

Then the other one told a similar story: "They killed us, too. I escaped. This is the reason: after this one fellow rapidly descended first, after he went, I followed down the hill behind him. As soon as my feet touched the ground— I hadn't taken a step yet—now another fellow landed on top of me as he slid down. Before I could even take a step, he landed on top of me. And here they must have seen us. Here they must have been watching down below there.

"Then they began shooting. They killed all the others in our party. Now I myself lay still. As soon as things were quiet, I got away. Then I came on. I'm tired now. I haven't eaten anything. I just don't have anything, not even a gun. I don't have any shells. I don't have a knife."

Well, then that Arikara gave him meat. "Now eat! But I'll go on." Then he gave meat to this Sioux.

Then the young man, this Arikara, came on. Then he arrived back home.

Meanwhile this other one, the Sioux, must have arrived there at his village, too. He must have told what happened.

Now that is how the people found out that the two Arikaras were the ones [who were the cause of Wet Moccasin being killed]. These two who shot him were older men. Now Wet Moccasin and the one who was named Old Bull were always companions. These two were the culprits when they killed him. They didn't know it. They thought, "The one we killed must be an enemy. And here he was one of us!"

Now this is what happened. Now this is what I myself heard.

34

Carries The Horn and the Sioux Raiders

Lillian Brave

When parties of Sioux men left their reservations to raid tradi-
tional enemies, seeking to count coups on them and steal horses, the
Arikaras living in Like-A-Fishhook Village were a primary target.
This story tells of one such raid, when a party of five Sioux men came
upon Ribs Woman, a lone Arikara who was picking buffalo berries on
a steep bank across the river from the village. Ribs Woman, a large
individual noted for her bravery, had bear power; and when the Sioux
assailed her, the bear spirit in her became manifest and she sent them
fleeing, catching one in the melee and pulling his legging off. Subse-
quently, when Ribs Woman lay unconscious in the Medicine Lodge,
three spirits—a bear, an elk, and a little Mandan boy—came to her
in her delirium and bestowed power on her. Akuke, the Mandan boy
spirit, chided her for previously having run away in fear from him,
and gave her a song as well as the name Carries The Horn, a refer-
ence to a horn that he himself carried attached to the end of a stick.
In addition to recounting the bravery of a woman, this story illus-
trates one circumstance in which spirits formerly came to individuals
and how personal names were derived from those encounters.

Now I am going to tell about the life of my grandmother. She was one of
the most courageous people of her time.

Once she was frightened by a spirit. And here it was bringing her a
message: "This is what is going to happen." But she did not pay any attention
to it.

Then she went to get buffalo berries. And so she crossed the river. Then
she went to get buffalo berries. After she and her sister had gone there, she hid
her sister. Then she turned the bullboat[1] over. She hid her sister under it. Then
she herself went up the hill to pick buffalo berries.

---

1. Bullboats, used by the village tribes of the middle Missouri for river transportation,
are tub-shaped vessels made of a buffalo hide stretched over a frame of willow poles.
See Brackenridge (1811:112) and Weitzner (1979:247–52).

There was a steep bank there. That was where the buffalo berries grew. That was where the thickest bushes were.

Then all at once she was quickly surrounded by Sioux. She was quickly surrounded by them. Then they were all just screaming.

But now here my grandmother Ribs Woman was a bear! And here she would imitate the sound of the bear.

Then they hurt the little finger on her hand. They cut her finger. Then that is when she became a bear. Then the bravery of this courageous woman manifested itself. She was a big woman when she went around—a big woman when she went around the village. She was noted for her bravery. And here a bear, a black bear, had pitied her!

As it was, the Sioux quickly surrounded her. Poor thing, then she was injured after they had cut her in several places—after they had stabbed her in various places and were counting coups on her. The Sioux were counting coups on her. There were five of them.

After they had cut the little finger on her hand, that is when the bear in her came out. The bear in her showed itself. Then she overcame the Sioux. She overcame them. She whipped them. Then she caught one. She threw him to the ground. Then she took one legging off him. She made him barelegged.

Then after a while one of the Sioux said, "*Hiyúpo! Hiyúpo!*[2] Come on! *Mat'ó wanáġi*. She has a bear spirit. She has become a bear. And here that's what she is! And here she's a bear!"

Then they became frightened. Then the Sioux ran off.

Then Ribs Woman went down the bank. Then she went down the bank. Then she turned the bullboat over. Then she turned it over. Then her sister got out, and she and her sister went home. Then they crossed the Missouri River. Then they crossed it. When they were about to get to the shore, she began calling out and calling out, and then some men came to the shore.

Then they took her out. Then they took her up the bank to the earth lodge in the center of the village.[3] That is where they took her. Then they took her inside.

While she was lying there dying, a [cottonwood] leaf dropped down. Then it became a bear. And there stood a bear.

Then it said, "You're doing the wrong thing. You shouldn't just be lying on your back, but you should move about! You should be going around in the woods. That's what we bears always do, and there we are just scattered around.

2. Italicized words are in the Sioux language.
3. The Medicine Lodge.

Even if my entrails are hanging out—even if my entrails are dragging—I go in the direction I'm facing."

Then Ribs Woman moved.

Now again a leaf dropped down, and when she looked, there was an elk.

It said, "You did wrong. Why, even if my guts are dragging, I go on, grazing on green grass—grazing on green grass. But you're doing wrong. You're just lying on your back."

Then the elk disappeared.

Then someone rubbed her eyes to revive her.

Then a leaf came in, and there stood a little boy. He had a stick, and on the end of it was a horn.

He said, "Why are you lying here? This is the reason I wanted to tell you something previously, but you became frightened. You ran away. You ran away from us. We came as spirits to tell you something, but you all ran away. You ran away."

When she regained consciousness she sat up. Then she wanted to walk around. Then the doctors took hold of her. Then they knocked her to the ground [because she was delirious].

Then the Bear doctors treated her.[4] Then the Bear doctors revived her when they were cooling her. Then they revived her.

Then the Elk doctors also began to sing. Then they rubbed up against each side of her. Then they rubbed up against each side of her.[5]

Then she got up. Then she was looking around the way elks do. Here she had now become an elk!

And then Akuke came last, the one named Akuke. And here he was a Mandan child.

And then he said, "This is what I meant. You ran away. If you had realized what I was trying to tell you, the Sioux wouldn't have hurt you, but you ran away. You became frightened. You became frightened. You ran away. But now this time I'll tell you. I'm giving you a song."

The song, a Mandan song, used to belong to Akuke. Now I don't know the song, whatever it was.

And then he said, "Now I'm going to name you. You'll be named Carries The Horn. You won't be named Ribs Woman any longer. No. You'll be named Carries The Horn."

And this is the reason they called my grandmother Carries The Horn when she was alive. My grandmother was the most courageous.

---

4. Doctors who had bear power and were members of the Bear society.
5. The Elk doctors were members of the Elk society. By rubbing against her, imitating the elk, the doctors imparted their powers to revive her.

When her brother, Little Crow Chief, was killed, he was the first one to be killed in a battle.[6] And his two cousins ran out into the battle, there where the battle was. They ran out into the battle. Then they picked up her brother, Little Crow Chief. Then they took him to the earth lodge there in the center of the village, where the medicine bundles used to hang. Then that is where they laid him [on a bed of sage in front of the altar] so that he would not become a scalped man.

This is what happened to Ribs Woman when she was courageous.

Well, now she was no longer named Ribs Woman. She had been named Yellow Cedar Woman. But now she was named Carries The Horn. She was named Carries The Horn by the spirit.

Comparative reference: ARIKARA Parks 1991, 4:754-56.

35

The Scalped Man Who Stole Things

DAN HOPKINS

Although the scalped man is portrayed as a benefactor in many Arikara traditions, the historical character was popularly perceived to be a thief, no doubt because his solitary lifestyle encouraged him to steal from people the things that social isolation denied him. In this story, which occurred when the Arikaras were living in Like-A-Fishhook Village, a scalped man repeatedly slipped into the village at night to steal hides and meat that were hanging on racks outside. People who lost things blamed one another for the thefts until one man determined to catch the culprit and discovered it was not a fellow villager but a scalped man.

6. The battle described in story 47, Parks 1991, 3:409-20.

Now I am going to tell the story of a scalped man who used to lurk around the village on the river bank—the one they called Fishhook—when people in the village were losing things to him.

When someone would be tanning a hide, she would hang it out at night to dampen and become pliable. And in the morning it would not be hanging there. "Why, someone must have stolen my hide!"

And especially when hit was dried meat, when someone would hang meat out to dry, then the person would pick out the big pieces of dried meat. Then he would pick them out. Then he would take them off. And in the morning: "Someone must have stolen my biggest pieces of dried meat!"

While this was occurring—while people were blaming each other for the things they were losing—one man said, "Now!" Whatever it was—a buckskin—he said, "Hang it up! Hang it up outside!"

Then his wife said, "Say, someone might steal it from me!"

"No. Hang it up!"

Then the woman did that: then she hung it up. After she had hung it up, the man hid near there in a shaded area that night. The moon shone brightly, wherever it was up in the sky.

Then the man saw a person come into sight—when the person came into sight. Then he came to where the buckskin was hanging. Then he picked it up with a stick, wanting to take that buckskin down with it.

But then this man came charging out. Then the scalped man ran off. Then the man chased him. He chased him and chased him until it became daylight. It isn't known how far he chased him.

And then the human tracks disappeared. There must have been snow, since it was spring, when the ice floats down the river. Then the human tracks disappeared. Then the tracks turned into those of a coyote.

Then this man was wandering around there aimlessly. Then he was running back and forth.

Then again the tracks became human. Now again he ran after the scalped man.

After he had chased the scalped man all day, chasing after him, well, the scalped man did it again: he changed his tracks into those of a coyote. But now the man knew what he was doing. He kept on going.

Then this scalped man killed a deer, thinking, "Surely you will stop for it. You'll pick up the meat." Then he took the hind legs off the deer. Then he took the hind legs off the deer.

But still the man who was pursuing him came on. And there lay the deer. There were no hind legs.

But then the man continued running, chasing him as he pursued him. Then he chased him to the bank of the river where the ice was floating downstream.

There in the distance the scalped man was jumping on the ice, jumping from one piece onto another. Then he motioned, "Go home! Go home!" Then he crossed over the river.

Then this man turned around. And then he came back to where the deer lay. Then he picked it up. Then he put it on his back. Then he brought it home. Then he arrived with it. Then he butchered it. Then he cooked all of it.

Then he said, "Now call the people! Let them come!"

The crier called it out. People came into his lodge. After they were inside, they began eating and eating. They ate everything up.

Well, then this man told the story of what had happened. He said, "The things you were losing when you were blaming each other were due to a different person. A scalped man was the one who was stealing things. He is the one I chased last night. I chased him that way all day, and he killed this deer that you have eaten. Then he crossed the river and I turned back. After I returned, my woman cooked the meat that you have eaten here. The scalped man is the one who was stealing things. No one here is the one. He is the one who was stealing things from you."

Narratives of the Past

Of Mysterious Incidents

Plate 20. Virgin's Breasts Buttes, Morton County, North Dakota. Photograph by Raymond T. Haas, 1990.

36

The Origin of Virgin's Breasts Buttes

ALFRED MORSETTE, SR.

On the level prairie not far west of Glen Ullin, North Dakota, on the south side of U.S. Highway 94, is an isolated pair of prominent, pointed hills known to Arikaras as Young Woman's Breasts Buttes and over the last century to whites as The Twins or Virgin's Breasts Buttes. The latter is their designation today, a more poetic translation of the Arikara name, and no doubt derives from this story, which explains not only these geographical formations but also the reason why hawks make a cry like that of a human baby.

When our people used to travel around while they were moving upriver, they were living somewhere, but I do not know just where it was. But this story here is one they used to tell. It happened there at the place they call Virgin's Breasts Buttes. It tells why they are called Virgin's Breasts Buttes.

It is a nice place there where the camp was located. A coulee goes through, and there are trees here and there. It is nice land. <The people used to go there on hunting trips.>

Well, one time there was a group of young women. There was a village there. Then they went up onto the prairie to go around digging for wild turnips.

And one young woman carried a baby on her back. It was a young baby. The baby was sleeping, and so she laid it down on the ground. Then she fixed up a nice spot where it could lie while she went around digging turnips.

The young woman must have gone quite a distance away. She must have somehow separated from the others. She must have wandered far off.

Finally she said, "Now I'll go back. I certainly have enough turnips now."

Then she went to where her baby lay. And there it was crying far up above! Then she looked, and the baby was not lying there on the ground! But there lay the shawl that had been wrapped around it! There her child was, flying up there with wings!

Then she began to call it. Then she began showing it her breasts. "Come quickly! Maybe you are hungry."

But it went on up there. It began flying higher. Then this young woman, the poor thing, gave up.

Now after that it is not known what happened.

And after the women went back home, the young woman's husband asked, "Where is the baby?"

Then she told her husband, "This is what happened. It flew up into the sky. Now it's flying around. It's become a bird."

Now from here I do not know what happened.

There are two hills sitting prominently there where the highway passes by today. The two hills are there on the prairie. They are pointed hills. That is where they are. That is where they used to say the young woman's baby—I don't know whether it was a little boy or a little girl—flew up and became a hawk.

And sometimes when a hawk calls out, it seems as if it is a baby crying. I myself heard it when I used to herd horses. When they used to brand around here, there were many horses. We were on a hill there once while the horses were grazing. It seemed as if someone were crying. It turned out to be a hawk flying around. It was calling out as it was making its sound. Now it sounded just like a baby. Maybe that incident is the reason why.

Now that is what I heard. And the two hills are prominent between Glen Ullin and Hebron.

Comparative reference: SIOUX Gilmore 1929:156–58.

37

The Priest Who Turned into Stone

ALFRED MORSETTE, SR.

Formerly, when the people of a village were returning from a communal buffalo hunt, the priests and others who had remained at home in the earth lodge village came out to meet the party. The priests carried the village sacred bundles, and people customarily

presented offerings of dried meat to them to offer to the deities in
return for blessings. This story tells of a priest who is ignored by all
the members of a returning party save for the last couple, who are
hurrying home suffering from thirst and hastily give him a tongue
rather than dried meat. Deeply offended, the priest pouts and turns to
stone. This story is admonitory in intent, emphasizing the gravity of
taking proper note of a priest in prescribed contexts. It is also the
explanation of a landmark whose location is no longer remembered.

Now I certainly don't know where it was that this story happened in the country there, when long, long ago our people were in the south migrating this way toward where we live today, but I used to hear about it when they told stories where my grandfather and grandmother lived—when the old-timers were living. Now I heard it when they told what happened with those sacred bundles that they had long ago.

Once after the village had gone on a communal buffalo hunt, after they had traveled far off, the young men returned to the village ahead of the others. "Now the hunting party is returning. The hunting party is coming." There were people who had remained behind in the village,[1] wherever it was that the Arikaras were living then.

And then the leading priest—one of the old men who possessed the holy things, the sacred bundles they had at that time—went out to meet the returning people as the priests would do.

Then someone would be sitting there, and he would say to a priest, "Now, open the bundle for me!" That is apparently what they used to say. When someone had given birth to a baby on the hunt, the old men who had the holy ways prayed for it while they incensed it. Also [another person might say], "Bless my boy. He became sick while we were traveling around out there." That is what the returning people would do<, asking for a blessing or making an offering of thanks to the bundle>.

But no one paid any attention to this one priest as he went by family after family. Then as he went on, the last members of the party were coming along. As one man and woman came, they stopped; and when the priest reached them, the man said to him, "Sit down for a while!" Then the priest sat down.

"Ah, my wife and I are dying of thirst. We don't have any water," said this man. "But here is a cooked tongue." It was a whole buffalo tongue. Then they put it down for him.

---

1. A reference to the elderly and infirm who were unable to go on the hunt.

Now it is not known what the priest said—they never told it—but then this couple arose to continue on their way home. They were thirsty for water.

Then this priest picked up a stick. Then he stuck it through the tongue. He felt hurt because no one had offered him some dried meat or had paid any attention to him [by asking for a blessing]. Then he went off. Then he climbed up it. A hill was there. Then he sat down on top of it. After he planted the stick with the tongue on it in the ground, he sat down by it. His feelings were hurt.

Then people began to look for him. "Where did he go?"

"He went out there. He went out to meet the returning people."

That is the reason priests used to go out to meet the returning people: that they would be invited somewhere <and that people would ask them for a blessing and present an offering of dried meat to them>.

Then they began looking for that man after he had not been seen around the village for however many days it was. "Surely you two were the last ones to see him," [they said to the couple].

"Eh, he reached us as we were coming. We were dying of thirst and wanted to come back quickly. So we put a cooked tongue down for him. I thought he would follow and we would all get back and then we would cook something nice for him here in the lodge. When we were coming we were in a hurry. And here he did not come with us. Now I don't know where he went."

"Perhaps he was killed." That is what people were saying.

And here he was sitting on top of that hill. Then they went up onto the prairie looking for him after he had not been seen around for however many days it was. Then they found him. There he sat on top of the hill, on a high hill. It was a high hill where he was sitting on top. There was the stick, set upright in the ground. The tongue hung from the end of it. And there he was, a rock! Why, here this man had become stone after pouting because no one had invited him to take some meat or had noticed him! And he had the holy things—he had the sacred bundle.

Now this is what the other priests were saying: "None of you noticed him. You were wrong to do that. <We have been praying for you people to get plenty of meat. You should have taken out some dried meat for him instead of giving him that tongue.> Now it has happened. You have offended the priest."

Then they offered him smoke.

Now, whatever had happened, he was no longer alive. No one knows what happened after that—only that he disappeared.

They used to call the place Where The Tongue Was On The Hill. They also used to say Where The Old Man Sat On The Hill.

This is what I used to hear from the man named Enemy Heart.

Comparative reference: ARIKARA G. A. Dorsey 1904a:119-20.

38

The Young Woman Who
Turned into Stone

ELLA WATERS

Today on a brick pedestal monument in Fort Yates, North Dakota, on the Standing Rock Sioux Reservation is a stone that, according to Arikara and Sioux tradition, was once a young woman. The story of her transformation recounted here is almost identical to other previously recorded Arikara versions and is probably the source for similar Sioux accounts.

Now I am going to tell about what happened where the standing rock is—when a young woman turned into stone.

There once was a young woman, a pretty young woman, but she did not want to marry. Her brothers would say, "You should get married." But she said no. When a man's relatives went to ask for her—taking horses like the old people used to do when they went to ask for a young woman, saying, "They will give you this many horses"—she would always say no.

Finally her brothers—she had brothers—began asking her, "Why don't you want to marry?"

But she would not tell. All she said was, "But I don't want to marry."

And then finally she said, "Alright," after her brothers continued to ask her to marry. "Now it will be as you wish. I'll marry."

So the young woman consented to marry a certain man after his relatives brought horses and asked for her.

And here the reason she had not wanted to marry was because she was not like other women are! Here she had a squash blossom for her vulva! Here she had a squash blossom for a vulva, and flying around inside it was a bee. And here that was her husband! The bee flying around inside the flower—here that was the young woman's husband!

Now after she married the man, the squash blossom wilted. Then it wilted. Then the young woman felt ashamed, and so she picked up her sewing bag. Then she put the bag on her back, and then went off. Wherever it was, she went off.

She also had a little puppy. Then she put the dog beside her after packing her sewing bag, after she felt ashamed, after her feelings were hurt.

Then she gradually began to turn into stone, beginning at her feet. And when people came after her, she told them, "It is impossible, the way I am now. Look at my feet!" She was stone there. "I can't go back to our village."

That is what happened. That is why the young woman felt ashamed after she got married, and became a rock.

Comparative references: ARIKARA G. A. Dorsey 1904a:120; Gilmore 1929:13-16; BLACKFOOT Cf. Holterman 1970:40; CHEYENNE Kroeber 1900:187; SIOUX Deloria 1932:221-23; McLaughlin 1916:40-41.

39

The Elk Doctor Who Called the Elk

ALFRED MORSETTE, SR.

A popular narrative form is the anecdote of a successful doctor's performance of his power to accomplish miraculous feats, thereby reinforcing people's faith in his ability to cure. This anecdote tells of one such performance witnessed by Jackrabbit, the narrator's uncle and a noted singer during the early part of this century. When he was still a boy, Jackrabbit and a companion watched the ritual summoning of an elk by a member of the Deer society, one of the eight doctors' societies composing the Medicine Lodge. This incident, related entirely in Jackrabbit's own words, occurred when the Arikaras were still living in Like-A-Fishhook Village.

Now I am repeating the words of the one called Jackrabbit. My mother— my father's sister—married him after her first husband died. Afterward she and the one who used to be called Jackrabbit married. He had no other name. I knew him by one name only, Jackrabbit. The man had a good voice when he sang songs at the old village. Now he told the story that I am going to tell. I was young yet. I was not going to school yet. I did not speak English. He told what I am going to relate.

"Among those who lived there in the village were medicine men, the different ones who used to perform mysterious feats.

"Now this boy and I were together. He was named Good Crow. Now I was fourteen winters old, but I don't know how old he was when we used to go around together here in the village, when we were in the combined village.

"Now he said that they were going into the Medicine Lodge to perform. My friend and I used to hear it from his father, or his grandfather, or his uncle, whichever one it was. He said, 'The Deer Society,' to which he belonged, 'is going to call an elk when it performs mysterious acts. Now they're going to call an elk. They're trying to see if it will happen—if an elk is going to believe them and to see if it will come.'

"Oh, it was just really dark! There was a fine rain. We were lying under the bed by the door, which faced east. We were lying there watching things. A man came out. Oh, they were singing while the drum was beating. A man came out. He faced the other way, the west. He stood there. He whistled, 'Uuuuuu.' It gradually faded out.

"He went on, going there. He went to the edge of the bluff on the river bank beside the village. We were hiding so that we would not be seen. It was really dark. He stood close by so that we could see him when he was talking. Again he whistled, 'Uuuuuu.' The sound echoed.

"After a while there in the west there was a whistle. We barely heard it when it whistled. He began speaking; he was singing.

"Again it whistled, and the sound echoed along the river. Now it must have been moving closer. Then it whistled close by. Oh, it was loud! There was an echo after it whistled.

"Now it had whistled twice; now once again it whistled after the human whistled, 'Uuuuuu.' It was barely audible at the end. The sound faded out after it whistled. It whistled nearby in the gardens in the brush. It seemed that we were actually seeing the elk. Oh, we opened our eyes wide so that we might see the elk.

"The other man began talking, talking, talking. He finished. Then he began to sing. Now it was not clear when the elk turned around. There were rustling sounds there in the brush where it went. Then there was a whistle over there in the distance where the end of the line of hills was, where the brush bordered the hills.

"And then this man turned around and entered the Medicine Lodge. We ran to the door. He began to tell about it. The Deer doctors ran around the inside of the lodge, and then they finished their performance. Now, this is what I saw."

This is what that man [Jackrabbit] said. And I myself heard what he told. That is why I know various stories.

40

The Young Man Who Did Not Believe in Ghosts

ALFRED MORSETTE, SR.

Fundamental to the Arikara worldview was a belief in an individual's continued existence, after death, as a ghost—an incorporeal spirit that might lurk around the living and influence their lives. This is the story of a skeptic, a young man who does not believe in an afterlife as a ghost. The experience convinces him that spirits do in fact exist and, moreover, are a source of good fortune when propitiated. Such a story functioned to reinforce cultural values and promote social conformity.

There once lived a boy—a young man—who did not believe in anything. No matter what might happen, he did not believe in ghosts. "Oh, you tell lies. There are no ghosts going around. When someone is killed, he is killed. What is he going to do if he becomes a ghost?" This young man just did not believe in them. He was living alone then.

Then one time he said, "I'll go hunting. I might kill a deer or an antelope," these animals being plentiful here in those times. And then this young man went off. He rode one horse and took two pack horses to carry his gear.

Then somewhere out there on the plains, in the west, wherever it was, he found a place to camp. It was a nice spot. "This is where I'll camp!" There was water there, and also woods. Oh, it was a nice, level place at the base of a hill.

Then he put up a lodge, a pointed lodge. They used to call it an "enemy lodge," a tipi. Then he put up the lodge. Then he tied his horses up. Then after making a fire, he began to fix a meal for himself, roasting dried meat.

Now it got dark, and as he sat there eating, someone came into the lodge. His shins were skinny. There were joints all over him. He was just bone. And he wore something over himself. Whatever it was, he wore it over himself.

Then the ghost began to make signs. Then this ghost said, telling him by motions, "I want you to give me some of what you're eating so I can eat."

Then this young man who did not believe in things said, "Why are you going around? And why don't you look around for your own food, just as I do. Don't just think that anyone is going to be giving you food! Go on outside!"

Then this ghost moved closer to where the young man was sitting, begging for food.

Then the young man who was a disbeliever said, "I don't like it. Just say, 'Throw me out now,' and I'll do it." Then he jumped up angrily, and he and the ghost grappled with one another.

Oh, the ghost was strong as they were wrestling. When it became daylight, the young man got on top of the ghost. And as soon as it became dark all over, the ghost got on top of the young man. Then the ghost became strong.

After they had been struggling, the young man with difficulty finally overcame the ghost. Then he grabbed the ghost's leg. Then he dragged him. He dragged him outside. There was a deep depression over there where he was dragging him, and then he threw him into it. "You're just pestering poor me when I am hungry!"

After he returned to his lodge, the young man began to eat. It was morning, and he ate a meal. After finishing, he said, "Why don't I water the horses first, and then I'll go hunting!" Then he proceeded to do that.

When he led the horses to the water where he was taking them to drink, there on the edge of the bank sat the ghost he had wrestled with. Then he charged the ghost. Then he kicked his ribs. "Now you're doing what you always do. I suppose you think you should be given food!"

The ghost, the poor thing, rolled over the bank, and there he went rolling down the bank.

Then the young man went on and watered the horses. Then he went to his lodge. He roped his best horse. Then he mounted his best horse. He went hunting.

When he would shoot at antelopes he could not kill any. Oh, so he came back to his camp. He had not killed anything.

Now it was morning again. When he went out hunting, he still could not kill anything. Even when he hit an animal he did not kill it: the deer or antelope just continued going on its way.

Then this young man felt like crying. He was now in his lodge. "Hey, why is it? Usually nothing is ever difficult for me, when I want to kill deer, antelope, and buffalo. Why is it that I'm not able to kill anything?"

Then a party of young men came along. There were seven of them. Among them were two older men.

"Now, hello! What are you doing?"

He said, "Why, it's difficult for me. Oh, there are lots of antelope, but I can't kill any. Or any deer or buffalo. Oh, they're plentiful. But no matter how I try, I can't kill any.

"But when I first arrived here, this is what happened: a ghost harassed me, begging for food while I ate. We fought, and I threw him down the bank. There's a deep depression there. That's where he's lying."

Then they went over there.

Then one of the two older men said, "Why, here's where you erred! The man lying down there at the bottom was with us when we were once camped here. It was long ago. This one was sick, and he died. We buried him here. And this is where it was, here where you are, when he was begging for some food to eat. The poor thing, he was sick and then died. That must be the reason he was hungry. That's why you didn't kill anything.

"Now, quickly, let's hurry!" Then they got ready. Then they prepared food for the ghost. They set food down for him, and then filled their pipe and offered it to him.

Now it was morning. "Now, hello! What's going to happen now? Let's go to where you were hunting, where you said there are plenty of antelope."

Then they went. There was a huge number of antelope. In no time they were shooting them and killing them. Oh, there was a large quantity of meat after they brought the carcasses back to their camp and made dried meat.

To this young man who had found it difficult to kill any, they said, "Now you'll believe it. You didn't believe in ghosts. Now you know how it is. This ghost, who is holy, was going to starve you to death, just as the situation was when he died."

For this reason, then, the young man said, "Now I believe it. Here it is that way! Here it is true! Ghosts do hear! Now I believe in them. Now from here on when I go around I shall believe everything. I'll be praying to the sacred powers to bless me."

Now that is what this young man did. The spirits blessed him, and after he prayed to them for what he wanted, it happened that way.

Now, this is how the story went.

41

The Dancing Ghost

ALFRED MORSETTE, SR.

This short story continues the theme of the existence of ghosts and how they are a potential source of good fortune. In it a party of Hidatsa hunters, having no luck finding game, camp near a bed of quicksand, where they are visited in the evening by a strange being. As they leave the next morning, they find a skeleton by the quicksand and then realize it had been the visitor, who is the spirit of the man whose remains are there. After caring for the skull and offering it smoke, they experience success in hunting and return home laden with meat.

I just don't know who I heard this story from that I am going to tell. It is one that was told when they used to tell stories. There were many old men who told them. Actually they were not old men; the men I used to see when they told stories were still young.

Now one time when a group of young men had gone off somewhere, however many there were, going out hunting to look for various things—now after they had been gone for so many days, they came to the bottomland of a river valley, wherever it was. Then they made a bullboat to cross the water. Then they floated across. Now they floated across. They came to the other bank. It was early evening now.

Then one of the men said, "Hey, it sure would be good if we were to stay overnight after we've crossed the river, and in the morning we can go back to our village."

"Now that's really a good idea. We'll do that," they said as they were floating across.

Then they went close to the bank. Then the one who sat in the front jumped onto a sandy spot. When he put his feet down, there was soft sand. Then his feet began to mire. And then he sang, "Ho, heya; ho, heya. I might get stuck in the mud." Then he quickly crossed over it.

Now the same thing happened to each of the others, but all of them came across the sand. Then they left the boat and went up the bank. It was a nice area there.

Then one of the men said, "We'll stay overnight here." Then they readied everything. Then they put up a hunting lodge—what they used to call a hunting lodge, whatever kind of lodge that was. Now they were inside the lodge telling stories while they were making a meal and meat was roasting over the coals.

Now after a while a man just came inside the lodge. Oh, what he was wearing must have been on him for a long time. When the men looked at the way he was dressed, they could see he had worn his clothes for a long time.

Then the stranger said, "Ah, I'll eat some of what you're eating and then I'll dance awhile. Ah, I like the song you were singing."

Then they gave him a piece of meat as he knelt with one knee on the ground. Oh, they did not know him.

Then he said, "Now sing it! I want to dance awhile and then I'll go."

Then the men were singing different songs.

Then he said, "No. It's a different song. That isn't the song I like."

Now there was one young man, a quiet one, who was sitting over there. Then he said, "Say, maybe he means the song we sang when we climbed up the bank: 'Ho, heya; ho, heya.'"

Then the ghost said, standing there by the fire, "That's the song that I want to dance to. Now sing it!"

While these men were clapping their hands and singing, "Ho, heya; ho, heya; ho, heya," oh my, this ghost was dancing and dancing. He was whooping as they were singing, "Ho, heya; ho, heya; ho, heya."

"Ah, say, now I'm thankful to you. Ah, I just like that song. Now I'll go." He went out.

"Whoever are you, you who are wandering around?" That is what the young men were asking now, wondering who he was.

Then they went to bed.

Then morning came. "Now let's go back to our village!" Then they went down the bank to where the boat was, the bullboat.

When they came to it, there was a pile of bones there. The skull was lying there, too. The person, whoever he had been, had got stuck in the mud over there where these young men had got stuck before.

"Ah, the poor thing, he must have died. He must have starved to death after he got stuck in the mud, just like what might have happened to us."

Then they picked up the skull and put it in a nice place. They offered smoke to it. After they fixed up a place for it, they set the skull nicely there.

Then they came on. Now nothing was difficult for them, as they were shooting deer and antelope on their way home. They had plenty of meat. Ah, then they arrived back at the Hidatsa camp, wherever it was.

This story I have told is a Hidatsa story. Now that is what happened when the Hidatsas were singing, "Ho, heya." It means 'to hurry up when one is getting ready to throw something away, to be prepared.' That is what they must have meant.

Now, I have told the story of this song "Ho heya" that I have sung. Now this is what happened.

42

The Eagle Trappers and the Scalped Man

ALFRED MORSETTE, SR.

When parties of men set out to seek their fortune—to raid, hunt, or trap eagles[1]—the leader generally took along religious objects that he used in rituals to insure the success of their undertaking. In this story of an eagle-trapping expedition, a buffalo skull (addressed as Grandfather) and an ear of corn (addressed as Mother) formed an altar in the hunting lodge where the men ate and slept. During the day, while the men were in their traps, a scalped man would slip into the lodge, scatter the furnishings about, and embellish the ritual objects. Here the scalped man appears as a comic character—one of the many roles in which he was cast—and both his antics and the men's reactions to them are sources of mirth. The story suggests how the tensions inherent in the seriousness of ritual were occasionally released as humor.

Back when we used to live in villages, a group of young men went off. They went to trap eagles like they used to do formerly when they caught eagles. They were eagle trappers. Now, however many young men there were, they went off to the badlands, where eagles ranged, out there on the prairie in the west.

"Now this is a place where we might find some eagles."

1. See story 30, pp. 282–88.

And then they built a lodge. They used to call it a hunting lodge, whatever kind it was, the hunting lodge. Then they fixed everything up. Now they used to pray to various things. There was a buffalo skull there. They had it sitting there. And there standing upright was Mother Corn. [These formed an altar.]

After the young men had fixed everything up in the lodge, getting everything ready, then each one said, "This is where I'll be." "This is where I'll be," [choosing their trap sites].

"Now all of you fix up the places where you'll be!"

[Then each one fixed up the trap he would sit in, where] he could watch things while he was inside, where he could watch all the other men, too, including the one farthest away [in case the enemy might come]. Then at sundown each one got out of his trap. Then they all gathered together. Now they came back to their lodge. That is what they used to do.

After a person had dug a hole and gotten into it, he laid willow sticks on top. There was a hole where the smokehole would be in the center, where the bait would lie—what they used to call bait, a rabbit. Now after skinning a rabbit, they tied it there. It was tied tightly so that an eagle could not snatch the rabbit away. He fixed things up. Now it was tightly secured.

Now when an eagle landed to eat the rabbit, that was the time to catch it by its legs. Well, then he would break its wings. Whatever it was that they used to do I surely do not know, but it is what I used to hear when they told stories.

But on this occasion those young men, after they had gone to their traps, came back to the lodge in the evening. "There aren't any eagles in this country."

Now they came back to their lodge. After each one had gone off to his trap, they returned to their lodge. Then they went inside where they had left ribs roasting over the fire, thinking "We'll be coming back."

Now the ribs were scattered along the far edge of the lodge. Things were in disarray. Wood was lying everywhere, and this buffalo skull was sooty black after someone had smeared it with soot. After he had smeared it, there it was, black! Also on the Mother Corn he had drawn a woman's face. And whatever else he had done.

Oh, then time went on with this happening repeatedly. Here the one bothering them was a scalped man.

"It's certainly not good; whoever he is, he's making fun of us, the one doing these things, ridiculing our grandfather Buffalo Skull and our Mother Corn. Now let's find out who it is going around making this mischief, scattering our things all around—the things we were roasting, while we thought they would cook nicely." He had thrown the ribs way over there. He had thrown them over there by the entry to the lodge.

"He must be one who really mocks people, whoever he is. Now let's catch him!"

Then they dug holes close by their lodge. Oh, then early in the morning they got into the holes, after they had arranged things in the lodge to look like they should.

Now it was sometime later. There was the sound of footsteps on the ground, coming fast. He arrived at the lodge, and, oh, he looked all around. It seemed as if he knew they were waiting for him. He put his head inside and looked all around. Then he went into the lodge again.

And then these young men got out of the holes. They went to the doorway. He was muttering in Arikara. And he said, "Why, say, I got everything fixed up for you, ah, so that you'd look nice. Ah, Mother, now they've spoiled the things I did. And this Buffalo Skull that I fixed up—they've changed it back. Oh my, it's certainly not good." That is what he was saying over and over.

He was kneeling down in the middle of the lodge. Then one man entered slowly . . . and then another . . . as they all came inside. The scalped man sat there facing the other way in front of the buffalo skull, talking to it and talking to himself. Then the young men stood in the doorway so that he could not run out.

"Hello! Hey, you who are wandering around far off, why, I wouldn't wander around if I had a village!"

When the scalped man jumped up and saw these young men, he fell over. Then he died of fright.

Then he was shaken by one of the young men. He never moved. "Let him lie there! Now quickly, let's be on our way!"

Then they picked up their things, the Mother Corn and the buffalo skull, and then they came home.

"What he's been doing to us—his making fun of us—is not good."

Then they remembered that a young man had died there long ago, and here he was living! I don't know what his name was. But they knew him when they saw him.

Ha, then the young men came home. After they returned home, one said, "Say,"—they meant that one—"he was ridiculing us, and here he must have been living there, and now he died of fright. Now this is what he did when we caught him. When we took him by surprise, he died of fright. He's still lying there, a left-behind. Then we came on."

Then the relatives of that young man went so that they could see him. He was not lying there inside the lodge. Here he had apparently jumped up again and gone off somewhere!

Ah, while they cried, saying "Ah, you yourself are the cause!" one of the young men said, "We should have grabbed him. Then we could have brought him back for whatever might have happened."

43

The Sioux Captive Tortured by Mosquitos

DAN HOWLING WOLF

This war tale recounts an unusual form of torture that an Arikara war party once inflicted on a captured enemy.

One time, wherever our village was, a group of men planned it. "Let's go on the warpath!" Then they got ready. They mounted their horses. Then they went off.

Then they went off. Then they found the Sioux. They fought. There was a fight with the Sioux. They got the best of them. Then the Sioux ran off.

But then they headed one man off, surrounded him, and caught him. Then they took him. They held him.

They were asking, "And what are we going to do with this one? We won't kill him. Let's tie him up to that tree and let the mosquitos kill him!"

Oh, there were hordes of mosquitos that summer.

And so that is what they did: then they tied him to it. They tied his hands and also his feet to it. They tied his body to a tree.

Then they went on.

"Now go on! The mosquitos will kill him."

Then the party did it: then they went on. They chased after the Sioux, pursuing them. Then, wherever it was, they caught up with the Sioux.

Then again there was a fight there where they were on the prairie. Then they killed and scalped them. Then they were waving the scalps on the ends of poles.

Now it isn't known where they went, but they traveled around out there in the west for a long time.

And then one said, "Now let's go home!"

They had gone there to steal horses, but then they had not taken any. Then they came back.

As they were coming along, one man said, "Let's go to where we tied up the Sioux enemy!"

"Fine."

Then they went. As they were running along,[2] they came out of the brush. "This is the place."

There he stood. The dead body hung there. His face was pallid after the mosquitos had sucked all his blood out. There where the grass was—when anyone walked on the grass by the tree, his feet became red. After the mosquitos had sucked the blood out of him and had become full, they died in the grass, and then it was bloody there. The mosquitos were really plentiful that summer.

His body was hanging there. Then they took him down and laid him in the brush.

Well, then that is what happened: then they went back to our village. Then they arrived there.

Then they told about it: "This is what happened: the mosquitos killed a Sioux. This is what we did: we tied him to a tree. There were hordes of mosquitos! They must have sucked all the blood out of him. When we came back, the body was hanging there. He was pallid all over. They must have sucked out all the blood. And when anyone went into the grass growing there, his feet became red."

There was a deep layer of mosquitos that had died there. This is what they did to the Sioux.

This is the end.

2. War parties usually set off on foot in the expectation of capturing horses on which to ride home triumphantly. The party here, however, has not taken any horses yet.

44

The Disliked Young Man
Who Went on the Warpath

DAN HOWLING WOLF

Another unusual theme is how members of a war party might deal with an unwelcome or disliked individual who joined them. In this story, a war party once gave an unwanted young man a contrived task and then abandoned him, hoping the enemy would find and kill him. Later, however, the members felt remorse after they discovered how seriously the young man had taken his task.

There in our village, wherever our village was then, they said, "Now let's go on the warpath!"

Now there was one boy going around there. Then he joined the party and said, "I'll go with you."

They did not like the boy—the young man—however many winters old he was.

They resented him as they were going along. After he came, why, things were not good.

After they had gone a long way off, wherever it was, they killed some deer that they hunted. Oh, then there was a large quantity of meat piled up. The meat was piled up.

And then they said to the disliked young man, "Now we're going to give you the task of brushing the flies away."

Then they gave him leaves. "You'll use these to fan back and forth, and you must go around the meat as you brush the flies. But now we'll go first, and then we'll bring back more meat. There isn't enough here. There isn't enough to go around."

Then that is what they did: then they left him and went on.

"The Sioux will kill him there. They'll find him."

Then they went on, going around looking for Sioux, wherever it was. It isn't known how long they went around. Anyway it was a long time, and then they came back.

"Let's go back to where we left the young man fanning flies, where he's fanning them. Let's see what's happened to him."

Then they went back there. It was located there by a cluster of trees, at the edge of the brush. That was the place where he was fanning them with the leaves.

They arrived there. He was still going around. There was a depression where he had been walking around and around [the meat]. The meat that had been lying there was now only bones. And the leaves were now only sticks. And the main one [the boy] was all shriveled up. He was alive, but, ah, he was all shriveled up.

"Why, he's still standing here!"

Then they went up to him. Then they took him. Ah, they set him down. Now the ones who had medicines began giving him medicine to drink. He was dying of exhaustion from going around the meat. His moccasins were torn. He had become skin and bones from going around.

Then they gave him medicine to drink. They always carried medicines with them.

One said, "What did you do to stay alive?"

"At first things were good. I'd cut off a slice of meat to eat. Then I'd just hurriedly eat it raw. I wouldn't roast it. I'd take a slice of it raw. Then after a while, after the weather got hot and the meat spoiled, it became impossible for me. It became impossible for me to eat any meat after it became spoiled. Now it was really no good. There were maggots in it.

"Heh, this is what I did. At first it was good. I would just run down to the river there." The Missouri River flowed there. "I would drink hurriedly. Then I would come back. Well, then it really became difficult for me, so that I was barely able to go down to drink. Now that's what I did. That's what happened."

Then this is what they did: now they wrapped him up. Then they laid him on a travois that one horse pulled. Then they laid him on it. Then they took him home. Then they felt bad after they saw him there, regretting what they had previously done.

They hurriedly took him there into the village and to the Medicine Lodge, wherever the lodge was, where the doctors would meet. Then that is where they took him. Now this is what happened: then the members of the party that had gone just went there.

Then they told about it: "Now this is what we did. We made a mistake. That is what we did: we left this young man there. Ah, we feel bad about what we did."

Then that is what they did: then the ones who had medicines began doctoring him. Then he put on weight again. For quite some time they would not let go of him while they were giving him medicines to drink.

Then he regained his strength. Then he began to walk around. Then he began going about again.

Then he did it: after he became strong, he went back to his home. Then he became vigorous. And then he himself told about "when we went on the warpath."

Comparative references: ARAPAHO Dorsey and Kroeber 1903:23–28; CHEYENNE Grinnell 1908:273–74, 292–93; 1926:270.

45

The Woman Who Was Taken by a Bear

DAN HOWLING WOLF

This is an account of a woman who is mesmerized by a bear and taken to its den. Although it is not an explicit story of power bestowal—the woman is simply abducted—it has the typical elements of one: an animal changing into human form, the human wearing a feather, and the spirit resuming its animal form and then mesmerizing the person, here a woman.

There in a village where our people used to live, one man and his wife made plans. "Let's go off! Let's go look for meat! I think I'll hunt far away!"

Then they went. After the wife put their gear on a travois, they went off, wherever it was.

"Now let's camp right here! This is a good place. This is where there must be some deer."

And so they put up their dwelling here. They camped.

Oh, morning came. While the woman sat there working, the husband went off hunting far away. He went hunting. But the woman sat there sewing—making moccasins. She sat outside.

And then sometime later she saw a movement. When she looked, a man was going into the woods in the distance. He was at the edge of the woods. She sat by the edge of the woods where they had their lodge. She looked, and a man went into the woods over yonder. He had a plume on his head. He went into the woods when she saw him. She paid no attention to him but continued her sewing.

Then toward evening her husband came back. But she did not tell her husband, "This is what a man who came out of the woods did."

Well, then again the next day the man went hunting. And then the same thing happened again: there was the same man there. Then he went back into the woods in the distance.

"Hey, whatever is the matter? What's going on?"

But she did not tell her husband anything: "A man is doing this, coming out of the woods and then going back into them."

And again morning came. And again he did the same thing when she was sitting outside. It was hot there. Then she looked. There went the man in the distance. Then he went back into the woods.

Then she thought, "Why, I wonder what it is? There must be a camp over there. They must be our people. Surely, though, they would have come out of the woods. Perhaps they might be Sioux. Surely, though, they would have come out of the woods."

And then he got the best of the woman. And so she went. "Let me take a look at that person who always comes out of the woods. Maybe there's a camp there."

She went into the woods. When she was walking into them, it came out of the woods. There was a bear! Then this woman became frightened.

Then it came up to her. Then it said, "Now you must have come."

"Yes, I have come." Now the woman was mesmerized by it.

It said, "Now let's go over there to my lodge! Let's go over there!"

Then it did that: it took her to its lodge. There where they went was a cave.

"This is my lodge."

Then they went into it. There was meat lying all around. Then the woman was eating well.

Meanwhile her husband returned. He returned. His wife was not in the lodge.

"Hey, I wonder where you went."

Then he ran all around, going into the valley and going all around there looking for her. He looked everywhere. He did not find her.

Then he yelled. There was no sound.

"Why, the Sioux might have come here. The Sioux might have taken her." The man thought all those things.

Then at night he gave up. Then he went to bed.

«   »

Then early in the morning he got up again. Then he went running here and there, going around over there on top of the hills.

But then he gave up. He came back to camp. Then he thought, "I'll go home now!"

Then he did that: he gathered all his belongings together. There lay what his wife had been sewing. Then he gathered the things up. He put everything on the travois. Then the man went back alone to our village there. Then he went into the village. He went into the village.

After he arrived he went into the chiefs' meeting, and then he told about it: "This is what happened. My woman has disappeared. They must have taken her somewhere. I don't know what happened to her. I want to gather a group of men to go look for her."

Then that is what they did: then the crier called out, "Now this is what is going to happen."

Then a party gathered. "We're going to go. This man has lost his woman. She isn't around any more."

Then that is what they did: then they got ready and went. Then the man took them to where they had camped.

Then he said, "Now this is where we were staying."

Then they scattered out, going there into the hills, the high hills. Then they found it: there was the cave. Dirt was dropping down from the top of the entrance.

Then they said, "A bear must be in here."

Then they did that: then they went up the bank to the cave. Then they became frightened.

"Who's going to go into it? Why, a bear is no good."

They became afraid of it.

"Ah, it might not even be inside!"

Then another man became angry. "I'll go inside."

Now he had a gun, and a knife. Then he did it: then he charged inside. After he went inside, it was light in the cave. And there sat the woman they were looking for.

Then he called out, "And here you are."

Then she said, "Yes, here I am."

Meanwhile the bear was sleeping by the wall. It was lying there asleep.

Then he said, "Now go! Now you go first! Hurry! I'll kill that one."

And so that is what the woman did: she jumped up. Then she went out. Then she went out.

Then the bear woke up and got angry. This man was waiting for it. Then he shot it. He killed it. He charged it and then really slit its throat with his knife. Then he went out.

There they stood, the woman among them. There the woman stood among the party.

Then the man said, "I have killed it. It's lying there inside. I killed it. I don't know what's going to happen, so let it lie there! It did wrong. Now go on!"

Then they took the woman. Then the man took her back to our village. They arrived there at the village.

Then the woman told what happened. "This is what happened. Here it must have been a bear—a bear—that I had been seeing. Then it was a man who was going into the woods. And it got the best of me. 'I think I'll go there. I wonder who you are, you who are coming out of the woods and then going back into them?'

"This is what I did: I went and walked into the woods. He passed in front of me. And there it was a bear! This is what it said: 'Now you must have come.'

"'Yes, I did come.'

"'Now let's go over there to my dwelling!'

"And this is what I did: it took me to its den where you found me. It took me inside where you found me. Now this is what the bear did."

Comparative reference: KIOWA Parsons 1929:9-10.

46

The Vision Quest of
Green Grass and Bull Neck

DAN HOWLING WOLF

*This is the story of two undisciplined young men who are urged
to fast on a hilltop in hopes that a religious experience might help*

them to mature and become men. Their effort, which ends in failure, is a story of irreverence and cowardice, in which they break the rule of fasting during the period of their ordeal and then run home frightened when they discern something strange approaching them, running away from the very spirit they are seeking to attract and thereby depriving themselves of any future spiritual blessings.

Once they went off. Then our people went on a communal hunt, to travel around hunting. Among them were two young men. They were named Green Grass and Bull Neck. They had no sense and were always doing various things, whatever they might be, and always acting wild.

Then the people were going along, and then they camped at the base of some hills. The hills were high there.

Then one old man said, "Say, you two, why don't you go up onto one of these hills somewhere? Make yourselves pitiful. Then something might bless you, since you don't have any sense. If you are pitiful, something might help you. You must cry. You must go up on a hill at night. You must cry."

Then they both said, "Oh, no!"

Then that Green Grass said, "Well, alright, we'll go tonight."

Then after dark they went up onto one of the hills. They went up on top.

Then one of them said, "Say, I'll stand right here. You stand up over there. Then you'll come [towards me] from that way. When you come from there, then I'll go that way and we can cross each other's paths. When you get over there, you'll turn around and come back again."

Then Green Grass said, "Fine."

Then that is what they did as they cried there that night. That is what they were doing there: then they were crossing each other's paths [as they went back and forth].

Now one never used to eat when one fasted. However, one of these two ran down into the camp. He entered a lodge over there. Then he took some food to eat. Then he went back up the hill.

"Now it's your turn."

Then the other one ran down to eat during the night, too.

Then morning came. Then they both went home to sleep. Now at night they went back up and did the same thing.

On the third night, while they were crying, Green Grass came one way and this Scabby [Bull Neck] went the other way, and then they crossed each other's paths. When he looked, there was something coming where the cut bank was. Something was coming up it. They both stopped.

This one said, "Do you see something coming?"

That other one, Green Grass, said, "Yes, I see it."

Then all of a sudden the other one [Scabby] said, "He'll catch us. He'll catch us." And, oh my, then they both ran off! Then they ran down the hill to the village. They ran inside.

After they were inside, this Scabby said, "Oh, say, now you've spoiled it. Did you see it coming up?"

"Yes, I saw it. Yes, something was coming. Something must have been pitying us. Something would have blessed us. Now we've spoiled it. Now don't say anything about it. Don't tell what we've done. Oh, the old man will scold us. He'll get really angry with us."

Then morning came.

"Well, hello! Did anything happen? Did anything pity you two?"

"Yes, but it didn't amount to anything. I'm still tired. My ribs are tired from so much crying."

"Yes, but did you see anything?"

Then he said, "No."

Later, as the two young men were going around, the old men found out. Then they called the two. Then they took them inside the lodge. They set food before them. Oh, now the two ate.

Then Scabby asked, "Why did you call us?"

Now the old men stared at the two of them. "Yes. You did badly by doing what you did. Look here, they must have been pitying both of you. They surely were going to bless you. Now look! Here you two spoiled it!"

Now they were just sitting there. Scabby said, "Yes, that's what I did."

Oh, then the old men scolded them. "Look here, it's not good. It's a mysterious thing. What you were doing you were doing well. Why, it would have pitied you. But now you have spoiled it! Hereafter nothing will be done for you again."

Now that's what they did: Scabby and Green Grass spoiled it for themselves.

Tales

Of Human Actors

47

How Bear Man Became a Chief

MATTHEW WHITE BEAR

This fable, told to children by Hidatsas and Mandans as well as Arikaras, illustrates many common folkloric themes on the northern Plains, the dominant one being the rise to chieftaincy of the protagonist, Bear Man, the progeny of a female human and a male bear who, like his father, possesses extraordinary power even though he has all the human attributes of his mother.

They tell that there once was a village, and then a group of young women said, "Let's go gather ground beans!"

Then that is what they did: then they went into the woods to gather ground beans.

But there were two young women who were friends. Then they came to a big rock.[1] Oh, there were many ground beans indeed by the rock!

Then one of them said, "You go around the rock that way, and I'll go around this other way! Then we'll meet each other."

After she went around it, the one did not meet her friend as they had planned. She reached the end of the rock and her friend was not there.

And then she began looking for her friend. "Perhaps you might have gone somewhere."

Then she asked the other young women who were here and there, "Have you seen anything of her?"

They had not seen her.

After they had all gone back home, the one young woman went to the lodge of her friend's mother.

Then the mother said, "She hasn't returned."

《　　》

---

1. A large rocky outcrop.

337

It was a long time later.

Meanwhile about the young woman who had disappeared: here a bear had its den where the rock was, the big rock. It had taken her into its den there.

Meanwhile this tale goes fast.

Then this young woman became pregnant and had a baby. And then it was a boy.

Now as time passed and the boy grew up and became aware of things, when he looked at himself he saw that he was only slightly hairy. But then he looked at his father: he was hairy all over. And then he looked at his mother: she was not that way.

Then he began to question his mother about it. Then he asked her, "Why is it that I'm not very hairy and you're not hairy at all, but my father is hairy all over?"

Then his mother told him what had happened.

The boy said, "Alright, when I become a man, I'll kill him."

Then the boy began doing it: when his father went out of the den, he began tracking him.

Now the tale goes fast.

Then the boy made a club for himself so he could hit his father on the head with it. When his father brought back a deer he had killed and he came into the den—when he came crawling into it—he hit his father on the head. Then he killed him.

Then he and his mother ran out of the den. Then they ran away. Then they arrived back at the village, and then they went to her mother's lodge.

Then she called out, "Father, mother, I've come back! Here I am."

They doubted her words, but then finally they opened the door for her. And so the young woman and her son went inside. She had her boy with her.

Now the boy began to mingle among the children. He went among the children when they were playing. But he played roughly and he would always hurt someone.

Finally the children began to fear him. They thought, "You shouldn't be among us." Then they began shunning him.

But he himself knew what they were thinking.

Then he told his mother, "I just think I'll go off somewhere. I'll go somewhere alone. But I want a blacksmith to make a club for me to carry."

Then his mother did that: then she went there. Then they made a club.

When the boy took hold of it, he said, "It isn't heavy enough. They should make me a bigger one!"

Then they did that: then they made one a little bigger, just as he wanted. Then he quickly disappeared.

《   》

He was going along, and as he was going through the woods he went to a grove of trees.

Then he saw a person coming. Wherever there was a tree in front of him he would just knock it down and continue on his way. This man was the one they call Whirlwind. Whirlwind. He was the one.

Then the two met each other.

Then Bear thought, "Why, I'm as good as you are."

Then they befriended each other after they were together.

Then they went on. And while they were going along, there was another person ahead of them. Wherever there was a stone, even if it was a boulder, he would just roll it around.

Then Bear thought, "I'm just as good as you over there."

Then the two men got to where this other one was. Then they all got together. Now there were three of them.

And then when they went on they found another man. There he was, going around.

The previous one was now named Stone Roller. And the fourth one was now named He's Strong.

Then the four of them—Bear, Whirlwind, Stone Roller, and He's Strong—went on.

And there was a lodge. "There's a lodge!"

Then they reached it. They went inside, and there were four beds—four beds.

Then Bear said, "You'll sleep on that bed there." And to another, "You'll sleep on that one." That was the way it was: each had a bed to sleep on.

The next morning, well, after morning came, Bear said, "We'll go hunting, but you, Whirlwind, you'll stay. You'll make a meal for us."

Then they went hunting.

Meanwhile as Whirlwind was going about, making fires and doing whatever it was that he thought he should do, a little old man came charging into the room. It was a little old man.

Then he said, "Now you've spoiled my room here! This is my lodge."

Then Whirlwind got angry. Then they did it: they wrestled. Then the little old man threw him down. Whirlwind was knocked unconscious by him. Then the little old man ran outside and went somewhere, wherever it was.

Then Whirlwind, the poor thing, awoke. And here the food he had been cooking was burned!

And now his companions who had gone hunting returned.

Then Whirlwind said, "I must have fallen asleep. All of what I was cooking must have burned." He did not want to tell them that the little old man who knocked him out was the reason.

Then Bear said, "Stone Roller, now it's your turn. You'll cook."

Then these three went out hunting.

And just as he had done previously, the little old man came charging inside. He knocked Stone Roller unconscious. Then he ran away.

And now the men returned. When Stone Roller awoke, all his food was burned.

Then he told them, "I must have fallen asleep," just as Whirlwind had said.

Again the next morning Bear said, "He's Strong, now it's your turn."

Then they went off.

Just as he had done before, the little old man came charging inside again. "Now you've spoiled everything for me. All of you get out!"

Then the two fought. He knocked out He's Strong. He got the best of him. Now the others returned.

Then He's Strong said, "All my food must have burned. I must have fallen asleep."

Then Bear said, "Now it's my turn. Now see if I go to sleep! You can go on."

Then they went off. They were laughing as they went. "Well, he must have been killed by now. He must have laid him out by now." That is what they were now saying.

Oh my, then the little old man came charging into the lodge. Then they fought. But Bear had the club! Then he hit the little old man on the head.

While they were still fighting, the little old man had a string around his neck. Hanging from it was a bag with liquid in it.

Then Bear cut the string. When he cut it, the little old man became pitiful. "Give me the liquid!"

Then he chased the little old man out, whipping him as he went, while the little old man ran to where there was a rock. He ran into a hole under the rock. Then the rock covered the opening.

Then Bear turned back. After he returned and went into the lodge, all the food was nicely cooked.

And now they returned.

Then Bear said, "You're going to eat well now. I didn't fall asleep. I've found out what the little old man did to you. We'll go there after you finish eating. We'll catch him."

After they had eaten, he led them to the rock.

Then he said, "Whirlwind, lift it up! Open the door!"

It was too difficult as he struggled to lift it.

"You, Stone,[2] now it's your turn."

Then he did it: he lifted it up a little. But it got the best of him.

And the other one, He's Strong. "It's your turn now."

Then it was too difficult for him, too.

And now Bear. "It's your turn."

Now Bear uncovered it.

Then they brought a rope. Then they dropped it down into the hole. The hole was deep.

Then Bear said, "Whirlwind, you be the first one! You'll go down into it."

Then he took hold of the rope.

"When you get to the bottom, shake the rope! Then we'll know you're there."

After he took hold of the rope, he went down. Before he reached the bottom, he shook the rope when he became frightened. It was dark in there. Then they pulled him back up.

Then he told them, "It's really dark there!"

"Now you, Stone Roller!"

Then he also did the same thing: then he became frightened; then he shook the rope; then they pulled him up.

And now the other one. "It's your turn, He's Strong."

Then he also did that: then he became frightened.

And "Bear, it's your turn."

Then he reached the bottom. He did not do what they had done.

Then he went off. When he went, he went in a direction different from the main one. Then it was getting light as he went there.

Then the little old man came charging again. Now he stood there. Then he pleaded for his liquid.

Then Bear hit him. He knocked him unconscious.

After he had knocked him unconscious, Bear went on. Now he found out where his dwelling was. There were four young women standing outside it over there in the distance. Then Bear arrived there.

---

2. A shortened form of his name.

Then the young women became frightened. "He'll kill you. The little old man is evil."

Then Bear said, "There he lies over there. I've killed him."

Then they said, "He's the one who has kept us. He's the one who captured us."

These were the daughters of the chief of their village.

Then Bear said, "Go! Get out of the cave!"

And then they went.

"The oldest one," he said, "you'll be first! You must shake the rope."

Then the men above pulled her out, and then they fought over her. After they calmed down, they put the rope back down into the hole.

"Now you!"

Then they pulled her out. Then they did the same thing: then they fought over her after they pulled her up.

"And now you!"

There were now three of them who had gone up.

Then the youngest one was last. Now she went up.

And then Bear was left. Then it was his turn.

And then the men said, "If we pull him up, he'll take all the young women from us."

After they pulled him half way up, they let go of the rope. Bear was knocked out.

When he was rolling around as he revived, the little old man came charging again. He must have revived somehow. And now he had the liquid. Here that was what was making the little old man strong!

Then it was impossible for Bear to get out. Meanwhile the others had run off.

Now while he was going around, a bird found him, whatever kind of bird it was. Then that one pitied him and took him out.

Then Bear got out. Then he began looking for the others. They were not in the lodge where they had been living. Then he went to the village and went home.

But some coyotes—there are always coyotes around—then they told Bear everything. The other three men were chiefs now, since they had brought the young women back. This was now their village.

But the youngest one knew what they had done to Bear. Now she did not like it. Then they saw Bear. Then the youngest one arrived there and she told about it. Then the youngest one told about it.

The youngest one said, "This Bear is the one who saved us, and here this is what they did to him. This is what they said: 'He'll take all the young women away from us.'"

Then those others got the worst of it. They were removed as chiefs, and then the youngest young woman married Bear. Then *he* was the one who became chief of that village.

Comparative references: ASSINIBOINE Lowie 1909:191–92; IOWA Skinner 1925: 480–81.

48

When Bloody Hands Went on the Warpath

LILLIAN BRAVE

The theme of social and economic differences among individuals permeates Arikara oral traditions. Nowhere, however, is the stratification of Arikara society more vividly portrayed than in the stories of Bloody Hands, the poor, ugly, misshapen boy who lives by the dung heaps with his grandmother. Hands's ugliness and poverty, however, are only superficial, for in fact he frequently discards this appearance to reveal himself as a handsome young man. And he always succeeds at what he undertakes, no matter the odds, because of the holy powers he possesses. In this story, which the narrator learned from her father, Hands goes to war and is victorious over the enemy despite the degrading treatment he receives from the wealthy members of the war party. Forcefully articulated here is the moral lesson that it is the poor person, not the affluent one, who ultimately triumphs.

Although Hands and his grandmother lived near the dung heaps, the poor things, they always managed to mingle with the wealthy families. Although they lived among them, he and his grandmother were poor and had their lodge by the dung heaps.

And then one time Hands thought, "I want to go on the warpath."

Then he said, "Grandma, I want to go on the warpath."

Then his grandmother said, "No. We are poor and you have an ugly horse. The one you ride is ugly."

"Oh, no, but I want to go." He was determined to go.

"Now go on then! Let it be! Go! Go!"

"Listen, grandma, when I return you can go through the village. Then you can go through the village. Then you can smear your face with soot. You can tie your hair up in braids over your forehead."[3]

"Oh, how you do talk this way, Hands! Look, we are poor."

Then he said, "No. I mean it, grandma. I want you to be prominent—to be prominent and go in front—since we always go around in the rear. Now I want you to be prominent."

Then she said, "Alright. Now go on! Go there!"

Then, the poor thing, she filled a pouch with parched corn. Then she filled it with parched corn. Now he carried it hanging below his arm. Then she also made corn balls.

Then his grandmother said, "Now go on! Go there, grandson! But we are poor. I don't want you to go with them. Look! Those others have beautiful horses, but yours, the horse you ride, is ugly."

"No. He's a beautiful horse. You don't know."

Then that is what he did: then he just went with the party. Oh, then he went with the men who traveled in the lead, but then they sort of left him behind. They did not want him to be among them since he was certainly ugly. And so that is what they did.

Now no sooner had they gone over a hill, than he, the poor thing, would just be coming up it. Those others would already have gone over the hill. Just now he himself would be coming up it. That is what he was doing.

Then he caught up with them when they had reached the place where they intended to scatter the Sioux. So that is what he did, the poor thing: he had traveled in the rear. Then he took himself off his horse. Then he got down from the horse that he was riding. Then he lay down to sleep.

Then one man said, "Hands, I want you to tell tales."

Then he said, "No, I can't tell tales on the warpath. I can't tell stories."

"Come now! Look, your grandmother and you are the foremost ones for telling stories."

Then he said, "No. My grandmother said, 'Don't tell a story when you go around on the warpath. You can't tell tales.'"

---

3. Members of a returning Arikara war party smeared soot over their faces for their trimphant procession into the village. Here, Hand's grandmother joins the war party for its procession into the village and, like the returning warriors, she blackens her face with soot and also ties up her braids over the forehead.

Then he flung off the cap he wore over his head. It was a tripe.[4] He threw it way over there. Then he took a frying pan. It was on the fire. Then he took it off it. Then he held it in his hand. Then he also took a ladle. Then he took a ladle. Then he put the frying pan under his arm.

They asked, "Why have you done this?"

"Well, you want me to tell a story. I can't tell a story."

Oh my, then he sang,

> These cuts in my hair represent battles.
> Ii a hai ra iree,
> Ii a hai ra.

"Now that's what I thought. I was afraid of doing it."

Then the Sioux were whistling. Wherever it was, they were whistling. Then the Arikaras were ambushed. Then the Sioux killed half of them. Half of them were killed.

And then he said, "Now, see, that is what I feared. But you wanted me to tell tales."

Then he sang again as he danced around. Then he was dancing around while he was singing.

Then he sang and danced harder. They tried to stop him. "Let that be all, Hands! Let that be all!"

"No. You wanted me to tell a tale; that's the reason I'm doing it. I'm not going to be afraid."

There was his cap over yonder. And here he had long, beautiful hair. Now he had long, beautiful hair, whereas before he had had a head just full of sores. He had had a head full of sores when they had seen his head before. Poor thing, he had had a scabby head. He had not had any hair. Now he had long locks of hair.

Now they were offering the pipe to him, the poor thing, and said, "Let that be all, Hands! Surely they've killed a lot of us already."

Then he put the cap back on his head now that the Sioux were whistling while they were disappearing. Oh my, then Hands charged around, killing Sioux and killing them.

Now the scalps that he had taken were piled high. The scalps were piled high.

Then he said, "Now, see, you have all seen this. Do something!"

They now picked up all the scalps.

"This one is yours. This one is yours."

---

4. Hands wears the reticulum to give the appearance of having a head covered with sores. From that appearance comes the name Sore Head (see story 5).

The scalps were piled high.

He said, "Now let's go home! Truly let that be all!"

Then the party grouped together. Then they came home.

《   》

Just as they were approaching the village, Hands said, "Now one of you go ahead! Go tell my grandma to come through the village. I have returned as I said. Now she can do it! Let her smear her face with soot! Let her tie her hair up in braids over her forehead! Then she can come through the village."

Then that is what they did: then the leader was the one who sent word. They told his grandmother, "'Now I am coming. Now I am coming. We have returned.' And he wants you to have a pole that you will carry at the head of the procession.'"

Then the man gave her the willow pole that Hands had had. There were the scalps he had tied to it. They were there on top. The scalps extended the full length of the willow pole, however long it was.

Then the man said, "'Let my grandmother come! Let my grandmother take the lead!'" That is what he said when he took word to her. "'My grandmother will come at the head of the procession, and then we'll go into the village.'"

And then that is what they did: when they arrived there at the village, when they arrived there, his grandmother came out.

"Now, grandson, what did you do? Poor thing, you are always doing things."

"No, grandma. Did you do as I said?"

Oh my, then his grandmother just smeared her face with soot. Then she tied her hair up over her forehead.

"Now that is what I meant. Grandma, I want you to be prominent."

Then they went into the village. His grandmother was in the lead. Then Hands followed. Of these chiefs, the different ones, the leader was at the end of the procession. Then the leader was at the end after Hands, the poor thing, had outdone them all.

When they saw this horse that had been scrubby, oh my, it was now so big! It had such slender legs and hoofs! Oh my, a beautiful horse!

When he and his grandmother went through the village, Lucky Man over there said, "Now, Hands, you and your grandmother come here! Come here! This is where you're going to live, here where I live."

And then they were offered another [small] lodge [of their own], too.

Then she said, "No. He and I can't live here. We are poor. We will go back to our own lodge by the dung heaps."

Then he said, "Alright. Now that is how it will be. For that is what you two want."

Then Lucky Man laid the pipe before Hands, the poor thing. Then Hands picked up the pipe and smoked.

Then he said, "Grandma, now we are going to do it. We're going to move into the lodge of Lucky Man, the wealthy man."

"Now it will be thus, grandson, but we, poor things, were poor, and you were ugly. When I see you now, grandson, here you are a handsome man! Oh my, a handsome man!"

Here he was Hands! Where he had had sores on his head there were now none. Now he was a fine-looking person.

And now today that is the reason that the person who is poor is the one who becomes a chief. And the one who is a chief is the one who will come last. The poor person is the one who will arrive in the lead. This is the reason that when one of us is poor, that person comes in the lead. For this is what Hands did.

Now the gut went in.[5]

Comparative reference: ARIKARA G. A. Dorsey 1904a:69-70.

49

When Bloody Hands Became an Eagle

LILLIAN BRAVE

This is the fourth, and last, of the stories of Bloody Hands in the narrator's repertoire, and according to her it is to be told in April, at the end of the storytelling season. In it his grandmother deeply offends Hands by her refusal to allow him to join a war party. In retaliation he turns himself into an old eagle and flies off to the Black Hills. When his grandmother follows him, pleading for him to return home with her, he steadfastly refuses. In a final desperate attempt to

5. A formulaic ending for a story (see p. 108).

force him back, the old woman turns into a bear and jumps up to grab her eagle grandson who is on top of Devils Tower—a motif found in the stories of the origin of that landmark (stories 10, 86, 141). Finally Bloody Hands flies off to live in the southwest, where as a remembrance of him he promises to give turquoise to the Indian people living there to use for their jewelry.

The village was coming in a long procession, and Hands and his grandmother, the poor things, were living among them, living pitifully on the outskirts of the village by the dung heaps, alone there where the pitiful people, the poor things, lived.

And then a war broke out. Then a war broke out.

Hands said, "Grandma, I'll go with them, too. I'll go with the young men when they go. The young men, however many there are, are going on the warpath. I'll go with them, too."

"No. No, Hands, you are pitiful. You are ugly. You aren't the type to be among them—for you to be among them on the warpath. You are pitiful. You are ugly."

"No, grandma, I want to go." He was repeating himself as he pleaded with his grandmother. "I want to go with them on the warpath."

"No, grandson, you are the ugliest baby. Why, you have a scarred belly. You are just ugly all over. You aren't one to go with them."

"No, grandma, you've just hurt my feelings by not giving me your permission to go. But now I want to go anyway—to be with them on the warpath."

And then Hands said, "No, grandma, you've hurt my feelings. I wanted to be with all the young men there where they're going. I wanted to be with them."

And then his grandmother said, "Surely I have already said that you cannot go. You are certainly ugly. I don't want the men to tease—to tease you and call you names. I don't want it."

"No, grandma, I wanted to go with them. I'm always successful when I go with them on the warpath. I'm always successful. But now for whatever reason it is that you won't allow me to go, that's how it will be. You've really hurt my feelings, grandma. You've really hurt my feelings."

Now when the old lady turned around, why, here he had become an eagle!

Then he sang,

> Now I'm going to become an eagle, grandma.
> Now I'm going to become an eagle, grandma.

Then his grandmother said, "Oh, ho! As ugly as you are, how can you become an eagle!"

When she turned around to look—when she saw her grandchild—there there was the head of an eagle attached to his body.

"No, grandson, no! I love you, grandson. You can go off with them. You can go off with them."

But he had already become an [old] eagle.

Then the old woman ran outside. She tied the tipi up. She staked it down. She staked the tipi down with great vigor.

Oh my, then there were flapping sounds up above in the smokehole. The smokehole is where the eagle flew out as he flew away. Then he was flying higher and higher. He was really flying high up there in the sky.

"Come down, grandson! I love you. You and I are pitiful together. It isn't good for poor me to live here alone pitifully."

Then the eagle said, "No. But that's what you wanted. This is what you want—that you live alone in solitude. Now that's how it will be. Now it will be that way: you'll live all alone in solitude. And now I'll go to the Black Hills. The Black Hills are the direction in which I'll fly. Where the highest of the Black Hills are is where I'm going."

After some time as he was flying along, the eagle flew down to the ground, but his grandmother was there. She had turned herself into a rabbit—a rabbit lying on top of a hill. Then the eagle flew down to the ground.

There he saw his grandmother.

"Grandma, I always like to eat a rabbit that's dead, but this one is alive. This rabbit lying here is alive."

Then he soared back up into the sky. Then he flew back up high.

Not long afterward, after he had flown back up high and was going along, there lay a stag off in the distance. Ah, it lay there in the distance. It lay on top of a hill far off. The eagle flew down to the ground again. Again the eagle flew down to the ground.

When he saw it, "Grandma! I always like to take bites out of a deer that's dead, but this one is just looking! This stag is just looking. It's just looking."

Then he flew up high again.

"Ah, grandchild, I want you to come. I want us to be together since I am pitiful. It is not good for me to live alone. But it was good when we were together. Poor things, we were pitiful when we lived and ate by the dung heaps."

His grandmother said, "Well, go on!"

Again he flew up high. As he went on flying, he flew high up against the sky.

His grandmother said, "Ah, Haaands! Haaands! I'm watching you here. I'm watching you here. You are just wishing that the buzzards would come to eat me up."

And then the old woman became frightened of them.

She said, "No. I'll just stay here, and when the buzzards come, I'll just scare them away. I'll just scare the buzzards away. And no matter what happens, grandson, listen: I'll follow you. I'll follow you there, wherever you go. Meanwhile I'll be flying behind. I'll fly behind, no matter where you go."

Then he reached the Black Hills there. He reached the Black Hills.

"Ah, grandma, no matter where you go, I'll always be up ahead. I'm going where the highest mountain is—where the very highest mountain is."

His grandmother said, "Now there will be one favor I ask of you, grandson. Come to the ledge and let me see you for the last time, and then I'll see your face, grandson."

Well, so then that is what the eagle did. He went there on top of the highest mountain. It was a rock. It was a tall rock [Devils Tower]. There on top is where he landed.

"Now, grandma, here I am now. But I let it be known. I said, 'But I'm going there to the Black Hills.' That's how it is. This is where I'm going to be. This will be my territory here. The Black Hills here will be where I roam around, but you'll live over there. You forbade me to go with them on the warpath. And now while the wars are going on, I'll be sitting here. I won't pay any attention to them, but, poor thing, I'll sit on top."

Then the old woman arrived there. Then she arrived. The old woman arrived there.

"Nooow! Haaands! Just peek over! Let me just get a glimpse of you!"

Then that is what he did: then Hands, the poor thing, perched on the ledge. Now he sat on the ledge. But when he saw his grandmother—but when Hands saw his grandmother—here she had become a bear! And there there was a bear, a big black bear—his grandmother.

"Now come to the ledge! Let me get a glimpse of your face!"

Then Hands moved over. When he looked at his grandmother, they looked at one another. Oh my, then the bear leaped up into the air. Then she clawed against it. Then she fell down. Now there was a thump on the ground when she fell down.

"Now wait, Hands! I want to touch your hand. I want to touch you anywhere."

"Now try harder, grandma! Why, surely that's what you want to do there. It's your own fault. You yourself are the cause. You hurt my feelings. You really hurt my feelings. That's the reason I turned myself into an eagle. I'll fly around over here permanently. Meanwhile I'll go about over here in the Black

Hills. Meanwhile you can live over there with them! You people can be making wars over there! But I'll go around here in the Black Hills. I'll go around here in the Black Hills. But you can live over there with them."

And then the old woman said, "Ah, Hands, I'm going to say it once more. I'm going to say it once more, 'Come to the ledge! Why, let me see you for the last time!'"

Now he went there again. Then he sat down on the ledge. Oh my, then the bear leaped up angrily. Then the bear leaped up angrily against the rock. This time she almost reached the top. Then she did it: then she fell down scratching it with her claws again.

"Now, grandson, why, here you have gone!"

"Yes, I've done it. But I've gone now. There to the south is where I'll head. There to the south is the direction in which I'll go. Over there is where human beings will have rings that they make. A rock—turquoise—is a stone that will be set in it, too. And that is what they can remember: what I, the eagle, have done for them, too—what I have done for them."[1]

Again that is what the old woman did: she leaped angrily up into the air. Then she scratched him. And then she scratched him a little. She fell down again. Well, now this was the last time.

"Now, Haaands! I loved you. We were pitiful. Poor things, we were pitiful."

And then the old woman cried.

"Now, grandson, this will be the end. I'm tired. I'm tired from jumping. And now that's the end. I'll let you go. I'll let you go, and you can go off there to the south where you have said. You can go off there. You've made it hard for me. I can't get there where you're going. It's a rocky land. It's too difficult. That's where you're going. You're really leaving me. And that's how it will be, too. You've hurt my feelings. We both have hurt each other's feelings."

Both the old woman and the eagle had hurt each other's feelings. That is all.

And now the eagle was headed southward. "And that is where I am headed, but here is where you'll go about."

"Now, grandson, grandson, you have made it hard for me. It is impossible to go over there. It is only rocky land. It is only rocky land. That is where you are headed there. Now what you yourself want to happen—and now I'm going to ask them over there to use those different kinds of precious metals, the precious metals inside the ground. I myself pity them. That is how they will be, too: the Indians living over there will be rich. But you have hurt my feelings

1. A reference to Navajos and Pueblo Indians, who make silver and turquoise jewelry.

here. And now we've separated. It is truly the way it is: we have separated. The eagle is going all around. He is going around in the Black Hills. But I'll go around pitifully over there."

And then the old woman went home. Then the old woman went home.

《   》

Then she arrived there. And there her lodge was.

"Eh, Hands used to live here. Here is where Hands used to live. Well, so now you have made plans for yourself. You have made plans for yourself, the way you wanted. That is also what I myself want to happen. You have made plans for yourself, the way you wanted."

But now she was talking to a spirit. The old woman was speaking to the eagle. "So you have made plans for yourself. You'll travel around there. Over there you are holy where you are going around far away. Now you have left me. Now you have made me feel miserable. And I'll live pitifully over here, whatever it is that I myself am going to do."

That is the end.

Tales

Of Coyote

50

Coyote and Lucky Man

ALFRED MORSETTE, SR.

Hungry, always seeking gratuitous meals for himself, deceitful, inept—these are the most common traits of the trickster, Coyote— traits well illustrated in this story.

They always tell about Coyote and his pranks when he wandered around looking for meals for himself.

One time when Coyote was running along, he saw smoke rising up. There was a lodge there. When he went up to it, he looked at the lodge.

Ah, the food smelled good to him. It smelled like boiling meat. "Why, oh my!" Coyote said.

Then Coyote went there. Then he went to the entrance of the earth lodge. Then he made a sound in his throat, "Ha, ha, uha!" as he tried to get the attention of whoever was inside. Now he was making this sound over and over.

Then the person inside finally said, "Say, whoever you are going around out there, you should come inside. Come in!"

Then Coyote went inside. "Hey, it certainly is good that I've finally found you, uncle, while I'm traveling around on the warpath. I've just come from the Black Hills. Our war just ended. We were warring with the enemy, and we counted coups on them." That is what Coyote was saying.

And then this man said—this man was named Lucky Man—"Say, sit down now!"

Then Lucky Man took some meat out of the pot. Then he dished some meat out for Coyote.

And here this is just what Coyote wanted: something to eat. Oh, he began eating while he told stories, telling all kinds of fibs.

Finally Coyote said, "Now I sure am full. I'll go now."

"Alright."

Then Coyote went out.

《　》

After he went outside, he swung around. "Hey! I wish I could find something good for myself. I wonder what I should do?" That is what Coyote was thinking over and over.

"I should hurt myself in some way so that Lucky Man will give me some meat!"

Oh, Lucky Man had lots of dried meat. Coyote just looked at it there, wanting to steal some dried meat, a tongue, or, oh my, one of the many other pieces.

Then Coyote said, "Say!" He charged up to the door. Then he sang a song there. While he was singing, he was jumping and dancing around, bothering Lucky Man inside and teasing him. He sang:

> Lucky Man, I am pleading for your food.
> Fox is dancing well.
> Fox is dancing well.[1]

Lucky Man came outside. Then he gave Coyote a rib to eat.

But Coyote was determined to continue jumping around while he was singing. Again Lucky Man gave him something to eat.

Now Coyote continued to sing:

> Lucky Man, I am pleading for your food.
> Fox is dancing well.
> Fox is dancing well.

Now Lucky Man was giving Coyote things—giving him dried meat and different things.

Then Lucky Man said, "Say, you sure are a pest! You must not be at all thankful for what I've given you. Hey! Now I'm going to kill you."

Then Lucky Man nocked an arrow. Coyote, the poor thing, fell to the ground screaming when his leg was shot. Then Lucky Man went and dragged him inside. He took the arrow out of Coyote's leg.

Coyote said, "Now, uncle, I just want to be around here because you have such good meals."

Then Lucky Man replied, "Yes, that's alright. You can fetch water for me. And if you stay here for a while your leg will get well."

《　》

1. The name Fox in this lyric is synonymous with Coyote. Among the Pawnee, Coyote stories are often designated Fox stories.

But when Lucky Man went out hunting, Coyote was greedy and got into things to eat. He ate everything up. And here that is what he wanted: to eat all of Lucky Man's food!

That is the way Coyote was, always telling lies when he was looking for food for himself.

51

Coyote and the Two Blind Men

ELEANOR CHASE

Even when Coyote's life is spared after committing some mischievous act, he cannot resist disobeying a simple injunction placed on him, no matter the consequences.

It is not known where our villages were along the Missouri River when this story occurred.

Then two men became friends. Both of them were blind, and so their relatives made a lodge for them in one of the villages. So that is where they built the lodge for them.

And while the two men lived in the lodge, they had piles of wood to make fires for themselves when they cooked the food that their relatives brought for them. They did nothing but stay inside their home. When one was sleepy, he proceeded to do it: then he lay down to sleep. And when the other one was sleepy, then he lay down to sleep. They did not know when night came. They only knew the time when someone came to their home to bring them food. Then they would wake up and go outside.

Now as they usually did when it was perhaps late in the afternoon, both of the blind men went outside to urinate. After they finished doing it they went back inside. They were doing this day after day, and then one time Coyote came trotting along.

Coyote is the one we have who always does wrong things.

And then Coyote came trotting along. Now he was looking at the faces of these two men. Then he thought, "Why, you can't see!"

Then Coyote entered their lodge. It was a small lodge. Then he ate up everything of theirs. Now it is always the case that Coyote is hungry wherever he goes. So he ate up all their food.

When the blind men came back inside, one said, "Shut the door!"

Then the other one shut it.

Meanwhile there was a fire burning in the fireplace in the center of the lodge where their things were. Then as time went on and on they sat by the fire telling stories and talking to each other.

Well, then after a while Coyote picked up a stick. Then he began to burn the end of it in the fire. Then he took it and burned the hand of one of the blind men.

Now when the blind man's hand was burned, he thought, "An ember must have popped up. It burned my hand."

It was not long before Coyote burned the hand of the other blind man. Then this one said, "Hey! You burned my hand. Why did you burn it?"

And then the other blind man said, "Why, you burned my hand first. You hurt my hand."

And then he said, "Why, I'm not the cause!"

The other one said, "Someone must be inside. Lock the door!"

Both knew the location of everything in the lodge as well as where the door was. So the other blind man went to the door and locked it.

Then both blind men began to chase the intruder around inside the lodge. And here it was Coyote! Then they caught him.

Then they both asked Coyote, "Why did you burn our hands?"

Now Coyote just sat there.

Then one of the blind men asked, "What shall we do with him?"

And then the other one said, "Let's pierce his ears."

And then his friend said, "Fine."

Then they pierced Coyote's ears. Then they made two holes in two small pumice stones. Then they hung them from Coyote's ears.

Now Coyote just sat there. Then he began bobbing his head up and down. Then the pumice stones were shaking.

Then one of the blind men told Coyote, "When you go outside and go on your way, don't look back at these villages, no matter where you go. But just continue going there, wherever you're headed, wherever you're going. Then things will be fine for you."

And then the other one said, "You're lucky we didn't kill you."

Then the blind men opened the door, and Coyote went outside.

As Coyote was hurrying along, jumping up and down as he went, he came to a long, high hill, and then Coyote went up it. As he was going along he thought, "You two men won't know if I do it. You're both blind."

Then Coyote looked back toward the villages where the lodge of these two blind men was. After he looked at their lodge back there, he ran down the hill.

As Coyote was going along after he arrived at wherever it was, the pumice stones he had hanging from his ears began to expand.

As he continued on his way, the stones finally got heavier. Now he was barely able to go . . . barely able to go, as he thought, "I want to go home," wherever his lodge was.

Then he thought, "Something must be wrong with me." The pumice stones were even bigger now as they continued to expand.

Finally Coyote's face touched the ground as the stones continued to expand.

Then Coyote fell to the ground. Now he lay there, not able to do anything, not able to shake them off as they continued to expand.

Now, after he lay there for a long time, Coyote died of starvation.

Now this is the reason that whenever there is a pile of bones near pumice rocks, we know that Coyote, who had no sense and who did mischievous things, came there. And so that is where his bones are. Now Coyote is the one who came there and starved to death.

Comparative references: ARAPAHO Dorsey and Kroeber 1903:227; HIDATSA Beckwith 1937:287; PAWNEE G. A. Dorsey 1904b:52; SIOUX Deloria 1932:174-75.

52

Coyote and Buffalo

DAN HOWLING WOLF

Here is Coyote again, appearing now in the common role of the envious, never satisfied trickster. Once he is transformed into a buffalo by a bull he has been admiring, he deludes himself into believing he has the same power, and as usual he goes too far.

Then Coyote went there. Buffalo were standing there in a large herd. It was a huge herd! Coyote was starving to death as he watched them. He was so hungry that his stomach was drawn in while the buffalo ate the green grass growing there.

Coyote admired what the buffalo were able to do. "I wish I were you. I wish I were a buffalo like you. Then I wouldn't get hungry. I would just be able to eat anything, like this green grass or hay, or anything."

Then one buffalo came toward him. Then a buffalo bull came toward him.

Then Buffalo said, "It seems like you're wishing for something while you're sitting here."

Coyote said, "Yes, yes. I just wish I were like you, just as you are there, just eating the grass, the leaves, and everything. You're really full. But, poor me, I'm just a coyote sitting here starving to death. I wish that I might eat some meat. I wish that I might kill a rabbit. I wish that I might have some good luck. It's just hard for me."

Then Buffalo said, "Surely it isn't hard. Surely you can be the same way that I am. Now let's go up the hill over there to where the ground is smooth!"

Oh, Coyote was happy. Then both of them went there.

Then Buffalo told him, "You sit right here! I'm going to go over there. I'll stop over there and then I'll come to you. I'll do it four times. Each time I'm going to hook you with my horns."

Then that is what Buffalo did. Then he went over there. Then he turned around.

Meanwhile Coyote sat there. "I wonder what you're going to do to me?"

Then Buffalo charged. Oh, when he reached Coyote, the poor thing, he hooked him and threw him into the air. Then Coyote, the poor thing, got hurt after he was thrown into the air and landed.

Then Buffalo said, "Now there are three more times for this to happen."

Now Coyote hurt all over. He was limping as he went back to where he had been. Then he sat down. "What did you do?"

"Don't move around. If you do, you'll lose your luck. You won't be the way I am. It doesn't matter to me what happens."

Then Buffalo went over there again. Then he stopped. Well, then he charged again. Then he hooked Coyote. He threw him up into the air. After he threw Coyote up, he let him go.

"Now sit down again!" Coyote, the poor thing, got up. Then he staggered. Then for the third time he sat down again.

Well, then Buffalo charged again. Then he hooked Coyote. He threw him up higher. After throwing him up, Buffalo let him go.

"Now there remains only one more time. Then you'll be the same as I am," Buffalo said.

But then Coyote thought, "Certainly you're telling a fib, you who are going there."

Buffalo turned his back to Coyote. He turned around. "Now this is the last time," he said. Well, then he did as before: then he charged Coyote and hooked him. Coyote flew high into the air. Then he became a buffalo. After being hooked by Buffalo, Coyote became a buffalo.

"Well, now you're like I am. You won't have to be hungry any more."

Now Coyote, the poor thing, had been starving, but now he was eating the green grass. Oh, then he got full!

Then the herd of buffalo moved on. Buffalo Coyote followed them as they went.

Sometime later it seemed that someone was on a hill nearby. When Buffalo Coyote looked, there was a coyote sitting on the hill.

Then Coyote thought, "I was once just like you, just as you are sitting there. But now I'm different. Perhaps I'll tell you this."

Then Buffalo Coyote went over there. He arrived where the other coyote was. "It seems that you're feeling bad. Why are you sitting here?"

This other coyote said, "I'm just wishing I were like you are, eating the green grass or whatever it might be. Nothing is hard for you. You're just really full."

Then Buffalo Coyote said, "It certainly isn't hard. I was once the way you are now. I was, and I really am now, a coyote. Why is it that way? Now I'll tell you. Let's go up the hill over there to where the ground is level!"

Well, then both of them went up. As they went the coyote asked, "What are you going to do to me?"

Then Buffalo Coyote said, "You'll know. Sit down here! I'll tell you. I'm going to go over there, and then I'll come and hook you. It will happen four times. When it happens on the fourth time, you'll be just like I am."

Well, then they went on. Then Buffalo Coyote went off, and while the other coyote sat there he charged him. When he hooked him, the coyote flew into the air and then landed, writhing around on the ground.

Well, then the coyote sat down again. "Now you have three more times that I must hook you."

Buffalo Coyote went over there. Then he turned around. Then he charged. Then again he threw the coyote into the air. When he landed he rolled around and around. Buffalo Coyote let him go.

"Now you have only two times remaining. You have two times remaining." Then Buffalo Coyote went over there. Then he did the same thing again.

"Now this is the last time. Be tough! You'll be just like I am. This is what they did to me."

Then Buffalo Coyote went over there again. When Buffalo Coyote charged and hooked him, things changed! The one who was a buffalo became a coyote again.

And then the two coyotes, the poor things, went down fighting each other, for the buffalo changed back into a coyote.

This is what happened.

Comparative references: ARIKARA G. A. Dorsey 1904a:138-39; CHEYENNE Kroeber 1900:170; MANDAN Beckwith 1937:277-81; OMAHA J. O. Dorsey 1890: 102-6; OSAGE G. A. Dorsey 1904d:10-11; PAWNEE G. A. Dorsey 1906a:449-51; Weltfish 1937:234-38; SIOUX Beckwith 1930:437; Wissler 1907:125-26; WICHITA G. A. Dorsey 1904c:278-80.

53

Coyote and Beaver

DAN HOWLING WOLF

Once again Coyote is foiled in his presumptuous attempt to emulate the capabilities of others in this version of the bungling host tale.

Then Coyote was going along the bank. There was a mound of dirt there. Then he sat down on top of it.

While he was looking around, someone called out over there, "Hey, you're causing the dirt to drop off my house. You must come inside."

"Where's the door?"

"Go around this way."

Then Coyote went to the other side. There was a door there. Then he entered. There sat Beaver.

"Hey, sit down!"

"Oh, poor me, I'm hungry."

"Yes, you will eat." Beaver had a pile of kindling in the corner. Then he began to pound the wood. Oh, now there were small chips lying there in a pile.

"Now you can eat, Coyote, poor thing."

Then Beaver lifted his leg up. Then he picked up an awl. Then he took hold of his testicles, and then he pricked them. Oh, tallow came out. The liquid flowed onto the kindling. Then it became pemmican.

Well, then while he stood there, he put the pemmican into a bowl for Coyote, and now Coyote ate.

"Now, say, Grandfather, I think I'll go home!"

And then Coyote went home.

Why, he had children! He went inside his home. He went inside his home.

"Now pick up the kindling! Oh, I was given a wonderful power."

Then the children, poor things, picked up the kindling. Then Coyote sat down to do what he planned while they were pounding the wood.

"What are you doing?"

"You'll learn. You're going to eat."

Oh, they filled the bowl up after they had pounded the kindling.

Then Coyote lifted his leg up. "Give me an awl!"

Then they gave it to him.

Oh, then he took hold of his testicles and pricked them. Poor thing, then blood spurted out. "Uh, it didn't happen!" Then he staggered. Now he fell over and died. All his blood had drained out.

Then Beaver came along. "Perhaps I'll go to see Coyote."

And there Coyote lay dead.

"This is what happened."

Beaver said, "You didn't say anything. You should have asked me and I would have told you what to do so that you wouldn't die. I would have told you what to do."

But this is what Coyote did: he killed himself when he stole [i.e., imitated] Beaver's power to make pemmican. Then he killed himself.

Now the gut went in.

Comparative references: ARAPAHO Dorsey and Kroeber 1903:118-20; ARIKARA Parks 1991:465-68; COMANCHE Curtis 1907-30, 19:191; CROW Lowie 1918:38-41; 1960a:182-85; IOWA Skinner 1925:491-93; KIOWA APACHE McAllister 1949: 74-76; OMAHA J. O. Dorsey 1890:552-58; PAWNEE G. A. Dorsey 1904b:239-53, 267-68; 1906a:439-45; PLAINS CREE Bloomfield 1934:298-301; SIOUX Wallis 1923:90.

54

Coyote and the Ghosts of the Dead Sioux

DAN HOWLING WOLF

For Coyote, sometimes the good fortune he thinks he has acci-
dently found is not what it seems after all.

Coyote, that vagabond, was wandering around hungry. Then he was going
along a creek, as he was wandering along a creek. Then Coyote came upon
them. There lay some dead bodies.

There must have been a fight. They were Sioux. Then he went among
them. Their clothing was nice.

One Sioux lay there. His moccasins were nice. So Coyote took them off
him. Then he put them on his own feet. Now he looked at his feet. Now he was
jumping around as he danced.

Then he went farther on, and there lay another one. His breechcloth was
nice. Then Coyote took it off him. Then he took it off him. He put the
breechcloth on himself. While he was looking at himself, he appeared nice.

As he went on, there lay another Sioux. He had a bow and arrows. Coyote
took them from him, too. Then he kept them.

As he went on, there lay still another one. He wore a roach headdress.
Then Coyote took it off him. Then he put the roach on himself.

Now Coyote danced and danced among the dead Sioux. He danced so well
that he would have received donations.[1]

In the evening he went off into the woods near the river. Now it was
evening. There were coyotes howling in the woods. Oh, then he went there.
They were dancing around a fire in the middle of a clearing. Then he joined
them.

Now Coyote, too, was dancing around, all dressed up in his finery. Then
the others watched him when they saw him.

"Hey, where did you get the things you're wearing?"

He said, "I made all of them myself!"

Then Coyote was tired. And so he went into the woods. All tired out, he
lay down there. Then he lay down.

---

1. Among Arikaras it is customary to give something to an especially good dancer
in appreciation of his effort. These gifts are referred to as donations.

Oh, after it got dark, why, then someone came! Then it grabbed Coyote's feet, and then it was tugging at them. It took the moccasins off Coyote. Then Coyote sat up, and there sat a person. Here it was the one whose moccasins he had first taken! There he sat!

Coyote did not say a thing when the moccasins were taken off. It was a ghost who took the moccasins off him! Then the ghost put the moccasins on himself, and then he went into the woods.

Then another touched him. Then he removed the breechcloth. Then it was taken from him.

Here they were all ghosts! Then Coyote jumped up. Then he sped off. As he ran off he looked back. There they were chasing him. As he went through the woods, he thought, "Why, I don't know how to climb a tree."

Then it became difficult for him. "Now the river is the only way to save myself. I'll jump into the water."

Then he ran, going to the river. Now they were about to catch up with him. Then he leaped into the air and landed in the water. But Coyote did not know how to swim. When he went into the water, wherever he landed, he began to sink.

Meanwhile, the ghosts who were chasing him for stealing their things stood by the water. After he went in the water, why, Coyote began to drown!

And these ghosts waded into the water. It is not known how far Coyote went into it; but, the poor thing, then he drowned.

No one knows where Coyote went from there. No one knows where he floated.

That is all. Now the gut went in.

55

Coyote and His Reflection

DAN HOWLING WOLF

Here again Coyote falls victim to his own inability to distinguish between a real adversary and a reflection he sees in the water.

One time when Coyote was starving he was going along the bank of a creek. The water was just calm. It looked like a mirror. Oh, as he went along he was looking for frogs to find and eat when he was starving. While he was trotting along, he looked; and when he looked, there went another Coyote over there. There it was, alongside him. He did not like it when he saw the other coyote. "Hey, you'll take half my food," he said to the other one.

As he continued going along, Coyote finally looked again. He was going along the edge of the bank, and the other coyote was doing the same thing, too.

Then Coyote peeked over the bank. The other coyote did that, too. "Aw, you sure are hateful for coming here," Coyote said.

And then Coyote went on. As he was going along, he looked. And there came the other coyote again. Then finally Coyote became angry. Then he jumped at him. Then the other coyote did the same thing: then he, too, became angry. Then they both became angry when they saw each other.

Coyote said, "Aw, you sure are hateful! Well, let me go this other way! Then if I find something I won't have to give any of it to you."

When Coyote was going along the bank there, he looked again. Now it was the same as before: the other coyote was coming alongside him. Then Coyote said, "Gee, you sure are hateful for coming alongside me like this!"

Then Coyote went farther on along the bank. Then he just stared angrily at the other coyote. "Gee, you sure are hateful! You'll take part of my food if I find any for myself."

Then Coyote charged the other coyote, wanting to fight him. When he sprang at him angrily, here there was water! Then he jumped angrily into the water! Oh my, Coyote, the poor thing, did not know how to swim, and so he drowned.

Comparative references: CHEYENNE Grinnell 1926:282–83; SIOUX McLaughlin 1916:144.

Tales

Of Others

56

Grasshopper, Ant, and Mosquito
Go on the Warpath

DAN HOWLING WOLF

The humor of this popular children's story rests on both the initial presumption of three insects going to war and on the subsequent ways in which each of the three accidently kills himself.

Then Grasshopper, Ant, and Mosquito went on the warpath. While they were going around, while they were hunting, it began to get cold. Then it rained.

Then Grasshopper said, "Now let's go home! Why, this is no good! It's raining."

Then another one said, "Fine."

Oh, it was muddy!

Then Grasshopper said, "Let's get ready!"

Then he said, "Alright."

Oh, Grasshopper's feet were big with mud. Now he just stood there with the mud stuck to his feet. Now he just stood there.

Then he said, "Now!"

Then he lifted his leg, thinking he would take it out of the mud. But his foot was stuck in the mud and then his leg broke off, the poor thing. Then he fell over and died.

Then Ant and Mosquito wrapped Grasshopper up.

Then they said, "Now let's bury Grasshopper!"

Then Grasshopper was buried by them.

Then one said, "Well, let's cry awhile and then we'll go. You and I are left now."

Now they stood there crying.

"Well, that's enough! Let's stop crying! That's enough! Now let's go on!"

Then they began to get ready. Then Ant put his belt on. As Ant did it, the poor thing, he broke off his rump. He also fell over dead.

Then only Mosquito remained. Oh, Mosquito went around crying.

Then he thought, "First let me bury you and then I'll go! Now I'm left alone. I'm going to go home alone."

Well, then he went and dug a hole. Then he wrapped up Ant and buried him.

Then he thought, "Well, let me just cry once more and then I'll go home. Now only I remain."

He stood there crying. Then he stopped crying. Then water was running from his nose. Then he did it: when he wanted to clean it, he took hold of his nose and then pulled it off. Oh my, he, too, fell over dead.

It isn't known who buried Mosquito, and it isn't known who brought back the story of their dying when they went on the warpath.

Comparative references: ARIKARA Parks 1991, 4:771-72; CHEYENNE Grinnell 1926:134-35; Kroeber 1900:189.

57

Lumpy Toad and the Rain Storm

LILLIAN BRAVE

A humorous anecdote told to amuse children.

When they were going around, Toad was among them.

Then they said, "Lumpy Toad, look! The rain is coming. A rain cloud is coming."

There he sat, breathing and looking all around. The cloud was coming a little closer.

"Why, now let me splash into the water so that I won't get wet." When he took a leaping dive, he splashed into the water over there.

After the rain had passed over, Lumpy Toad surfaced.

Then they said, "Hello! Did you get wet?"

Then he said, "No. I didn't get wet at all."

Now he was just covered with mud.

They said, "Why, now you're just covered with mud!"

"Yes, I didn't want to get wet!"

Song

58

A Love Song

MARY GILLETTE

This love song came to a man in a dream in which he heard the spirit of a deceased man sing about the woman he had courted before his death.

> There are days when I feel lonely.
> Then I just feel like going to you when I see you.

In this song which I have sung the lyric tells about a man after he died. It must be that we still live here, even though we are not living visibly. And that man's spirit was the one they heard when he told it. The woman he had been courting is the one he is singing about.

He says, "There are days when I feel lonely. I just feel like going to you when I see you."

This is the story. The man must have died long ago. And he is the one they began singing the lyric about. It must be true that we hear in our sleep. And they are singing about that man, the one who was singing about the woman he had been courting.

Concordance

This concordance presents a complete numerical list of the narratives as they appear in the original edition (Parks 1991). The corresponding numbers of narratives reprinted in this abridged edition appear at the right. A dash indicates that the narrative is not included in this edition.

Traditional Narratives of the
Arikara Indians (1991)

Myths and Traditions of the
Arikara Indians (1995)

STORY NO.

STORY NO.

ALFRED MORSETTE, SR.

1.	How Summer Came to the North Country	2
2.	The Holy Boy Who Stopped Animals from Killing Humans	3
3.	The Race between the Horse and the Buffalo	4
4.	Long Teeth and Drinks Brain Soup	—
5.	Bloody Hands and the Star Boy	5
6.	Bounding Head and the Four Young Women	—
7.	The Young Woman Who Swallowed a Stone	—
8.	The Man with the Sharpened Leg	6
9.	The Young Woman Who Married the Moon	—
10.	The Young Woman Who Became a Bear	7
11.	Corn Woman and Buffalo Woman	8
12.	The Boy and the Hoop Game of the Buffalo	10
13.	When the Bears Attacked the Arikaras	11
14.	The Foolish Ones Who Killed the Beloved Snake Child	12
15.	Hidden Man and the Two Holy Men	13
16.	Baby Chief and the Two Holy Men	—
17.	The Young Man Pitied by the Spotted Buffalos	14
18.	Red Dog and the Four Stars	—
19.	The Young Man Who Became a Snake and Carries The Antelope	15

DAN HOWLING WOLF

DAN HOPKINS

Bibliography

Abel, Annie Heloise, ed.
  1939   *Tabeau's Narrative of Loisel's Expedition to the Upper Missouri.*
          Norman: University of Oklahoma Press.
Beckwith, Martha W.
  1930   Mythology of the Oglala Dakota. *Journal of American Folk-Lore*
          43:338–442.
  1937   *Mandan-Hidatsa Myths and Ceremonies.* Memoirs of the Ameri-
          can Folk-Lore Society, no. 32. New York: J. J. Augustin.
Bloomfield, Leonard
  1930   *Sacred Stories of the Sweet Grass Cree.* National Museum of
          Canada Bulletin no. 60. Ottawa.
  1934   *Plains Cree Texts.* Publications of the American Ethnological
          Society, no. 16. New York: G. E. Stechert.
Boller, Henry A.
  1959   *Among the Indians: Four Years on the Upper Missouri, 1858–
          1862.* Ed. Milo Milton Quaife. Chicago: Lakeside Press.
Bowers, Alfred W.
  1950   *Mandan Social and Cermonial Organization.* Chicago: Univer-
          sity of Chicago Press.
  1965   *Hidatsa Social and Ceremonial Organization.* Bureau of Ameri-
          can Ethnology Bulletin 194. Washington, D.C.
Brackenridge, H. M.
  1811   Journal of a Voyage up the Missouri. Vol. 6 of *Early Western
          Travels, 1748–1846,* ed. Reuben Gold Thwaites. Cleveland:
          Arthur H. Clark Co., 1904.
Bradbury, John
  1817   *Travels in the Interior of America, 1809, 1810, and 1811.* Vol.
          5 of *Early Western Travels, 1748–1846,* ed. Reuben Gold
          Thwaites. Cleveland: Arthur H. Clark Co., 1904.
Bright, William
  1987   The Natural History of Old Man Coyote. In *Recovering the*

Word: Essays on Native American Literature, ed. Brian Swann
and Arnold Krupat, pp. 339-87. Berkeley: University of California Press.

Canonge, Elliott
1958　　*Comanche Texts.* Norman, Okla.: Summer Institute of Linguistics.

Catlin, George
1848　　*Illustrations of the Manners, Customs, and Condition of the
North American Indians: In a Series of Letters and Notes.* 2 vols.
7th ed. London: Henry G. Bohn.

Cooper, John M.
1957　　*The Gros Ventres of Montana: Part II. Religion and Ritual.* The
Catholic University of America Anthropological Series, no. 16.
Ed. Regina Flannery. Washington, D.C.

Culin, Stewart
1907　　*Games of the North American Indians.* Twenty-Fourth Annual
Report of the Bureau of American Ethnology to the Secretary of
the Smithsonian Institution, 1902-1903. Washington, D.C.

Curtis, Edward S.
1907-30　*The North American Indian.* 20 vols. Norwood, Mass.: Plimpton.
Reprint ed. New York: Johnson Reprint Corp., 1970.

Deloria, Ella C.
1932　　*Dakota Texts.* Publications of the American Ethnological Society,
no. 14. New York: G. E. Stechert.
1944　　Short Dakota Texts, Including Conversations. *International
Journal of American Linguistics* 20:17-22.

DeMallie, Raymond J., ed.
1984　　*The Sixth Grandfather: Black Elk's Teachings Given to John G.
Neihardt.* Lincoln: University of Nebraska Press.

Denig, Edwin Thompson
1961　　*Five Indian Tribes of the Upper Missouri.* Ed. John C. Ewers.
Norman: University of Oklahoma Press.

Densmore, Frances
1929　　*Pawnee Music.* Bureau of American Ethnology Bulletin 93.
Washington, D.C.

Dorsey, George A.
1902　　Letter to W. A. Jones, Commissioner of Indian Affairs, 10
November. Correspondence files, Department of Anthropology,
Field Museum of Natural History, Chicago.
1902-4　Wichita Tales. *Journal of American Folk-Lore* 15:215-39, 16:
160-79, 17:153-60.

1904a   *Traditions of the Arikara.* Carnegie Institution of Washington Publication no. 17. Washington, D.C.

1904b   *Traditions of the Skidi Pawnee.* Memoirs of the American Folk-Lore Society, no. 8. Boston: Houghton, Mifflin and Co..

1904c   *The Mythology of the Wichita.* Carnegie Institution of Washington Publication no. 21. Washington, D.C.

1904d   *Osage Traditions.* Publications of the Field Columbian Museum, Anthropological Series vol. 7, part 1. Chicago.

1905   *Traditions of the Caddo.* Carnegie Institution of Washington Publication no. 41. Washington, D.C.

1906a   *The Pawnee: Mythology (Part I).* Carnegie Institution of Washington Publication no. 59. Washington, D.C.

1906b   Pawnee War Tales. *American Anthropologist* 8:337-47.

Dorsey, George A., and Alfred L. Kroeber
1903   *Traditions of the Arapaho.* Publications of the Field Columbian Museum, Anthropological Series, no. 5. Chicago.

Dorsey, George A., and James R. Murie
1940   *Notes on Skidi Pawnee Society.* Ed. Alexander Spoehr. Field Museum of Natural History Anthropological Series vol. 27, part 2. Chicago.

Dorsey, James Owens
1888   Osage Traditions. *Sixth Annual Report of the Bureau of American Ethnology to the Secretary of the Smithsonian Institution, 1884–85.* Pp. 373-97. Washington, D.C.

1889a   Teton Folk-Lore. *American Anthropologist,* o.s. 2:143-58.

1889b   Teton Folk-Lore Notes. *Journal of American Folk-Lore* 2:133-39.

1890   *The Ƈegiha Language.* Contributions to North American Ethnology, no. 6. Washington, D.C.

Dusenberry, Verne
1962   *The Montana Cree: A Study in Religious Persistence.* Stockholm: Almquist & Wiksell.

Fletcher, Alice C.
1904   *The Hako: A Pawnee Ceremony.* Twenty-Second Annual Report of the Bureau of American Ethnology to the Secretary of the Smithsonian Institution, 1900-1901, Part 2. Washington, D.C.

Fletcher, Alice C., and Francis La Flesche.
1911   *The Omaha Tribe.* Twenty-Seventh Annual Report of the Bureau of American Ethnology to the Secretary of the Smithsonian Institution, 1905-1906. Washington, D.C.

Gilmore, Melvin R.
1927   Notes on Arikara Tribal Organization. *Indian Notes* 4:332–50.
1929   *Prairie Smoke.* New York: Columbia University Press.
1933   The Plight of Living Scalped Indians. *Papers of the Michigan Academy of Science, Arts, and Letters,* vol 19, pp. 39–45. Ann Arbor: University of Michigan Press.

Grinnell, George Bird
1889   *Pawnee Hero Stories and Folk-Tales.* New York: Forest and Stream.
1891   The Young Dog's Dance. *Journal of American Folk-Lore* 4:307–13.
1892a   *Blackfoot Lodge Tales: The Story of a Prairie People.* New York: Scribner's.
1892b   Development of a Pawnee Myth. *Journal of American Folk-Lore* 5:127–34.
1893a   A Blackfoot Sun and Moon Myth. *Journal of American Folk-Lore* 6:44–47.
1893b   Pawnee Mythology. *Journal of American Folk-Lore* 6:113–30.
1894   A Pawnee Star Myth. *Journal of American Folk-Lore* 7:197–200.
1901   The Girl Who Was the Ring Hoop. *Harper's Monthly Magazine* 102:425–30.
1907   Some Early Cheyenne Tales. *Journal of American Folk-Lore* 20:169–94.
1908   Some Early Cheyenne Tales II. *Journal of American Folk-Lore* 21:269–320.
1915   *Blackfeet Indian Stories.* New York: Scribner's.
1921   Falling-Star. *Journal of American Folk-Lore* 34:308–15.
1923   *The Cheyenne Indians: Their History and Ways of Life.* 2 vols. New Haven: Yale University Press.
1926   *By Cheyenne Campfires.* New Haven: Yale University Press.

Hall, C. L.
1891   Ree Cosmology. *The Word Carrier* 20(9):32. Santee, Nebr.: Santee Indian Training School.

Harrington, John P.
1946   Three Kiowa Texts. *International Journal of American Linguistics* 12:237–42.

Henry, Alexander
1897   The Manuscript Journals of Alexander Henry and David Thompson, 1799–1814. In *New Light on the Early History of the Greater Northwest,* ed. Elliott Coues. 3 vols. New York: Francis P. Harper.

Hodge, Frederick Webb, ed.
   1907-10   *Handbook of American Indians North of Mexico.* Bureau of
              American Ethnology Bulletin 30. 2 vols. Washington, D.C.
Hoffman, Charles
   1887   Tusks and Drinks Brains: An Arickaree Story. *The Word Carrier,*
              n.s., 4(7):3-4. Santee, Nebr.: Santee Indian Training School.
Hoffman, W. J.
   1884   La fête annuelle des Indiens Arikaris. *Société d'Anthropologie de
              Paris, Bulletins et Mémoires,* series 8, no. 7, pp. 526-32.
   1892   The Water Babies, an Arickaree Story. *American Antiquarian
              and Oriental Journal* 14:167-69.
Hoijer, Harry
   1972   *Tonkawa Texts.* University of California Publications in Lin-
              guistics, no. 73. Berkeley.
Holder, Preston
   1970   *The Hoe and the Horse on the Plains: A Study of Cultural
              Development among North American Indians.* Lincoln: Univer-
              sity of Nebraska Press.
Holterman, Jack
   1970   Seven Blackfeet Stories. *Indian Historian* 3:39-43.
Hymes, Dell
   1981   *"In vain I tried to tell you": Essays in Native American Ethno-
              poetics.* Philadelphia: University of Pennsylvania Press.
Josselin de Jong, Jan P.
   1914   *Blackfoot Texts from the Southern Piegans Blackfoot Reserva-
              tion, Teton County, Montana.* Koninklijke Akademie van
              Wetenschappen, Afdeeling Letterkunde, Verhandelingen, n.s. vol.
              14, no. 4. Amsterdam: Johannes Müller.
Kennedy, Dan
   1972   *Recollections of an Assiniboine Chief.* Toronto: McClelland and
              Stewart.
Kennedy, Michael Stephen, ed.
   1961   *The Assiniboines from the Accounts of the Old Ones Told to First
              Boy (James Larpenteur Long).* Norman: University of Oklahoma
              Press.
Kercheval, Geroge Truman
   1893   An Otoe and an Omaha Tale. *Journal of American Folk-Lore*
              6:199-204.
Killoren, John J., S.J.
   1994   "Come, Black Robe": De Smet and the Indian Tragedy. Norman:
              University of Oklahoma Press.

Knox, Robert H.
  1923   A Blackfoot Version of the Magic Flight. *Journal of American Folk-Lore* 36:401-3.

Kroeber, Alfred L.
  1900   Cheyenne Tales. *Journal of American Folk-Lore* 13:161-90.
  1907   Gros Ventres Myths and Tales. *Anthropological Papers of the American Museum of Natural History,* vol. 1, no. 3. New York.

Krupat, Arnold
  1987   Post-Structuralism and Oral Literature. In *Recovering the Word: Essays on Native American Literature,* eds. Brian Swann and Arnold Krupat, pp. 113-28. Berkeley: University of California Press.

La Pointe, James
  1976   *Legends of the Sioux.* San Francisco: Indian Historian Press.

Lesser, Alexander, and Gene Weltfish
  1932   Composition of the Caddoan Linguistic Stock. *Smithsonian Miscellaneous Collections,* vol. 87, no. 6. Washington, D.C.

Lévi-Strauss, Claude
  1968   *The Origin of Table Manners: Introduction to a Science of Mythology, 3.* New York: Harper & Row.

Libby, O. G.
  1910   The Story of Corn Silk: An Ancient Mandan Legend. *Collections of the State Historical Society of North Dakota,* vol. 3, pp. 688-707. Bismarck.

Libby, O. G., ed.
  1920   *The Arikara Narrative of the Campaign against the Hostile Dakotas June, 1876.* North Dakota Historical Collections, no. 6. Bismarck.

Linderman, Frank B.
  1915   *Indian Why Stories.* New York: Scribner's.
  1931   *Old Man Coyote (Crow).* New York: John Day.

Lowie, Robert H.
  1909   The Assiniboine. *Anthropological Papers of the American Museum of Natural History,* vol. 4, no. 1. New York.
  1915   Societies of the Arikara Indians. *Anthropological Papers of the American Museum of Natural History,* vol. 11, no. 8. New York.
  1918   Myths and Traditions of the Crow Indians. *Anthropological Papers of the American Museum of Natural History,* vol. 25, no. 1. New York.
  1935   *The Crow Indians.* New York: Farrar and Rinehart.

1939   Hidatsa Texts. *Indiana Historical Society, Prehistory Research Series,* vol. 1, no. 6. Indianapolis.

1942   Studies in Plains Indian Folklore. *University of California Publications in American Archaeology and Ethnology,* vol. 40, no. 1. Berkeley.

1960a   *Crow Texts.* Berkeley: University of California Press.

1960b   A Few Assiniboine Texts. *Anthropological Linguistics* 2:1–30.

McAllister, J. Gilbert

1949   Kiowa-Apache Tales. In *The Sky Is My Tipi,* ed. Mody C. Boatright. *Publications of the Texas Folklore Society,* no. 22, pp. 1–141. Austin and Dallas.

McClintock, Walter

1910   *The Old North Trail.* London: MacMillan.

1933   Blackfoot Legends (As Related by Bull Plume, of the Northern Peigan). *Masterkey* 7:41–46, 70–73.

McLaughlin, Marie L.

1916   *Myths and Legends of the Sioux.* Bismarck: Bismarck Tribune.

McLean, John

1890   Blackfoot Indian Legends. *Journal of American Folk-Lore* 3:296–98.

1893   Blackfoot Mythology. *Journal of American Folk-Lore* 6:165–72.

Marriott, Alice

1945   *The Ten Grandmothers.* Norman: University of Oklahoma Press.

1963   *Saynday's People: The Kiowa Indians and the Stories They Told.* Lincoln: University of Nebraska Press.

Marriott, Alice, and Carol K. Rachlin

1975   *Plains Indian Mythology.* New York: Thomas Y. Crowell.

Mattina, Anthony

1987   North American Indian Mythography: Editing Texts for the Printed Page. In *Recovering the Word: Essays on Native American Literature,* eds. Brian Swann and Arnold Krupat, pp. 129–48. Berkeley: University of California Press.

Maximilian, Prince of Wied

1843   *Travels in the Interior of North America.* Vols. 22–24 of *Early Western Travels, 1748–1846,* ed. Reuben Gold Thwaites. Cleveland: Arthur H. Clark Co., 1906.

Meeker, Louis L.

1901   Siouan Mythological Tales. *Journal of American Folk-Lore* 14:161–64.

1902   White Man. A Siouan Myth. *Journal of American Folk-Lore* 15:84–87.

Michelson, Truman
1911   Piegan Tales. *Journal of American Folk-Lore* 24:238-48.
1916   A Piegan Tale. *Journal of American Folk-Lore* 29:408-9.
Mooney, James
1898   *Calendar History of the Kiowa Indians.* Seventeenth Annual Report of the Bureau of American Ethnology to the Secretary of the Smithsonian Institution, 1895-1896, Part 1. Washington, D.C.
Morgan, Dale L., ed.
1964   *The West of William H. Ashley.* Denver: Old West Publishing.
Moulton, Gary, ed.
1987   *The Journals of the Lewis and Clark Expedition.* Vol. 3. Lincoln: University of Nebraska Press.
Murie, James R.
1914   Pawnee Indian Societies. *Anthropological Papers of the American Museum of Natural History,* vol. 11, no. 7. New York.
1981   *Ceremonies of the Pawnee.* 2 vols. Smithsonian Contributions to Anthropology, no. 27. Ed. Douglas R. Parks. Washington, D.C. Reprint ed. (2 vols. in 1). Lincoln: University of Nebraska Press, 1989.
Nye, Wilbur S.
1962   *Bad Medicine and Good: Tales of the Kiowa.* Norman: University of Oklahoma Press.
Packeneau, Joseph
1908   The Story of Corn Silk—A Mandan Legend. *Collections of the State Historical Society of North Dakota,* vol. 2, pp. 494-97. Bismarck.
Parks, Douglas R.
1979a   Bands and Villages of the Arikara and Pawnee. *Nebraska History* 60:214-39.
1979b   The Northern Caddoan Languages: Their Subgrouping and Time Depths. *Nebraska History* 60:197-213.
1982   An Historical Character Mythologized: The Scalped Man in Arikara and Pawnee Folklore. In *Plains Indian Studies: A Collection of Essays in Honor of John C. Ewers and Waldo R. Wedel,* ed. Douglas H. Ubelaker and Herman J. Viola. *Smithsonian Contributions to Anthropology,* no. 30, pp. 47-58. Washington, D.C.
Parks, Douglas R., ed.
1977   *Caddoan Texts.* International Journal of American Linguistics, Native American Texts Series, vol. 2, no. 1.
1991   The Reminiscences of a Skiri Pawnee Priest: The Roaming Scout Narratives. Unpublished collection of linguistic texts recorded by

George A. Dorsey and James R. Murie, reelicited and translated by the editor.

in press   A Fur Trader among the Arikara Indians on the Upper Missouri: The Journals and Description of Jean-Baptiste Truteau, 1794-96. Lincoln: University of Nebraska Press.

Parsons, Elsie Clews

1929   *Kiowa Tales.* Memoirs of the American Folk-Lore Society, no. 22. New York: G. E. Stechert.

1941   *Notes on the Caddo.* Memoirs of the American Anthropological Association, no. 57. Menasha, Wisc.

Radin, Paul

1915   *Literary Aspects of North American Mythology.* Canada Department of Mines, Geological Survey, Museum Bulletin no. 16, Anthropological Series 6. Ottawa.

1956   *The Trickster: A Study in American Indian Mythology.* New York: Philosophical Library.

Riggs, Stephen Return

1893   *Dakota Grammar, Texts, and Ethnography,* ed. James Owen Dorsey. Contributions to North American Ethnology, no. 9. Washington, D.C.

Robinson, Doane

1928   Tales of the Dakota: One Hundred Anecdotes Illustrative of Sioux Life and Thinking. *Collections of the State Historical Society of South Dakota,* no. 14, pp. 485-537. Pierre.

St. Clair, H. H.

1909   Shoshone and Comanche Tales. *Journal of American Folk-Lore* 22:265-82.

Salzmann, Zdenek

1956a   Arapaho II: Texts. *International Journal of American Linguistics* 22:151-58.

1956b   Arapaho III: Additional Texts. *International Journal of American Linguistics* 22:266-72.

1957   Arapaho Tales III. *Midwest Folklore* 7:27-37.

Salzmann, Zdenek, and Joy Salzmann

1950   Arapaho Tales I. *Hoosier Folklore* 9:80-96.

1952   Arapaho Tales II. *Midwest Folklore* 2:21-42.

Schultz, James W.

1974   *Why Gone Those Times? Blackfoot Tales.* Norman: University of Oklahoma Press.

Schultz, James Willard, and Jessie Louise Donaldson

1930   *The Sun God's Children.* Boston: Houghton Mifflin.

Simms, S. C.

1903   *Traditions of the Crows.* Publications of the Field Columbian Museum, Anthropological Series vol. 2, part 6. Chicago.

1904   Traditions of the Sarcee Indians. *Journal of American Folk-Lore* 17:180-82.

1906   Myths of the Bungees or Swampy Indians of Lake Winnipeg. *Journal of American Folk-Lore* 19:334-40.

Skinner, Alanson

1916   Plains Cree Tales. *Journal of American Folk-Lore* 29:341-67.

1920   *Medicine Ceremony of the Menomini, Iowa, and Wahpeton Dakota, with Notes on the Ceremony among the Ponca, Bungi Ojibwa, and Potawatomi.* Museum of the American Indian, Indian Notes and Monographs, vol. 4. New York.

1925   Traditions of the Iowa Indians. *Journal of American Folk-Lore* 38:425-506.

Taylor, Allan R.

1977   Arikara Texts. In *Caddoan Texts,* ed. Douglas R. Parks. *International Journal of American Linguistics, Native American Texts Series,* vol. 2, no. 1, pp. 20-26.

Tedlock, Dennis

1983   *The Spoken Word and the Work of Interpretation.* Philadelphia: University of Pennsylvania Press.

Teit, James A.

1921   Two Plains Cree Tales. *Journal of American Folk-Lore* 34:320-21.

Thompson, Stith

1953   The Star Husband Tale. *Studia Septentrionalia* 4:93-163.

Uhlenbeck, C. C.

1911   *Original Blackfoot Texts from the Southern Piegans Reservation, Teton County, Montana.* Koninklijke Akademie van Wetenschappen, Afdeeling Letterkunde, Verhandelingen, n.s. vol. 12, no. 1. Amsterdam: Johannes Müller.

1912   *A New Series of Blackfoot Texts from the Southern Piegans Blackfoot Reservation, Teton County, Montana.* Koninklijke Akademie van Wetenschappen, Afdeeling Letterkunde, Verhandelingen, n.s. vol. 13, no. 1. Amsterdam: Johannes Müller.

Vestal, Stanley

1934   *Warpath: The True Story of the Fighting Sioux Told in a Biography of Chief White Bull.* Boston: Houghton Mifflin. Reprint ed. Lincoln: University of Nebraska Press, 1984.

Voegelin, Erminie W.
    1933   Kiowa-Crow Mythological Affiliations. *American Anthropologist*
                35:470-74.
Voth, H. R.
    1912   Arapaho Tales. *Journal of American Folk-Lore* 25:43-50.
Walker, James R.
    1917   The Sun Dance and Other Ceremonies of the Oglala Division of
                the Teton Dakota. *Anthropological Papers of the American
                Museum of Natural History,* vol. 16, no. 2. New York.

Wallis, Wilson D.
    1923   Beliefs and Tales of the Canadian Dakota. *Journal of American
                Folk-Lore* 36:36-101.

Weitzner, Bella
    1979   Notes on the Hidatsa Indians Based on Data Recorded by the
                Late Gilbert L. Wilson. *Anthropological Papers of the American
                Museum of Natural History,* vol. 56, no. 2. New York.

Weltfish, Gene
    1937   *Caddoan Texts: Pawnee, South Band Dialect.* Publications of
                the American Ethnological Society, no. 17. New York: G. E.
                Stechert.

    1965   *The Lost Universe: Pawnee Life and Culture.* New York: Basic
                Books.

Will, George F.
    1912   Some Hidatsa and Mandan Tales. *Journal of American Folk-Lore*
                25:93-94.

    1913   No-Tongue, A Mandan Tale. *Journal of American Folk-Lore* 26:
                331-37.

    1916   The Story of No-Tongue. *Journal of American Folk-Lore* 29:
                402-6.

    1934   *Notes on the Arikara Indians and their Ceremonies.* Denver:
                John VanMale.

Will, George F., and George E. Hyde
    1917   *Corn among the Indians of the Upper Missouri.* St. Louis: Wil-
                liam H. Miner Co.

Will, George F., and H. J. Spinden
    1906   The Mandans: A Study in Their Culture, Archaeology and Lang-
                uage. *Papers of the Peabody Museum,* vol. 3, no. 4. Cambridge,
                Mass.

Wilson, Gilbert L.
  1924   The Horse and Dog in Hidatsa Culture. *Anthropological Papers of the American Museum of Natural History,* vol. 15, no. 11. New York.
  1928   Hidatsa Eagle Trapping. *Anthropological Papers of the American Museum of Natural History,* vol. 30, no. 4. New York.
  1934   The Hidatsa Earthlodge. *Anthropological Papers of the American Museum of Natural History,* vol. 33, no. 5. New York.
Wilson, R. N.
  1893   Blackfoot Star Myths—The Pleiades. *American Antiquarian and Oriental Journal* 15:149-50, 200-203.
Wissler, Clark
  1907   Some Dakota Myths I-II. *Journal of American Folk-Lore* 20: 121-31, 195-206.
Wissler, Clark, and D. C. Duvall
  1908   Mythology of the Blackfoot Indians. *Anthropological Papers of the American Museum of Natural History,* vol. 2, no. 1. New York.

Index